# REVOLUTIONS ACROSS BORDERS

RETHINKING CANADA IN THE WORLD

Series editors: Ian McKay and Sean Mills

Supported by the Wilson Institute for Canadian History at McMaster University, this series is committed to books that rethink Canadian history from transnational and global perspectives. It enlarges approaches to the study of Canada in the world by exploring how Canadian history has long been a dynamic product of global currents and forces. The series will also reinvigorate understanding of Canada's role as an international actor and how Canadians have contributed to intellectual, political, cultural, social, and material exchanges around the world.

Volumes included in the series explore the ideas, movements, people, and institutions that have transcended political boundaries and territories to shape Canadian society and the state. These include both state and non-state actors, and phenomena such as international migration, diaspora politics, religious movements, evolving conceptions of human rights and civil society, popular culture, technology, epidemics, wars, and global finance and trade.

The series charts a new direction by exploring networks of transmission and exchange from a standpoint that is not solely national or international, expanding the history of Canada's engagement with the world.

http://wilson.humanities.mcmaster.ca

1 Canada and the United Nations
Legacies, Limits, Prospects
*Edited by Colin McCullough and Robert Teigrob*

2 Undiplomatic History
The New Study of Canada and the World
*Edited by Asa McKercher and Philip Van Huizen*

3 Revolutions across Borders
Jacksonian America and the Canadian Rebellion
*Edited by Maxime Dagenais and Julien Mauduit*

# Revolutions across Borders

## *Jacksonian America and the Canadian Rebellion*

*Edited by*

MAXIME DAGENAIS AND JULIEN MAUDUIT

Afterword by Amy Greenberg

McGill-Queen's University Press
Montreal & Kingston • London • Chicago

ISBN 978-0-7735-5664-5 (cloth)
ISBN 978-0-7735-5665-2 (paper)
ISBN 978-0-7735-5774-1 (ePDF)
ISBN 978-0-7735-5775-8 (ePUB)

Legal deposit second quarter 2019
Bibliothèque nationale du Québec

Printed in Canada on acid-free paper that is 100% ancient forest free (100% post-consumer recycled), processed chlorine free

This book has been published with the help of a grant from the Canadian Federation for the Humanities and Social Sciences, through the Awards to Scholarly Publications Program, using funds provided by the Social Sciences and Humanities Research Council of Canada.

Funded by the Government of Canada | Financé par le gouvernement du Canada | Canada

Canada Council for the Arts | Conseil des arts du Canada

We acknowledge the support of the Canada Council for the Arts, which last year invested $153 million to bring the arts to Canadians throughout the country.

Nous remercions le Conseil des arts du Canada de son soutien. L'an dernier, le Conseil a investi 153 millions de dollars pour mettre de l'art dans la vie des Canadiennes et des Canadiens de tout le pays.

---

Library and Archives Canada Cataloguing in Publication

Title: Revolutions across borders : Jacksonian America and the Canadian Rebellion / edited by Maxime Dagenais and Julien Mauduit ; afterword by Amy Greenberg.
Names: Dagenais, Maxime, 1979– editor. | Mauduit, Julien, 1979– editor.
Series: Rethinking Canada in the world ; 3.
Description: Series statement: Rethinking Canada in the world ; 3 | Includes bibliographical references and index.
Identifiers: Canadiana (print) 2018906630X | Canadiana (ebook) 20189066318 | ISBN 9780773556645 (cloth) | ISBN 9780773556652 (paper) | ISBN 9780773557741 (ePDF) | ISBN 9780773557758 (ePUB)
Subjects: LCSH: Canada—History—Rebellion, 1837–1838—Influence. | LCSH: Canada—History—Rebellion, 1837–1838—Social aspects. | LCSH: Canada—History—Rebellion, 1837–1838—Economic aspects. | LCSH: United States—Politics and government—1829–1837—Influence.
Classification: LCC FC450 .R48 2019 | DDC 971.03/8—dc23

---

This book was typeset in 10.5/13 Sabon.

# Contents

propel that country toward Civil War, and later fought for the property rights of freedmen – but in the end, he was largely forgotten, just another man named Smith.

But *who* was Abram Daniel Smith, what qualified him to become the president of the new northern republic, and how did he manage to keep his identity in the Hunters' movement under wraps to such an extent that no one realized the radical past of the judge who adjudicated one of the most important legal cases of the antebellum period?

Studies of the so-called Patriot War and its connections to the Canadian Rebellion are limited and dated, and investigations into the leaders of the Patriot War are even more sparse. And an examination of the man elected to lead the country that was the very object of that war has been non-existent. Most mentions of A.D. Smith are in passing and in reference to his accomplishments in later life, long after the Patriot cause had been silenced and the Hunters' Lodge had collapsed and, for the most part, been forgotten.

But Smith's disappearance also mirrors the disappearance of his Hunter comrades from scholarship related to the Rebellion. Their thoughts, philosophies, and contributions to history on both sides of the border have become a footnote to more common investigations of the social and political machinations taking place on Canadian soil, even though, as this volume proves, their movements and members provide much-needed context for the Rebellion that preceded their mobilization. It is only with a trans-national perspective on the Rebellion that we are able to open new avenues of interpretation, analysis, and, perhaps, a better understanding of the time period in general.

This is best illustrated by two key events in Smith's life mentioned earlier: the landmark ruling that set in motion the *Ableman v. Booth* case and a lengthy (and, at times, nasty) battle for the property rights of freedmen in occupied South Carolina during the Civil War. Remarkably, no one who has written about either event – both of which have received scholarly analysis – has explored Smith's radical past with the Hunters. And yet these experiences in Smith's youth can tell us much about why he acted the way he did in later years. And they also reveal how often events in the 1850s and 1860s may have been shaped by radicals of the late 1830s.

It would be easy to dismiss Smith as just one of so many eccentric characters of his age – worthy of no further examination than the other Hunters who gave their time, and sometimes their lives, to the Patriot cause. But Smith's life, and the lives of the many other characters in this volume, provide a greater lesson on nineteenth-century America, offering a snapshot of men who carried with them the impulse to free the oppressed and live out, in all things, Winthrop's vision of a shining city on a hill. Smith and the other Hunters undoubtedly saw their role not simply as an opportunity to help those they deemed less fortunate, but rather as a moral imperative thrust upon them as Americans.

Members of the Hunters' Lodge saw their efforts much like a second American Revolution – an attempt to liberate Canadians from what they believed was the oppression of British rule. With clandestine meetings and a Masonic-like structure that demanded underground meetings and secret handshakes, the Hunters were, according to historian Donald Creighton, "the most formidable of all the secret associations formed for the forcible republicanization of Canada."

And they believed they would be remembered for their efforts, even if their contemporaries dismissed them. For people of the nineteenth century, who often waited weeks for letters and took months to travel, had a tendency to be less concerned about the present than they were, as Smith said in one letter, about the "eternal record."

In an 1857 letter to his wife, Smith wrote that his efforts to overturn the Fugitive Slave Law were undeserving of praise, for their ultimate impact would not be felt for generations. "I am afraid that Mr. (Wendell) Phillips and others go too far, and are too exultant," he said. "It is, indeed true that the effect, the *ultimate* effect, of my decisions can not *now* be estimated – long years hence when you and I are sleeping in our graves their full value, their full weight will be felt and appreciated."

None of Smith's writings from the Hunter period have surfaced, but it would seem likely that he felt the same way about efforts to free Canadians from British thraldom. His fellow Hunters were clear that those who took part in the Rebellion would have been revered, if only they had been successful. "Papineau would have been the Jefferson of his age, and Nelson and Mackenzie would have had their names enrolled on the scroll of fame in the niche with Washington and Lafayette, as the deliverer of their country," read an excerpt from the *Bald Eagle*, an Ohio-based Hunter publication, in 1839. "Davington and Demaray would have been hailed as martyrs of liberty, and the butchery of St Eustache and St Charles would have been stigmatized as a disgrace to the civilization of the age.

The name of McNab, of Colborne and of Gosford, would have been 'damned to everlasting fame,' as unfit associates even of the butcherer Santa Anna."

It is as if, in many ways, Smith lived two lives. In the first life, he was a key player in the drama that unfolded in the borderlands as a secret society plotted guerrilla warfare – the president of a republic that never existed. In the second life, he was a respected lawyer and abolitionist, a man who fought for the rights of former slaves. That no one had pieced these two lives together suggests that, perhaps, Smith might have preferred it that way all along, and that historians can be forgiven for never noticing. But what if we *could* successfully stitch those two lives together – what would the overlap between the two reveal? And more importantly for this work, what would the overlap between separate visions of the Rebellion reveal about the gaps in our understanding of the people and events that shaped them?

A.D. Smith carried his secret Hunter past to his grave, and yet, once known, it provides a new way to view the turbulent years in the United States that followed the Rebellion in Canada. Smith, of course, is just one such story – but how many other prominent American men of the antebellum period also supported, or were actively involved in, the Patriot War? If they spent their youth along the Canadian border, the odds are good that they, too, carried the same secret that A.D. Smith once did. This generation's secret is well protected by an organization that was so guarded that it often documented itself in code and ordered that all traces of its existence be burned should it be disbanded. The Hunters and their radical philosophies fell so far out of favour that it served no one, including former participants and their family members, to ever speak of them again.

But it is certain that Smith was not alone among men of the antebellum era who shared the dubious distinction of being former members of the Hunters' Lodge. These men shaped the laws, pushed for reforms, and fought for their own vision of America. And their Patriot pedigrees are most likely hidden in plain sight – their so-called eternal record written in invisible ink.

Each time I managed to track down a Smith descendant by phone, I held my breath as I told the unsuspecting Americans of their ties to Canadian history.

"This is going to sound odd, but bear with me," I would say, hoping they would not mistake me for a telephone scam artist with a vivid imagination. "But I think you are a descendant of a man who wanted to be the president of Canada in 1838."

This was always followed by silence.

And then, sometimes, laughter.

But it was telling that in all cases, Smith's descendants had no idea that a president was part of their family tree. And then, when I told them the whole story (as much as it is possible to tell the whole story of A.D. Smith in a brief phone conversation), they were incredulous. I'm not sure that any of them was aware of the Canadian Rebellion, the Hunters' Lodges, or the great cross-border drama that unfolded in the late 1830s. I realized over the years that it was not just A.D. Smith who had been forgotten by history, but also the window of time in which he participated in this great story that had gripped two nations.

But it was hard to fault these descendants for not knowing, because historians, generally speaking, had forgotten Smith, too. When I sought out experts on the Hunters' Lodges, for example, they were few and far between and those who had taken a good look at them, such as Oscar Kinchen, Albert Corey, and Edwin Guillet, were long dead.

The abandonment of A.D. Smith is a living analogy of the wider disinterest on the part of American – and often Canadian – scholars to examine the Rebellion in anything but a Canadian context. It is a situation finally addressed by the research in this volume, and the ongoing work of our colleagues across the United States and Canada who are finding new lenses through which to see the volatile period of the Rebellion.

And what of A.D. Smith? I fear there will be much more Abraming in my future as I continue the struggle to resurrect his memory and his contribution to history. Smith's portrait, which he himself presented to the State Historical Society of Wisconsin in 1856, once stared down from a wall above a stairway landing at the Society. I saw it while on a research trip to Madison and was impressed by its size and prominence, though most people shuffled past without giving it a second glance. A few years later, an employee of the Society emailed to tell me the portrait had been removed and placed in storage indefinitely – a turn of events that did not surprise me, and that would not likely have mattered to Smith. For him, it was not the people who mattered, but rather what they said and did that was critical to understanding the motivations of the past. And he desperately wanted those who followed to be able to make that connection.

In 1857, more than two decades after leaving the Hunters behind, he closed a letter to his wife, agonizing over decisions he had made in the past and how they might be viewed in the years ahead. "The principles and doctrines there inculcated and taught are for the far distant future, and it sometimes alarmes [*sic*] me to see such present importance attached to them," he wrote. "But I fear that the exultant, and apparently inconsiderate tone in which they are quoted, will tend to lessen their *present* weight and importance. But, Dearest, you I trust know that they have gone forth with an honest and faithful purpose, and there we must leave them, – on their way in the Providence of God to find their just place in the history of nations, long after you and I their authors are gone and forgotten."

# Foreword

RUTH DUNLEY

Many Friday evenings, my husband asks a question that I dare say would sound a bit odd if anyone could overhear us.

*"Are you with Abram this weekend?"*

"Yes," I usually say. "I'm with Abram."

Sometimes, he turns it into a verb, as in, *"Are you Abram-ing this weekend?"*

It is the shorthand we use to indicate that I will be researching or writing about Abram Daniel Smith, a man I now know more about than my own ancestors.

I've been Abram-ing for more than a decade now, but the story of Abram Daniel Smith is still as perplexing to me as it was when I first encountered his name at the beginning of my doctoral studies. It was then that my adviser pointed me to a passage in a book that mentioned "one Smith," who had been named the president of the Republic of Canada in the aftermath of the Canadian Rebellion, the violent political upheaval in Upper and Lower Canada in the late 1830s. Ever since then, I've been trying to find out who "one Smith" was, and why – or if – he mattered. But his secret past and common surname have made it exceedingly difficult to track him, much less define him. For despite his notable role in both Canadian and American history, Abram Daniel Smith remains a forgotten man on both sides of the border.

And I have tried everything to find and understand him.

Initially, when I was trying to establish that an A.D. Smith I had found in one state was the same A.D. Smith I subsequently found in another, I consulted a handwriting expert to analyze the two signatures. When I located a code that I thought might refer to his involvement in a secret society, I asked a colleague in IT at the newspaper where I worked to show it to a hacker acquaintance to try to decipher. I have consulted professional genealogists, tracked down and spoken with several of Smith's descendants, and written columns in local newspapers urging people to check their attics for any traces of him. As a journalist, I felt compelled to tell a story that, it seemed to me, had been wrongfully neglected. As a historian, I found it difficult to believe that the story had been overlooked by so many for so long.

And, as this volume illustrates, Smith's story is just one of many connected to the Rebellion that have disappeared over time, overshadowed in American minds by scholarship on the American Revolution on one side, and the Civil War on the other. The life of A.D. Smith, for that was the name he preferred, began a generation after the first conflict, and ended shortly after the conclusion of the second. He left a wife, three daughters, and a story to be told.

Smith was born, to the extent that I have been able to verify his birthplace, in upstate New York in June 1811, taking a path that led him through Vermont, back to New York, Ohio, Wisconsin, and eventually South Carolina. He was – like so many of his time – a man on the move, always seeking the next opportunity, the next place to make his mark. He died in the spring of 1865 aboard a northbound steamer headed from Hilton Head to New York. He was presumably on his way home to his family in Milwaukee after a long period of service in the Sea Islands of South Carolina. His cause of death is not known.

He is a little bit like a nineteenth-century Forrest Gump – just as the character at the centre of the eponymous 1994 film had an uncanny ability to cross paths with some of the twentieth century's most influential characters and historical moments, A.D. Smith also managed to insert himself into situations with the movers and shakers of his time. Prominent abolitionist Wendell Phillips was a fan ("Seward, Wilson, Giddings, Sumner rolled into one, don't make one Chief Justice Smith, who defied the United States Court to the utmost"). So, too, was outspoken anti-slavery senator Charles Sumner ("I note with pleasure the vigor and clearness with which you sustain your original position"). And, in 1861 Smith wrote to his son-in-law that he had been called by "special appointment" to meet with "Old Abe" (the president, Smith noted, "would halt the grand army while scaling the ramparts of sessessiondom to listen to, or crack a joke upon rail splitting").

Smith is best known, if he is known at all, as the maverick judge on the Supreme Court of Wisconsin who dared to declare the Fugitive Slave Act unconstitutional.

For a time, his decision brought him national acclaim in the United States – so respected was Smith that his name even surfaced as a possible candidate for vice-president in 1859.

Later, he became a political appointee, serving the Lincoln administration as a member of the Direct Tax Commission in federally occupied South Carolina. He fought for the property rights of freedmen, arguing that they had a God-given right to the land they had once worked as slaves, "their lands yearning for the plow and the spade" – a position that put him at odds with his colleagues and that eventually, along with his alcoholism, created a negative undercurrent that ultimately led to his dismissal from the commission.

At the time, people around Smith were shocked by what was then considered radical thinking. In South Carolina, it led to an ongoing conflict that pitted Smith against his fellow commissioners in a bitter and angry battle that went on for months. "This wild scheme," Smith's colleague on the Direct Tax Commission lamented about Smith's position on land rights for the former slaves, "out radicals all the radicalism I ever heard of in agrarian history."

In Wisconsin almost a decade earlier, and in the context of a southern-sympathizing federal government, Smith's rejection of the Fugitive Slave Act *was* radical – a bold act of defiance against central power. His willingness to challenge the nation, for that was really what he did, probably caught some off guard.

But it should not have surprised anyone. Challenging a federal government in one country would have meant very little for someone who had previously tried to foment revolution in another.

As legal scholar Jenni Parrish has noted, understanding "the motivations of all the judges involved" in what came to be known as *Ableman v. Booth* (a case that made it all the way to the United States Supreme Court) might provide greater insight into their mindsets. In particular, it might answer questions about their willingness to flout federal authority. But historians have routinely failed to connect Smith's landmark decision with a past that was rife with radical leanings and a strong distaste for centralized power. Had they looked, they would have discovered that when Smith was in his late twenties, he was involved with the Hunters' Lodge, an American paramilitary group born in the aftermath of the failed Canadian

Rebellion that had grandiose ideas about freeing Canadians from Crown rule. The secretive group attracted the working class and professionals alike, united in a cause for which they were willing to die – and unafraid to kill. Dismissed by some, the Hunters' exploits gained enough attention to become a diplomatic concern that exacerbated tensions throughout the borderlands. (The Hunters, it should be noted, were western based, primarily in Ohio, Michigan, and New York, and focused their attention on Upper Canada. There is no evidence that Smith had any direct connection to their eastern equivalent, the Frères Chasseurs, who focused on Lower Canada through lodges based in New England, particularly Vermont.)

The Hunters believed they could rally not only Americans to the cause of creating a republic north of the border, but also Canadians, who would be so inspired by the Hunters' appeals to liberty that they would scramble to bear arms in bloody revolt. Hunter military forces would capture key Canadian cities with fine precision and, in the process, lay the groundwork for a new republic. And in this new republic, Canadians would live under a flag that bore the symbol of American liberty – the bald eagle – and celebrate the end of British control.

A.D. Smith was to be their first elected president – the president of the Republic of Canada, so chosen at a Hunter convention in the fall of 1838. There is no mention of his election in the press of the time and very little is known about what took place or why Smith emerged victorious. Presumably, though, Smith was designated president so that, when a border incursion was finally successful, he would be ready to lead the newly formed republic.

At least, that was the plan.

The reality, of course, played out quite differently.

The Hunters' Lodge did exist. But its ambition far outpaced its ability in terms of its sad-sack military (which bungled more than it accomplished), its political goals (which failed to find a positive reception north of the border), and its internal structure (which ultimately crumbled).

And the bitter story of the disappearance from history books of A.D. Smith, the man who intended to become Canada's George Washington, tells a tale of a mysterious figure whose thinking mirrored political and social movements of the day and reveals much about attitudes toward republicanism in the United States and Canada. Smith wanted to become Canada's first president, rose to national prominence in the U.S. for a bold legal decision that helped

# Acknowledgments

As a parent, I have always felt uncomfortable with the saying "it takes a village to raise a child." As a historian, however, I have come to appreciate it. Though historians are typically regarded as solitary creatures, every project is a team effort, with numerous people playing key roles at key moments, each pushing our projects closer to completion.

First of all, I would like to thank all of our contributors. Without your commitment and hard work, this book would have never been possible. I would also like to thank Karen Marrero, Eric Schlereth, and Taylor Spence, who were all initially involved in this project, but for various reasons are not represented in this final draft. I would also like to thank Stephen Smith, Elsbeth Heaman, Marise Bachand, Yvan Lamonde, and Gavin Taylor for commenting on our chapters at our winter 2017 workshop at McGill.

I would also like to thank everyone at the McNeil Center for Early American Studies at the University of Pennsylvania. I spent two of the greatest years of my life at the McNeil Center, and in many ways, this book is the result of this time. In between our many Friday Seminars, numerous brown bags, frequent visits to New Deck, one haunted prison, and the odd game of "poor kitty," I learned a lot about early America, which forced me to rethink Canada, North America, and the Rebellion. Sarah (G and R), Jess Linker, Christine, Brendan, American Max, Carolyn, Sonia, Lori, Rachel (Go Habs!), Alex F, Chris, Alex M, Tommy, Gabriel, Ala, and even you Jamie, thanks for making these years so memorable. James, Liz, Rachel, and Dan, thanks for being willing participants in our continuing texting shenanigans. I would also like to thank Dan Richter, my postdoctoral supervisor. What can I say about Dan that we don't already all know? If everyone in academia was like Dan, it would be a much better place. Barbara and Amy, thanks for allowing me to use the fax machine too frequently.

I would like to thank Dallett Hemphill. Before Dallett passed away, I proposed her this project as a special issue for *Early American Studies*. At that point, it was only an idea, an idea that Julien and I were still unsure of. Dallett's enthusiasm for this project gave us the confidence that we were onto something. If I have one minor regret about this project, it's the fact that we didn't publish with *EAS* as she hoped. As the project grew and became too big for a special issue, the move to MQUP was necessary.

I would also like to thank all of my friends at McMaster University and the Wilson Institute. Coming back to McMaster in 2016 in a non-academic position was a tricky transition. Thanks to Debbie, Wendy, and Aurelia, who helped and continue to help me navigate this new world, and Ian, for encouraging me to remain an academic, I was able to strike a nice balance between my academic and non-academic lives. To my fellow Wilson fellows – Asa, Phil, Amanda, Stacy, Jenn, Mary, and Kass – and to our Winstitute grad students – Jenna, Mack, Brandon, Carly, Kloiber, Chelsea, Mica, and Graydon – thanks for making our days together entertaining and enjoyable. Sam, thanks for editing my work, including those grammatically correct five-line sentences that you love so much. I owe you all my "Maxnowledgments."

I'd also like to thank Julien. Julien and I have spent years, and incidentally too much money on coffee, discussing this project. Your espresso-fuelled creative energy was a joy to work with. Julien and I hope that this book will encourage historians of the Rebellion to look beyond the Canadian border, beyond the typical stories associated with the event, and push the Rebellion in new directions. For instance, though race plays a major role in this volume, the Rebellion's connection with Indigenous populations remains elusive.

Finally, I would like to thank Seve, Renton, and Tristan for listening to me rant about this project, the Rebellion, and Jacksonian America for four long years, which is incidentally also Tristan's entire life.

Maxime Dagenais

J'aimerais remercier en premier lieu deux personnes qui ont, pour différentes raisons, permis à ce livre de prendre son envol. Maxime, tout d'abord, qui, depuis Philadelphie, a lancé cette aventure collective. Son indéniable savoir-faire, sa maitrise de la pratique de l'histoire, ainsi que son énergie, ont agréablement et efficacement rythmé les étapes menant au manuscrit final. Jason Opal, ensuite, qui a été le « troisième directeur » de ce livre. Jason a indéfectiblement soutenu le projet, il a largement contribué à la qualité du travail collectif, et ses conseils ont été extrêmement précieux.

J'ai souvent eu le sentiment, à tort ou à raison, que les évènements de 1837 et des années subséquentes ne sont pas considérés comme ils le devraient – j'espère d'ailleurs que ce livre révèlera aux lectrices et aux lecteurs l'étendue de notre méconnaissance du sujet et contribuera à démontrer son importance historique. C'est pourquoi je tiens à remercier celles et ceux qui ont manifesté leur intérêt pour ce projet ou qui y ont directement participé. Je remercie Ruth, Robert, Tommy, Andrew, Albert, Louis-Georges et Amy pour leur texte et leur participation active, ainsi que Karen Marerro, Eric Schlereth et Taylor Spence pour avoir pris part au projet à ses débuts. Je suis très reconnaissant envers Yvan Lamonde, Elsbeth Heaman, Marise Bachand, Gavin Taylor et Stephen Smith pour avoir pris de leur précieux temps pour nous aider à améliorer le manuscrit. Je remercie également Allan Greer, Martin Petitclerc, Jean-Philippe Garneau, Julie Guyot, Éric Bédard et celles et ceux que nous ne pouvons mentionner ici, dont les réflexions et les remarques ont contribué à façonner le livre. Je remercie Dan Richter pour nous avoir ouvert les portes du McNeil Center for Early American Studies à l'Université de Pennsylvanie, de même que Ian McKay et Sean Mills qui ont su nous convaincre de publier ce travail dans la collection Rethinking Canada in the World. Je suis également extrêmement reconnaissant envers l'Institut Wilson et le département d'histoire de l'Université McMaster pour leur soutien et leur confiance. Et je tiens tout particulièrement à évoquer ma gratitude envers les deux évaluateurs anonymes pour leur travail qui a pleinement contribué à l'amélioration du manuscrit.

Last but not least: Sophie, Lila, Jack, voilà quelques pages qui peuvent expliquer certains moments qui n'ont pas été passés ensemble. J'espère que vous les lirez un jour, c'est aussi votre histoire.

Julien Mauduit

REVOLUTIONS ACROSS BORDERS

INTRODUCTION

# The Canadian Rebellion and Jacksonian America

## *A Connection Decades in the Making*

MAXIME DAGENAIS

To many historians of early America, the year 1837 stands out as the start of a major financial crisis commonly referred to as the Panic of 1837: a financial crisis that resulted in a long recession, the collapse of numerous banks and businesses, and high unemployment rates in the United States. To historians of colonial Canada, however, 1837 is the beginning of an armed uprising known as the Canadian Rebellion, which pitted reformers in Lower and Upper Canada against a local conservative elite and lasted until late 1838 – with sociopolitical repercussions lasting decades longer.

In November 1837, following a political impasse that had paralyzed Lower Canada for decades, the more radical members of the Parti patriote – a local reformist political party comprised of mostly (but not exclusively) French Canadians – revolted against British rule. Craving a more representative and accountable government, the patriotes no longer believed that such reforms could be obtained through peaceful means – the British government had, until then, rejected almost all of their demands and even ordered the arrest of several patriote leaders. Rebellion was their final option. Though the insurrection began with a patriotes victory at Saint-Denis, east of Montreal, on 23 November, the outnumbered and out armed rebels were subsequently defeated at Saint-Charles, south of Montreal, on 25 November, and finally at Saint-Eustache, north of Montreal, on 14 December.

In the meantime, Upper Canadians seeking similar reforms also revolted. On 5 December 1837, William Lyon Mackenzie and a small force of reformers took up arms in Toronto. A few days later, near the town of London, Dr Charles Duncombe gathered his men and marched to Toronto. His aim: link up with Mackenzie's force. However, on 13 December, near Hamilton, after receiving news that Mackenzie's uprising had failed and that a force of loyalists under the leadership of Col. Allan MacNab had been sent to defeat him, Duncombe's force dispersed. Following these defeats, Mackenzie, Duncombe, and their followers fled to Navy Island (on the Upper Canadian side of the Niagara River) where they proclaimed the Republic of Upper Canada. The republic was short-lived as the rebels were soon forced to evacuate.

In the aftermath of this failed rebellion, several rebel leaders, including Louis-Joseph Papineau, Ludger Duvernay, Mackenzie, and Robert Nelson sought refuge in American border towns like Burlington, Buffalo, St Albans, and Watertown, and assistance from the American population. At this point, the Rebellion crossed the border and became a transnational phenomenon with consequences in the United States. In fact, as soon as the rebels escaped to Navy Island, Americans became – whether they wanted it or not – involved in the Canadian conflict. In late December 1837, a group of loyalist and British militiamen under the leadership of Allan MacNab and Royal Navy Capt. Andrew Drew crossed the Niagara River into American territory, captured an American vessel (the *Caroline*) rumoured to have been smuggling arms and ammunition to the rebels on Navy Island, set it on fire, and cast it adrift off Niagara Falls, killing at least one American in the process. In the aftermath of the destruction of the *Caroline*, newspapers all over the country – including as far south as Virginia, the Carolinas, and New Orleans – hotly debated how the federal government should respond to this act of aggression on American soil. Column after column was spent covering the event and articles on the Canadas became front-page material.[1] Newspaper editors frantically attempted to figure out what happened, printed numerous extracts from borderland newspapers, debated how the government should respond, and struggled to separate fact from fiction. While some viewed this as an act of war on the part of Great Britain and called for immediate military action, others feared that the United States was in no position to go to war against a powerful British army, nor could it risk losing its most important economic ally – Great Britain – in the aftermath of the debilitating economic crisis known as the Panic of 1837.[2]

In the months that followed the *Caroline* Affair, American newspaper editors continued to discuss the Rebellion, which remained one of the most covered events until the end of hostilities in December 1838, with reports and updates often taking up more than two full columns per day.[3] More importantly, Americans, from all over the borderland and beyond, pledged to assist the rebels in their fight against the British. Following their escape to the United States, Upper and Lower Canadian rebel leaders, hoping to take advantage of the anti-British sentiments that followed the *Caroline* Affair, sent letters and met with local leaders and politicians and travelled to major cities such as Boston, New York City, Philadelphia, and Washington seeking financial and/or military support. Though they failed to secure the assistance of the federal government and President Martin Van Buren, who vowed to remain neutral throughout the uprising, they had more success at the local level. Throughout Michigan, Vermont, New York, Maine, and Ohio, Americans living in the borderland expressed sympathy for the Canadian rebels and joined secret societies, known as the Hunters' Lodges. By the hundreds and thousands, they pledged to free Canada from the yoke of "British Thraldom" and assist the rebels in what they and many favourable newspaper editors called the "Canadian Revolution."[4] Supporters of the Canadian patriots even equated rebel leaders, like Papineau and Mackenzie, with the "heroes of 1776" – men like George Washington, Thomas Jefferson, and Benjamin Franklin. The rebels were fighting for something just; they were fighting for their freedom.[5]

Support for the rebels along the border was significant. All along the border states, Americans joined Hunters' Lodges and provided rebels with a safe haven, money, supplies, weapons, and volunteers. Putting an actual figure on this support is very difficult, however. Since the main source of support came from the very secretive Hunters' Lodges – secret societies that unfortunately left historians with little archival material – it is almost impossible to put a number on the support. However, we do know that support for the rebels was significant enough that it forced Martin Van Buren to – on more than one occasion – publicly denounce American participation in the Rebellion and remind American citizens that the United States was officially at peace with Great Britain. Any military aggression against the British, he warned, was strictly illegal and would be severely punished. American sympathy and participation was also significant enough that it forced Van Buren to send a military force under one of its most famous generals, General Winfield Scott, to arrest anyone – Canadian or American – causing a disturbance along the border. The United States was at peace with the British and the president was adamant that every American remain neutral.

Despite this, Americans nonetheless participated in numerous military raids against the British along the borderland. For instance, in May 1838, a group of American and Canadian hunters, under the leadership of the infamous pirate Bill Johnston, destroyed a British ship – the *Sir Robert Peel* – that was en route to Toronto. Stopped at Wells Island (known today as Wellesley Island) in the Thousand Islands for a new supply of wood, Johnston's group captured the ship, allowed all passengers and deckhands off the ship, pillaged it, and finally set it on fire. Their aim: provoke a war between the United States and Great Britain, which, they hoped, would benefit the Rebellion. They failed. Military activities escalated in November and December 1838 when three separate forces, which included numerous Americans, attempted to invade Upper and Lower Canada. First, a force led by Robert Nelson crossed the American border into Lower Canada, and on 4 November, arrived at Napierville (in the Richelieu valley) where they settled. Short on weapons and manpower, Nelson's men were quickly defeated at Lacolle (7 November), Odelltown (9 November), and Beauharnois (10 November). Following these crushing defeats, rebel forces dispersed, and on 10 November, a week after Nelson arrived, British troops entered an empty Napierville. The last rebel stronghold in Lower Canada had been overrun without a fight. The two invasions of Upper Canada also ended in failure. On 11 November, Nils Von Schoultz, a Finnish-American immigrant, unsuccessfully led a group of 250 hunters at the Battle of Windmill (across from Ogdensburg). A few weeks later, on 4 December, a group of 400 hunters crossed the Detroit River and faced the British at the Battle of Windsor. The battle ended in a quick, resounding defeat and was the last major encounter of the Canadian Rebellion. Though some American supporters continued to hope that the United States and Great Britain could be pushed to war and there was the odd raid into Canada – such as at Queenston Heights where Americans destroyed the Sir Isaac Brock Monument – the "Canadian Revolution" was over.

Despite the failures of American intervention, the attempted "Canadian Revolution" did leave an imprint on the United States. For over one year, it was a phenomenon: Canada and the Canadian rebels dominated the American news cycle and were on the front page of several newspapers, often taking up to two columns. And despite Van Buren's belief that Americans should remain neutral, many supported the rebels and were directly involved in the Canadian struggle, with thousands joining Hunters' Lodges and hundreds participating in military campaigns against the British. Yet, despite such an obvious connection between the Canadian Rebellion and the United States, our understanding of this connection and of the mutual influence each had on the other remains limited.

Though historians have paid a great deal of attention to the Rebellion, the American perspective remains under-examined. First, Canadian scholars have generally considered the event from a local and national perspective. In Canada, we are all familiar with the story of the 1837–38 Rebellion. We know about the social, political, and economic implications, its importance in Canadian history, and its impact on nascent Canadian nationalism and nation building. Its causes and consequences are rooted in Canadian context and historiography.[6] For instance, the last three monographs on the Rebellion – Gilles Laporte's *Brève histoire des patriotes*, François Deschamps's *La "rebellion de 1837" à travers du prisme du Montreal Herald*, and Mylène Bédard's *Écrire en temps d'insurrections* – focus exclusively on the Canadian perspective.[7] Regardless, and as is suggested by the publication of three major monographs on the subject in a twelve-month period, the Rebellion remains an important topic of study in Canada. This is especially the case in Quebec where the Rebellion has become an important part of the collective identity of the French-speaking population. The Rebellion is everywhere in Quebec: it is celebrated every May with La Journée nationale des patriotes, in numerous songs, plays, and poems, and it is even celebrated with a beer, Unibroue's 1837, brewed in honour of the memory of those that sacrificed their lives in the name of liberty at Saint-Eustache.[8]

With so much on the line, it is no surprise that historians still debate the impact, meaning, and memory of the Rebellion in Canada. To make matters even more complicated, we still do not have a truly national (or pan-Canadian) interpretation of the Rebellion as events in Upper and Lower Canada are still often treated separately, each fitting into two competing collective identities and memories. In the case of Upper Canada, the Rebellion and its connection with Lower Canada is often minimized to fit the image of an Upper Canada that was loyal to the empire.[9] The Rebellion is described as an anomaly, first led by Mackenzie as an unpopular *coup d'état* and then by invading Americans as the Patriot War.[10] It was a limited, unpopular, and foreign event. In the case of Lower Canada, the Rebellion is treated separately due to, in large part, the involvement of French-Canadian nationalism.[11] As a significant part of the national identity of the Québecois, many have defended the Rebellion's nationalist interpretation and therefore minimized its connection with Upper Canada.

Some historians – most notably Allan Greer and Michel Ducharme – have challenged this interpretation. In "Rebellions Reconsidered," for instance, Greer argued that historians would gain a much better understanding of the uprising and the period in general by presenting a "pan-Canadian view of the Rebellion."[12] Despite "internal diversities," the Rebellions are, to Greer, a "single historical phenomenon" with similar causes, similar political, social, and economic contexts, and similar aims. Two decades later, Ducharme confirmed Greer's assumptions and demonstrated that a pan-Canadian view did, in fact, lead to a better understanding of the event. When studied as a single phenomenon, Ducharme showed that both were part of a similar ideological struggle, a struggle between supporters of "republican liberty" and supporters of a "modern concept" of liberty.[13] Yet, despite such important steps, as recently as 2015 historians still question whether the Rebellion should be regarded as a singular event. In *Brève histoire des patriotes*, Gilles Laporte continued to defend a separate interpretation based on the fact that events in Upper Canada were not as intense, claiming that the Upper Canadian Rebellion was a mere "walk" led by Mackenzie with significantly less support than the Lower Canadian rebels, and no coordination with its counterpart.[14]

Since historians in Canada still debate the concept of a pan-Canadian Rebellion, often focusing on more local histories, it is not surprising that studying the Rebellion beyond the Canadian/Quebec border has not attracted the attention of many historians. However, this topic has not flourished in the United States, either – most studies on the Jacksonian period limit their analyses of the Rebellion to a few pages.[15] Even James Kloppenberg's 700-page overview of the history of democracy in the Western world barely mentions Canada.[16] This is perhaps not surprising since the Rebellion coincided with a momentous and turbulent period in American history: the United States was in the midst of the Jacksonian democracy; the Locofoco movement was strengthening; the Panic of 1837 and the broader economic transformations that some historians have called the "Market Revolution" were causing acute economic anxiety; Texas had seceded from Mexico; debates regarding slavery raged on; and the American territory was in full expansion. These are all events that, upon first glance, appear to have more dramatic consequences in the United States, and which as a result have garnered the attention of historians.

However, we posit that it is precisely as a result of this turbulent period that the Rebellion mattered even more in the United States. In this volatile context, when every element of American society was questioned and challenged, Canada's Rebellion added to the internal pressures felt by the young republic. Canada's Rebellion became front-page material, with newspaper editors and citizens around the nation struggling to figure out what happened (and why) as well as debating the position the federal government ought to take. The Rebellion mattered, but it also did more. As we will see, it offered many Americans – disillusioned with the United States – the opportunity to do something about it. The Rebellion thus became entangled with conflicts and disagreements surrounding Jacksonian democracy, the Market Revolution, the Locofoco movement, American expansionism, Manifest Destiny, and slavery. This collection of essays demonstrates just how connected events in Canada and the United States were during this period. By taking the Rebellion out of its Canadian context and placing it in a North American one, we suggest that not only did this regional and limited rebellion have significant consequences beyond the Canadian border and in the United States – and vice versa – but it can also provide a new window through which we can examine the major social, political, and economic changes that were taking place in the United States during the period. Though most of the chapters in this collection focus on Jacksonian America, several place the Rebellion in the context of the Age of Revolutions, making direct links between it and the American Revolution as well as Patriot discourse and the ideologies of Thomas Paine and Thomas Jefferson. These chapters also contribute to the field of comparative borderlands history, an approach that encourages borderland historians to study the Canadian-U.S. and Mexican-U.S. borders together in a continental, comparative methodological framework.

Therefore, this collection of essays not only forces early American borderland historians that generally focus on the Mexico-U.S. border to turn their attention to Canada, but by comparing events along the Canada-U.S. border in 1837–38 with those in Texas in 1836, it reveals the many and oftentimes contradictory ways the American government handled disputes and enforced its will along its borders and the overall flexibility of its foreign policy during this period. Finally, it demonstrates that borderlands were not at the mercy of decisions taken by central governments, but they too could influence central authority and be an important source of social, political, and intellectual change.[17]

Though we would like to claim to be the first, we are not breaking new ground. Some very important foundations have been laid, and historians have taken important steps. The first analyses that connected the Rebellion to the United States were produced in the first half of the twentieth century by Orrin Tiffany, Edwin C. Guillet, Albert Corey, and Oscar A. Kinchen.[18] However, these are very descriptive and focus almost exclusively on the Hunters' Lodges and their military activities. Albert Corey's work is the most analytical of this group and it still remains one of the best syntheses of American-British relations during the era of the Rebellion. Regardless, by demonstrating that the Rebellion did have a real impact south of the border, these works laid foundations that *should* have allowed historians to push their analyses even further and fully explore the connection between Jacksonian America and the Canadian Rebellion. This did not happen, however, and in the decades that followed, historians produced very descriptive and episodic studies, still focusing on the Hunters' Lodges and their activities along the border. The geographic scope of this work is also limited, focusing on Vermont, New York, and Michigan, leaving us with an incomplete picture.[19] Lillian F. Gates, Marc L. Harris, and Yvan Lamonde are exceptions here.[20] While Gates discovered several links between William Lyon Mackenzie's ideology and the anti-bank, anti-monopoly Locofoco movement, Harris suggested that the Rebellion pushed many Americans to question their commitment to the young republic and the values it embodied following the Market Revolution. Yvan Lamonde, on the other hand, considered the impact of *américanité* and *américanisation* (or Americanness and Americanization) on French-Canadian society and Lower Canadian political leaders, particularly Louis-Joseph Papineau.[21]

Since the publication of Tiffany's *The Relations of the United States to the Canadian Rebellion of 1837–1838*, over one hundred years ago, our understanding of the connection between the Canadian Rebellion and Jacksonian America remains inadequate. However, in the last ten years, some historians – many of whom are in this collection – have taken important steps to remedy this as they further investigated the relationship between the United States and the Canadian Rebellion. One of the most important was Andrew Bonthius's "The Patriot War of 1837–38: Locofocoism with a Gun?" Bonthius was, at the time, the only historian to draw an explicit link between Jacksonian ideology and the patriotes' agenda. Focusing on Hunters' Lodges in Ohio, Bonthius proposed the hypothesis that radical Democrats – also known as the Locofocos – participated in the Canadian Rebellion and joined Hunters' Lodges to express their frustrations with the changes brought by the "Market Revolution" and the disappearance of traditional socio-economic values.[22] Louis-Georges Harvey, Albert Schrauwers, and Charles-Phillipe Courtois also produced studies that considered the influence of *américanité*, republicanism, the American model, and Andrew Jackson's Bank War on Lower and Upper Canadian reformers.[23]

More recently, historians have pushed our understanding of the Rebellion and Jacksonian America beyond its ties with the radical democrats and republicans, looking instead at slavery, abolitionism, and international diplomacy. For instance, David Shields considered the "dissenting voice" of *The Liberator*, one of the Unites States' leading abolitionist newspaper.[24] Shields maintained that the newspaper heavily condemned the Rebellion because of a reverence that abolitionists held for British principles and liberties, "painting a northern utopia in which the genius of persons of color blossomed when permitted to order their own lives."[25] Abolitionists feared that if the rebels were successful – and if the Canadas were added to the United States – fugitive slaves would lose this land free of slavery, and "find themselves again subject to … the coercive power of the constitutional stipulation that fugitive slaves be returned to their owners in their home states."[26] In 2017, Maxime Dagenais and Jason Opal produced two articles that further deepened our understanding of the link between the Rebellion and the United States. While Dagenais suggested that the fear of losing its most important economic ally – Great Britain – and concerns over the survival of slavery influenced many, including the American government, to outlaw American intervention, Jason Opal considered how the Panic of 1819 shaped Andrew Jackson's conservative political economy, his need to maintain friendly diplomatic relations with Great Britain, and its consequences for Canadian republicans.[27]

Finally, many recent dissertations from emerging scholars have also pushed our understanding of the connection between the Canadian Rebellion and Jacksonian America, the most significant of which is Julien Mauduit's "'Vrais républicains' d'Amérique: les patriotes canadiens en exil aux États-Unis (1837–1842)." Mauduit examines a trans-border community of radical republicans, Canadian and American, and their general goal to build an "alternative" republic in the Canadas and the United States, based on "true" democratic principles. By connecting the attempted Canadian Revolution to several American events, such as the 1840 presidential election, he suggests that the Canadian crisis had a significant impact on the United States.[28] In a chapter on the Upper Canadian Rebellion, which is part of a larger dissertation on breakaway republics in North America, Thomas Richards Jr suggests that many Americans participated in the Rebellion because they sought the creation of an Upper Canadian Republic that was a political, economic, and social alternative to a United States that they had grown alienated with.[29] Ruth Dunley also examined the mysterious life of American Abram Daniel Smith, from his time as the chosen president of the future Republic of Canada to his groundbreaking role as an abolitionist on the state Supreme Court of Wisconsin.[30] And finally, Stephen Smith recently defended a dissertation on the use of the press by patriot voluntary organizations, on both sides of the border, from 1834 to 1842.[31]

Though we are not the first to make explicit links between the Canadian Rebellion and Jacksonian America, this collection provides the most in-depth and complete analysis connecting the Canadian Rebellion – and pre-Confederation Canada in general – to Jacksonian America. After decades of sparse, limited, and episodic analyses and loosely founded hypotheses – with the majority focusing on the relationship between the Canadian rebels, the Hunters' Lodges, and radical democrats – this collection provides a wide selection of case studies – each dealing with important social, economic, political, and cultural issues – that showcase how closely the history of Canada and the United States evolved and how our nations mutually influenced one another during this turbulent period. Each of the following essays draws from this tumultuous time in North American history and demonstrates how the Rebellion became a source of conflict, concern, and debate amongst Americans. They not only allow us to reframe the Canadian Rebellion as an important North American event, but also challenge established historiography on the period and suggest new ways of thinking about borders and borderlands, American expansionism, the "Market Revolution," slavery and abolitionism, and Jacksonian ideology. These essays, more importantly, illustrate the value of transnational approaches. Each one is part of a flourishing conceptual framework that considers regional events from an international perspective and each demonstrates the value in studying old subjects from new theoretical and contextual perspective. Studies on the Rebellion have stalled in the past decades as they remain, for the most part, firmly rooted in nationalist historiography. By continuously looking at the Rebellion as a Canadian event, with exclusively Canadian consequences, we shortchange the importance of the event. We limit its scope, its importance, and our understanding of it. These essays bring new life to this historiography and new significance to the event.

We have named this collection *Revolutions across Borders: Jacksonian America and the Canadian Rebellion* for several reasons. First, we use "revolutions," plural, to refer to more than one revolution. The first, of course, refers to the Canadian Rebellion. Historians have used many terms to describe the armed insurrection that took place in Upper and Lower Canada in 1837–38: rebellion, revolt, insurrection, civil war, Patriot War, and revolution. In fact, even as late as 2016, historians were still redefining what happened in 1837–38 as François Deschamps suggested that we use the expression "major political crisis."[32] We settled on the term revolution because, as will be demonstrated in our chapters, to many of the actors involved in the conflict what was happening in 1837–38 was a revolution, one that if successful would result in a dramatic, monumental change to North America. Moreover, many Americans – newspaper editors, patriots, and hunters, for instance – referred to the insurrection as the "Canadian Revolution," even comparing events in Canada with the American Revolution. Captivated readers around the United States were told that the Canadians were experiencing their own revolution, and Mackenzie and Papineau were Canada's versions of George Washington and Thomas Jefferson. Since our collection focuses on the impact of the Rebellion on the

United States, we thought that using their own terminology to describe the insurrection was appropriate.

Along with the Canadian Rebellion, "revolutions" also refers to the major, fundamental changes that took place (and were still taking place) in the United States during this period. The most dramatic of these were the broader economic transformations that some historians have called the "Market Revolution." In his seminal *Market Revolution*, Charles Sellers argued that the Jacksonian era was a period of conflicts between the proponents of a market economy – the seaboard entrepreneurial classes that endorsed industrialization and national economic development – and those who opposed it – rural yeoman and craftsmen that favoured locally based economies based on egalitarianism and self-sufficiency. Sellers argued that as this "Market Revolution" fanned out of eastern seaboard cities towards the interior, it caused great distress and was rejected by a number of Americans. Opponents had an ally in Andrew Jackson who led what Sellers called a "democratic revolt" against capitalism in the 1830s. Though many historians have questioned and challenged this interpretation – the most significant are Daniel Walker Howe and John Lauritz Larson – it is undeniable that in the period between 1815 and 1840, the United States underwent major socioeconomic transformations. These transformations, as some of our chapters suggest, had a significant impact across the border in Canada.[33]

"Across borders" suggests that we are not only considering the impact of the Rebellion on the United States. Though much of our book considers the many ways the Rebellion played out in the United States and influenced the young republic's social, political, and economic environment, some of our chapters will also focus on the manner in which the major transformations that defined Jacksonian America impacted Canada and influenced the rebels. The Canadian Rebellion and Jacksonian America are treated as two equal agents of change. Finally, we refer to the events covered in this book – the 1837 Upper Canadian Rebellion, the 1837 and 1838 Lower Canadian Rebellions, and the Patriot War – as one major event, and as a result use the default term "Canadian Rebellion."[34] This is not an attempt to impose a Canadian national dimension to a complex series of events with local American, Upper Canadian, and Lower Canadian specificities, but to emphasize that a transnational approach can bridge these often-separate historiographies, by highlighting their connections rather than their distinctions.[35] Though historians have often underlined the differences between these various events,[36] some historians – including several in our collection – have focused on their similarities. Julien Mauduit, for instance, has recently suggested that these events were perhaps even more connected than previously thought as Upper and Lower Canadians and their American supporters shared similar republican, egalitarian, and socioeconomic ideals and goals.[37] Since this collection examines these events simultaneously, as one single transnational, continental event, we felt that the use of "Canadian Rebellion" was appropriate in this case. The same also goes for the term "patriot." By default, it is assumed that it refers to every individual involved in the event – whether American, Upper Canadian, or Lower Canadian – as well as to the totality of events in 1837–38. Nevertheless, we are aware that connecting these events remains a hotly contested issue with several interpretations.[38] As a result, although we took the editorial decision to link them and use the term "Canadian Rebellion" in our title, we did not impose our terminology on our contributors. Each can use the designation they wish.

Though our collection includes many case studies on a variety of different social, economic, cultural, and political issues, there are central themes that we believe transcend each chapter. First, and most obvious, they demonstrate how significant the Canadian Rebellion was for North America and North American politics in the 1830s and 1840s. Each also illustrates how fluid and volatile the concepts of "nations" or "states" were in the 1830s. Nations were in a constant state of flux and unsteadiness as borders were constantly shifting and loyalties were fleeting and frequently changing. For instance, many Americans, disillusioned with what the United States had become, broke away on their own, forming (or attempting to form) their own independent republics, such as those in California, Utah, Madawaska, or Texas.[39] The Canadas and the Rebellion provided another opportunity for disillusioned Americans – and Canadians – to rebuild and break away from the United States. Finally, these chapters further illustrate how fluid North America's borders were during this period, allowing for an easy exchange of ideas and people.

This collection is divided into three categories. The first section, titled "Economic Concerns," focuses on the many ways the Rebellion either influenced economic policies on a continental level or was directly influenced by the major economic transformations that defined the era. In fact, some of these chapters demonstrate how economic changes and transformations on a continental and international level shaped the Rebellion and played a major role in whether it would succeed or fail. In "Patriots No More," Jason Opal discusses the economic *rapprochement* between the British and Americans in the years leading up to the Rebellion. In the tense economic period that followed the War of 1812 and the Napoleonic Wars, American and British merchants searched for new markets to sell and trade goods. As Americans sought "economic security," they looked at a former foe: Britain. Unfortunately for the rebels and their allies, this economic rapprochement had terrible consequences for the Rebellion, guaranteeing its failure in the United States. In "Bank War in Lower Canada," Robert Richards examines the impact of the Market Revolution, via the controversy over paper-money banking, on the patriotes of Lower Canada. Though not as significant as in the United States, Richard explains that the Market Revolution moved beyond the American border, causing a similar Market Revolution in Canada. Many patriotes reacted to it the same way as the radical democrats – also known as the Locofoco – did during the Age of Jacksonian Democracy, paving the way to the Rebellion.

The second section, titled "Alternative Republics," examines how many used the context of the Rebellion to create – or at the very least discuss the creation of – new republican institutions that were different than Upper Canada, Lower Canada, and the United States in the 1830s. Many had grown disillusioned with the Canadas and the United States and sought to create what they believed would be better alternatives. In "Bald Eagle over Canada," Andrew Bonthius examines the popularity of William Lyon Mackenzie's "radical Jacksonian and agrarian" platform. Through the writings of Dr Samuel Underhill, Bonthius demonstrates how Mackenzie's platform reverberated in Ohio, shaking the fragile bonds of the American union and causing many to discuss an alternative, a nation of "yeoman-farmer producers" as a counterweight to the "ruthless monied aristocracy" that now dominated the United States. In "The Lure of a Canadian Republic," Thomas Richards Jr discusses the motivations behind American participation in the Rebellion. Many Americans – whose attachment to the United States was "ambivalent" – had grown extremely frustrated with the changes that resulted from the Market Revolution. Witnessing the disappearance of their own political and financial authority, they sought to create a social, political, and economic alternative to the United States. The Rebellion provided the perfect opportunity to create an alternative republic outside of the United States and in Upper Canada. In "'The Road Not Taken,'" Albert Schrauwers offers the banking alternative presented by Dr Charles Duncombe. Though often forgotten and ignored in favour of William Lyon MacKenzie, Duncombe offered his own interpretation of an Upper Canadian Republic, largely influenced by the American "equal rights" and Locofoco movement. Seeking to make "free banking" the staple of his republic, Duncombe sought the creation of a society that would benefit all members equally and one in which banking and hard money were accessible to all.

Our third section, titled "Continental Impact," investigates the impact of the Rebellion beyond the Canadian border. Though the Rebellion is frequently thought to be a localized event with little to no impact outside of Canada, the final two chapters demonstrate that the Rebellion changed the American political and ideological landscape. In "John L. O'Sullivan's 'Canadian Moment,'" Louis-Georges Harvey looks at the place of the Canadian Rebellion in *The United States Magazine and Democratic Review*, an American journal closely associated with the genesis of "Manifest Destiny." With what he calls "the Canadian Moment," Harvey demonstrates how though the notions associated with "Manifest Destiny" were especially prevalent in the mid-1840s and the annexation of Texas, the newspaper used the context of the Canadian Rebellion to start developing the notions that would eventually define "Manifest Destiny." In "Canadian Interference in American Politics," Julien Mauduit examines the impact of the Rebellion on the 1840 Presidential election and argued that it was a major cause of William Henry Harrison's stunning victory over Martin Van Buren. To Mauduit, Van Buren's response to the Rebellion – more particularly, his unpopular foreign policy towards the patriots – cost him the support of his radical base. Siding with Harrison in 1840, these radical republicans undermined Van Buren's strength in the northeast, destroying the delicate alliance that Andrew Jackson had previously secured between his supporters in the slave-owning south and the populist elements in the "free states." Finally, our collection ends with an afterword by Amy Greenberg, titled "'The Practicability of Annexing Canada': Or, the Manifest Destiny of Canada, According to the United States," which places Canada in a more general continental post-1838 historical context and examines how many Americans continued to push for the annexation of Canada, despite the failures of 1837–38.

When we first conceptualized this project, in a café in Montreal in early 2015, we initially expected that it would be difficult to find enough authors working on the Rebellion from an American perspective to produce an entire volume; as stated, studies on the Rebellion in Canada are generally confined to the national context and we assumed American historians would not be interested in a failed and limited Canadian Rebellion, especially when considering the many important changes that were taking place in the United States during this period. We were wrong. Not only did we find many contributors, but in the process we discovered an emerging community of scholars interested in the Canadian Rebellion and the United States. These scholars are not only pushing the Rebellion's history forward, but they are forcing us to reconsider our understanding of key concepts, such as banking, nation-building, citizenship, Manifest Destiny, and republicanism.

## NOTES

1 For more information on the newspaper coverage of the *Caroline* Affair and the Rebellion, see Maxime Dagenais, "'[T]Hose who had money were opposed to us, and those who were our friends were not the moneyed class.' Philadelphia and the 1837–38 Canadian Rebellions," *American Review of Canadian Studies* 48, no. 1 (Spring 2017): 1–18; Arthur L. Johnson, "The New York State Press and the Canadian Rebellions, 1837–38," *American Review of Canadian Studies* 14, no. 3 (1984): 279–90; Julien Mauduit, "'Vrais républicains' d'Amérique: les patriotes canadiens en exil aux États-Unis (1837–1842)" (PhD diss., Université du Québec à Montréal, 2016); Yvan Lamonde, "Le Bas-Canada et *Le Courrier des États-Unis* de New York (1828–1840)," *Cahiers des dix* 56 (2002): 217–33.

2 Dagenais, "[T]Hose who had money were opposed to us," 8–9.

3 Ibid., 3–4.

4 For more information, see Dagenais, "[T]Hose who had money were opposed to us."

5 Ibid.

6 For instance, see: George Bellemare, *Saint-Charles 1837 et la survie d'un peuple menace* (Montreal: Guérin, 2005); François Deschamps, *La "Rébellion de 1837" à travers le prisme du Montreal Herald* (Quebec:

Presses de l'Université Laval, 2015); Allan Greer, *The Patriotes and the People: The Rebellions of 1837 in Rural Lower Canada* (Toronto: University of Toronto Press, 1993); Gilles Laporte, *Patriotes et loyaux, mobilisation politique et leadership régional en 1837–1838* (Quebec: Septentrion, 2004); Gilles Laporte, *Brève histoire des patriotes* (Quebec: Septentrion, 2015); Julien Mackay, *Notaires et patriotes, 1837–1838* (Quebec: Septentrion, 2006); Elinor Kyte Senior, *Redcoats and Patriotes: The Rebellions in Lower Canada, 1837–38* (Ottawa: Canadian War Museum Historical Publication 20, 1985).

7 Mylène Bédard, *Écrire en temps d'insurrections: pratiques épistolaires et usages de la presse chez les femmes patriotes (1830–1840)* (Montreal: Les Presses de l'Université de Montreal, 2016); Deschamps, *La "Rébellion de 1837" à travers le prisme du Montreal Herald*; Laporte, *Brève histoire des patriotes*.

8 Mauduit, "'Vrais républicains' d'Amérique," 3.

9 See for instance Alan Skeoch, *United Empire Loyalists and the American Revolution* (Toronto: Grolier, 1982); David Mills, *The Idea of Loyalty in Upper Canada, 1784–1850* (Montreal: McGill-Queen's University Press, 1988); Norman Knowles, *Inventing the Loyalists: The Ontario Loyalists Tradition and the Creation of Usable Pasts* (Toronto: University of Toronto Press, 1997); Alan Taylor, *The Civil War of 1812: American Citizens, British Subjects, Irish Rebels, and Indian Allies* (New York: Alfred Knopf, 2010).

10 Several historians are guilty of this, but most significant is Colin F. Read. See Colin F. Read, *The Rising in Western Upper Canada, 1837–38: The Duncombe Revolt and After* (Toronto: University of Toronto Press, 1982).

11 Gérard Filteau, *Histoire des Patriotes* (Queebec: Septentrion, 2004 [1938])

12 Alan Greer, "1837–38: Rebellion Reconsidered," *Canadian Historical Review* 76, no. 1 (1995): 8.

13 Michel Ducharme, *The Idea of Liberty during the Age of Atlantic Revolutions* (Montreal: McGill-Queen's University Press, 2014).

14 Laporte, *Brève histoire des Patriotes*, 95–8.

15 Most overviews of the Jacksonian period either ignore the Rebellion or discuss it in a mere few paragraphs. For instance, Daniel Walker Howe, *What Hath God Wrought: The Transformation of America, 1815–1848* (Oxford: Oxford University Press, 2009); John Lauritz Larson, *The Market Revolution in America: Liberty, Ambition and the Eclipse of the Common Good* (New York: Cambridge University Press, 2010); Melvyn Stokes and Stephen Conway, *The Market Revolution in America: Social, Political and Religious Expressions, 1800–1880* (Charlottesville: University Press of

Virginia, 1996); Charles Sellers, *The Market Revolution: Jacksonian America, 1815–1846* (New York: Oxford University Press, 1991); Henry Watson, *Liberty and Power: The Politics of Jacksonian America* (New York: Hill and Wang, 2006). Finally, recent studies on filibustering expeditions also ignore or limit their analyses of the Rebellion to a few pages: Amy S. Greenberg, *Manifest Manhood and the Antebellum American Empire* (Cambridge: Cambridge University Press, 2005); Robert E. May, *Manifest Destiny's Underworld: Filibustering in Antebellum America* (Chapel Hill, NC: University of North Carolina Press, 2002). The most serious article on the issue of filibustering and Canada was produced by Samuel Watson, who examined how United States Army Officers, under the order of President Van Buren, prevented Americans from intervening in the Rebellion. Samuel Watson, "United States Army Officers Fight the 'Patriot War': Responses to Filibustering on the Canadian Border, 1837–39," *Journal of the Early Republic* 18 (Fall 1998): 485–519.

16 James Kloppenberg, *Toward Democracy: The Struggle for Self-Rule in European and American Thought* (Oxford: Oxford University Press, 2016).

17 For an example of a comparative approach to North American borderlands history, see: Benjamin H. Johnson and Andrew R. Graybill, eds, *Bridging National Borders in North America: Transnational and Comparative Histories* (Durham, NC: Duke University Press, 2010). For a more theoretical, conceptual, and methodological discussion on borderlands, including the comparative approach, see: Pekka Hämäläinen and Samuel Truett, "On Borderlands," *Journal of American History* 98, no. 2 (September 2011): 338–61.

18 Albert B. Corey, *The Crisis of 1830–42 in Canadian-American Relations* (New Haven: Yale University Press, 1941); Edwin C. Guillet, *The Lives and Times of the Patriots: An Account of the Rebellion in Upper Canada, 1837–1838, and The Patriot Agitation in the United States, 1837–1842* (Toronto: Thomas Nelson & Sons, 1938); Oscar A. Kinchen, *The Rise and Fall of the Patriot Hunters* (New York: Bookman Associates, 1956); Orrin Tiffany, *The Relations of the United States to the Canadian Rebellion of 1837–1838* (Ann Arbor: N.A., 1905).

19 For instance, see Jean-Paul Bernard, "Vermonters and the Lower Canadian Rebellions of 1837–1838," *Vermont History* 58, no. 4 (1990): 250–63; John Duffy and Nicholas Muller, "The Great Wolf Hunt: The Popular Response in Vermont to the 'Patriote' Uprising of 1837," *Journal of American Studies* 8, no. 2 (1974): 153–69; Peter G. Marshall, "George Bancroft and the Canadian Rebellions and the American Revolution,"

*New England Quarterly* 63, no. 2 (June 1990): 302–8; Roger L. Rosentreter, "Liberating Canada: Michigan and the Patriotic War," *Michigan History* 67, no. 2 (March 1983): 32–4; Roger L. Rosentreter, "Brigands and Paragons: Michigan Officials during the Patriot War," *Michigan History* 73, no. 5 (September 1989): 24–31; Stuart D. Scott, "The Patriot Game: New Yorkers and the Canadian Rebellion of 1837–38," *New York History* 68, no. 3 (July 1987): 281–95.

20 Lillian F. Gates, "The Decided Policy of William Lyon Mackenzie," *Canadian Historical Review* 40, no. 5 (1959): 185–208; Marc L. Harris, "The Meaning of Patriot: The Canadian Rebellion and American Republicanism, 1837–1839," *Michigan Historical Review* 23, no. 1 (1997): 37.

21 For instance, see: Yvan Lamonde, "Conscience coloniale et conscience internationale dans les écrits publics de Louis-Joseph Papineau (1815–1839)," *Revue d'histoire de l'Amérique française* 51, no. 1 (Summer 1997): 3–37; Yvan Lamonde, *Histoire sociale des idées au Québec* (1760–1896), vol. I (Montreal: Fides, 2000); Lamonde, "Le Bas-Canada et *Le Courrier des États-Unis* de New York (1828–1840)." The influence of American Republicanism on Louis-Joseph Papineau was also an important part of a 2012 book Lamonde published with Jonathan Livernois: *Papineau: Erreur sur la personne* (Montreal: Les éditions du Boréal, 2012). The influence of "americanité" and "américanisation" (or Americanness and Americanization) on Quebec has also been the subject of several studies. Yvan Lamonde has written particularly extensively on the topic. "Americanité," as a historiographical concept, insists on the influence and impact of the American model and American culture on the evolution of Québecois and French-Canadian identity, society, and heritage, to this very day. With regards to the patriotes in Lower Canada, Lamonde maintains that the American republican experience served as a model and provided the answer to their frustrations with Britain and their political aspirations on the continent. They admired their neighbour to the south and looked to it for inspiration and guidance. See for instance: Yvan Lamonde, "A One-Way Mirror: American Cultural Influence in Quebec," *Problems and Opportunities in US-Quebec Relations*, eds Alfred Hero Jr and Marcel Daneau (Boulder, CO: Westview Press, 1984): 106–26; Gérard Bouchard et Yvan Lamonde (dir.) *Québécois et américains: la culture québécoise aux XIX et XX siècles* (Montréal: Fides, 1995); Yvan Lamonde, *Avec eux ni sans eux: le Québec et les États-Unis* (Quebec: Nuit blanche éditeur, 1996); Yvan Lamonde, "Pourquoi penser l'américanité du Québec?" *Politique et Sociétés* 18, no. 1: 93–8; Yvan Lamonde, "Antiaméricanisme

européen et anti-américanisme vus du Québec," in *Américanisations et anti-américanismes compares*, eds Olivier Dard and Hans-Jürgen Lüsebrink (Lille, France: Presses universitaires du Septentrion, 2008), 79–86. Others have also worked on the topic. For instance: Gérard Bouchard, *La nation québécoise au futur et au passé* (Montreal: VLB éditeur, 1999); Jean-François Côté, "L'identification américaine au Québec: de processus en résultats," in *L'américanité* et les *Amériques*, ed. Donald Cuccioletta (Sainte-Foy: Éditions de l'IQRC, 2001), 6–27; and Joseph Yvon Thériault, *Critique de l'américanité: mémoire et démocratie au Québec* (Montreal: Québec Amérique, 2002).

22 Andrew Bonthius, "The Patriot War of 1837–1838: Locofocoism with a Gun?" *Labour/Le Travail* 52 (Fall 2003): 9–43.

23 Louis-Georges Harvey, *Le printemps de l'Amérique française: Américanité, anticolonialisme et républicanisme dans le discours politique québécois, 1805–1837* (Montreal: Boréal, 2004); Albert Schrauwers, *Union Is Strength: W.L. Mackenzie, the Children of Peace, and the Emergence of Joint Stock Democracy in Upper Canada* (Toronto: University of Toronto Press, 2009); and Charles-Phillipe Courtois, "Nation et république chez les Patriotes," in *La culture des Patriotes* (Quebec: Septentrion, 2012), 85–118. In a more recent article, Harvey also found important links between some Lower Canadian rebels, particularly Edmund Bailey O'Callaghan, and the anti-bank sentiments of the New York Locofoco movement, men such as journalist William Legget. Louis-Georges Harvey, "Banques, société et politique dans le discours politique d'Edmund Bailey O'Callaghan, 1833–1837," *Cahier des dix* 69 (2015): 251–79.

24 David Shields, "The Power to Be Reborn," in *The American Revolution Reborn*, eds Patrick Spero and Michael Zuckerman (Philadelphia: University of Pennsylvania Press, 2016), 294.

25 Ibid., 296.

26 Ibid., 297.

27 Dagenais, "[T]Hose who had money were opposed to us," and Jason Opal (avec la collaboration de Julien Mauduit), "La Panique financière de 1819 et les patriotes de 1837: nouveau regard sur le rapprochement anglo-américain et la 'démocratie jacksonienne,'" *Bulletin d'histoire politique* 25 (Winter 2017): 193–221.

28 Mauduit, "'Vrais républicains' d'Amérique."

29 Thomas Richards Jr, "The Texas Moment: Breakaway Republics and Contested Sovereignty in North America, 1836–46" (PhD diss., Temple University, 2016).

30 Ruth Dunley, "A.D. Smith: Knight-Errant of Radical Democracy" (PhD diss., University of Ottawa, 2008).

31 Stephen Smith, "Within Arm's Reach: Political Violence, Voluntary Organizing, and the Borderland Press during the Canadian Rebellion, 1834–1842" (PhD diss., Queen's University, 2017). Based on his PhD dissertation, Taylor Spence's book project, *Cataraqui: Dominion, Possession, and Land Rights in the Borderland of North American Empires*, also promises to push our understanding of the Rebellion in a transnational framework forward. Taylor Spence, "The Endless Commons: Indigenous and Immigrant in the British-American Borderland, 1835–1848" (PhD diss., Yale University, 2012).

32 In what he calls "la refondation par les armes des institutions canadiennes," Deschamps argues that the tories used the context of the 1837 insurrections to enact their own plans, a "second conquest" that would, once and for all, turn Lower Canada into a full British colony. Under the guise of an "anti-insurrectional" movement, the radical tories themselves rebelled against the Executive Council, the "politics of conciliation" of the Colonial Office, and the French Canadian population in general. Deschamps, *La "rebellion de 1837" à travers du prisme du Montreal Herald*, 243.

33 Daniel Walker Howe, *What Hath God Wrought: The Transformation of America, 1815–1848* (Oxford: Oxford University Press, 2009); John Lauritz Larson, *The Market Revolution in America: Liberty, Ambition and the Eclipse of the Common Good* (New York: Cambridge University Press, 2010); Charles Sellers, *The Market Revolution: Jacksonian America, 1815–1846* (New York: Oxford University Press, 1991).

34 In this context, the Canada we are referring to is Upper and Lower Canada, not Canada in the modern, present sense.

35 Allan Greer was one of the first modern historians – although older historians such as Frank Underhill, Stanley Ryerson, and S.D. Clark also made similar claims – to seriously consider the connections between events in Lower and Upper Canada. To Greer, there were similar social, political, economic, and even "ethnocultural" tensions in both colonies, both events developed and unfolded in a similar fashion, and both Upper and Lower Canadian rebels supported one another. See Greer, "1837–38: Rebellion Reconsidered."

36 For instance, see Laporte's very recent overview of the 1837 and 1838 Lower Canadian Rebellion: *Brève histoire des patriotes*.

37 See Julien Mauduit, "L'économie politique des patriotes, entre capitalisme et socialisme," *Bulletin d'histoire politique* 25, no. 2 (Winter 2017) : 172–92.

38 For instance, in October 2017, we hosted a roundtable discussion at the annual meeting of the Institut d'histoire de l'Amérique française titled "Entre le national et le transnational: les Rébellions de 1837–38." Though our panelists touched upon a variety of topics, the issue of connecting these events was the most hotly debated, with most arguing against it, pointing out that Upper and Lower Canada were two very different colonies, with two very different populations.

39 For instance, see Béatrice Craig and Maxime Dagenais, *The Land in Between: The Upper St John Valley, Prehistory to World War One* (Thomaston, ME: Tilbury House Publishers, 2009); Amy Greenberg, *Manifest Manhood and the Antebellum American Empire* (Cambridge: Cambridge University Press, 2005) and Richards, "The Texas Moment."

SECTION ONE

# Economic Concerns

I

# Patriots No More

## *The Political Economy of Anglo-American Rapprochement, 1815–1846*

JASON M. OPAL

In early 1820, a Virginia newspaper summarized the recent history of the Atlantic world this way: "the transition from war to peace was sudden." Andrew Jackson won glory at New Orleans on 8 January 1815, and Napoleon met his Waterloo on 18 June of the same year. All at once, the vast struggle between revolutionary France and the British-led coalitions was over, along with the proxy war in North America. To be sure, violence persisted along the Gulf Coast, where Jackson wiped out British-allied Seminoles and black regulars. The "Old Hero" also executed two Britons captured in Florida in early 1818, moving patriotic Englishmen to call for a third war against the republican traitors. But cooler heads prevailed. The American minister to London credited the Tory leadership for holding firm against the "almost universal" call to arms, thus keeping a rational – and profitable – peace.[1]

The sudden change made people think about patriotism more generally. As Noah Webster puts it in his first dictionary, patriotism was "the noblest passion that animates a man in the character of a citizen." It was a "zealous" desire to serve one's country, "either in defending it from invasion, or protecting its rights and maintaining its laws and institutions in vigour and purity." If the world crisis and total wars of 1793–1815 had made the first part of that definition self-evident, the ensuing peace left the rest open for interpretation. A patriot defended his homeland: that was obvious. But what did that mean when the threat of invasion passed? What was *peacetime* patriotism? How should it inform foreign and domestic policy and their intersection in the new field of political economy?[2]

During the long years of war and its close aftermath, agricultural producers of all kinds – tenant farmers in East Anglia as well as slave-owners in Alabama – had taken full advantage of high prices and easy money. They had put marginal lands under plough and bought new estates on credit, counting on the insatiable demands of full-spectrum militaries and long-deprived consumers. In the English midlands, entire industries had grown up to equip the fleets and troops. Here again, peace changed everything. From 1815 to 1819, prices for wheat, corn, tobacco, and cotton fell. Idled sailors and soldiers flooded the labour force. Arms-makers looked for new buyers among South American rebels.[3]

In British domains, these economic shocks sparked a wide range of rebellions and protests, which Prime Minister Liverpool and his "liberal Tories" vigorously repressed. British policy then cohered around an imperial interest defined within the "natural" laws of a global economy, calling for free trade abroad and austerity at home. In the more open political context of the United States, hard times instead gave rise to state-level efforts to secure the people from such an economy. These efforts were self-consciously patriotic in their focus on local autonomy and hostility to the British.

After surveying all this unrest and reaction in the post-war years, this essay argues that the national leader and regional interests who emerged victorious in the United States changed their minds about the traditional British foe. They did so quietly but definitively from the mid-1820s to the mid-1830s. Among the victims of this subtle rapprochement were the Canadian and American "Patriots" of 1837–38, who assumed that the United States would support their anti-British revolution. Instead they found that the American republic was allied in all but name with Queen Victoria's vast and vigorous empire.[4]

## REBELLIONS

The end of war in 1815 glutted labour markets in Britain. Prices and wages fell faster than rents, making landlords even less popular than usual. Those resentments were enhanced by the 1815 Corn Law, which forbade the importation of grains until domestic prices hit 80 shillings per quarter (Canadian wheat could enter at 67 shillings). The ruling Tories saw this as a temporary measure, for they increasingly embraced the "invisible hand" as the best way to enrich the empire and discipline the people. Young conservatives and liberals alike also took aim at what they saw as excessive poor relief, while creditors called in loans and denounced paper currencies. In Barbados, the oldest part of the British West Indies, planters intensified production to satisfy their debts. Combined with rumours that the Crown wanted to free them, this pushed large numbers of slaves to rebel on Easter Sunday 1816.[5]

The spring of 1816 also brought Luddite vandalism in Midlands towns and unemployment riots in East Anglia. Unlike eighteenth-century bread rioters, these rebels questioned the deeper relations of the market, including the right of employers to set wages and replace winter workers with threshing machines. Scottish farmers and tenants did somewhat better in the post-war doldrums. As the magistrates of one county boasted, the people were "too much of an agricultural cast for the spirit of *radicalism*" to take root. But Scottish workers led by an unemployed weaver set up a new government in Glasgow in April 1820. They reached out to their English counterparts around Manchester, who were still reeling from the "Peterloo" massacre of the previous year. Everywhere, Prime Minister Liverpool worried, the transition to peace revealed new and frightening class divisions and a general teetering of "established authority."[6]

By contrast, the United States boomed. Slave-grown cotton from the Gulf Coast lands conquered by Andrew Jackson fetched high prices in England, setting off a rush on public land offices. The good times vindicated Jackson's vision of "growing greatness," in which people like him could pursue lands and profits wherever they wanted. Once export prices dipped as imperial markets recovered, however, both American and British bankers sought to retire risky debts and currencies. The steep rise in personal indebtedness during the boom made the resulting "Panic of 1819" a general depression, not just a credit crisis. "All things are changed, the rich have become poor," one Ohio banker summated. "['Tis] want, and fear and prosecution and suspicion and terror and dismay and bankruptcy and pauperism on all sides and on all hands." Blame fell variously on the Bank of England, the Second Bank of the United States (BUS), the many smaller banks chartered by the states, and – more accurately – the neocolonial character of the American economy.[7]

Besides the northern cities, where liberal reformers denounced aid to paupers, the depression hit hardest where people had been buying public land at inflated prices. As of the 1820 nadir, citizens in Alabama, Mississippi, Ohio, and other western states owed the U.S. government some $22 million dollars, or about ten times the sums outstanding to the BUS in Ohio and Kentucky. "The whole population trembled upon the brink of ruin," one westerner recalled. Had the government acted like a "rigid creditor," tens of thousands of people would have faced foreclosure. Instead, Congress passed a Relief Act in early 1821 enabling people to walk away from plots they could not afford.[8]

The more radical wave of "relief" ideas swept through the state legislatures, challenging the gentry-dominated factions that normally ran things. In June 1819, for instance, a "numerous public meeting" in Frankfort, Kentucky urged quick action to stop property auctions. Its obscure leaders spoke of their patriotic duty to protect the "general welfare." In July, a similar rally took over the steps of the Tennessee state house, presenting a slate of new candidates. This mobilization brought a 40 per cent surge in voter turnout in Davidson County, home of an appalled Andrew Jackson. By the end of the year, the new legislature passed a stay law that gave a debtor two years to repay, unless the creditor accepted current bank notes rather than specie.[9]

During the summer of 1820, the Governor of Tennessee, Joseph McMinn, called for the further "care and protection of government" in the face of general distress. Individuals would and should pursue "private gain," he said. "But public prosperity should not be sacrificed to the gratification of a few," as when good farms went for a song at sheriffs' auctions. Economic emergency called for an "indulgent policy" for the "debtor class," an "extraordinary effort" by and for the people. In Kentucky, the uprising had begun as an effort to tax the charter banks along with the BUS, which both the federal district courts and the Supreme Court disallowed. As the crisis deepened, though, "Relief" became a more proactive project led by the Governor and legislature against the courts.[10]

Many states had used stay laws during the post-war depression of the 1780s and again during the embargo of 1807–09, even though Article I, Section 10 of the U.S. Constitution – the "Contracts Clause" – more or less forbade these interventions. What made such measures during the "hard times" of 1819–22 different was that they came with a deeper critique of the *laissez faire* rule of law, a wider call for patriotic solidarity and general well-being. Experience had shown the need for a "visitorial superintending authority" above private interests, a Kentucky leader announced. The people had to secure "the safety of the community" against uncaring outsiders and impersonal forces. Another relief leader spoke of a "fatal tendency in the progress of society" to make life harder on the poor and unfortunate, while the Frankfort public meeting called for "merciful forbearance" to head off "*general* calamity." A Virginia assemblyman used his state's patriotic record against British creditors during the Revolution to argue for the people's ongoing authority over "*legal process* within her domain."[11]

In Kentucky and Tennessee, especially, this movement also tried to challenge the private, state-chartered banks with public, state-owned banks. The mission of the Bank of the State of Tennessee, opened in the fall of 1820, was to help small settlers buy and keep small tracts of land. It was to increase the sum of money that answered to the "public welfare," shifting economic power away from the large planters and interstate merchants who normally controlled credit. This "New Bank" would be "a blessing to the people of this State," its supporters insisted. It was indeed "the PEOPLE'S BANK," distinct from the older banks in that it served and answered to Tennessee voters. The notes of the Bank of the Commonwealth of Kentucky began to circulate in early 1821. This, too, was a "republican bank," a patriotic measure for a peacetime emergency.[12]

These new state banks relied on land sales and taxes to underwrite their notes. They also attached themselves to the new stay laws: creditors who would not accept their bills were barred from suing their debtors for two years. In this way, too, the legislature propped up the people's money and declared a new kind of independence from market rules and forces. Of course, out-of-state lenders and foreign merchandisers might still refuse or discount the notes and demand specie. But so what? Governor McMinn dared to ask. The goal was to secure the well-being of state residents, not to ease transactions across state or national lines. It was to let Tennesseans "command the common destinies of the soil they tread," recycling the values they created for the mutual benefit of those who lived and laboured there.[13]

A second, more constitutional form of economic patriotism to emerge from the hard times was "Protection." Among its champions was Henry Clay of Kentucky, whose manufactories had suffered from the post-war influx of Scottish and Russian hemp and cordage. By holding on to its western lands and imposing higher tariffs, he argued, the national state could pay for new roads and canals, fostering home markets. Without such an "American System," Clay warned, the United States and its southern (but not northern) neighbours would continue to cower under the invisible fist of European capital. The Irish-born Mathew Carey of Pennsylvania argued that the government's duty was to "step in" and favour American workshops over British factories. "Patriotism" demanded no less. Delegates from nine states attended a Convention of Friends of Domestic Industry in New York in early 1820, making Protection an electoral force that ran north of Relief.[14]

And yet the United Agricultural Societies of Virginia also held their first meeting in 1820. Denying the "patriotic motives" of protectionists, these wealthy planters warned that this was no time for "an experimental course of political economy" in which nations altered the flow of goods and credit to finance their own development. Rather it was time to unleash "a most unrestricted" trade over Creation, to preserve traditional social relations by giving slave-owners and other businessmen more markets. God wanted the oceans "traversed and overcome," just as he demanded that the debts incurred through such trade be redeemed in gold or silver specie. Any imposition on commercial pursuits was as "artificial" as paper money. That same year, some two hundred London merchants signed a petition for free trade, while the Bank of England prepared to resume specie payments for the first time since 1797.[15]

## REACTIONS

Although Liverpool's government spent modest sums to employ idled workers – most fittingly with the Church Building Acts of 1818 and 1824 – it preferred to inflict law and order through show trials and deportations. Tory leaders also fought the "democratic tyranny" of trade unions and Luddites by spying on dissidents and spreading pro-government news. The Scottish rebellion of 1820 also ran into state repression and popular ambivalence. British troops easily quelled the Glasgow rising, executing three leaders and sending others to Botany Bay. Many more Scots chose exile. Among them was William Lyon Mackenzie, who settled in Upper Canada. Over the next decade, the British government offered North American lands to English and Scottish men who would otherwise cause trouble at home. Upper Canada's population surged fourfold in the twenty years after the war, a rate of growth comparable to the frontier states to the south.[16]

The aftermath of the 1816 uprising on Barbados was far bloodier: several hundred slaves were massacred over several weeks. "Very horrid," one planter reported. "Heads sticking all about the country." As more rebellions followed in Demerara and Jamaica, British opinion turned against the slave-owners, if not against slavery itself. As one critic noted, the empire had spent too much blood and treasure on the West Indian planters, much as Napoleon had wasted whole armies on Haiti. Now His Majesty's subjects were paying once again for those planters' sugar monopoly. Perhaps the "true interest" of Britain was instead to free both the slaves and the colonies, enabling a "voluntary, unconstrained interchange of commodities" within and even beyond the Empire. The Tory government thus moved towards free trade during the early 1820s while preserving protections for Canadian wheat and timber, drawing in Montreal merchants while cutting out West Indian planters.[17]

In the southern and western United States, the post-war uprisings had wider and deeper support. Their opponents therefore had to bide their time, chipping away at Relief and exploiting its latent tensions. Public banking was the first target. "There are, no doubt, some hard cases of oppression and embarrassment, which require relief," conceded the September 1820 *Gazette* of Nashville, a mouthpiece for the state's older banking interests. But the times were not so bad as to excuse such an "alarming violation of the Constitution of the United States" as a public bank. This resonated among both right-thinking businessmen and isolated farmers who tended to shun all banks. A month later, with the people's bank up and running, the *Gazette* hardened its tone. Only "broken merchants, negro traders [and] land mongers and speculators" had suffered in the Panic. Why should others have to pay – or not be paid – for their mistakes? Why should the people bail each other out?[18]

Stay laws helped most during their first year, enabling debtors to complete a season without losing time and capital to lawsuits and foreclosures. In Jackson's mid-Tennessee county, for example, the number of prosecutions for debts and ejectments dropped 40 per cent from late 1819 to late 1820. After that the number of people they annoyed grew. Two small petitions in the summer of 1820 declared that further interventions would only help "the Rich and speculating Class." And while poorer settlements balked at a state bank, tradesmen in town centres objected to the stay law. One group of tradesmen and villagers noted that they had "allready Suffered a sacrifice of our property to pay our just Debts" and simply wanted their own debtors to do the same. For his part, Mathew Carey deplored these "*acts of legislature, suspending the collection of debts*" for depriving tradesmen of their pay.[19]

Popular fatigue with Relief also reflected its fine print. Missouri's stay law, for example, enabled a citizen to reclaim foreclosed property within thirty months, at 6 per cent interest. This brought little help to poor settlers and may have enabled speculators to cut overhead during the crisis and then reclaim the land after someone else had improved it. In Tennessee, the public bank was tied to the earlier stay law, which had also encouraged creditors to accept the notes of the two older banks. Relief legislation thus buoyed the "money" of the very people most blamed for the Panic along with that of the new, unproven "Bank of the people." Anti-Relief legislators also pushed through some last-minute revisions to trim its scope. These new bank notes were not backed by the "faith of the state," one conservative stipulated, but only by a limited number of land sales. Future legislatures were thus free to defund the experiment. This lawmaker also attacked Relief in court.[20]

Federal judges had used the Contracts Clause against debtor relief since their inception in the late 1780s. They cited the "sacred" principles of national credit just as the Public Accounts Commissioners of Britain did that same decade. Such precedents guided the Tennessee Supreme Court's ruling on the people's bank in May 1821. Both the stay law of 1819 and the public bank act of 1820 were void, the judges ruled. One added that it would be "unconscionable" of creditors to press too hard during this "extraordinary" depression, but that he could not *force* them to show any patriotic forbearance. Similar decisions followed in Kentucky and Missouri. Supporters could only hope that "liberal and patriotic merchants" who identified with their fellow citizens would still support the public banks.[21]

Relief leaders in Kentucky dug in their heels during 1823, even burning some $770,000 in public bank bills to bolster the value of those still in circulation. That autumn, however, an appellate court scolded the legislature that its real obligation was not so much to Kentucky as to every individual who owned property in Kentucky, resident or not. The protection of that property was the defining duty of any state under the U.S. Constitution, indeed of "all civilized states." A creditor's right to outstanding debts moved with him; the state had no right to challenge this "international principle" in the name of its own well-being. The key attribute of the Federal Constitution, one judge explained, was "to impose an obligation upon all the states to give free course to the coercion of contracts." *Free course to the coercion of contracts*: this was exactly what out-of-state creditors, not to mention British investors, wanted to hear.[22]

By then, the hard times had passed, and the rush to explain what had happened began. The founder of Tennessee's state bank credited both the Relief measures and the people's industry with reducing private debts by three-fifths from 1819 to 1821. He saw no need for further interventions, not least because he had larger political ambitions. "The relief measures sprang from the great mass of the people," the Kentucky-based *Argus of Western America* declared in 1823, "and are by them sustained." The legislature best reflected popular will, and by extension "the eternal principles of *justice* and *mercy.*" Surely they could authorize emergency departures from legal principles born in England. What patriot would say otherwise? The *Argus* tried to name them: "Is there an Englishman in the country? He is one of them. Is there a non-resident land speculator? He is one of them. Is there an advocate for the surrender of the power of the states to tax the United States Bank? He is one of them. Is there an advocate for the many and flagrant usurpations of the Supreme Court? He is one of them ... Is there a man who denies the power of State Legislatures to grant indulgence to debtors even in times of the greatest calamity? He is one of them." Stunned by the judicial backlash, one Relief leader asked how any law that would "*grind to death* the debtor" could be better than one that applied "the feelings of humanity" to social and economic relations among patriotic citizens.[23]

In response, anti-Relief leaders drew bright contrasts between the foolish experiments in Kentucky and the promised land of Ohio, which had stood firm against the popular call for more money. Ohio's legislature, one paper opined, had honoured the Constitution's rules. It had "put down a host of swindling banks, banished a spurious medium, and restored the good old currency." Presumably, the "good old currency" was coin, while the "spurious medium" referred to the bills printed by the public banks, or by the "swindling" banks, or both. Americans were now done with "spurious banks" and "ridiculous" stop laws. Through such vehement generalities, opponents of

Relief appealed to everyone who disliked one part or another of the legal and monetary tangles it left behind.[24]

Beyond the quintessentially conservative theme of personal accountability to non-negotiable rules, anti-Relief forces had another weapon: Andrew Jackson, "the Hero" himself. He had made his name as a lawyer and judge before launching an ambitious import-export business in early Tennessee. He blamed delinquent debtors and federally protected "Indian Country" for its disappointing returns. The Battle of New Orleans made him a legend, of course, but he never changed his hardline views about the "duties of strict justice" that followed commerce around the world. When the depression hit in 1819, the fifty-two-year-old grumbled that there was "no escape" besides "industry and economy." In this he sounded much like Lord Liverpool, who shrugged that everyone just had to wait "'till trade comes round" and employment returned "in a natural way."[25]

Possibly in military uniform, Jackson had waited for the Tennessee lawmakers as they entered the statehouse for their emergency session of 1820. There he warned them that voting for the public bank would mean violating the oaths they had taken to the Tennessee and U.S. Constitutions. Jackson also authored an anti-Relief petition with other wealthy men from Nashville. Wondering why "so much sympathy should be indulged for the *debtor*, and none for the *creditor*," it denied the legislature's right to interfere on behalf of either party. Citing "judicious" rules of political economy, Jackson's treatise also celebrated the "enterprising commercial adventurers" who risked their fortunes while seeking "markets abroad." Only by enabling such men to collect and sue could Tennesseans preserve "our respectability abroad as well as our confidence at home." As for the people at large, they should rediscover "our former habits of industry and simplicity," saving themselves rather than helping each other.[26]

Beaten in 1820, Jackson kept up his resistance in letters to key allies in the legislature. Relief laws were "not voidable, but absolutely void," the spawn of "demagogues" and "despots." He would oppose them "as long as I live." Sometime between late 1821 and early 1822 he decided to run for president. His campaign began with a 4 July 1822 address in Nashville, during which he accepted a sword for patriotic service – and refocused public debate on "the whole British and Indian War" that had ended at the gates of New Orleans. He had acted as "the humble instrument in the hand of Divine Providence" to save the frontiers from "savage cruelty" and the Crescent City from "ravages and pollution," he declared. The "*holy* zeal" that his soldiers had shown "ought to be fostered and cherished, not dampened, by the government." For it was "this *zeal alone*," Jackson insisted, "that can defend and preserve the liberties of our country."[27]

Most people wanted to think that Jackson was on their side, which made it all the easier for his handlers to build a national coalition upon his few known positions. In 1820, *Niles' Weekly Register* approvingly published his tirade against public banks and stay laws, while Jackson spelled out that opposition to the men who organized his campaigns. Chief among these was Tennessee's leading jurist, who made clear that Jackson had always been a "firm and inflexible judge," as well as future cabinet member John Eaton, who in a revised and authorized biography of 1824 noted that the General was "scrupulously attentive" to financial obligations. In addition, the *National Intelligencer* had published Jackson's 1819 toast to "Domestic Manufactures." The nation's most connected readers thus knew him as safely anti-Relief and vaguely sympathetic to Protection. Everyone else simply knew him as America's "great avenger," the fearless patriot who had made the British invaders bathe in their own blood.[28]

Jackson's legend was most powerful in the same western and southern regions where Relief had been most radical, burying that movement as no judicial reaction ever could. In 1824, for example, a Relief supporter from Kentucky compared anti-Relief conservatives to the New England Federalists who had almost committed treason during the War of 1812. These were the unpatriotic men, the writer noted, "whom General Jackson says he would have hanged if it had been the last act of his life." The article thus identified Jackson with the most impassioned ways of dealing with Britons and Federalists, sweeping away the key distinctions over where, when, and against whom the American people should be patriotic.[29]

## REALIGNMENTS

Jackson's ascent is often linked to that of the frontier west in American politics, but he was no less a product – and servant – of the slaveholding south. The political ferment in this region began with the wrenching debate over whether to admit Missouri as a state in early 1819. Northern congressmen tried to stop the spread of slavery in this new land beyond the Mississippi, outraging southern delegates. The economic crisis that followed hit Virginia, the oldest and most prestigious slave state, especially hard. Yet its conservative leaders turned back Relief measures as "warring with the very principles of the social compact." The answer, they insisted, was freer trade and more rigorous debt collection. Here again they echoed the British government.[30]

Once cotton prices began to recover, southern planters made enough profits to reassure their British creditors while Upper South planters found new domestic markets for their slaves. One big season could turn everything around. For Andrew Jackson that was 1824, when he shipped enough to cover his most pressing debts and buy more slaves; the next year the total value of the U.S. cotton crop soared past its 1818 level. Especially as Great Britain moved away from wartime protectionism in the early 1820s, its industrial and technological supremacy no longer worried southern exporters. Instead it offered a new lease on life for the beleaguered slaveholders.[31]

Two other developments reinforced the great turn to cotton. The first was the 1820 creation of *Gossypium barbadense* in Mississippi, a hybrid of superior "pickability." The second was the spread of steamboats, the American answer to Britain's industrial wonders. Still a curiosity on the Mississippi River a decade after its 1811 introduction there, these privately owned vessels proliferated as flush times resumed. They conquered space without public investments or state charters, defying winds and currents and answering only to the "natural" laws of commerce. Andrew Jackson was among their biggest enthusiasts, and not only because one of the first steamboats operating near Nashville was the *General Jackson*.[32]

The presidential election of 1824 revealed the diversity of southern opinion at this key moment. The safest choice was William H. Crawford of Georgia, a longtime cabinet member who generally called for strict construction and states' rights. But Crawford had a stroke before the campaign heated up, leaving the field to three other conventional candidates: John C. Calhoun, a South Carolina firebrand; Henry Clay, the protectionist with strong support in the Upper South; and John Quincy Adams, a New Englander with an impeccable record of political service. And then there was Jackson, that "patriot ... of the first class" and anti-British hero. "He is honest, he is independent," commented the rising judge Roger B. Taney. "He is taken up spontaneously by the people." Jackson took the popular vote but lost out as Congress installed Adams as president, who in turn chose Clay as secretary of state.[33]

In his youth, Taney had been a Federalist in much the way Jackson was: a sentinel of global commercial order over unruly states and local demands. Sometimes he criticized slavery. He changed that tune shortly after moving to the racial hotspot of Baltimore in 1823, the year after the Vesey conspiracy terrified the haughty free-traders of South Carolina. Abolitionist agitation in that seaport pushed Taney and other young conservatives into a kind of anti-black fundamentalism. Obsessed with the bodily safety of white women and men, this viewpoint named all black people as inherently and permanently degraded, no matter what political and legal changes happened around them.[34]

Historically, the British Empire had been the one to force such changes. Its ships and troops had targeted American slavery during both the War of the Revolution and the War of 1812, and its native and black proxies had fought on in East Florida even after the British gave up on them in 1818. In the eternal frontier of slave country, Thomas Jefferson's shocking charge from 1776 – that the king had set black and native men to murder white families – remained a vivid scenario even as the microeconomic interests of southern masters began to align with the macroeconomic approach of British rulers. Simply put, southern whites feared and hated Britain. When in 1823 the British government offered to go "hand in hand" with the United States in preventing France, Spain, and Russia from re-colonizing the Americas, however, all of that changed.[35]

As Jefferson told President Monroe, this possibility of an Anglo-American alliance was "the most momentous" question to face Americans since the American Revolution. Momentous, but obvious: the United States, Jefferson counselled, should jump at the chance for real friendship with the empire. Knowing how deep Anglophobia ran among the American people (and his own cabinet), the president opted for his independent-sounding "Monroe Doctrine" rather than a formal alliance. As such the sea change in Anglo-American relations was quiet and subtle. Even the news from late 1826 that His Majesty had agreed to pay $1.2 million for slaves carried off during the last war drew only muted praise.[36]

If southern Anglophilia had a founding text, it was *The Crisis; Or, Essays on the Usurpations of the Federal Government*, published in Charleston in 1827 by the low country planter and lawyer

Robert J. Turnbull. Writing as Brutus, Turnbull questioned the very notion of the "*national welfare*," except during times of war or rebellion. Because the era of patriotic defence was over, at least as far as the British Empire was concerned, any effort to favour American over British producers was unjust and unwise. "Now, that we are independent," he noted, "Nature has bound us together in cords of mutual friendship." He cited Adam Smith to demand "a free and uninterrupted commerce with the whole world, and particularly with England."[37]

These were not mere questions of political economy, Brutus warned, but of subjects "ten thousand times ten thousand more important." Adams's plans for domestic progress would be the "the ENTERING WEDGE" for abolition. Canals, observatories, national universities, colonization societies: all of them threatened white families like "the secret dagger of the midnight assassin." Brutus likened tariff men such as Henry Clay to pirates and robbers. And when such criminals came to his home, he reserved the right to "BLOW OUT their BRAINS." Until then he urged the "real patriot" to see the danger and support Jackson over Adams and Clay in the election of 1828.[38]

Still, Brutus had his reservations about Jackson because the general had voted for tariffs during a brief Senate tour in 1824. During his second run for the White House, Jackson still signalled his support for "judicious" tariffs and national works, not least because these were very popular in "the great leading state of Pennsylvania." Always the general, he wanted to ensure that the United States could produce enough guns, ships, and uniforms to stop the next British invasion. As this threat quickly faded after 1823, however, Jackson gradually pulled back from Protection, indeed from the wider concept of economic patriotism within U.S. borders. As such he made a point of praising Great Britain in his First Inaugural and of negotiating more open trade with His Majesty's possessions in North America.[39]

During his first term, Jackson solidified southern support through his Indian Removal Act of 1830. Immediately after the vote, he vetoed federal support for an interstate road. Just after his re-election he struck down a more comprehensive plan for improvements. And after a tense showdown with anti-tariff extremists from South Carolina, Jackson and his party demoted the tariff to a mere source of revenue. For his next priority after native deportation was to retire the national debt, which would make the United States just as credit-worthy as him. As he told his adopted son, "farmers" like him had to pay every debt exactly as promised, or else their properties "must go" to auction. That was the rule of law, period.[40]

Rigid as ever about the stakes of commercial exchange, Jackson did everything he could to expand its range. He urged the overwhelmed War Department to use steamboats to hurry the natives out of the Deep South, enabling more planters to rush in. All the while he pushed hard for new access to British and Canadian markets, and indeed to the entire world – with an enlarged U.S. Navy offering protection and deterrence. Upon leaving office he also recommended sending a warship to the coast of Mexico, authorized to open fire if that republic refused to pay outstanding claims to American merchants.[41]

Much of Jackson's second term was taken up with his "War" on the BUS, which an English business agent, among others, found puzzling. By redirecting the government's revenue from the BUS to riskier and smaller "deposit banks," Jackson further diminished the scope of national economic policy. He even called for an entirely hard-money economy, with payments made only in Mexican or British coins or in gold pieces mined from what had been taken from the Cherokee lands of Georgia. What kind of nationalist would pursue such a radically decentralized policy? No matter, the Englishman shrugged: Jackson had retired the national debt in early 1834, another good sign for the republic "in point of national credit." British investors could lay their old fears of the "law of debtor and creditor in the U.S." to rest, so long as they did not mind dealing with a slave-owning power.[42]

## PANICS AND PATRIOTS

British investors had preferred the resource-rich South American republics to the United States. In the late 1820s, however, those new states defaulted on a range of loans to mining and pearl companies. Then, just as the factories of north Briton increased output, Jackson forced open millions of new acres of cotton land. This pushed the value of the precious fibre to more than half of America's total exports and erased old memories of the revolutionary republic that had renounced debts and confiscated properties. A minor recipient of British capital during most of its brief history, the United States became the main overseas market for English and Scottish capitalists during the 1830s.[43]

Giving up on a national system of public works under President Jackson, state governments turned to private funding for their canal, turnpike, and railroad projects. They wanted to imitate New York's smashing success with the Erie Canal and to provide their residents with faster, cheaper ways to market. This drove them into the arms of investors in London as well as New York. Even as the president celebrated his nation's golden credit rating, then, state debts grew by 660 per cent between 1830 and 1838. At least half of this growing sum was held by foreign creditors.[44]

In the slave states where native deportations were in full swing, over 85 per cent of state debts were incurred to open or expand banks. More money was in high demand in Mississippi and Alabama because the white invaders had to get cotton to England as fast as possible, while prices were high. They could not wait for public investments or internal markets. The rapid rise in the number of deposit banks – from seven to twenty-two in late 1833 alone – and the removal of the BUS as a monetary clearing house further encouraged this new profusion of paper, which in turn accelerated the purchase of land. More land under whip and plough meant that more product shipped to Britain, opening credit lines still wider and driving a steep increase in America's trade deficit with the mother country.[45]

Toward the end of his second term, the president began to worry that the full-throttle expansion he required was encouraging the full-throttle speculation he deplored. He explicitly recalled the economic crisis of 1819 as the history that could not be allowed to repeat itself, not least because it had spawned Relief and Protection. Beginning in 1835, then, the administration scrambled to take small bills and unreliable money out of circulation. The following summer it ordered that land offices only accept gold or silver coin. Upon leaving office in the spring of 1837, Jackson told his successor as president, Martin Van Buren of New York, to "check the paper mania," as if Van Buren could do much without an effective BUS. "The safety of the great body of the importing Merchants [of New York], and possibly of some of the Banks," the new president shuddered in April 1837, "is supposed to depend upon the next arrivals from England." Bank runs hit the city a few weeks later.[46]

It is hard not to feel sorry for Van Buren. Shortly before taking office, he had witnessed another Missouri-like crisis, which Congress avoided by admitting slave-owning Arkansas in advance of free Michigan. ("We of the South want a hostage," one Alabama

Democrat noted, "to protect us on a delicate question.") Bound to satisfy the Democracy's southern base, which now itched for Texas, Van Buren also had to keep New York's Jacksonians in the fold. Neither they nor he thought any more of public banks or stay laws. Instead the president pressed on with the hard-money faith. "All communities are apt to look to government for too much," he scolded as the Panic bit deep. Among the few people who liked the message was Nathaniel T.W. Carrington, a visiting planter from Barbados who generally disdained "Yankees" as a matter of reactionary principle. Yet he had to credit Van Buren and Jackson for their stance against debtors and deficits.[47]

Carrington also noted that a rebellion had just broken out in the Canadas, the fault of "the patriots, as the rebels are called." In Nova Scotia in January 1837 he had seen a regiment arrive to "intimidate the disaffected inhabitants" of Lower Canada. The French subjects had always vexed "the loyal part of the population," he sighed. Now their assemblymen were calling for embargoes and homespun, embracing patriotic self-sufficiency as the faithless Americans once had. Another true-blue Tory agreed: the unhappy ones were the pro-American *habitants*, not the 520,000 North American colonists of "British origins." Except for radical outcasts like Mackenzie, he trusted, the Upper Canadians were loyal consumers no less than loyal subjects. And they would remain so, unless they joined the tariff-charging states.[48]

For many thousands of Americans, of course, a Canadian revolution was a matter of democratic destiny. The empire would be swept out of North America, they were sure, creating new republican states where patriots could win land and glory all at once. In a not-so-subtle dig at Anglo-Texans, one Pennsylvanian said that the northern patriots "did not go to secure cotton plantations, or to introduce slavery, where it was prohibited." Rather, "[they] went to a country, barren, when compared with their own, to strike off the shackles of their neighbors, friends, and kindred." Watching the people of Buffalo welcome the desperate Patriots after the initial fighting in December 1837, one of Henry Clay's friends in the area worried: "We are in the midst of a revolution!" From New York City, Carrington guessed that "every American almost in his heart wishes [the Patriots] success."[49]

"Alas! Alas!" the Barbadian gloated. The U.S. government would never cross the British Navy – or, for that matter, the British economy.

"Where would you find markets for your lumber and numberless articles of export?" he taunted. If the Americans had supported the rebels, the British would have cut back on American imports, precisely when Americans were most in need of financing their debts to British creditors. If the violence along the northern borders had intensified, British warships could have retaliated from New Orleans to New York. A prolonged conflict might have moved the imperial rulers to replace American staples with South Asian, Egyptian, and Brazilian cotton, as they would during the Civil War.[50]

As early as November, Van Buren had quietly approved the passage of British regulars through disputed lands to Quebec City. In that way, the Crown could stamp out this latest rising as discretely as possible. Events in Upper Canada the next month – specifically, the destruction of the steamboat *Caroline*, during which an American stage-driver was killed – forced Van Buren to show his pro-British hand more openly. Both Canadian and American patriots were certain that the administration would avenge this insult in the Jacksonian way, just as they had assumed that American authorities would support the wider cause.[51]

Instead the president denounced the "dangerous excitement" and warned that America's pro-British neutrality would be "rigidly enforced." He then sent a new Neutrality Act to Congress, strengthening the 1818 version by enabling federal officials to pre-emptively seize men or materials that might be used for filibustering. Such seizures would not be easy, because the U.S. Army was searching for a few hundred Seminoles in the swamps of Florida, fighting once again to expand and secure slavery. So, Van Buren leaned on selected marshals and officers, pressured the relevant governors and justices, and said nothing over the next year when twenty Americans were killed in the Canadas and another eighty exiled to Tasmania. He was similarly effective in defusing a later dispute over the Maine-New Brunswick border.[52]

Defeated in the Canadas and abandoned by the states, the Patriots went under cover. In New York they formed the "Canadian Refugee Relief Association." In Ohio they preferred "Hunters' Lodges." Whig and Democratic leaders sometimes cheered their patriotic passions but always renounced their revolutionary project. Travelling to Montreal and Quebec in the summer of 1839, for example, Henry Clay told a Buffalo crowd that the *Caroline* incident "remains to be satisfactorily atoned for" by the British.

The protectionist Whigs, he declared, were the real patriots of a new, post-colonial age in which "foreign competition" rather than foreign invasion was the main threat. Back in the Senate the next year, Clay changed his tune, calling any group that might invade British lands "a criminal party."[53]

Clay's delicate game bore fruit in the presidential election of 1840, when the Whigs defeated "Martin Van Ruin" in part because of mass defections from Democrats along the Canadian border. One Irish-born "Hunter" said that he had once believed in Van Buren, if only as the rightful heir to Andrew Jackson. Who could doubt the anti-British patriotism of such men? Alas, the president was a "Queen's Man," awestruck by the newly crowned Victoria. "I could see him lynched with pleasure," the Hunter swore. Mackenzie went on to write a book-length exposé of Van Buren, and to admit that he had been wrong about America.[54]

For their part, the Whigs pursued a watered-down form of economic patriotism, proposing in early 1841 to limit the right of pre-empting public lands to American citizens. (The motion to exclude aliens was defeated, 30–12, whereas a companion measure to exclude black Americans passed 37–1.) Otherwise they formalized Anglo-American rapprochement with the Webster-Ashburton Treaty. The next Democrat in office, James K. Polk, pretended to cross sabres with the British while carefully avoiding conflict in the Oregon territory. Conversely, he struck a diplomatic tone with Mexico while manoeuvring for war in 1846, ultimately claiming that "American blood" had to be avenged. By then, many Democrats and some Whigs spoke of a shared "Anglo-Saxon blood" that joined the old country and the new republic, a racial nationalism that had no need for the patriotic dreams of revolutionary times.[55]

## NOTES

1 "Agricultural," *American Beacon and Norfolk and Portsmouth Daily Advertiser* (Norfolk, VA), 28 January 1820; Richard Rush quoted in James Parton, *Life of Andrew Jackson*, 3 vols, vol. 2 (New York, 1861), 488.

2 Noah Webster, *An American Dictionary of the English Language*, 2 vols. (New York, 1828), volume 2. On Webster's politics, see Jill Lepore, *A Is*

*for American: Letters and Other Characters in the Newly United States* (New York: Vintage Books, 2002).

3 Boyd Hilton, *A Mad, Bad, and Dangerous People? England, 1783–1846* (New York: Oxford University Press, 2006); Caitlin Fitz, *Our Sister Republics: The United States in an Age of American Revolutions* (New York: Liveright Publishing Corporation, 2016).

4 Julien Mauduit, "'Vrais républicains' d'Amérique: les patriotes canadiens en exil aux États-Unis (1837–1842)" (PhD diss., Université du Québec à Montréal, 2016); Marc L. Harris, "The Meaning of Patriot: The Canadian Rebellion and American Patriotism," *Michigan Historical Review* 23, no. 1 (Spring 1997): 33–69; Alan Taylor, *The Civil War of 1812: American Citizens, British Subjects, Irish Rebels, and Indian Allies* (New York: Vintage Books, 2010).

5 Hilton, *Mad, Bad, and Dangerous People*, 264–8; Peter Mandler, "Tories and Paupers: Christian Political Economy and the Making of the New Poor Law," *Historical Journal* 33, no. 1 (March 1990): 81–103; Anthony Webster, "The Political Economy of Trade Liberalization: The East India Company Charter Act of 1813," *Economic History Review* 43, no. 3 (August 1990): 404–19; Robert Morris, "The 1816 Uprising – A Hell-Broth," *Journal of the Barbados Museum and Historical Society* 46 (December 2000): 1–39; Jerome S. Handler and Ronald Hughes, "The 1816 Slave Revolt in Barbados and the Petition of Samuel Hall Lord," *Journal of the Barbados Museum and Historical Society* 47 (November 2001): 267–86.

6 T.M. Devine, "Social Stability and Agrarian Change in the Eastern Lowlands of Scotland, 1810–1840," *Social History* 3, no. 3 (October 1978): 332 ("agricultural cast") and 331–46; Liverpool quoted in Hilton, *Mad, Bad, and Dangerous People*, 251; A. Temple Patterson, "Luddism, Hampden Clubs, and Trade Unions in Leicestershire, 1816–1817," *English Historical Review* 63, no. 247 (April 1948): 170–88; Carl J. Griffin, "East Anglican Wheat Riots, 1816," *International Encyclopedia of Revolution and Protest*, ed. Ness Immanuel, *Blackwell Reference Online* (accessed 31 March 2017); Gordon Pentland, "'Betrayed by Infamous Spies': The Commemoration of Scotland's 'Radical War' of 1820," *Past and Present* 201 (November 2008): 141–73; Peter Berresford Ellis and Seumas Mac A'Ghobhainn, *The Scottish Insurrection of 1820* (Edinburgh: John Donald Publishers, 1970).

7 Andrew Jackson to John Coffee, 26 December 1816, in *Papers of Andrew Jackson*, ed. Daniel Feller et al., 10 vols, vol. 4 (Knoxville: University of Tennessee Press, 1984), 77 (hereafter PAJ); Banker quoted in Donald F.

Carmony and Sam K. Swope, "From Lycoming County, Pennsylvania, to Parke County, Indiana: Recollections of Andrew TenBrook, 1786–1823," *Indiana Magazine of History* 61, no. 1 (March 1965): 4; Daniel Feller, *The Public Lands in Jacksonian Politics, 1815–1840* (Madison: University of Wisconsin Press, 1984); Murray N. Rothbard, *The Panic of 1819: Reactions and Policies* (New York: Columbia University Press, 1962). See also Cathy Matson, "Mathew Carey's Learning Experience: Commerce, Manufacturing, and the Panic of 1819," *Early American Studies* 11, no. 3 (Fall 2013): 455–85; Edwin J. Perkins, "Langdon Cheves and the Panic of 1819: A Reassessment," *Journal of Economic History* 44, no. 2 (June 1984): 455–61; Charles Sellers, *The Market Revolution: Jacksonian America, 1815–1846* (New York: Oxford University Press, 1991), 163–71; Sean Wilentz, *The Rise of American Democracy: From Jefferson to Lincoln* (New York: W.W. Norton and Company, 2005), 181–217; Samuel Rezneck, "The Depression of 1819–1822, A Social History," *American Historical Review* 39, no. 1 (October 1933): 28–47 (hereafter *AHR*); Andrew R.L. Cayton, "The Fragmentation of 'A Great Family': The Panic of 1819 and the Rise of the Middling Interest in Boston, 1818–1822," *Journal of the Early Republic* 2, no. 2 (Summer 1982): 143–67 (hereafter *JER*).

8 James Hall, *Notes on the Western States* (Philadelphia, 1838), 175 ("whole population") and 174 ("rigid creditor"); William H. Crawford, "State of the Finances, Communicated to the Senate," 5 December 1820, in *American State Papers: Finances*, 38 vols, vol. 3 (Washington, DC: Gales and Seaton, 1832–61), 551 (hereafter *ASP*); Merrill D. Peterson, *The Great Triumvirate: Webster, Clay, and Calhoun* (New York: Oxford University Press, 1987), 67 (BUS casework); Priscilla Ferguson Clement, "The Philadelphia Welfare Crisis of the 1820s," *Pennsylvania Magazine of History and Biography* 105, no. 2 (April 1981): 150–65.

9 "Public Meeting," *St Louis Enquirer*, 9 June 1819 ("numerous" and "general welfare"); *Journal of the House of Representatives at the First Session of the Thirteenth General Assembly* (Murfreesborough, 1819), 22–3, 131–3, and 236; *Nashville Gazette*, 10 November 1819. For the stay law: "An Act Regulating proceedings on Judgements and for other purposes," ch. XIX, *Acts of a Public or General Nature, Passed at the First Session of the Thirteenth General Assembly* (Nashville, 1819), 44–5. The total number of votes cast for state representative in Davidson County jumped from 2,179 (1,339 vs 840) in 1817 to 3,082 (1,163 vs 991 vs 928) in 1819. Although population increase in Davidson (some 29 per cent between 1810 and 1820) accounts for some of this jump, voter turnout was volatile in the county, surging during the War of 1812 before actually declining

in 1817. From 1819 to 1821, voter turnout again jumped 31 per cent before stabilizing. See "Tennessee 1817 House of Representatives, Davidson County" and "Tennessee 1819 House of Representatives, Davidson County," in *A New Nation Votes: American Election Returns, 1787–1825*, http://www.elections.lib.tufts.edu (accessed 21 July 2016).

10 Governor's Address to Special Session of General Assembly, 26 June 1820, in box 1, Governor's Papers: Joseph McMinn, 1815–1821, Tennessee State Library and Archives, Nashville (hereafter TSLA); William G. Leger, "The Administration of John Adair" (MA thesis, University of Kentucky, 1951), 21–35; Message from Lt. Governor and Acting Governor, 8 December 1818, *Journal of the House of Representatives of the Commonwealth of Kentucky* (Frankfort, 1819), 16–18; Sandra F. VanBurkleo, "'The Paws of Banks': The Origins and Significance of Kentucky's Decision to Tax Federal Bankers, 1818–1820," *JER* 9, no. 4 (Winter 1989): 457–87; Rothbard, *The Panic of 1819*, 42–5; Harry R. Stevens, "Henry Clay, the Bank, and the West in 1824," *AHR* 60, no. 4 (July 1955): 843–8.

11 Address by Gabriel Slaughter, Lt. Governor, 8 December 1818, in *Journal of the House of Representatives of the Commonwealth of Kentucky* (Frankfort, 1818), 19 ("visitorial" and "safety,"); Gov. Adair quoted in Leger, "Administration of John Adair," 39 ("fatal tendency"); "Public Meeting," *St Louis Enquirer*, 9 June 1819 ("merciful forbearance" and "*general* calamity," emphasis in original); "Execution Law," *Enquirer* (Richmond), 1 February 1820 ("*legal process*," emphasis in original); Sandra Frances VanBurkleo, "'That Our Pure Republican Principles Might Not Wither': Kentucky's Relief Crisis and the Pursuit of 'Moral Justice,' 1818–1826" (PhD diss., University of Minnesota, 1988). For earlier relief legislation and its foes: "A Friend of the People," *Carthage Gazette and Friend of the People* (Carthage, TN) 13 February 1809; [McMinn], Address to Fellow-Citizens, 18 September 1821, in *Journal of the House of Representatives at the … Fourteenth General Assembly*, 17.

12 [McMinn], Governor's Address to Special Session of General Assembly, 26 June 1820; Nashville supporters quoted in John Wooldridge, *History of Nashville, Tenn.* (Nashville, 1890), 266 ("New Bank"); VanBurkleo, "'The Paws of Banks,'" 485 ("republican bank"); William Graham Sumner et al., *A History of Banking in all the Leading Nations: The United States*, 4 vols, vol. 1 (New York 1896), 149; Rothbard, *Panic of 1819*, 57–111; Walter Johnson, *River of Dark Dreams: Slavery and Empire in the Cotton Kingdom* (Cambridge, MA: Harvard University Press, 2013).

13 [McMinn], Governor's Address to Special Session of General Assembly, 26 June 1820, ("common destinies"). For the bank charter: "An Act to Establish a Bank of the State of Tennessee," ch. VII, *Acts of a Public or General Nature, Passed at the Second Session of the Thirteenth General Assembly* (Nashville, 1820), 9–16. See also Patrick Bolton and Howard Rosenthal, "Political Intervention in Debt Contracts," *Journal of Political Economy* 110, no. 5 (October 2002): 1103–34.

14 Mathew Carey, *Essays on Political Economy* (Philadelphia, 1822), 326 ("step in"); "On Manufactures," *Charleston Courier*, 14 September 1820 ("Patriotism"); James L. Huston, "Virtue Besieged: Virtue, Equality, and the General Welfare in the Tariff Debates of the 1820s," *JER* 14, no. 4 (Winter 1994): 523–47; Daniel Peart, *Era of Experimentation: American Political Practices in the Early Republic* (Charlottesville: University of Virginia Press, 2014), 73–107. For Clay's opposition to Relief: Henry Clay to Langdon Cheves, 14 November 1819, in *Papers of Henry Clay*, ed. James F. Hopkins, 10 vols, vol. 2 (Lexington: University Press of Kentucky, 1959–92), 722, hereafter *PHC*; Henry Clay to Langdon Cheves, 20 November 1820, in *PHC* 2: 903.

15 "Agricultural," *American Beacon and Norfolk and Portsmouth Daily* (Norfolk, VA), 28 January 1820; "On Manufacturers," *Charleston Courier*, 14 September 1820 ("traversed and overcome"); William D. Grampp, "How Britain Turned to Free Trade," *Business History Review* 61, no. 1 (Spring 1987): 86–112; Hilton, *A Mad, Bad, and Dangerous People*, 251–64. The Bank of England resumed specie payments in 1821.

16 Lord Melbourne quoted in Hilton, *A Mad, Bad, and Dangerous People*, 499 ("democratic"); Ellis and Mac A'Ghobhainn, *Scottish Insurrection of 1820*, 292–3; Paul Knapland, "Colonial Problems and Colonial Policy, 1815–1837," in *Cambridge History of the British Empire: Volume II, the Growth of the New Empire, 1783–1870*, ed. J. Holland Rose et al. (Cambridge, UK: University Press, 1940), 275–307. Upper Canada's rate of population growth between 1820 and 1840 resembles those of Alabama (462 per cent) and Indiana (466 per cent) and exceeds that of the more settled Ohio (261 per cent). Then again, Michigan's population shot up by an incredible 2386 per cent.

17 Planter quoted in Handler and Hughes, "1816 Slave Revolt in Barbados," 268; John Taylor, *Negro Emancipation and West India Independence, the True Interest of Great Britain* (London 1824), 8, 10; *The Honourable Address and Petition of the Council and Assembly of Barbados*, 17 January 1816, original at Barbados National Archives; C.R. Fay, "The

Movement toward Free Trade, 1820–1853," in *Cambridge History of the British Empire*, vol. 2, 388–414.

18 "The Bank of the State of Tennessee, No. 1," *Nashville Gazette*, 16 September 1820; "The Bank of the State of Tennessee, No. 6," *Nashville Gazette*, October 21, 1820; Petition #62, June 30, 1820, ser. 3, roll 6, Tennessee Legislative Petitions, Tennessee State Library and Archives (hereafter TSLA). On the *Gazette*, see Charles Grier Sellers Jr, *James K. Polk, Jacksonian, 1795–1843* (Princeton: Princeton University Press, 1957), 501; Michael O'Brien, *Conjectures of Order: Intellectual Life and the American South, 1810–1860*, 2 vols, vol. 2 (Chapel Hill: University of North Carolina Press, 2004), 799–816.

19 Jackson and Smith Counties, Petition #18, 20 June 1820, ser. 3, roll 6, Tennessee Legislative Petitions, TSLA; Carey, *Essays on Political Economy*, 318 ("*acts of legislature*," emphasis in original); Proceedings of 11 July 1820, *Journal of the House of Representatives at the Second Session of Thirteenth General Assembly of the State of Tennessee* (Murfreesboro, 1820), 65–73. Prosecution figures from Davidson County Circuit Court Minute Books: First Circuit, Minutes Civil and Criminal, roll 522, Volume C, 1817–1820, 137–93 (November 1818) and 243–302 (November 1819); Davidson County Circuit Court Minute Books, Volume D, 1820–24, 1–50 (November 1820), TSLA. The records of these circuit courts, created in 1809 as a level between the Common Pleas courts and the Supreme Court of Errors and Appeals are messy and ambiguous. I counted all cases that were categorized as "ejectment" and "debt" matters and clearly concerned such actions. But other cases that were categorized differently also dealt with sums owed. Therefore, I made the most conservative counts possible, and offer the figures cautiously. In the case of Greene County, ejectments seem to have been categorized as *scire facias* cases. I found eight cases for debt and ejectment in September 1818, nineteen in September 1819 (fourteen categorized as scire facias), and just two scire facias in March 1820. See Greene County Circuit Court Minute Book, Civil, roll 36, vol. 1, November 1809 to May 1820, 341–74, 378–438, and 439–83, TSLA.

20 "An Act, Supplemental to an Act, entitled, 'An act to establish a Bank of the State of Tennessee,'" 29 July 1820, in *Acts of a Public or General Nature Passed at the Second Session of the Thirteenth Assembly*, 17 ("faith"); Pleasant M. Miller to AJ, 9 August 1820, ser. 1, reel 29, Andrew Jackson Papers, Library of Congress (AJ had written to Miller on 3 August, but I cannot find this letter). Miller was either the lawyer or security for Taylor Townsend, the East Tennessee man who brought his long-standing dispute

over how his sons should pay him for lands to the courts. See Bond agreement, 28 May 1819, Taylor Townsend and Pleasant M. Miller, in "James Townsend et al. vs Taylor Townsend," Supreme Court Records, East Tennessee, box 58, TSLA. For Missouri terms: W.J. Hamilton, "The Relief Movement in Missouri, 1820–1822," *Missouri Historical Review* 22, no. 1 (October 1927): 63, 75, 79, and 51–94. See too Charles G. Sellers Jr, "Banking and Politics in Jackson's Tennessee, 1817–1827," *Mississippi Valley Historical Review* 41, no. 1 (June 1954): 61–84; Lewis E. Atherton, "The Services of the Frontier Merchant," *Mississippi Valley Historical Review* 24, no. 2 (September 1937): 165, 167, and 153–70.

21 *Townsend vs. Townsend and Others*, Peck 1, 7 Tenn. 1, 1821 ("unconscionable" and "extraordinary,") available at Tennessee Judicial Museum, Nashville; "Missouri Loan Office," *St Louis Enquirer*, 8 September 1821; Hamilton, "Relief Movement in Missouri," 80. Early uses of the Contracts Clause: Saul Cornell and Gerald Leonard, "The Consolidation of the Early Federal System, 1791–1812," in *The Cambridge History of Law in America: Volume I, Early America (1580–1815)*, ed. Michael Grossberg and Christopher Tomlins (New York: Cambridge University Press, 2008), 1: 541–2. My thanks to Trent Hanner and Tom Kanon of the TSLA for helping me with this case. See also Rothbard, *Panic of 1819*, 92–6 and Gouge, *Short History of Paper Money and Banking*, 133–9. On the Public Accounts Commissioners, see Hilton, *Mad, Bad, and Dangerous People*, 262–4.

22 *Lapsley vs. Brashears and Barr*, 4 Litt. 61 (1823), Court of Appeals of Kentucky ("civilized states"); "Opinion of Judge Mills, in the Two Proceeding Cases," [11 October 1823] in *Lapsley vs. Brashears and Barr*, 4 Litt. 102, 84 ("international principle" and "free course to the coercion"); John Boyle, William Owsley, and B[enjamin] Mills to Honorable Representatives, 9 December 1824, in *Journal of the House of Representatives of the Commonwealth of Kentucky* (Frankfort 1824), 311–48; Rothbard, *Panic of 1819*, 109 (bonfires).

23 *Argus of Western America* (Frankfort, KY), 22 October 1823 ("Is there an Englishman?" and "sovereignty"); "Speech of Samuel Daveiss," *Kentucky Gazette*, 13 May 1824 ("*grind to death*" and "feelings"); "Speech of Samuel Daveiss," *Kentucky Gazette*, 20 May 1824; Report by Felix Grundy, 21 September 1821, in *Journal of the House of Representatives at the … Fourteenth General Assembly*, 49–53. See also Donald B. Cole, *A Jackson Man: Amos Kendall and the Rise of American Democracy* (Baton Rouge: Louisiana State University Press, 2004), 67–94.

24 *Providence Gazette*, "By the Mails," 17 August 1822, reprinted this praise of Ohio from a Kentucky paper, where it was originally titled

"Manufactures of Ohio"; Timothy Flint, "A Condensed Geography and History of the Western States, or the Mississippi Valley," [1828] in *Indiana as Seen by Early Travelers*, ed. Harlow Lindley (Indianapolis: Indiana Historical Commission, 1916), 462 ("spurious banks" and "ridiculous"); AJ to Andrew Jackson Donelson, 8 February 1823, in *Correspondence of Andrew Jackson*, ed. John Spencer Bassett, 7 vols, vol. 3 (Washington: Carnegie Institution, 1926–35), 187 (hereafter CAJ); Thomas H. Greer, "Economic and Social Effects of the Depression of 1819 in the Old Northwest," *Indiana Magazine of History* 44, no. 3 (September 1948): 227–43.

25 AJ to Andrew Jackson Donelson, 17 September 1819, in PAJ 4: 323; Liverpool quoted in Hilton, *Mad, Bad, and Dangerous People*, 253; J.M. Opal, *Avenging the People: Andrew Jackson, the Rule of Law, and the American Nation* (New York: Oxford University Press, 2017).

26 "Tennessee Bank and Relief Law," *Niles Weekly Register*, 2 September 1820 (hereafter NWR); "General Jackson," *Alexandria Gazette*, 27 April 1827 quotes the outraged legislators who felt threatened by Jackson's personal intervention, and stresses that Jackson presented himself as "a *major general in the United States army*!" See also Rothbard, *Panic of 1819*, 95–6; PAJ 4: xxxi–xxxvii; Sellers, "Banking and Politics in Jackson's Tennessee"; William M. Gouge, *A Short History of Paper Money and Banking in the United States*, ed. Joseph Dorfman (New York: A.M. Kelley, 1968 [1833]), 133–9.

27 AJ to Andrew Jackson Donelson, 8 February 1823, in CAJ 3: 187 ("not voidable"); AJ to William B. Lewis, 16 July 1820, in PAJ 4: 380 ("as long as I live"); "Hero of New Orleans," NWR, 3 August 1822 (from July celebration; "*holy* zeal" and "*zeal alone*," emphasis in original); AJ to AJ Donelson, 25 July 1822, in PAJ 5: 206. See also AJ to AJ Donelson, 17 September 1819, in PAJ 4: 323; AJ to James Gadsden, August 1, 1819, in PAJ 4: 307. Jackson's disgust at relief measures may well have been intensified by repayment demands made by the U.S. government on him for earlier military and treaty expenditures. See William Lee to AJ, David Meriwether, and Jesse Franklin, 10 May 1820, ser. 1, reel 29, Andrew Jackson Papers, Library of Congress. For a superb discussion of fiscal and monetary ideas in the early republic, see Jessica M. Lepler, *The Many Panics of 1837: People, Politics, and the Creation of a Transatlantic Financial Crisis* (New York: Cambridge University Press, 2013).

28 "Reception of General Jackson," *Nashville Gazette*, 22 April 1825 ("firm and inflexible," from Judge John Overton's reception speech); John Eaton, *The Life of Andrew Jackson* (Philadelphia 1824), 432–3;

quotes from 25 June 1819 toasts and 19 July 1819 *National Intelligencer* in PAJ 4: 537; "Tennessee Bank and Relief Law," NWR, 2 September 1820. Besides Overton, William B. Lewis was a key member of the so-called "Nashville Junto," which later became the Nashville Committee for Jackson's campaign. Pleasant M. Miller had helped nominate Jackson for President on behalf of the Tennessee assembly in 1822. Jackson had written to both Lewis and Miller about Relief and banking in 1820. For various accounts of the "Junto" and the "Nashville Committee" that succeeded it, see PAJ 6: 14n, 15n; Mark R. Cheathem, *Andrew Jackson, Southerner* (Baton Rouge: Louisiana State University Press, 2013), 99–100; Donald B. Cole, *Vindicating Andrew Jackson: The 1828 Election and the Rise of the Two-Party System* (Lawrence: University of Kansas Press, 2009), 79–80; Lynn Hudson Parsons, *The Birth of Modern Politics: Andrew Jackson, John Quincy Adams, and the Election of 1828* (New York: Oxford University Press, 2009), 139.

29 "Abridged from *The Telegraph*," *Frankfort Argus and Western Reporter*, 14 July 1824; Squire Turner to Henry Clay, 7 January 1827, in PHC 6: 25 ("Military chieftain" and "Jackson was the man"). In a series of articles under the name "Patrick Henry," a Relief Party supporter attacked the "Court Party" as latter-day Federalists and traitors. Besides NWR, which published Jackson's June 1820 screed against relief, the only direct mention of the General's fierce opposition that I have found is "General Jackson," *Alexandria Gazette*, 27 April 1827.

30 *Richmond Enquirer*, "The Times," 6 January 1821; Cheathem, *Andrew Jackson, Southerner;* Robert Pierce Forbes, *The Missouri Compromise and Its Aftermath: Slavery and the Meaning of America* (Chapel Hill: University of North Carolina Press, 2007); Michael Schoeppner, "Navigating the Dangerous Atlantic: Racial Quarantines, Black Sailors, and United States Constitutionalism" (PhD diss., University of Florida, 2010).

31 Andrew Jackson to Andrew Jackson Donelson, 21 January 1824, in PAJ 5: 343; "Memorandum of Slaves and Land in Davidson County, Tennessee," [1 June 1825], in PAJ 6: 3–5; Alexander Trotter, *Observations on the Financial Position and Credit of such of the States of the North American Union as have Contracted Public Debts* (London 1839), 400 (cotton figures).

32 Johnson, *River of Dark Dreams*, 151–2 and 73–96; Robert H. Gudmestad, *Steamboats and the Rise of the Cotton Kingdom* (Baton Rouge: Louisiana State University Press, 2011), 8 (*General Jackson*).

33 [John Eaton], *The Letters of Wyoming* (Philadelphia 1824), 87; Taney quoted in Mark H. Haller, "The Rise of the Jackson Party in Maryland, 1820–1829," *Journal of Southern History* 28, no. 3 (August 1962): 312 and 307–26 (hereafter *JSH*); Thomas Coens, "The Early Jackson Party: A Force for Democratization?," *A Companion to the Era of Andrew Jackson*, ed. Sean Patrick Adams (Malden, MA: 2013), *Blackwell Reference Online*.

34 Timothy S. Huebner, "Roger B. Taney and the Slavery Issue: Looking beyond – and before – Dred Scott," *Journal of American History* 97, no. 1 (June 2010): 17–38; Peart, *Era of Experimentation*; Donald J. Ratcliffe, "Popular Preferences in the Presidential Election of 1824," *JER* 34, no. 1 (Spring 2014): 45–78; Seth Rockman, *Scraping By: Wage Labor, Slavery, and Survival in Early Baltimore* (Baltimore 2008); Edward B. Rugemer, "The Southern Response to British Abolitionism: The Maturation of Proslavery Apologetics," *JSH* 70, no. 2 (May 2004): 221–48; Philip M. Hamer, "Great Britain, the United States, and the Negro Seamen Acts, 1822–1848," *JSH* 1, no. 1 (February 1935): 3–28.

35 Ernest R. May, *The Making of the Monroe Doctrine* (Cambridge, MA: Belknap Press of Harvard University Press, 1975), 3 and 12–64.

36 Thomas Jefferson to James Monroe, 24 October 1823, in *The Life and Selected Writings of Thomas Jefferson*, ed. Adrienne Koch and William Peden (New York: Modern Library, 2004), 646; Don E. Fehrenbacher, *The Slaveholding Republic: An Account of the United States Government's Relations to Slavery*, completed and edited by Ward M. McAfee (New York: Oxford University Press, 2001), 94–6. For a telling reply to the 1826 convention, see *South Carolina State Gazette* (Columbia), 20 January 1827.

37 [Brutus], *The Crisis: Or, Essays on the Usurpations of the Federal Government* (Charleston, 1827), 87 ("*national welfare*," emphasis in original), 51 ("cords of perpetual friendship"), 115 ("free and uninterrupted"), reference to Smith on 120; Michael Schoeppner, "Peculiar Quarantines: The Seamen Acts and Regulatory Authority in the Antebellum South," *Law and History Review* 31, no. 3 (August 2013): 559–86.

38 [Brutus], *The Crisis*, 12 ("ten thousand"), 131 ("ENTERING"), 121 ("secret dagger"), 159 ("BLOW OUT"), 164 ("real patriot"). Brutus mentioned the eastern states' distaste for slavery on 48 but did not explicitly describe the threat to the institution until 95. Jabez Z. Rabun and James Harvey Young, "William H. Crawford on the Election of 1828: Two Letters," *Georgia Historical Quarterly* 37, no. 4 (December 1953): 344.

39 AJ to AJ Donelson, 18 January 1824 in PAJ 5: 340 ("great leading state" in P.S.); [Brutus], *The Crisis*, 118. For Jackson's views on the tariff: AJ to John Coffee, 18 June 1824, in PAJ 5: 417; AJ to AJ Donelson, 11 April 1824, in PAJ 5: 391; and AJ to Littleton H. Coleman, 26 April 1824, in PAJ 5: 398–400.

40 AJ to Joel R. Poinsett, 7 February 1833, in CAJ 5:15 ("Repleven laws"); AJ to Andrew Jackson, Jr, 12 February 1834, in CAJ 5: 247. On the unexpected costs of Removal: Ethan Davis, "An Administrative Trail of Tears: Indian Removal," *American Journal of Legal History* 50, no. 1 (January 2008–2010): 96–7 and 49–100; Matthew T. Pearcy, "'The Ruthless Hand of War': Andrew A. Humphreys in the Second Seminole War," *Florida Historical Quarterly* 85, no. 2 (Fall 2006): 153 and 123–53.

41 AJ, "Fourth Annual Message," 4 December 1832, in *A Compilation of the Messages and Papers of the Presidents, 1789–1897*, ed. James D. Richardson, 20 vols, vol. 2 (New York 1897), 596 (hereafter CMP); AJ, "Sixth Annual Message to Congress," 1 December 1834, in CMP 3: 106–7; AJ to the Senate and House of Representatives of the United States, 6 February 1837, in CMP 3: 278. See also John M. Belohlavek, *"Let the Eagle Soar!": The Foreign Policy of Andrew Jackson* (Lincoln: University of Nebraska Press, 1985); Davis, "An Administrative Trail of Tears," 95–6; Gudmestad, *Steamboats and the Rise of the Cotton Kingdom*; and David F. Long, "'Martial Thunder': The First Official American Armed Intervention in Asia," *Pacific Historical Review* 42, no. 2 (May 1973): 143–9.

42 Trotter, *Observations on the Financial Position and Credit*, 1 ("national credit"); *Morning Post* from 1837 quoted in Leland Hamilton Jenks, *The Migration of British Capital to 1875* (1927; London: Nelson 1963), 365n ("law of debtor and creditor").

43 Peter Temin, "The Economic Consequences of the Bank War," *Journal of Political Economy* 76, no. 2 (March–April 1968): 263 and 257–74; Temin, "The Anglo-American Business Cycle, 1820–60," *Economic History Review* 27, no. 2 (March 1974): 207–21; Namsuk Kim and John Joseph Wallis, "The Market for American State Government Bonds in Britain and the United States, 1830–43," *Economic History Review* 58, no. 4 (November 2005): 736–54; J. Fred Rippy, "Latin America and the British Investment 'Boom' of the 1820s," *Journal of Modern History* 19, no. 2 (June 1947): 122–9; *Historical Dictionary of the Jacksonian Era and Manifest Destiny*, ed. Terry Corps (Lanham, MD: Scarecrow Press, 2006).

44 Dorothy R. Adler, *British Investment in American Railways, 1834–1898*, ed. Muriel E. Hidy (Charlottesville: University of Virginia Press, 1970), 8–9 (total state debts from $26 million to $172 million, 1830–38).

45 Adler, *British Investment in American Railways*, 9–11 (Alabama, Mississippi, Arkansas, and Florida have $22.3 million in debts by 1838, of which $19.3 million in banking, or 86.5 per cent and figures on foreign holdings); Robert V. Remini, *Andrew Jackson and the Bank War* (New York: W.W. Norton and Company, 1967), 125 (number of deposit banks); Trotter, *Observations on the Financial Position and Credit*, 377 (total land sales); Jenks, *Migration of British Capital*, 65–98 (trade from 1832 to 1836). See also Daniel Walker Howe, *What Hath God Wrought: The Transformation of America, 1815–1848* (New York: Oxford University Press, 2007), 363; Major L. Wilson, *The Presidency of Martin Van Buren* (Lawrence: University of Kansas Press, 1984), 45–6.

46 AJ to Martin Van Buren, 30 March 1837, in CAJ 5: 467; Martin Van Buren to AJ, 24 April 1837, in CAJ 5: 479; Peter L. Rousseau, "Jacksonian Monetary Policy, Specie Flows, and the Panic of 1837," *Journal of Economic History* 62, no. 2 (June 2002): 457–88; Lepler, *Many Panics of 1837*; Alastair Roberts, *America's First Great Depression: Economic Crisis and Political Disorder after the Panic of 1837* (Ithaca, NY: Cornell University Press, 2012); Donald B. Cole, *Martin Van Buren and the American Political System* (Princeton: Princeton University Press, 1984), 277.

47 Remarks by Rep. Lewis (Alabama), 8 June 1836, in *Register of the Debates of Congress*, 24th Congress, 1st Session, 4209; Martin Van Buren, "Special Session Message," 4 September 1837, in CMP 3: 344 ("All communities") and 324–45; Entries for 29 July 1837 and September 8, 1837, in "The Journal of Nathaniel T.W. Carrington: A Barbados Planter's Visit to Canada and the United States in 1837," 44, 75–7; ed. James Collins Brandow, typescript at Barbados Museum and Historical Society; Jack B. Scroggs, "Arkansas Statehood: A Study in State and National Political Schism," *Arkansas Historical Quarterly* 20, no. 3 (Autumn 1961): 227–44.

48 Entries for 29 June 1837 and 21 December 1837, in "Journal of Nathaniel T.W. Carrington," 16, 207; [A Canadian Merchant,] *A Letter on the Insurrection in Canada, to Edward Baines, Esq., M.P., January 8, 1838* (Leeds 1838); Allan Greer, "From Folklore to Revolution: Charivaris and the Lower Canadian Rebellion of 1837," *Social History* 15, no. 1 (January 1990): 25–43; Mauduit, "'Vrais républicains' d'Amérique," 260, 256–66.

49 William J. Duane, *A Letter to a Friend* (Philadelphia 1838), 6; Peter B. Porter to Henry Clay, 15 December 1837, in PHC 9: 104; Entry for 21 December 1837, "Journal of Nathaniel T.W. Carrington," 208; Mauduit, "'Vrais républicains' d'Amérique"; Andrew Bonthius, "The Patriot War of 1837–1838: Locofocoism with a Gun?" *Labour/Le Travail* 52 (Fall 2003): 9–43; T.P. Dunning, "The Canadian Rebellions of 1837–1838: An Episode in Northern Borderland History," *Australasian Journal of American Studies* 14, no. 2 (December 1995): 31–47.

50 Entry for 21 December 1837, "Journal of Nathaniel T.W. Carrington," 209; Sven Beckert, "Emancipation and Empire: Reconstructing the Worldwide Web of Cotton Production in the Age of the American Civil War," AHR 109, no. 5 (December 2004), 1405–38.

51 Mauduit, "'Vrais républicains' d'Amérique," 82; Samuel Watson, "United States Army Officers Fight the 'Patriot War': Responses to Filibustering on the Canadian Border, 1837–1839," JER 18, no. 3 (Autumn 1998): 485–518; Stuart D. Scott, "The Patriot Game: New Yorkers and the Canadian Rebellion of 1837–1838," *New York History* 68, no. 3 (July 1987): 281–95.

52 [President Van Buren], "A Proclamation," 5 January 1838, in CMP 3: 481; Willis Hall to Henry Clay, 14 December 1838, in PHC 9: 255; Wilson, *Presidency of Martin Van Buren*, 157–69; Scott, "Patriot Game"; Dunning, "Canadian Rebellions of 1837–1838."

53 Henry Clay, "Speech in Buffalo," 17 July 1839, in PHC 9: 331; Clay, "Comment in Senate," 14 April 1840, in PHC 9: 405. For Clay's voyage, see PHC 9: 330n. For his worries about war, see Henry Clay to Alexander Hamilton, 24 February 1839, in PHC 9: 291 and Clay to Ambrose Spencer, 25 February 1839, in PHC 9: 292–3.

54 Harris, "The Meaning of Patriot," 57 ("Queen's man"); Mauduit, "'Vrais républicains' d'Amérique," 261 ("lynched") and 259–63; William Lyon Mackenzie, *The Life and Times of Martin Van Buren* (Boston 1846).

55 Remarks by Sen. Benton in *Abridgment of the Debates of Congress from 1789 to 1856*, ed. Benton, 16 vols, vol. 14 (New York, 1857), 192; *Congressional Globe*, "General Prospective Pre-Emption Law," 26th Congress, 2nd Session, 77–8; Howe, *What Hath God Wrought*, 740–3; Robert W. Merry, *A Country of Vast Designs: James K. Polk, the Mexican War, and the Conquest of the American Continent* (New York: Simon and Schuster, 2010).

2

# Bank War in Lower Canada

## *The Rebellion and the Market Revolution*

ROBERT RICHARD

> The two things came together [in 1837]. The impact of the political crisis was driven home by the dead weight of the financial and commercial collapse. Canada was at once a member of the British Empire and a minor partner in the system of British and North American trade; and she had as little chance of escaping the influence of the American business cycle as she had of avoiding the interference of the imperial authorities ... The end, towards which the two Canadas had been travelling for a generation, was now at hand. These two brusque movements, political and financial, precipitated the crisis in Canadian affairs.[1]
>
> Donald Creighton, 1937

Eight decades ago, in *The Commercial Empire of the St Lawrence*, Donald Creighton justified the armed uprisings in Upper and Lower Canada as a practically inevitable outcome of what he called the "Canadian economic revolution." This phrase was ill-fitting, however, for Creighton rightly insisted that Canada's commercial development in the early nineteenth century, like the outbreak of the Canadian Rebellion itself, could never be disentangled from corresponding events in the United States or the greater British Atlantic world. The Panic of 1837 represented one acute and especially harmful result of vast economic transformations enveloping the North American landscape – what U.S. historians now label the "Market Revolution." If that financial crash "precipitated" the Rebellion of

1837–38 by exacerbating political conflict in the Canadian colonies, as Creighton suggested, then it begs the larger question of scholars who prioritize the early history of international capitalism: to what extent was the Canadian Rebellion a direct or indirect consequence of the American Market Revolution?[2]

Creighton's magnum opus first appeared back in 1937, but histories of nineteenth-century Canada and the United States remain stubbornly segregated today. This academic partition only reinforces Alan Taylor's historical claim that the War of 1812 "decisively divided the continent between the republic and the empire." Such a division was hardly conclusive for American and Canadian peoples living in the Jacksonian era, from 1815 to the mid-1840s. Yet despite a recent transnational turn (thanks to several authors in this volume, among others), the complex relationship between Canadians and their southern counterparts in this period is still poorly understood. In college history departments across the United States, the subject is almost completely ignored. American readers may be surprised to discover, therefore, that the British Province of Lower Canada, with its relatively insulated and agrarian francophone majority embedded in a seigneurial system of hereditary lords and feudal taxes, nonetheless participated in the same economic processes comprising the Market Revolution as those which transformed the early American republic. Notwithstanding key disparities in manner and magnitude, the Canadian (including the *French* Canadian) version of the Market Revolution also involved the rise of banks and canals, corporations and credit, and other capitalist trappings so familiar to historians of the early United States.[3]

This essay considers some of the ways in which the Market Revolution transcended national borders in eastern North America, pulling Canada and the United States closer together, rather than pushing them apart, in the aftermath of the War of 1812. Taking the fiery controversy over paper-money banking as a case study, it demonstrates how French- and English-speaking subjects in Lower Canada responded to the emergence of modern finance capitalism in terms similar to their American neighbours to the south. Finally, by approaching the origins of the Lower Canadian Rebellion from the commercial perspective of the Panic of 1837, this analysis jettisons traditional historiographic barriers of language and culture, and suggests new prospects for integrating these "distinct, national histories" through mutual economic experiences. This transnational project becomes even more urgent if we meet Alan Taylor halfway, by recognizing that revolutionary-era affinities between the United States and Canada no longer carried the same cultural weight by the 1830s as they had through the War of 1812.

Although the Upper Canadian Rebellion remains a crucial component of this shared history, as other contributions in this volume well illustrate, it pales in comparison to the closely linked but far more significant Lower Canadian Rebellion. With a population of roughly 550,000 in 1831 – compared to Upper Canada's 400,000 as late as 1837 – Lower Canada would have been the sixth most populous state in the American republic at this time (in terms of overall free population). Nonetheless, most U.S. historians fail to appreciate that Lower Canada experienced a decisive political contest beginning in the late 1820s between a predominant mass of mostly francophone patriotes and a small minority of Anglophone colonial and merchant elites. Fought over nothing less than "the very framework of state power," according to Allan Greer, this quarrel reached a sudden and bloody culmination in the ill-fated Rebellion of 1837–38. After the demise of about 250 patriotes and the forced exile of many others (fewer patriots died in Upper Canada, where the fighting was lighter), the political and economic landscape of British North America would never look the same again.[4]

American scholars *are* familiar, of course, with the vaguely parallel atmosphere that characterized U.S. politics after Andrew Jackson's presidential election in 1828. Though neither a rebellion nor a revolution, a heated conflict known as the Bank War became the focal point of Jackson's eight-year presidency, with permanent political and economic upshots. Reflecting an essential debate over the limits of liberty and power in American society – "a question of transcendental importance," in Old Hickory's words – the Bank War signalled a turning point in the public discourse of the early republic. While banking institutions and financial credit were indispensable tools of the Market Revolution, Jackson's feud with the Second Bank of the United States exploited a profound resentment among rural and working-class citizens regarding the unfair methods and unequal rewards of modern capitalism. By the time Jackson left office in 1837, the nascent Whig and Democratic Parties had begun to coalesce around his epic dispute with the "Monster" Bank, with both parties upholding distinctive and often clashing visions of commercial prosperity in a republican society.[5]

As it turns out, Lower Canadian patriotes paid close attention to the bitter confrontations between Democratic and Whig politicians south of their border, and they fully grasped the significance of the Bank War for their own state of affairs. One reported how "every political move that occurs in the neighbouring Union is most interesting to the people of this Province."[6] Partisan rhetoric and economic reform proposals during the Bank War helped the patriotes to envision their contest with the British colonial regime in an American or continental context. As Yvan Lamonde and other researchers have illuminated, this awareness was part of a broader recognition of shared transnational values in 1830s Lower Canada; but above all, "a political consciousness of the American republican experience."[7]

Then again, what really constituted the "American republican experience" according to the patriotes? Ever since Allan Greer established the contextual relevance of the "Age of Revolution" for the Canadian Rebellion, some historians have embraced this revolutionary paradigm hook, line, and sinker. They construe the 1830s in Lower Canada as politically equivalent to the 1770s in the Thirteen Colonies or the 1780s in France, while giving insufficient consideration to the economic and ideological developments of nineteenth-century North America. "Although the Canadian uprisings occurred much later, they were not ideologically different from the upheavals that preceded them," one scholar concluded. "Had they succeeded, they would have been known as the Canadian Revolution." This academic fixation on the continuity between the American and French Revolutions and the Lower Canadian Rebellion partly reflects the public discourse of the patriotes themselves. By the summer of 1837, patriote leaders often referenced revolutionary arguments by Thomas Paine or Thomas Jefferson in local meetings and newspapers, in order to justify boycotts of British goods or taking up arms against the colonial government. Like the participants of other uprisings in the Age of Revolution, the patriotes were liable to imitate the experiences of their revolutionary forebears. Hence in 1937 (the same year Donald Creighton arrived on the scene), Chester New cautioned his colleagues in the Canadian historical profession that "there are times when one is tempted to feel that the Rebellion of 1837 *is* the American Revolution in the Canada colonies."[8]

Meaningful though it may be, the patriotes' own revolutionary republican rhetoric obscures the complex nature of their movement, as well as their material incentives for armed rebellion in 1837.

Their reaction to pressing economic concerns in Lower Canada during the 1830s – an unstable paper currency, growing socioeconomic inequality, and a lack of access to financial credit among the francophone population – increasingly emulated the political outlook of Jacksonian Democrats fighting in the Bank War, rather than Founding Fathers fighting in the Revolution. Like so many of their American contemporaries, the patriotes adopted an anti-corporate, hard-money response to the unwanted consequences of an evolving commercial society. To be sure, this critique contained explicit ideological ties to the eighteenth-century English "Country party" and to Jefferson's agrarian republicanism.[9] Yet the radical platform jointly promoted by Lower Canadian patriotes and Jacksonian Democrats was very much a product of its own age – "a crisis of republican values," according to Sean Wilentz, "born of the Market Revolution." When the North American economy abruptly collapsed during the Panic of 1837, partisans of the Bank War on both sides of the Canadian-American border championed the sweeping alternative of a "democratic commerce." In the end, however, the two sides achieved dissimilar and disappointing results.[10]

## MARKET REVOLUTIONS ACROSS BORDERS

In the generation after the War of 1812, both the United States and Canada experienced a rapid acceleration of economic changes that had been underway since the late eighteenth century. By the time of Andrew Jackson's election, the dizzying pace of commercial development in eastern North America, fuelled by massive population growth, had created a society more or less alien to that of Thomas Jefferson's day. It was not always a smooth process.

The Market Revolution brought astonishing advances to the early American republic in terms of transportation, communication, and the overall scope of production, as foreign immigration boosted the nation's territorial expansion and manufacturing capacity. In 1820 only 8,385 immigrants came to the United States, but that annual figure nearly tripled to 23,322 by 1830, and almost quadrupled to 84,066 by 1840. To facilitate the mass movement of people and the ever-increasing amount of goods they produced, state governments and state-chartered corporations built roads, canals, and (somewhat later) railroads; in John Larson's estimation, "the 1820s and early 1830s saw an explosion of internal improvement projects wherever vacant land lured settlers who in turn demanded access to markets." Just as critically, steamboat technology combined with these improvements – there were seventeen steamboats in the Ohio and Mississippi river valleys in 1817, more than 100 by 1828, and an incredible 536 by 1840 – to lower domestic shipping rates dramatically for basic commodities and consumer goods across the United States, whether travelling by land, river, or canal.[11]

Escalating market demand created corresponding applications for financial credit and legal protections for entrepreneurs. For the most part, the U.S. federal and state governments were more than willing to satisfy such requests. Among the striking transformations in industries like manufacturing, insurance, and shipping, state-chartered banks with the power to print paper money – and whose lucky investors were shielded by the privilege of limited liability – suddenly proliferated across the early republic in the two decades after 1815. In addition to the Second Bank of the United States, which the U.S. Congress officially chartered in 1816, the total number of incorporated banks increased nationally from 327 with $55 million in outstanding loans in 1820 to 788 with $525 million in loans by 1837. "All an enterprising American needed ... was credit," the late historian Robert Wiebe observed of this era, "and Americans now demanded it as their right – not a privilege to be granted but a right to be claimed by every individual whose reputation earned it."[12]

Unfortunately, this "right" to financial credit did not extend evenly to all Americans, and fluctuations in the value of bank paper often caused extreme distress. The working classes of New York, Philadelphia, and other eastern cities, as well as small farmers across rural America, counted the fortunes of corporate stockholders and directors from afar as they held depreciated banknotes during economic downturns. Over time, they acquired a sophisticated self-awareness of their inequitable position within the commercial marketplace. William Leggett, editor of the *New York Evening Post* and a leader of the radical Locofoco wing of the Democratic Party, became an outspoken critic of the so-called "Paper Dynasty" and its subjugation of working-class Americans. He once declared (in typically defiant prose) that "our people – we mean emphatically the class which labours with its own hands – is in possession of a greater portion of the property and intelligence of this country, ay, ten times over, than all the creatures of the 'paper credit system' put together." For Leggett and other Americans of his time, an earlier financial crisis called the Panic of 1819 remained a searing reminder of the potential pitfalls and lopsided profits wrought by the Market Revolution. Their grim experience would not be lost on Lower Canadian patriotes during the 1820s and beyond.[13]

It is no coincidence that Leggett, one of the loudest detractors of corporate capitalism in this era, resided within the very heart of Jacksonian America's burgeoning commercial empire. New York City not only epitomized the Market Revolution but drove it forward, with its myriad entrepreneurs "fostering round after round of business innovations that ... made New York by far the best place in America to engage in commerce." The completion of the Erie Canal in 1825 made all the difference, both for the future of New York *and*, as will be explained below, for the British provinces of Upper and Lower Canada. Less publicized but still enormously significant was the growth of state-chartered banking throughout the State of New York, particularly after the passage of the Safety Fund Act in 1829. By creating a common insurance pool for the creditors of failed banks, placing key restrictions on investment and loan operations, and making the whole system more transparent, New York legislators paved the way for a well-regulated banking network that expanded swiftly to meet the credit demands of their state's booming economy. The twenty-seven original banks chartered under the Safety Fund had a combined capital of less than $8 million, but by 1837 there were ninety Safety Fund banks with a combined capital exceeding $32 million and total assets over $82 million. Many of these banks were located along the Erie Canal and other waterways of upstate New York specifically to finance the prosperous trade in western agricultural goods, as well as the unprecedented real estate boom accompanying it.[14]

Although Canada experienced its own distinctive version of the Market Revolution in the decades after the War of 1812, Donald Creighton and subsequent historians have underscored the colossal influence of New York when evaluating its northern neighbour's economic trajectory. The sheer movement of people, goods, and money between Lower Canada, its smaller but fast-growing sister province Upper Canada, and the United States greatly intensified in the first half of the nineteenth century as each region became more dependent (or interdependent) upon the markets of the others. Beginning in the mid-1820s, the Canadian-American border gradually if haphazardly evolved into a free trade zone after years of tariff battles between the U.S. Congress and British Parliament. In the meantime, as Andrew Bonthius and other scholars have noted, the international boundary "was poorly guarded and scarcely more than a political formality to which [contemporaries] gave little practical consideration." The border was fluid, in other words, for purposes of both commerce and settlement.[15]

What this fluidity really *meant*, however, was that the rising agricultural and timber industries of the vast North American Great Lakes region – formerly the domain of eighteenth-century Canada's fur trading empire – steadily fell into the hands of New Yorkers rather than Canadians. The latter scrambled to rival New York's western route via the Erie Canal with improvements along the Great Lakes and St Lawrence River system such as the Lachine (1825), Welland (1829), and Rideau (1832) canals – but to no avail. The impressive Welland Canal in Upper Canada even received a majority of its initial capital from New York investors, for they predicted (correctly) that it would become an extension of the Erie system by way of the Oswego feeder canal. Simply put, New York's physical and financial infrastructure made the Erie Canal irresistible for shippers, buyers, and sellers of all commodities along the Great Lakes. The numbers speak for themselves: in the above-average year of 1832, the Lachine Canal – "the bottle-neck of the entire St Lawrence system" – conveyed only 91,862 barrels of flour and 293,968 bushels of wheat; while in the below-average year of 1834, the Erie Canal transported 977,027 barrels of flour and 748,433 bushels of wheat. "The Empire State was becoming a reality," Creighton famously wrote, "and the commercial empire of the St Lawrence remained a remote ideal." He attributed Canada's relative economic decline in North America to a popular and misguided resistance to commercial development, especially among representatives of the rural French Canadian population. But who actually benefitted from the Market Revolution in Lower Canada? Did the patriotes resist economic development outright, or were they merely opposed to the unjust manner in which it unfolded in their province?[16]

Many immigrants arriving in Lower Canada during these years journeyed on to Upper Canada or the United States, but Lower Canada still received a whopping 400,000 new arrivals from 1815 to 1840, mainly from the British Isles. Meanwhile, the native francophone population also swelled by 250,000 from natural increase. Unlike the sprawling western frontiers of its neighbours, Lower Canada had a severe shortage of good farmland, so overcrowding became a major problem in the regions surrounding Montreal and Quebec City. To make matters worse, the province faced a long-term agricultural crisis owing to insufficient wheat production by francophone farmers (*habitants*) as a result of overpopulation and soil exhaustion. Yet amid these multiple setbacks of urban and rural crowding as well as diminishing farm incomes, the Lower Canadian lumber industry expanded dramatically in the early decades of the nineteenth century. Combined with rising wheat imports from Upper Canada and the United States, which became increasingly necessary to sustain the Lower Canadian population, the flourishing timber trade fostered rapid growth in the shipping and shipbuilding operations of Montreal and Quebec City. A mere 362 ships went through the port of Quebec City in 1812, whereas 1,213 vessels cleared the same port in 1834. Though minuscule compared to New York, this expansion of Lower Canadian commerce encouraged the growth of the urban merchant class at a rate far exceeding the total provincial population. Accordingly, Quebec City had just 370 merchants in 1805 but 961 in 1831, while Montreal boasted 648 merchants in 1819 and 1,203 by the latter year. Fernand Ouellet has shown how this enlargement of the commercial sector, thanks to British immigration and the exclusivity of imperial trade, worked "mostly to the advantage of the English-speaking." Indeed, Montreal had a budding Anglophone majority by the early 1830s, and Quebec City was not far behind.[17]

As in the United States, such sweeping economic developments in Lower Canada produced unequal socioeconomic outcomes. Above all, a serious predicament emerged for the francophone habitants who resided on seigneurial estates along the St Lawrence valley from Quebec City to Montreal. Eighty-nine percent of Lower Canadians lived in the countryside in 1831, and French Canadians in the seigneuries comprised the bulk of them. The intensifying demand both for sturdy timber and arable farmland placed heavy pressure on seigneurs (who technically owned the estates in an arrangement vaguely analogous to the old patroonships of New York's Hudson Valley) to start behaving more like capitalists in their transactions with habitants. In addition to raising rents on new grants of land, stripping it of timber beforehand, and even selling uncultivated tracts contrary to law and custom, seigneurs adopted "increasingly hard-nosed styles of estate management" that involved petty exactions and other indignities toward their habitants. Following the pioneering work of Fernand Ouellet, Allan Greer has documented how the seigneurs' mounting jealousy of their property rights became especially flagrant in the Montreal region by the 1830s, where many habitants were deeply indebted to their seigneurs. Not surprisingly, this area was a hotbed of rebellion in 1837. A less dire situation also developed outside the seigneuries in the Anglophone Eastern Townships, where the British American Land Company obtained a charter from Parliament in the early 1830s to monopolize the sale of immense tracts of Crown real estate to newly arrived English immigrants. While temporarily propping up the economy of the Eastern Townships through price inflation and spending on internal improvements, the British American Land Company clearly favoured the profits of its London-based investors over the high prices and likely indebtedness faced by local Anglophone farmers.[18]

On the one hand, the rural francophone population bore the brunt of the agricultural crisis while urban Canadians faced stiffer job competition from recent immigrants. On the other hand, the soaring profits from the import (and re-export) trade, the lumber industry, and shipbuilding largely flowed into the pockets of elite Anglophone merchants with close ties to the imperial metropole. The booms in immigration and shipping were intertwined because the same vessels that transported Canadian timber to Great Britain filled their cargoes with destitute migrants for the return voyage. Seeking an investment outlet for their profits and new sources of financial credit, such merchants spearheaded the chartering of the Bank of Montreal in 1817 and the Bank of Quebec one year later. By 1830, French Canadians owned just 19 per cent of the total stock in the Bank of Quebec and 2.9 per cent in the Bank of Montreal, leaving the balance to wealthy Anglophone investors. It is instructive, moreover, that francophone patrons only owned 2 per cent of shares in the nine largest Lower Canadian transport companies during this period.[19]

As the rich grew richer, skilled and unskilled workers in Montreal and Quebec City (including many Irish and English labourers) responded to this rising inequality by cultivating a collective identity that translated into strikes, riots, and the formation of trade unions. Mirroring the 1827 creation of the Mechanics' Union of Trade Associations in Philadelphia and the 1833 founding of the General Trades Union in New York, striking carpenters in Montreal joined forces with tailors, shoemakers, bricklayers, and other craftsmen to establish (albeit briefly) the Montreal Trades Union in 1834. For various reasons, these urban workers remained ambivalent about their political allegiance leading up to the Rebellion of 1837–38 – an event in which they played only a marginal role – as Robert Tremblay has recently illustrated. Nonetheless, the monopolization of economic power by Anglophone elites fomented "a sense of injustice" among Lower Canadian labourers, according to Tremblay, which prompted them "to move closer to the democratic platform of the *Parti patriote*."[20]

By and large, the Parti patriote itself was managed by middle-class professionals in the cities. Yet patriote leaders knowingly derived their political strength from habitants suffering in the countryside and (to a lesser extent) the disgruntled sectors of the urban working class. Like William Leggett, they became crucial voices for "the class which labours with its own hands" – those Lower Canadians who felt most oppressed by the costly changes and doubtful benefits of the Market Revolution.

## THE PATRIOTES AND THE BANKS

With these polarizing effects of the Canadian Market Revolution as a backdrop, the patriote press closely monitored U.S. political developments, including the first major skirmish of the Bank War: Andrew Jackson's July 1832 veto of the congressional bill to recharter the Second Bank of the United States. In the official view of his administration (notwithstanding the president's personal history as a speculator and corporate stockholder in Tennessee), "exclusive privileges" were the bane of American civilization. Boldly articulating the core message of his political movement, Jackson noted that a certain degree of social disparity was to be expected in any country; but, when "the rich and powerful too often bend the acts of government to their selfish purposes," he wrote, then "the humble members of society – the farmers, mechanics, and labourers ... have a right to complain of the injustice of their Government."[21] Compounding the problem, Jackson argued that the Second Bank's small cadre of unelected officials remained wholly unaccountable to the interests of the American people. The president surmised in his veto message that more than a quarter of the Second Bank's stockholders were foreigners (i.e., British investors), so the danger of "European monied domination" in the United States, as he later said in a cabinet meeting, seemed not only possible but imminent.[22]

The next year, almost as an addendum to Jackson's veto message, Philadelphia economist William Gouge demonstrated in convincing detail how a national network of incorporated banks fostered the institutional corruption and social deterioration that the president had so elegantly protested. Gouge's best-selling treatise, *A Short History of Paper Money and Banking in the United States*, became the bible for anti-bank critics in the Jacksonian period and a fundamental blueprint for the economic policy of the Democratic Party. It went through five editions before 1840 and was published in French from Brussels; moreover, extracts appeared in newspapers throughout North America over the course of the 1830s, including William Lyon Mackenzie's reform-oriented *Colonial Advocate* in Upper Canada. The Library of the Lower Canadian Legislative Assembly ordered a copy of *Short History of Paper Money and Banking* in 1834, and a London edition published in 1833 has been found in the personal library of the famous patriote Speaker of the Assembly, Louis-Joseph Papineau.[23]

Gouge's thesis was simple and compelling: banks had to be excluded from control over the national currency through their printing and circulation of paper money, by which they "lay the foundation of an *artificial* inequality of wealth."[24] His anti-bank (but really anti-*corporate*) program embodied a direct response to the Market Revolution – a revised Jeffersonian outlook deliberately tailored for a new era in which the sovereignty and welfare of "the humble members of society" assumed a central place. Gouge's critique thus appealed especially to the beleaguered working classes of Lower Canada, for he insisted that with the help of incorporated paper-money banks, a handful of privileged, non-producing capitalists continually pocketed "the earnings and savings of many of their frugal and industrious neighbors." For patriote leaders and their mostly francophone constituents, this process of economic extortion plainly originated in the unelected, Anglophone membership of the provincial Legislative Council and its potent alliance with British merchants from Montreal and Quebec City. Indeed, the patriotes' general disdain for corporate banking in Lower Canada during the 1830s remained inexorably linked to the "*political, tory monopoly*" entrenched in the Legislative Council.[25]

To some extent, the political and socioeconomic conditions of Lower Canada exemplified Andrew Jackson's worst fears for the

American republic. While U.S. politicians during the Bank War knowingly exaggerated the "aristocratic" and "monopolistic" behaviour of their opponents for political gain, the political opponents of the Parti patriote on the Legislative Council actually *were* aristocratic monopolists. Assisted by imperial connections and powerful banks incorporated by the British Parliament, Anglophone merchant elites channelled most of their profits toward the accumulation of land or luxury goods. According to scholars Gérald Bernier and Daniel Salée, this mercantilist relationship with Great Britain "undermined the establishment of manufactures or industries" and "smothered the blossoming of a domestic market." Lower Canada was an aristocracy of merchant-landowners, Bernier and Salée maintain, "enmeshed in a structure of authority and domination which invariably turned to the advantage of the large landowners."[26] Like the Legislative Council itself, the provincial banking system formed an integral part of that structure, for both were staffed by the same network of affluent Anglophone elites. Thus, the "artificial distinctions" and "special privileges" so detested by Jacksonian Democrats permeated the very heart of Lower Canada's political economy, rendering Lower Canadian habitants and urban labourers even more susceptible than their American counterparts to the sort of economic exploitation described by William Gouge. Patriote orators acknowledged this dilemma when they referred to "the aristocracy of Banks, of government, and of money."[27]

Against this bleak picture, the patriotes – mirroring their anti-bank neighbours in the United States – envisioned a brand of "democratic commerce" by which a popularly elected government would only regulate the economy to ensure that all members of society participated on an equal footing. They imagined an economy without drastic fluctuations in the market, without unequal access to financial credit, and where tradesmen and farmers alike could reap the benefits of their daily labour. Michael Connolly, an Anglophone patriote running for an Assembly seat in Quebec City in 1837, best summed up the patriotes' notion of democratic commerce: "In short, I shall always be found, as I am now, the determined opponent of MONOPOLY – whether the Monster appears under the alluring mask of a speculating Land Company, or any other of the too numerous petty Companies which infest this Province, to the great injury of the producing classes, who are in reality the *bone* and *sinew* of society; and who it should be the special care of the Legislature to foster, encourage and protect." Whether they called the working classes the "*bone* and *sinew*" or the "humble members of society," Connolly and the patriotes had the same audience in mind as Andrew Jackson and his Democratic followers. Though surely influenced by an eighteenth-century republican discourse of virtue and corruption, the patriotes' anti-corporate message was distinctly egalitarian and carefully directed at systemic inequities in Lower Canada amplified by the Market Revolution.[28]

In the spring of 1833, some patriotes briefly supported the incorporation of a new bank in Lower Canada – the City Bank of Montreal – in the belief that it would break the monopoly of the Bank of Montreal and further the objectives of democratic commerce by expanding access to financial credit for the working-class population. "The City Bank is to ... act in competition with the Bank of Montreal," its patriote sponsors declared, adding that the Bank of Montreal "is composed of all the principal members of a powerful party well known in this country by the opposition it has consequently made to the wishes of the mass of the population."[29] Almost immediately, however, the patriote press learned of the "*sham* election" of the bank's new directors: a group of Anglophone merchants with ties to the Bank of Montreal apparently made use of dubious electoral techniques in order to seize control of the City Bank. The patriotes were furious, having insisted that the City Bank "not be under the control of any persons interested in the other institution, for if it be, it cannot but prove a drag upon commerce, and add to the power of the Montreal Institution, already too much felt." Such protests were futile; by 1837, French Canadians owned merely 4 per cent of City Bank shares. Due to their disappointment with the monopolistic takeover of the City Bank, patriote leaders began moving toward William Gouge's denunciation of all incorporated banks while continuing to push for a more democratic diffusion of financial credit in their province.[30]

This shift in the patriotes' outlook coincided with the escalating events of the Bank War – namely, President Jackson's removal of federal deposits from the Second Bank of the United States in late 1833 – as well as the famed passage of the Ninety-Two Resolutions by the Lower Canadian Legislative Assembly in early 1834. The latter achievement marked a radical turning point for the patriote movement, and even garnered the support of the Montreal Trades Union, for patriotes now demanded nothing less than the modification of the

1791 Constitutional Act (only amendable by the British Parliament) in order to transform the Legislative Council into a democratically elected body.[31] "Give us a council that is suitable to the people of the colony," the patriote chief Louis-Joseph Papineau demanded of lawmakers in England. "It must therefore be drawn from the people, and restored to the people ... [for] it must not form a particular class, influenced by authorities beyond the Ocean, but must have its interests here as we do." In addition to Papineau's populist, class-infused vision of good government, the Ninety-Two Resolutions displayed a firm conviction among patriotes that there was no better validation for democratic reform than the obvious success of their southern neighbour. In Resolution 44, they asserted that "the unanimous consent with which all the American States have adopted and extended the elective system, shows that it is adapted to the wishes, manners and social state of the inhabitants of this continent."[32]

While turning to the United States for a proper model of republican government, Ludger Duvernay, the veteran editor of Montreal's main patriote newspaper, *La Minerve*, also revealed his keen understanding of Gouge's hard-money critique and its singular relevance for Lower Canadian society. He began an editorial in late 1834 with a recognition of the historical benefits of paper-money banking for American industry and commerce; but Duvernay quickly cautioned his readers that "there is evil beside the good."[33] He reviewed the process by which banks with minimal specie in their vaults circulated paper notes greatly exceeding the specie-to-liability ratios stipulated in their legislative charters. The eventual economic crisis was inevitable, Duvernay concluded, for once the public began to demand hard money in return for their banknotes, the fatally overextended banks had little choice but to suspend specie payments. "The Banks," Gouge had written, "by expanding their [paper] issues, give aliment to the wild spirit of speculation when it begins; and by their contractions, they aggravate the evils of the natural reaction."[34] The patriote editor agreed that the ensuing contraction of credit and declining value of bank paper were devastating – but not necessarily for those same individuals who benefitted in the first place. "This easy creation of paper money which makes some people rich," Duvernay declared ominously, "may cause the ruin of others."[35]

The editor of *La Minerve* reminded his readers that Lower Canada's paper-money circulation, like that of the United States, was nowhere close to 100 per cent convertible into specie. He noted how the incorporated banks in the province officially maintained a one-to-three specie-to-liability ratio under the terms of their charters, which seemed far too risky in his opinion; and like Gouge, Duvernay also remained skeptical of the banks' willingness to abide by the legal ratio. (Unlike many U.S. bank charters, those in Lower Canada did not forbid the banks from suspending specie payments, perhaps exacerbating the editor's fears.) As for the situation in the United States, Gouge himself bleakly estimated that "not more than one-twentieth of the [bank] paper is actually 'convertible' at any one time." Regardless of his accuracy, the manifest potential for monetary instability manufactured by the banks, plus its disproportionate impact on the middle and working classes, was a genuine concern for both William Gouge and his deeply knowledgeable Lower Canadian counterpart.[36]

Finally, Ludger Duvernay recounted Andrew Jackson's accusations against the Second Bank of the United States to show his patriote readers how British capital constituted their common enemy. He accepted the president's dire pronouncements of governmental corruption and the pressing threat of overseas influence, concluding that the Second Bank was less a national institution in its present form than "a weapon in the hands of foreigners, dangerous to public liberties."[37] This situation appeared all too familiar to Duvernay: "When you consider these fair complaints, against the [Second Bank], you cannot help but notice the perfect coincidence that exists between this bank and those established in Canada ... Like the [Second Bank], they are managed by enemies of the country; like many other banks, they can only guarantee the value of two-thirds below their paper circulation ... Finally, experience has proven that they do not discount nearly as generously to patriotes as to their own kind; therefore, their operations are tainted with a revolting bias in this country." The patriote editor emphasized an overwhelming commonality between the objections of American anti-bank Democrats and the grievances of his own countrymen against the Lower Canadian banks. Just as Old Hickory feared "European monied domination" by way of the Second Bank, so Ludger Duvernay identified the chartered banks in Lower Canada and wealthy merchants who controlled them as "enemies of the country." He also detected "a revolting bias" in the lending patterns of the corporate banks in favour of Anglophone colonial and merchant elites. Bolstered by national and class-based enmities, Duvernay's assessment of Lower

Canadian banking operations strongly reinforced Jackson's poignant observation that "the rich and powerful too often bend the acts of government to their selfish purposes."[38]

A few weeks prior to his editorial, Duvernay featured a lengthy campaign speech by Louis-Joseph Papineau on the front page of *La Minerve*. In his oration, Papineau expressed similar apprehensions about the state of banking in Lower Canada. "I would add that of all the devices now operating to harm the interests of the country," he announced unequivocally, "the most powerful is the bad direction of Banks."[39] Revealing an almost emotional distrust of paper money and pleading for Lower Canadians to crash the system by voluntarily redeeming all their banknotes in specie, Papineau demonstrated a deep resentment toward "[the] unequal division of wealth when banks favour the monopoly of a political clique." It was obvious to Papineau that collusion between the banks and the colonial government – especially the Legislative Council – facilitated the existence of a permanent, "monied" aristocracy in Lower Canada with interests linked to British investors. Moreover, Papineau's opposition to the "monopoly of a political clique" precisely reflected the ethno-demographic landscape in the province, for he cited special privileges favouring a "violent minority" of 34,000 Anglophone subjects over the "overwhelming majority" of 477,000 French Canadians. For patriote leaders like Papineau and Duvernay, the "humble members of society" were comprised, by and large, of Lower Canada's francophone labourers and habitants.[40]

Responding to this unfortunate situation in the winter of 1835, twelve reform-minded businessmen from Montreal with personal ties to Louis-Joseph Papineau and the patriote movement established Viger, DeWitt, and Company, also known as the Banque du Peuple (the People's Bank). Its primary founders were Louis-Michel Viger and Jacob DeWitt, two rare examples of non-English beneficiaries of the Canadian Market Revolution – DeWitt, a native-born American who voted for the Ninety-Two Resolutions in the Assembly, had made a fortune in the shipping industry around Lac St Louis. These entrepreneurs considered their bank to be an alternative to the two incorporated banks in that city, particularly in light of the hostile takeover of the City Bank. In their first public announcement for the Banque du Peuple, they stated their goal of "putting into circulation a capital that is now dormant and producing nothing, and to protect the industry, the Agriculture, Manufactures and Commerce of the country, the benefits of which extend indiscriminately to all classes in a community." The founders' commitment to democratic commerce was sincere, for unlike its predecessors, the Banque du Peuple was a *société en commandite* without a royal or legislative charter; thus, its principal partners were not protected by limited liability. While incorporated banks could print and circulate paper money far beyond the amount of specie in their reserves without considering individual risk, a société en commandite had to maintain a strict specie-to-liability ratio of nearly 100 per cent. Patriotes like Edmund Bailey O'Callaghan, editor of the radical Montreal newspaper *The Vindicator*, clearly understood both the financial vulnerability and consequent fidelity of such a bank. "Apart from every other consideration, the security offered to the public by this institution, beyond what is expected from chartered Banks, is not to be overlooked," O'Callaghan wrote in his endorsement of the Banque du Peuple. "There is every certainty that these individuals, for the safety of their own fortunes, thus at stake, will conduct the affairs of the Bank, and the funds committed to them by the stockholders, with the utmost prudence."[41]

If the founders of the Banque du Peuple hoped to advance the patriotes' democratic vision for Lower Canada by extending loans to the working-class population and doing their part to restrain harmful credit cycles, they evidently did so in full accordance with the views of radical anti-bank Democrats in the United States. William Gouge pinned the underlying evil of paper-money banks on the "exclusive privileges" of incorporation afforded them in their legislative charters. Because of those privileges, he argued, chartered banks "respect the laws and public opinion so far only as is necessary to promote their own interest." William Leggett felt the same way, concluding "that charters conferring partial or exclusive monopolies on small fractions of society are infringements on the general rights of society and therefore that the system ought to be abandoned as soon as possible as utterly at war with the rights of the people at large." The Banque du Peuple, lacking the financial immunity provided by a royal or legislative charter and governed solely by local shareholders, simply encouraged the widespread diffusion of credit necessary for a thriving democratic commerce. Even a biased observer like O'Callaghan (who also owned stock in the bank) could claim with some degree of legitimacy that "the people of the province have more confidence in the *People's Bank* than in those of any other Bank" in Lower Canada. Such optimism would not last long, however, either for the Banque du Peuple or the province's several incorporated banks.[42]

## THE PANIC AND THE PEOPLE

The turbulent year of 1837 witnessed a culmination of Jacksonian anti-bank, hard-money arguments in both the United States and Lower Canada. Thanks to the worst economic crisis in decades, countless North Americans watched their financial prospects evaporate as banknotes lost all value and procuring sufficient credit to cover one's debts suddenly became impossible. President Martin Van Buren, Jackson's chosen Democratic successor, seized on the general despair fomented by pervasive insolvency and unemployment to make a bold push for sweeping monetary reform in the United States. His plan for an "Independent Treasury" – originally William Gouge's idea – proposed that the federal government discontinue its relationship with banks altogether by storing federal funds in separate "subtreasuries" without the power to circulate paper currency.[43]

Gouge had argued both publicly and in private letters to Democratic officials that by accepting bank notes as payment for taxes, the federal government was primarily to blame for perpetuating the national circulation of paper money. "If the operations of the Government could be *completely* separated from those of the banks," he had recommended back in 1833, then "the system would be shorn of half its evils. If Government would neither deposit the public funds in the Banks, nor borrow money from the Banks; and if it would in no case either receive Bank notes or pay away Bank notes, the Banks would become mere commercial institutions, and their credit and their power be brought nearer to a level with those of private merchants." After the eventual passage of an amendment in the U.S. Senate offered by hard-money enthusiast John C. Calhoun, the Independent Treasury was strictly limited to carrying out its financial operations in specie. Although the Independent Treasury bill did not become law until 4 July 1840, it was the cornerstone of Jacksonian economic policy beginning in late 1837.[44]

The Lower Canadian patriotes likewise interpreted the Panic of 1837 as a wake-up call for radical reform of their provincial banking system. In Montreal, patriotes expressed disgust over the banks' mutual decision to suspend specie payments on 17 May – including the Banque du Peuple – and a desperate fear that "the loss falls upon the Mechanic, Labourer and *Habitant*." The vulnerability of working-class Canadians due to the specie suspension was profound, for they had few financial resources other than small earnings from daily wage labour or the sale of underpriced farm produce, both of which now came in the form of depreciated paper money. "If a rich man cannot sell his merchandise to-day [*sic*], he can sell it tomorrow," Gouge famously commented, "[but] labour is the poor man's only commodity ... [if] he cannot sell it to-day, it is lost to him forever." Thus, the patriote editor Edmund Bailey O'Callaghan publicized the most extreme hard-money arguments emanating from Jacksonian newspapers like the Washington *Globe*, which demanded the complete removal of paper-money banks from American shores. Occasionally, even O'Callaghan and his fellow Montreal patriotes delivered the hard money critique in its sharpest form: "*Take none of it*; nothing but *pure* copper ... and small silver coins, and they will soon be in abundance, and honest and hard working people will be no longer shamefully *cheated*." O'Callaghan firmly believed that suspending specie payments did nothing to stop the outflow of hard money from Lower Canada to the United States or Great Britain – the banks' official pretext – but that it "only prevents the Banks from paying their debts, and enables merchants to pay what they owe in a depreciated currency." Louis-Georges Harvey has found that O'Callaghan's public criticism of the Banque du Peuple for its specie suspension landed him in hot water with patriote friends of the bank, including Papineau. Nonetheless, his radical views in *The Vindicator*, and surely those of numerous Montreal readers, remained in perfect accord with Gouge's hard-money ideology.[45]

In Quebec City, meanwhile, patriotes attacked the Bank of Quebec after it too suspended specie payments in the midst of the crisis. Like O'Callaghan and Ludger Duvernay, contributors to the upstart patriote newspaper *Le Libéral* complained bitterly that the bank's corporate charter originated outside the province by an act of British Parliament – and was actually *renewed* along with the Bank of Montreal's charter at the end of May. They argued that the banks' interests, reflecting those of the Legislative Council, were utterly hostile to the Lower Canadian masses and the overall stability of the domestic economy. "Without any control on the part of the public to the issues of paper by the Banks here," the patriotes asked, "what security is there that one tenth of the bank notes now in circulation ever can be redeemed?"[46] The basic problem, they insisted, was that corporate bank directors cared nothing for the public good, for "in order to save a few monopolists from the abyss, [they] constantly bring ruin upon the masses." Did banknotes bring any advantages whatsoever for working-class Canadians? The patriotes replied decisively: "In general, they only serve the interests of the greedy speculator ... Moreover, the commercial class, far from opposing the circulation of these paper bills, or the scarcity of hard money, seems to maintain a very keen interest in sustaining the present system of Banks."[47]

The Panic of 1837 fully convinced the patriotes of Quebec City, just as Duvernay had predicted, that the perennial instability of paper currency inevitably led to utter devastation for the lower classes. "Thus [the working man] suffers a direct loss by a state of things to which he has in no way contributed," they exclaimed, "and as he is neither a merchant, nor a bank director, nor a stockholder he suffers *all* the loss, without receiving *any* of the advantages." In the wake of the financial collapse, these patriotes developed a passionate distaste for paper money no less vitriolic than that of Andrew Jackson's most radical Locofoco followers like William Leggett. They took great delight, for example, in the failure of Upper Canada's Kingston Bank in September: "We wonder when our monied (paper!) institutions here will have the decency to do likewise." Deeming corporate, paper-money banking essentially incompatible with their vision for democratic commerce in Lower Canada, some patriotes declared this crisis an opportune moment to banish forever "these paper-money aristocrats, who live so magnificently at the expense of an honest and overconfident people!"[48]

Unfortunately, we will never know just what sort of financial system the patriotes might have implemented in Lower Canada had they emerged victorious from the Rebellion of 1837–38. We can only speculate that they would have continued to embrace sociétés en commandite like the Banque du Peuple or, replicating their experiment with the City Bank, chartered their own financial corporations to achieve a broader distribution of credit among the middle and lower classes. Perhaps they would have considered an Independent Treasury like the United States, or even Dr Charles Duncombe's plan for a "Republican Bank of Canada" – detailed by Albert Schrauwers in chapter 5 of this volume – as an appropriately republican means of regulating the currency by Gouge's hard-money standards.

By the outbreak of the Rebellion in November 1837, the patriotes certainly viewed their struggle against Anglophone colonial and merchant elites in an American, continental context. They looked accusingly to Great Britain not only as the fountainhead of commercial banking in North America, but also as the source of all opposition to honest republican government on their side of the Atlantic Ocean. Therefore, when Whig newspapers in the United States criticized the Democratic press for supporting the Lower Canadian Rebellion, Quebec City patriotes retorted conspiratorially that those newspapers "are believed to be in the continual pay of the Barings [Bank in London], the United States Bank, and perhaps, through the secret service money indirectly conveyed to them, of the British Aristocracy." Pro-bank Whigs in the United States and the fiercely detested "*political, tory monopoly*" in Lower Canada both derived their political and economic power from aristocratic interests abroad, according to these patriotes. As a result, both parties could "scarce profess to be republicans."[49]

Historians should take their cue from the patriotes. We should cast aside restrictive or nationalist narratives isolating the Lower Canadian Rebellion from the Bank War and the Panic of 1837. Viewed within a larger framework of capitalist economic development and its political consequences in North America, the Rebellion appears less a product of the Age of Revolution than of the Market Revolution, and less ideologically linked to Jeffersonian republicanism than to Jacksonian democracy. Rural and urban workers on both sides of the Canadian-American border during this era became increasingly aware of unfair socioeconomic disparities emerging in the context of rapid commercial change. Though most members of the Parti patriote belonged to the middle classes of Montreal and Quebec City, they understood the grievances of the francophone masses – the "*bone* and *sinew*" of Lower Canadian society. Through their fiery speeches and editorials, patriote spokesmen disseminated anti-bank panaceas across the province not only in the service of armed rebellion, against the British, but also, they clearly believed, on behalf of a more participatory economy for all Lower Canadians. Too often veiled by discrete political and linguistic contexts, the mutual agendas of the Jacksonian Democrats and Lower Canadian patriotes should be seen as a loosely coordinated response to the unsettling effects of the Market Revolution, which, like so many revolutions throughout history, hardly confined itself to convenient national boundaries.[50]

## NOTES

1 Donald Creighton, *The Empire of the St Lawrence: A Study in Commerce and Politics*, 2nd ed. (Toronto: University of Toronto Press, 1956; first published 1937 by Ryerson Press as *The Commercial Empire of the St Lawrence, 1760–1850*), 310. Robert Richard would like to thank Jay Gitlin, Jason Opal, Taylor Spence, Yvan Lamonde, Louis-Georges Harvey, Julien Mauduit, Maxime Dagenais, and the other contributors in this volume for their insightful feedback throughout the many editorial stages of this essay.

2 Historians have argued extensively over the precise details of the Market Revolution. For a full discussion of this complex topic, see Melvin Stokes and Stephen Conway, eds, *The Market Revolution in America: Social, Political, and Religious Expressions, 1800–1880* (Charlottesville: University Press of Virginia, 1996). For scholarly fatigue with the Market Revolution in the U.S. historiography, see Daniel Feller, "The Market Revolution Ate My Homework," *Reviews in American History* 25, no. 3 (1997): 408–15.

3 Alan Taylor, *The Civil War of 1812: American Citizens, British Subjects, Irish Rebels, & Indian Allies* (New York: Vintage Books, 2010), 456–8.

4 Allan Greer, "1837–38: Rebellion Reconsidered," *Canadian Historical Review* 76, no. 1 (1995): 14–18; Greer, *The Patriots and the People: The Rebellion of 1837 in Rural Lower Canada* (Toronto: University of Toronto Press, 1993), 3–4; "Censuses of Canada, 1665–1871," Statistics Canada, last modified 26 August 2015, accessed 26 May 2017, www.statcan.gc.ca; U.S. Secretary of State, *Abstract of the Returns of the Fifth Census* (Washington: Duff Green, 1832), 46.

5 Jackson is quoted in Major L. Wilson, "The 'Country' versus the 'Court': A Republican Consensus and Party Debate in the Bank War," *Journal of the Early Republic* 15, no. 4 (1995): 619–47. See also Harry L. Watson, *Liberty and Power: The Politics of Jacksonian America* (New York: Hill and Wang, 1990), 132–71; and Charles G. Sellers Jr, *The Market Revolution: Jacksonian America, 1815–1846* (New York: Oxford University Press, 1991), 301–65.

6 *The Vindicator*, 3 July 1835. This analysis draws primarily from three patriote newspapers of the period: *La Minerve* (Montreal), *The Vindicator* (Montreal), and *Le Libéral* (Quebec City). For two brief considerations of their impressive influence in Lower Canada, see Allan Greer, *The Patriots and the People*, 139–41; and Maureen Slattery, "Irish Radicalism and the Roman Catholic Church in Quebec and Ireland, 1833–1834: O'Callaghan and O'Connell Compared," CCHA *Historical Studies* 63 (1997): 36–8.

7 Yvan Lamonde, *Ni avec eux, ni sans eux: le Québec et les États-Unis* (Quebec: Nuit blanche éditeur, 1996), 25–30; Louis-Georges Harvey, "Importing the Revolution: The Image of America in French Canadian Political Discourse, 1805–1837" (PhD diss., University of Ottawa, 1990), 344–50.

8 Allan Greer, "Rebels and Prisoners: The Canadian Insurrections of 1837–38," *Acadiensis* 14, no. 1 (1984): 145; Greer, *The Patriots and the People*, 4–6, 145–6; Michel Ducharme, "Closing the Last Chapter of the Atlantic Revolution: The 1837–1838 Rebellions in Upper and Lower Canada," *Proceedings of the American Antiquarian Society* 116, no. 2 (2007): 429–30; ibid., *Le concept de liberté au Canada à l'époque des Révolutions atlantiques (1776–1838)* (Montreal: McGill-Queen's University Press, 2009), 125; Chester New, "The Rebellion of 1837 in Its Larger Setting," *Report of the Annual Meeting of the Canadian Historical Association* 16, no. 1 (1937): 6–8, emphasis in original.

9 Without explicitly referring to the Market Revolution, Louis-Georges Harvey provides a superb analysis of the patriotes' banking principles and their relationship to Jacksonian America in "Banques, société et politique dans le discours politique d'Edmund Bailey O'Callaghan, 1833–1837," *Cahiers des dix* 69 (2015): 251–79. For an overview of republicanism in Lower (and Upper) Canada, see Allan Greer, "Historical Roots of Canadian Democracy," *Journal of Canadian Studies* 34, no. 1 (1999): 11–22; and Louis-Georges Harvey, "The First Distinct Society: French Canada, America, and the Constitution of 1791," in *Canada's Origins: Liberal, Tory, or Republican?* (Ottawa: Carleton University Press, 1995), 79–107.

10 Sean Wilentz, "Society, Politics, and the Market Revolution, 1815–1848," in *The New American History*, ed. Eric Foner (Philadelphia: Temple University Press, 1997), 72. Wilentz describes the Jacksonian hard-money program as "democratic commerce" in *The Rise of American Democracy: Jefferson to Lincoln* (New York: Norton, 2005), 440. The concept of "democratic commerce" is clearly shown, though not stated explicitly, in Julien Mauduit's recent interpretation of the patriotes' entrepreneurial and egalitarian political economy, in "L'économie politique des patriotes, entre capitalisme et socialisme," *Bulletin d'histoire politique* 25, no. 2 (2017): 172–92. Robert Tremblay sees a distinction between the patriotes' middle-class, "democratic capitalism" and the so-called "worker republicanism" of urban labourers, but the broader notion of "democratic commerce" in this essay embraces both concepts. See Robert Tremblay, "Artisans et ouvriers à l'époque des revendications démocratiques et

nationalitaires du Parti patriote dans le Bas-Canada, 1832–1838: un rendez-vous manqué avec l'histoire?," *Bulletin d'histoire politique* 25, no. 2 (2017): 146–71.

11 For a brilliant and concise account of the Market Revolution that includes many of these statistics, see John L. Larson, *The Market Revolution in America: Liberty, Ambition, and the Eclipse of the Common Good* (New York: Cambridge University Press, 2010), especially 46–91. For U.S. immigration figures, see U.S. Department of Commerce, *Historical Statistics of the United States: Colonial Times to 1970* (Washington: Bureau of the Census, 1975), 106.

12 Robert Wiebe, *The Opening of American Society: From the Adoption of the Constitution to the Eve of Disunion* (New York: Alfred A. Knopf, 1984), 151; Howard Bodenhorn, "Antebellum Banking in the United States," EH.Net Encyclopedia, Robert Whaples, ed., 26 March 2008, http://eh.net/encyclopedia/antebellum-banking-in-the-united-states/.

13 Theodore Sedgewick Jr, ed., *A Collection of the Political Writings of William Leggett*, vol. 1 (New York, 1840), 107; Harvey, "Banques, société et politique dans le discours politique d'Edmund Bailey O'Callaghan," 255–67.

14 Larson, *The Market Revolution in America*, 50. For the Safety Fund Act and its role within the larger evolution of credit, money and commerce in New York State, see Janet A. Riesman, "Republican Revisions: Political Economy in New York after the Panic of 1819," in William Pencak and Conrad E. Wright, eds, *New York and the Rise of American Capitalism: Economic Development and the Social and Political History of An American State, 1780–1870* (New York: New York Historical Society, 1989), 1–44. For the banking statistics and a more technical analysis of the Safety Fund, see Howard Bodenhorn, *State Banking in Early America: A New Economic History* (New York: Oxford University Press, 2003), 155–82.

15 Andrew Bonthius, "The Patriot War of 1837–1838: Locofocoism with a Gun?," *Labour/Le Travail* 52 (2003): 19–20. For transnational commerce and the growing dominance of New York over the British North American economy (next paragraph as well), see Creighton, *The Empire of the St Lawrence*, 205–87; and Daniel Patrick Glenn, "Facing West From Niagara's Shores: Competition, Commerce, and Expansionism on the U.S.-Canadian Border, 1810–1855" (PhD diss., University of Cincinnati, 2007).

16 See previous note. The quotation and comparative trade figures are from Creighton, *The Empire of the St Lawrence*, 251–4.

17 Fernand Ouellet, *Lower Canada, 1791–1840: Social Change and Nationalism*, trans. Patricia Claxton (Toronto: McClelland and Stewart, 1980), 117–65.

18 For economic change and hardship in the seigneuries, see Ouellet, *Lower Canada*, 142–51; and Greer, *The Patriots and the People*, 20–51, 258–93. For the Eastern Townships, see Ouellet, *Lower Canada*, 151–6; and J.I. Little, *Loyalties in Conflict: A Canadian Borderland in War and Rebellion, 1812–1840* (Toronto: University of Toronto Press, 2008), 57–106.

19 Ouellet, *Lower Canada*, 135. For a brief account of Lower Canada's incorporated banks in this era, see Bray Hammond, *Banks and Politics in America from the Revolution to the Civil War* (Princeton, NJ: Princeton University Press, 1957), 645–8.

20 Bryan D. Palmer, *Working-Class Experience: Rethinking the History of Canadian Labour, 1800–1991*, 2nd ed. (Toronto: McClelland & Stewart, 1992), 57–9; Tremblay, "Artisans et ouvriers à l'époque des revendications démocratiques et nationalitaires du Parti patriote dans le Bas-Canada," 152–4.

21 Andrew Jackson, "Veto Message," 10 July 1832, in *A Compilation of the Messages and Papers of the Presidents*, James D. Richardson, ed., vol. 2, part 3, Project Gutenberg, http://onlinebooks.library.upenn.edu/webbin/metabook?id= mppresidents. For patriote coverage of the recharter bill's passage in Congress, see *La Minerve*, 12 July 1832; for Jackson's veto, see *La Minerve*, 16 July 1832.

22 "Paper Read to the Cabinet, 18 September 1833," in *Correspondence of Andrew Jackson*, ed. John Spencer Bassett, vol. 5 (Washington, DC: Carnegie Institution of Washington, 1931), 200; Watson, *Liberty and Power*, 144.

23 Watson, *Liberty and Power*, 139; Wilentz, *The Rise of American Democracy*, 510; Benjamin G. Rader, "William M. Gouge Jacksonian Economic Theorist," *Pennsylvania History: A Journal of Mid-Atlantic Studies* 30, no. 4 (October 1963): 443–53; Harvey, "Importing the Revolution," 132, n84; Yvan Lamonde, e-mail communication with author, 27 March 2017.

24 William M. Gouge, *A Short History of Paper Money and Banking in the United States, Including an Account of Provincial and Continental Paper-Money. To Which Is Prefixed an Inquiry into the Principles of the System* (Philadelphia: T.W. Ustick, 1833), I, 91, emphasis in original.

25 Ibid., I, 25; *The Vindicator*, 12 July 1833, emphasis in original.

26 Gérald Bernier, "The Rebellions of 1837–1838 in Lower Canada: A Theoretical Framework," *Canadian Review of Studies in Nationalism* 18, nos 1–2 (1991): 131–43; Gérald Bernier and Daniel Salée, *The Shaping of Québec Politics and Society: Colonialism, Power, and the Transition to Capitalism in the 19th Century* (Washington, DC: Taylor & Francis, 1992), 34, 78.

27 Louis-Joseph Papineau, "Aux libres et indépendants électeurs du Quartier-Ouest de Montréal," *La Minerve*, 4 December 1834. French original: "L'aristocratie des Banques, du gouvernement, et du comptoir." Albert Schrauwers draws a similar picture of political and economic collusion perpetrated by members of the Family Compact, such as William Allan, in 1830s Upper Canada. See Albert Schrauwers, "Revolutions without a Revolutionary Moment: Joint Stock Democracy and the Transition to Capitalism in Upper Canada," *Canadian Historical Review* 89, no. 2 (2008): 223–55; and Schrauwers, *'Union Is Strength': W.L. Mackenzie, the Children of Peace, and the Emergence of Joint Stock Democracy in Upper Canada* (Toronto: University of Toronto Press, 2009).

28 Michael Connolly, "To the Free and Independent Electors of the Lower-Town of Quebec," *Le Libéral*, 21 June 1837. These general themes can be found in Harvey, "Banques, société et politique dans le discours politique d'Edmund Bailey O'Callaghan"; and Mauduit, "L'économie politique des patriotes, entre capitalisme et socialisme."

29 *Vindicator*, 19 March 1833. For further evidence of patriote support for the City Bank, see *Vindicator*, 5, 22, and 29 March 1833.

30 *Vindicator*, 19 July 1833. For more patriote objections to the City Bank election, see *Vindicator*, 9, 12, 23, and 30 July 1833; also Harvey, "Banques, société et politique dans le discours politique d'Edmund Bailey O'Callaghan," 262–3.

31 Greer, *The Patriots and the People*, 137–9. For patriote coverage of the Bank War during this period, see *Vindicator*, 11 December 1832; and *La Minerve*, 30 September 1833 and 28 April 1834.

32 "Conclusion du discours de M. Papineau sur la Première Résolution (18 Février)," *La Minerve*, 3 March 1834. French original: "Nous donner un conseil qui convienne au peuple de la colonie. Il faut donc qu'il soit tiré du peuple, et rendu au peuple ... qu'il ne forme pas une classe particulière, influencée par les autorités au-delà de l'Océan, mais qu'il ait ses intérêts ici comme nous." For the language of Resolution 44, see W.P.M. Kennedy, ed., *Statutes, Treaties and Documents of the Canadian Constitution,*

*1713–1929*, 2nd ed. (Toronto: Oxford University Press, 1930), 279, http://www.canadiana.org/view/9_03428/0004.

33 *La Minerve*, 22 December 1834. French original: "[à] côté du bien se trouve le mal."

34 Ibid.; Gouge, *A Short History of Paper Money and Banking in the United States*, I, 63.

35 *La Minerve*, 22 December 1834. French original: "Cette facilité de création d'un papier monnoyé qui faisait la fortune des uns, pouvait causer la ruine des autres."

36 Ibid.; Gouge, *A Short History of Paper Money and Banking in the United States*, I, 59; Hammond, *Banks and Politics*, 660; Creighton, *The Empire of the St Lawrence*, 311.

37 *La Minerve*, 22 December 1834. French original: "une arme entre les mains des étrangers, dangereuse pour les libertés publiques."

38 Ibid. French original: "Quand on examine ces justes plaintes, contre la banque des Etats-Unis, on ne peut s'empêcher de remarquer la coïncidence parfaite qui existe entre cette banque et celles établies en Canada … Comme la grande banque, elles sont administrées par les ennemis du pays; comme beaucoup d'autres banques, elles n'ont pour garantie que des valeurs des deux tiers inférieures à leurs circulations de papier … Enfin l'expérience preuve qu'elles n'escomptent point aussi largement aux patriotes qu'a leurs propres castes; par conséquent leurs opérations sont entachées d'une partialité révoltante au pays."

39 "Aux libres et indépendants électeurs du Quartier-Ouest de Montréal," *La Minerve*, 4 December 1834. French original: "J'ajouterai que de tous les engins maintenant en operation pour nuire aux intérêts du pays, le plus puissant est la mauvaise direction des Banques."

40 Ibid. French original: "[la] repartition inégale de la richesse lorsque des banques favorisent le monopole d'une coterie politique."

41 For the official notice of the Banque du Peuple and O'Callaghan's endorsement, see *Vindicator*, 20 February 1835. A highly useful but unpublished reference for the Banque du Peuple is Robert S. Greenfield, "La Banque du Peuple, 1835–1871, and Its Failure, 1895" (MA thesis, McGill University, 1968). My analysis of the Banque du Peuple as a société en commandite mirrors Albert Schrauwers's interpretation of the joint-stock banks in Upper Canada as vehicles for a democratic economy, in Schrauwers, "Revolutions without a Revolutionary Moment: Joint Stock Democracy and the Transition to Capitalism in Upper Canada"; and Schrauwers, *'Union Is Strength.'*

42 Gouge, *A Short History of Paper Money and Banking in the United States*, I, 137; [William Leggett], *New York Evening Post*, 3 January 1835, in *Social*

*Theories of Jacksonian Democracy*, Joseph L. Blau, ed. (New York: The Liberal Arts Press, 1954), 72; *Vindicator*, 4 August 1835 [emphasis in original]. For O'Callaghan's relationship with the Banque du Peuple, both political and financial, see Harvey, "Banques, société et politique dans le discours politique d'Edmund Bailey O'Callaghan," 265–78.

43 Wilentz, *The Rise of American Democracy*, 457–62.

44 Ibid.; Gouge, *A Short History of Paper Money and Banking in the United States*, I, 113, emphasis in original.

45 *Vindicator*, 19, 23, and 30 May, and 9 June 1837; Gouge, *A Short History of Paper Money and Banking in the United States*, I, 31 [emphasis in original]. *See also* Harvey, "Banques, société et politique dans le discours politique d'Edmund Bailey O'Callaghan," 272–6.

46 *Le Libéral*, 5 September 1837. For the charter renewals and additional attacks on the mismanagement of incorporated banks in Lower Canada on the basis of their violation of popular sovereignty, see *Le Libéral*, 5 July and 29 August 1837; and *The Vindicator*, 24 March and 22 August 1837.

47 *Le Libéral*, 19 September 1837. French original: "Nous n'avons cessé de nous élever contre ces Institutions de Banques, qui pour sauver de l'abime quelques monopoleurs, ruinent toujours les masses. – Que produisent sur le pauvre peuple ces billets crées par le besoin et l'intérêt? Ils ne servent en général qu'aux vues de l'avide spéculateur ... Aussi la classe commerciale, bien loin de s'élever contre la sortie de ces billets, contre la rareté du numéraire, parait avoir un intérêt bien vif à soutenir le système actuel de Banques."

48 *Le Libéral*, 5 July, 9 August, and 23 September 1837, emphasis in original. French original: "ces aristocrates de papier-monnaie, qui vivent si magnifiquement aux dépens d'un peuple honnête et trop confiant!"

49 *Le Libéral*, 9 September 1837.

50 These conclusions stand in contrast to those of the eminent Canadian historian Fernand Ouellet, especially in his books *Histoire économique et sociale du Québec, 1760–1850* (1966) and *Le Bas-Canada, 1791–1840* (1976). Ouellet unjustly dismisses the influence of Jacksonian political ideology in Lower Canada as wholly subservient to the conservative nationalism of the middle-class patriote leadership – e.g., "Despite the rationalizations based on liberal and democratic ideologies, [the *Patriotes*'] real intention was to preserve a society like the *Ancien Régime* on the banks of the St Lawrence ... The nationalist venture of 1837–38 was too tightly linked to the ambitions of specific individuals, to the immediate interests of the liberal professions, and to the particular

difficulties to the period to succeed. *It was not based on the elements which would have allowed the building of a better future.*" Fernand Ouellet, *Economic and Social History of Quebec, 1760–1850: Structures and Conjonctures*, trans. Institute of Canadian Studies (Ontario: Gage Publishing Limited, 1980), 442, emphasis added.

SECTION TWO

# Alternative Republics

3

# The Lure of a Canadian Republic

## *Americans, the Patriot War, and Upper Canada as Political, Social, and Economic Alternative, 1837–1840*

THOMAS RICHARDS JR

On 16 November 1838, soldiers of the Patriot Army of Upper Canada emerged with a white flag from their improvised redoubt, a stone windmill on the Canadian bank of the St Lawrence River, a few miles downriver from the Upper Canadian town of Prescott. For five days they had been besieged by British forces, and they held out until the arrival of British artillery rendered the formerly impregnable windmill now quite pregnable. The patriots had hoped to restart the failed Upper Canadian Rebellion of 1837, and anticipated thousands of Upper Canadian colonists coming to their aid when they crossed into Canada – but none came. They had also hoped for reinforcements or relief from the American shore, but U.S. officials patrolled the river, keeping the patriots isolated from any American sympathizers. They did receive moral support, as hundreds cheered on the patriots from the New York town of Ogdensburg just across the river, but inside the windmill this mattered little. All told, 161 men surrendered to the British – of whom sixty were exiled to Van Diemen's Land, and eleven were executed. Most of these men were American.

These men who fought – and died – in the Battle of the Windmill represented but a small sliver of the thousands of Americans who rallied to the cause of the Canadian patriots in the aftermath of the Canadian Rebellions, a vast majority of who came from counties neighbouring the U.S.-Canadian border. Because much Patriot activity in the United States remained both clandestine (due to U.S. authorities' anti-Patriot stance) and unfulfilled (because Britain's crushing victories over the patriots in 1838 prevented the patriots from taking further military activity), it remains impossible to gauge Patriot numbers with any degree of accuracy. A rough estimate suggests 2000 Americans fought in Patriot battles against the British, while another 2000 bore arms but never had the chance to fight. By way of comparison, in 1836, one year before the advent of the Patriot War, the Republic of Texas' forces numbered approximately 2000, and the U.S. Army totalled 8000. In the context of the late 1830s, therefore, the patriots were hardly an insignificant force. Moreover, Patriot volunteers were buttressed by thousands more Americans who joined the secret Hunters' Lodges organizations, and tens of thousands of Americans along the northern border who supported Patriot actions from a passive stance. Even these passive supporters, however, aided the patriots by refusing to report Patriot activity to U.S. authorities, or declining to testify against or convict the patriots' illegal actions in U.S. courts. In sum, American support for the Patriot War along the northern border was substantial, and just as importantly, this support was sustained for more than a year in the face of countless Patriot defeats and setbacks.[1]

Despite the substantial numbers of Americans who actively joined or tacitly supported the patriots, very few American historians have studied the Patriot War, and even the few who have studied it give cursory attention to the internal dynamics of the conflict, in particular the reasons why so many Americans staked their futures on the cause of a Canadian republic.[2] Most historians of the conflict fleetingly note reasons such as the pursuit of military glory, the need for money amidst the Panic of 1837, and an early display of the American desire to expand U.S. borders – what would come to be called Manifest Destiny. Yet, in almost all works, these motivations are stated perfunctorily, left unproven so the military aspects of the conflict can be detailed. Ultimately, to most U.S. historians, American patriots were simply another example of American filibusters – no further explanation needed.[3]

This treatment must change, particularly in light of recent work on filibustering that has demonstrated its participants' complex motivations, and American filibusters' complicated – and very ambivalent – relationship with the U.S. state. This ambivalence was especially prevalent in filibustering operations before the 1850s. Beginning with Florida in the 1810s, reaching its peak in Texas from the 1820s to the 1840s, Americans in the south and west moved into non-U.S.

territories and, over time, attempted to seize control. Although often defined as filibusters, their actions differed from the filibusters of the 1850s, who invaded Latin American countries with the unabashed goal of seizing immediate power and expanding slavery. Pre-1850s American filibusters, by contrast, took up arms only after prolonged settlement and accommodation with the sovereign power. For instance, in the most prominent example of Mexican Texas, it took fifteen years for American migrants to rebel, and then only after massive political shifts in Mexico itself. Although their actions often facilitated U.S. expansion in the long term, American settlers in Texas – and in Florida, California, and Oregon – did not migrate or fight at the behest of the U.S. state. Instead, they were motivated by a complex set of ideological and pecuniary factors that shifted in response to larger shifts in U.S. politics and North American geopolitics.[4] The thousands of Americans involved in the Patriot War were motivated by a similar set of factors, from abstract ideological commitments to republicanism and liberty, to more concrete motivations like free land and financial gain. Whatever their motives, key to the American involvement was the borderlands nature of their continual contact with Upper Canadians in the decades prior to rebellion; they were fighting for a people who they believed were just like themselves.

Based upon Patriot sources largely unexamined by American historians, this essay argues that, while the reasons Americans joined the patriots were myriad, they all revolved around one central factor: a potential Upper Canadian republic represented a political, economic, and social alternative to the United States, where Americans could achieve political power and financial gain that seemed no longer possible in a United States riven with depression and uncertainty. Unlike the southern borderlands that offered similar incentives for decades, the window of opportunity in the northern borderland arrived late and was remarkably brief. After 1810 the British discouraged American immigration to Canada, and thus there was no comparative migration north as there was south. The 1837 Canadian Rebellions finally provided this opportunity, holding out the prospects of a Canadian Republic. Of course, the patriots needed to win this republic first, and to do so they planned to use U.S. territory as a staging ground for multiple invasions of Canada. Not only did American patriots believe this undertaking was legal, it also represented the highest ideals of American citizenship, and was sanctioned by the federal structure of the American Union. Stunned and outraged at federal opposition to what they perceived as their righteous and lawful actions, American patriots responded with a vigorous defence of states' rights and individual liberty, avowing that the federal government had betrayed American principles. Indeed, these federal actions confirmed U.S. decline, and gave American patriots even greater incentive to realize a more perfect republic across the northern border.

## THE LINGERING GREAT LAKES BORDERLAND

Historians have argued that the War of 1812 augmented nationalism for both Americans and Canadians, and, as a result of these newly loyal populations, by the 1820s the United States and Great Britain maintained unchallenged authority on their respective sides of the international border. Pre-war accommodation and hybridity gave way to post-war uncontested sovereignty and imperial rivalry.[5] Yet, while the structures of power along the border were no longer fluid, the economic and social connections between Americans and Canadians remained so. Before 1837 these connections were hardly secret, and were especially acute along the Upper Canada-U.S. border. At the far western end of the St Lawrence River, Upper Canada (roughly, modern southern Ontario) was the most isolated of Britain's North American colonies. With a population of only 400,000, and encircled on three sides by a much more populated and economically robust United States, the colony was unsurprisingly much more a part of the U.S. than the British economic orbit. Most goods to Upper Canada travelled through New York via the Erie Canal and the Great Lakes, tying the burgeoning cities of Buffalo, Detroit, and Cleveland to the smaller towns of Upper Canada. Social ties amplified economic ties. Despite the fact that the British discouraged American immigration after 1810, even in 1837 a majority of Upper Canadians were either American migrants or their descendants. These people read easily obtained American newspapers, followed American politics, traded with Americans, and married Americans. Americans and Upper Canadians interacted on an everyday basis, and shared common language, culture, and customs.[6] By the 1820s British authorities feared this Americanization would seep into the political realm, and effectively disenfranchise all Canadian settlers of American background. Across the U.S. border, Americans had no need to reciprocally orient themselves north as Upper Canadians did south. After all, the Upper Canadian economy was marginal in comparison to that of the United States, and Americans were unwelcome as a matter of British policy. However, the sheer number of social and economic connections with Canadians meant that Upper Canada was not a foreign land to those Americans who lived along the Great Lakes. Although the two sides had grown further apart since the War of 1812, the region remained a borderland.

In some respects, Lower Canada's border with the United States mirrored Upper Canada's. The populations of both countries mingled, and trade travelled both ways along the Richelieu River-Lake Champlain that connected Lower Canada with Vermont and eastern New York. The Lower Canadian Eastern Townships especially, where many New Yorkers had settled in the 1810s, were firmly rooted in an American social and economic orbit.[7] Yet, with its French-speaking majority and its proximity to the Atlantic, Lower Canada was more isolated from the American population south of the border than Upper Canada, even though, as many of the chapters in this collection demonstrate, the Lower Canadian patriotes were certainly in tune with national events in the United States. From an economic standpoint, Vermont's economy hardly matched that of New York or Ohio, and was stagnant even before the Panic of 1837, and thus a majority of Lower Canadian commerce was oriented north via the St Lawrence, while Maine's border with Lower Canada, while extensive, was mostly uninhabited on the American side. No city comparable to Buffalo or Rochester existed along the Lower Canadian border; St Alban's, population 2,700, was the largest American town in close proximity to Lower Canada.[8] In terms of social ties, they certainly existed, for no geographic barrier separated much of Lower Canada and the United States. However, essential differences in language and religion created powerful barriers that prevented the deep integration of peoples found in the Great Lakes region.[9]

The differences between Upper Canada and Lower Canada, and in turn each Canada's relationship with the United States, is crucial for understanding why – and *where* – Americans along the northern border became enthralled with the Patriot movement. If Americans wanted to base their aid for the rebels on a rational military assessment of their potential success, then they should have looked to Lower Canada; after all, Lower Canadian patriotes achieved a military victory at Saint-Denis, and briefly threatened British sovereignty in the region. In contrast, the two Upper Canadian Rebellions, the first led by William Lyon Mackenzie in Toronto, the other by Charles Duncombe in Western Upper Canada, never did. Indeed, to an impartial observer, the incident at Montgomery's Tavern was more tragic farce than transformative rebellion.[10]

Americans across the border, however, were not impartial. To them, the inhabitants of Upper Canada were proto-Americans from a social and cultural perspective. Their continued contacts with Upper Canadians throughout the Great Lakes borderland made the Upper Canadian Rebellion a personal struggle. As one Detroit observer explained to his wife, Americans flocked to the Upper Canadian rebel ranks because "many of the citizens of this city and the adjoining country are Canadians, or have been, they have many friends there, and to a man they are opposed to the General Government."[11] Moreover, just as Americans had done decades prior, these Canadian friends and neighbours were overthrowing the tyrannical British, exhibiting – as several observers noted – a new manifestation of the "spirit of '76." Meanwhile, Americans living along the Lower Canadian border did not see Lower Canadian Rebellion as a personal, *American* struggle.[12] Certainly, when the patriotes crossed the Vermont border, they were heartily welcomed with rhetorical and material support, but in the end very few Americans – in comparison – joined Patriote armies, and those that did deserted before fighting began. Patriote armies in Vermont remained composed of mostly French-Canadian refugees.[13] Thus, the 1838 Patriote invasions of Lower Canada from Vermont were in many ways a second Lower Canadian Rebellion, while the American-supported – and soon American-dominated – Patriot War that took place along the Upper Canadian border was a different struggle than the Upper Canadian Rebellion that had preceded it.[14]

When William Lyon Mackenzie and his fellow Upper Canadian rebels crossed into U.S. territory, Americans living in cities and towns along the border welcomed them with open arms, pledging to support their cause by any means necessary. Indeed, some Americans were ready to assist even before rebel defeats, for Mackenzie had requested aid through a letter to the Buffalo press a day before the Toronto uprising.[15] After Mackenzie crossed the border and arrived in Buffalo, its citizens held the largest meeting ever assembled in the city in support of the Canadian patriots.[16] This support meant many things: a safe haven on American soil, money and provisions, weapons, and – most significantly – manpower. Within days of rebellion's failure, hundreds of Americans joined Patriot ranks throughout the Great Lakes borderland.[17] As one Detroit resident wrote, "Canada – Canada, is in the mouth of everyone, even the women have caught the torch of liberty and are passing it on from the other with as much enthusiasm as the most devoted Canadian revolutionist."[18] The patriots of Upper Canada had hoped for, even counted on, American support – and they found it.

In the weeks after their arrival in the U.S., Upper Canadian patriot leaders organized their mushrooming multinational forces. The largest patriot army, numbering anywhere from 500 to 1000 men, assembled on Navy Island on the outskirts of Buffalo. Lying in the middle of the Niagara River, the island was officially British territory, thus giving the patriots an aura of political legitimacy.[19] Canadians made up an important component of patriot forces, but from the outset Americans made up a majority of the patriot forces, as multiple sources attest. One Buffalo paper estimated the Navy Island force was two-thirds American and one-third Canadian, and Winfield Scott, sent to Buffalo in January to restore order, also perceived a preponderance of Americans.[20] A Michigan observer who opposed the Patriot War lamented that it was not Canadians but "American citizens ... creating warfare."[21] Of course, in massive gatherings like Navy Island, Americans and Canadians were most likely socially and culturally indistinguishable from one another, a result of the ubiquitous connections of the Great Lakes borderland. However, over the following year American dominance of the patriot movement only increased, to the point where it became obvious that the patriot movement was fundamentally American-led. By the following November Americans constituted a significant majority at a Cleveland patriot convention, and Americans outnumbered Canadians by six to one in the Battle of the Windmill a few weeks later.[22] Mackenzie and other Canadian rebels eventually perceived this American dominance as a problem. Hoping a patriot invasion would spur the rising of Canadians who had remained silent during the first rebellion, they realized that an army of American patriots looked much more like invasion than revolution.[23] Indeed, William Johnson, a Canadian patriot known as the "Pirate of the Thousand Islands," started rejecting American volunteers for the "Patriot Navy" in July 1838 in an effort to return the patriot cause to its Canadian roots. He and other Canadians perceived that, while Canadians had started a war for Canadian liberty, Americans had taken it over.[24]

## FREEDOM, FAME, AND FORTUNE

Why did Americans in such overwhelming numbers embrace the patriot cause in the first months of the conflict? It is a question historians have answered before, but almost always in a cursory fashion, because these motivations are seemingly straightforward: tangible incentives like money and power, coupled with more ideological motivations like liberty and republicanism. Yet the superficial nature with which historians have studied these various impetuses makes it appear as if the American patriots themselves were superficially motivated, and thought little about what they were getting themselves into. In point of fact, American patriots' reasons for joining the cause may have been obvious to the naked eye, but they were hardly superficial, reflecting a calculated rationality on what their involvement would bring for themselves and their families.[25]

Let us begin with the most prominent motivation as voiced by the American patriots themselves: Canadian freedom. Countless patriot letters and patriot newspapers argued that they were embarking on a glorious cause to liberate Canada from tyranny. A patriot soldier from Rochester wrote Mackenzie, "I am for liberty. My whole soul is in it and if I am called to defend it I am willing to shed the last drop of blood in my veins rather than surrender this glorious boon." [26] Americans at a patriot meeting collectively expressed their desire to help the rebels in their "difficult and arduous, but honourable and praiseworthy task to plant and sustain the tree of liberty."[27] Statements such as these were ubiquitous.[28] Certainly the fact that the patriots were fighting the British only added to the motivation. Many American patriots imagined themselves as heirs to the Revolutionary generation, none more so than the aptly named Thomas Jefferson Sutherland. Sutherland was a newspaper printer who quickly assumed a leadership position among the patriots, although he would almost immediately disappoint, for his actions rarely matched his rhetoric. Sutherland frequently compared himself and other patriots to "Lafayette, DeKalb, Steuben, Pulaski, Kosciusko, and other illustrious foreigners" who aided Americans during the Revolution.[29] Sutherland believed his mission was twofold: first, to spread democracy throughout North America, and second, to "oppose British influence" wherever it appeared.[30] Other volunteers noted that their fathers and grandfathers – or in a few cases, they themselves – had fought the British in the past, and now they would do so again. Clearly the combination of a fight *for* liberty, and also *against* the British, struck a chord for American patriot volunteers.[31]

Yet spreading liberty and opposing the British were not the sole explanations for why Americans joined the patriots. If they were, then we should expect Americans throughout the country to also volunteer, for they too hoped to spread liberty, and they too disdained the British – especially after the infamous "*Caroline* Affair."[32] Border inhabitants hoped the incident would increase recruitment, and immediately appropriated the *Caroline* Affair as a symbol of British perfidy – and by extension the righteousness of the patriot cause. "Remember the *Caroline*" became a patriot rallying cry, and when the patriots burned the British ship *Robert Peel* in July, many viewed it as justified revenge.[33] However, those who joined the patriots did not do so solely, or even primarily, because of the *Caroline*. Despite their public outcry, privately American patriots wrote little on the *Caroline* in weeks immediately following the incident. Indeed, out of dozens of letters Americans wrote to Mackenzie during the Navy Island campaign, only one mentioned the *Caroline*.[34] The lack of private correspondence suggests that, at its core, the patriot uproar over the *Caroline* Affair was propaganda, designed to induce Americans outside the Great Lakes region to also join the cause, or to at least offer wholehearted rhetorical support to the patriots' efforts. Unfortunately for the patriots it was ineffective; while the *Caroline* Affair outraged Americans outside the Great Lakes region, notably few clamoured for war, and fewer still acted on their impulse by enlisting in the patriot cause. To Americans living far from the conflict, this international outrage necessitated a national, not individual, response. Thus, the *Caroline* Affair neither initiated nor enlarged the Patriot War, and explaining the Patriot War as a response to the incident – as many historians have done – hides the complexity of the patriot cause.[35]

If the *Caroline* Affair did little to induce Americans to join the patriots, desire for U.S. annexation of Canada was even more insignificant, at least as an immediate reason for Americans along the border to volunteer. American patriots were not acting as early harbingers of Manifest Destiny, and no American patriot expressed an interest in the U.S. seizure of Canada; considering the frequently expansionist tendencies of many Americans, this silence was significant. To be sure, it would be wrong to state that annexation was not contemplated as a potential consequence of patriot victory in some American patriots' minds, for – as Mauduit's dissertation and Harvey's chapter demonstrate – Americans *outside* of the border region *were* contemplating the annexation of Canada in case of rebel victory. Yet, even for most of those American patriots who longed to annex Canada, annexation was an amorphous vision rather than immediate program.[36] Moreover, on the border, this vision – or, more accurately, many visions – of U.S. expansion took a backseat to the immediate concerns of patriot victory. Indeed, only the rare patriot discussed a potential U.S.-Canada union until nine months into the conflict, when Mackenzie broached the subject in his patriot newspaper, and the circumstances behind this demonstrated just how unusual the topic was.[37] Once against a U.S.-Canada union, Mackenzie changed his opinion after he had been marginalized within the patriot movement, and was clearly grasping at straws to reassert his leadership. Few patriots supported Mackenzie's idea, nor did his suggestion have any evidential increase on patriot recruitment. In response, one American sympathetic to the patriots admonished Mackenzie that a union was "incomprehensible," and Mackenzie had no chance to "convince the two people of the advantages to be gained."[38] To the writer, there was no reason that two separate republics could not exist side by side. Upper Canada would not be part of the Union, but rather become, as Americans defined both Texas and Mexico at the time, a "sister republic" – one that could join the United States immediately, eventually, or never.[39]

Of course, for most American patriots, interests augmented ideology: while the patriots wanted a liberated Republic of Upper Canada, they also saw an opportunity for themselves within that republic – perhaps glory and fame, perhaps wealth and personal independence. Many Americans who volunteered did so with the caveat that they assume a certain rank in the patriot army. For example, one volunteer with medical experience asked to be appointed surgeon or some other position of "reputable standing," while a lieutenant-colonel in the New York militia expressed his willingness to join the patriots as long as he kept his lieutenant-colonel rank.[40] Importantly, personal interests did not make ideological commitments false or hypocritical.

American patriots were undoubtedly committed to Canadian republicanism, as interests seamlessly coincided with ideology – a powerful combination that helps explain why so many Americans joined the patriots with such enthusiasm. Indeed, interests were often embedded within ideological statements. Major George Russell of the Ohio militia succinctly tied the two together when he wrote to patriot leaders, "[The commanding officer] and his staff are at your command, providing you can give them the same rank in your army, that they now hold in the militia of Ohio. Our reasons for tendering you our services are, that we are willing to aid in the cause of LIBERTY."[41] Whether Russell would fight for "LIBERTY" if he did not receive a proper rank, he did not say.[42]

It is impossible to pinpoint exactly what these men hoped to ultimately gain by their service, for complete defeat ensured no patriot gained much of anything. Some may have envisioned that, after defeating the British, they would return to the U.S. as American Lafayettes, and achieve national fame and universal acclaim. However, American patriots fought for a Canadian republic, and many more likely would have chosen to remain in Canada as national heroes. Considering the intimate connections between the two peoples, Americans from the Great Lakes region would not have felt out of place. In Canada, patriot fame could translate into a higher military rank or, as one observer put it, "offices of high honor and dignity."[43] Whether they planned to remain in Canada or return to the United States, clearly those who were already officers in state militias believed their prospects were greater in the Patriot Army than in their current positions.[44] This relentless quest for glory and power fit squarely with the ideals of the Jacksonian Age, indeed with the actions of Andrew Jackson himself. Hoping to mimic Jackson, American patriots sought military glory, which could then translate into political power down the road.[45]

For these would-be Jacksons, war alone provided reason enough to join the patriots. The examples of both Jackson and Washington taught Americans that war launched careers, yet these opportunities for glory had faded since the War of 1812. This was particularly the case on the northern border, where even Indian warfare had dwindled. Now the Patriot War provided a new opportunity that many had sought. Such was the case for the impressively named Rensselaer Van Rensselaer, who assumed command of the patriot army in the first months of the conflict. Van Rensselaer was a scion of New York's renowned family of Dutch origin and editor of the Albany *Daily Advertiser*, and as such clearly had little financial incentive to join the patriots. Instead, he claimed he joined because he hoped to emulate "the chivalrous example of the South in the Case of Texas."[46] Van Rensselaer's citation of Texas was an explicit attempt to portray the patriot cause as a similar fight for liberty and republicanism, yet his comparison was also revealing in a way he did not intend. For some soldiers in Texas, most famously Sam Houston and David Crockett, the conflict offered an opportunity to rebuild failed or failing lives in the United States. Canada could do the same thing for Van Rensselaer. Van Rensselaer had a drinking problem, and, judging by his letters, a continued insecurity about not living up to his family's reputation. Presumably this would all be changed after he led the patriot army to victory.[47]

Unlike Van Rensselaer and his type, many American patriots sought more immediately tangible incentives than personal glory, namely land and money. From the outset patriot leaders promised volunteers 300 acres in Canada after the British were overthrown, which was not unrealistic in sparsely populated Upper Canada.[48] During the Navy Island campaign Mackenzie also offered $100 in silver in several months' time, leaving unsaid that it would take Patriot victory to make good on this offer.[49] Later the patriots formed a "Bank of Upper Canada," with a proposed capital of $7.5 million, from which funds could be used to pay patriot soldiers their promised salary of $10 per month, about the same pay as a day labourer in the region.[50] Unsurprisingly the volunteers themselves rarely put these baser requests in letters to patriot leaders, although one police constable requested a "small salary" to become a recruiting agent.[51] Whether this person did become a recruiting agent is unknown, but actual patriot recruiters knew tangible incentives were needed. According to one recruiter, more men would come with "a little assistance."[52] Predictably, anti-patriot observers claimed money was the sole reason Americans joined the patriots, and they feared the effects of failure on the hundreds of armed men who had been promised rewards.[53] As one Detroiter who witnessed patriot activity firsthand wrote, the patriots wanted to "plunder neighbouring Canada or ourselves."[54] While the patriots were not bent solely on "plunder," this anti-patriot rhetoric possessed an important truth: the patriot cause was just as much about personal interest as it was republican ideology.

While freedom, fame, and fortune were all factors that pulled Americans into patriot ranks, there was also one crucial push factor: the Panic of 1837. By the time of the Canadian Rebellions in December, the United States was mired in the most severe depression in its short history. Many of the cities and towns bordering the Great Lakes, such as Buffalo and Detroit, were hit particularly hard.[55] In the midst of "hard times," Americans joined the patriots in the hope that somehow they could get out of financial distress if Canada were set free – even though Canada too suffered depression. Unlike the Van Rensselaer-types, for these men it was not the war itself, but what happened after that truly mattered. They hoped patriot service would eventually provide a financial restart, representing a northern counterpart to the concurrent "Gone to Texas" phenomenon in the South, during which Americans by the thousands fled to Texas in order to escape their debts, notifying their neighbours (and debt collectors) by writing "G.T.T." – "Gone to Texas" – on their doors. Michigan patriot officer W.W. Dodge illustrates the point. Dodge was captured by the British, but made a spectacular escape from Quebec and returned to Michigan. Unfortunately, Michigan did not provide a respite, for authorities wanted him for indebtedness. He then escaped to New York, but his luck finally ran out, and he was soon arrested.[56] For Dodge, and for many other American patriots, we can imagine that if Canada already provided opportunities for cheap land and debt evasion before the Patriot War, then they would have already "Gone to Canada" to rebuild lives decimated by the depression. Americans had done exactly that in the aftermath of the Revolution, when the British had welcomed American immigration. However, unlike Canada in the 1790s or Texas in 1837, Canada in 1837 did not welcome Americans – *unless* the Patriot War was won and a Canadian republic was consummated.[57]

Thus, all classes of men were represented in patriot ranks – elites like Van Rensselaer, yeoman farmers and labourers who desired land and economic opportunity, and the truly desperate like Dodge. In its class dynamic, therefore, the patriot army imperfectly resembled the other hodgepodge armies of the early American republic, such as George Washington's Continental Army, the various militias the United States raised during the War of 1812, and the volunteer forces in the U.S.-Mexican War in 1846. While British officers and Americans hostile to the patriot cause denigrated patriot volunteers as rabble, they were no more rabble than other American armies of the era – nor, for that matter, the ranks of the British Army.[58] As in these armies, elites provided the leadership, while labourers and anyone who simply needed work filled the bulk of its muster rolls.[59] Considering the patriots' persistence over several years in the face of both British and U.S. hostility, the multi-class composition of the patriot army is not surprising. The number of reasons for volunteering meant that there was no single panacea that would curb patriot activity: the British would simply have to defeat the patriots in the battlefield. Unfortunately for the patriots, the British would be aided in their efforts by the United States.

The United States government did not share the patriot desire for a Canadian republic. Behind the U.S. stance was a simple calculation that few Anglophobic Americans wanted to admit: the United States, mired in depression and possessing an army of only eight thousand men, did not have the strength for war with Great Britain. Therefore, the United States could not allow the patriots to use American territory as a springboard to invade Canada, which would make war much more likely. The Van Buren administration, with the full cooperation of Congress, tried to suppress the patriots with a series of escalating steps. In January 1838, immediately after learning of the *Caroline*, Van Buren dispatched Winfield Scott and other army officers to the border. While Scott succeeded in forcing the Patriot Army to disperse by cutting off supplies to Navy Island, patriot plans and invasions continued. In response, Congress passed a stronger Neutrality Act in March, which gave authorities more leeway to arrest would-be filibusters. Finally, with patriot activity still continuing in October, Van Buren sent two thousand U.S. regulars to the border. Meanwhile, across the border the British vastly expanded their military presence, placing thousands of troops in the Canadas within months of the rebellions, which augmented substantial numbers of loyalist militia already in arms. Facing the combined opposition of Great Britain and the United States, the patriot cause looked increasingly desperate.[60]

## UPPER CANADA: A MORE PERFECT AMERICAN REPUBLIC?

Yet, in spite of the odds, many American patriots rededicated themselves to the cause, and formed the secret Hunters' Lodges organization. In the guise of the Hunters, Americans patriots – along with a dwindling number of Canadian allies – carried on the struggle for many more months, sometimes even years, in the face of unrelenting opposition. This persistence requires explanation – one that can be found notably in American patriots' hopes and visions for a future Canadian Republic.

However, before investigating why thousands of American patriots continued the struggle, it is important to acknowledge how remarkable their persistence truly was. The Hunters were hemmed in from all sides, facing both overwhelming British and loyal Canadian opposition across the border, and a U.S. federal government overtly hostile to their future incursions into Canada. And yet, for most of 1838, the Hunters defeated the federal government for control of the U.S. side of the border region. The patriot cause remained so popular that it led to a complete breakdown of federal authority throughout the far northern United States. At first, with so few U.S. soldiers on the border, federal officials charged with enforcing order required local citizens to support them – juries in local courts, state and local officials, and local militia. All were undependable. State officials refused to enforce the Neutrality Act, and when they did so juries refused to convict. Their refusal was unsurprising, for, as one Canadian patriot commented on jury composition, "Young and old, and all classes ... are advocates of Canadian freedom."[61] General Hugh Brady was apoplectic over his inability to enforce the law: "What can a Military Commander do, towards maintaining the supremacy of the Laws, with a mere handful of men, when compelled to act in subordination to civil officers, a majority of whom to say the least are notoriously favorable to ... the Patriot cause?"[62] Patriot arms came almost exclusively from U.S. arsenals, where state officials left weapons "just where they might be stolen" by the patriots. Failing this, patriots forged letters from U.S. officials ordering for the weapons to be released.[63] State militias were entirely unreliable, so much so that Winfield Scott requested militias from non-border states that were "uninfected" with patriot sympathies.[64] Colonel William Worth also deemed the border state militias "infected," and mused to Secretary of War Joel Poinsett whether the militia would not only refuse to obey orders, but "openly ally themselves with the insurgent cause."[65] During patriot highpoints, such as the gathering of patriot soldiers in the New York town of Ogdensburg in November 1838 before the aforementioned Battle of the Windmill, it was the patriots, not the United States, who controlled the town.

In many ways, the patriots wrested the entire border region from U.S. control.[66] In response, British authorities began to argue that, because the United States failed to fulfill its role as the sovereign power in the borderland, then the British had a right to violate U.S. sovereignty in order to uphold British sovereignty over Canada. After the Caroline, the British never put this legal theory fully to the test, but their willingness to consider it demonstrated just how little ability the United States had to supress the patriots.[67]

Why was the patriot cause so popular along the northern border? Or was it? Clearly some Americans joined the Hunters' Lodges for the food, drink, and camaraderie of the meetings, and had little intention of fighting. They cheered on the cause of Canadian republicanism from the sidelines, donating money if they had the means. Yet simply because these men never fought does not mean they were uncommitted to the cause; under different circumstances, many may have indeed joined patriot armies. Any patriot victory could have led to a surge of patriot volunteers, mirroring the ebb and flow of the militia during the American Revolution. Unfortunately for the patriots, British military strength ensured most tacit support never became active support. However, even patriot supporters who never intended to fight under any circumstances played a significant role. If they had not existed in such numbers, then the United States would have suppressed the patriots within weeks, and Van Buren never would have needed to send federal troops. They acted as a sort of home front, providing economic and rhetorical backing to the patriots even as the United States tried to take it away from them. And, in case the patriots did emerge victorious, there is no reason to believe many of these tacit supporters would not have taken advantage of the prospects offered within an Upper Canadian republic.[68]

Take the example of Preston King. King was a prominent citizen from the New York town of Ogdensburg, and he would serve four terms in the House of Representatives in the 1840s, first as a Democrat, then as a Free Soiler, followed by one term as a Republican senator in 1856. In 1838, however, his political career was still in its infancy. In the early 1830s King was appointed the postmaster of Ogdensburg, and then was elected as a state representative in 1835. King's mother had emigrated from Upper Canada – which meant no more than crossing the St Lawrence River – but her family remained in Canada. In the first month after the rebellion King staunchly promoted the patriot cause, while across the border his cousin joined the loyal Canadian militia. After the initial patriot failures in early 1838, King actively abandoned the struggle, believing Van Buren's policy of strict neutrality was the most prudent course of action. It seems unlikely he ever joined the local Hunters' Lodges, despite rumours to the contrary. Nevertheless, judging by his continued support for Mackenzie and his paper, he maintained sympathy for the patriots.[69]

When the Battle of the Windmill erupted, King's belief in neutrality was put to the test. Unwilling to see the patriots captured, King led a rescue mission for the besieged men. Despite King's earnest endeavours, the mission failed, leaving the patriots to their fate. Perhaps unknown to him at the time, these same men whom he tried to rescue had killed his Canadian cousin during the battle. These events haunted King for the rest of his life. Immediately afterwards he checked himself into a Hartford asylum, and the battle's lingering effects may have even contributed to his suicide in 1865.[70] King was not an active patriot – indeed, he supported U.S. neutrality – but he was clearly invested in patriot victory. Although the rescue mission was not as risky as actually joining the patriots, it was risky nonetheless, and its failure devastated him. Considering his continuing interest in the cause and his family connections in Canada, it is not unreasonable to imagine that King would have tried to advance his fledging political career in the new Upper Canadian republic, rather than in the United States. Of course, such speculation can only be taken so far, but King's actions demonstrate a central point: simply because the thousands of patriot sympathizers and passive Hunters' Lodges members never fought did not mean their support was superficial. King's belief in neutrality made him a rather weak patriot sympathizer, but when the Patriot War came to his doorstep he could not help but get involved. There were significantly more dedicated but still passive patriots than King, and they represented a vast potential reservoir of support, one that was ultimately untapped due to continued patriot defeats.

As men like King urged on the patriots from the sidelines, the Hunters' Lodges met to fundraise, strategize, and implement the next patriot invasion of Canada. In September 1838, the Hunters clandestinely planned a three-front invasion of Canada, formed a provisional government for the Republic of Canada in Cleveland, opened pro-patriot presses throughout the border region, and frustrated U.S. officials who hoped to stop their actions. Importantly, while Americans dominated the organization, its very existence was based upon its opposition to the policies and actions of the United States. In essence, the Hunters' Lodges represented a breakdown of nationality, in which dedication to Canadian republicanism outweighed obedience to the laws of the United States. Many observers noted these skewed allegiances. As the anti-patriot *National Intelligencer* stated, the patriots "hovered between the two countries, not deserving the name of United States citizens, or subjects of Great Britain."[71] Daniel Webster observed, "If war breaks out [between the U.S. and Britain], [American patriots] do not propose to join the forces of the United States, but to unite themselves with the disaffected in Canada, declare the province free, and set up another government."[72] Eric Schlereth has recently demonstrated that Americans who moved to Texas in the 1820s and early 1830s were consciously expatriating themselves from the United States, drawn to Texas by the economic and political opportunities it offered.[73] While dedicated American patriots had not yet physically expatriated themselves as the Anglo-Texans had done, their membership in the Hunters' Lodges represented a preliminary ideological expatriation. An Upper Canadian republic, like Mexican-cum-independent Texas, represented a political, social, and economic alternative to the United States. Although this republic existed only as an idea, once the British were driven from Canada the expatriation would be consummated, and the idea would become reality.

But what would this reality look like? How did American patriots imagine the workings of the Republic of Upper Canada, and why did it continue to captivate so many after military victory looked increasingly unlikely? We have seen how republican ideology, military glory, political ambition, and financial gain pulled Americans of all classes into the patriot movement from the outset of the failed rebellions. Fighting for a republican Canada offered opportunities that the United States did not, both immediately and in the future. As the conflict continued, American patriot letters gave hints at what the future would hold once liberty was won – a future in which an Upper Canadian republic would solve many of the issues that the United States increasingly looked unable or unwilling to solve. Canada would become the ideal republic that the United States no longer was.

Certainly, this attitude was present in an amorphous sense in the initial weeks of the Patriot War, before the federal government became hostile to patriot activity. After all, American patriot hopes for fame and fortune could be realized in the new Republic of Upper Canada just as much as the United States. Yet American patriots' understanding of a Canadian republic as an alternative – and improved – republic truly crystallized when the federal government began implementing its anti-patriot measures. American patriots believed that, by trying to suppress them, the United States was betraying the principles of the Union, and now it was the patriots, not the U.S. government, who held true to American values. Central to their argument were the twin Jacksonian defences of democratic majority rule and the sanctity of individual liberty. With a majority of Americans along the border not necessarily joining but at least supporting the patriot cause, the imposition of federal power looked decidedly anti-democratic and authoritarian, especially when it came at the hands of 2,000 federal troops. Although the number of U.S. regulars did not compare to the 10,000 British soldiers across the border, it was a remarkable number by American standards. By comparison, 700 troops were placed in South Carolina during the Nullification Crisis, and only during the Whiskey Rebellion had more regulars been deployed against American citizens during the United States' short history.[74]

The patriots attacked this display of federal power. For example, Benjamin Kingsbury, editor of the *Detroit Morning Post* and a not-so-secret patriot, maintained federal troops had no right to arrest any patriots, for the patriots commanded majority support in the city – as Kingsbury maintained, "the people are sovereign."[75] If not the people, then at the least federal authorities had no right to supersede state power. As one patriot wrote, "We shall not let the U.S. authorities wrest the few rights which as a sovereign state we possess."[76] Moreover, federal imposition was a violation of constitutional rights and represented "shameful conduct of a free government."[77] At a Hunters' Lodges meeting in Detroit, one patriot proclaimed that, while he understood that the U.S. did not want war with Britain, there were "constitutional privileges" that could not be violated for any reason. Hunters at that same meeting issued a series of resolutions that condemned U.S. actions on the border, reiterated the importance of state sovereignty, free speech, and the right to bear arms, and warned of the dangers of "consolidation." Importantly, these resolutions expressed that allegiance to the United States was conditional on U.S. actions: "We are for sovereignty of the states, and for the union of the states; but we will not submit to martial law in a time of peace."[78] How the Hunters would respond if martial law were implemented was left unsaid.

This language mirrored that of the radical wing of the Democratic Party, and it was not surprising that a majority of American patriots were Democrats.[79] As Andrew Bonthius and Albert Schrauwers argue in this volume, many patriots were drawn to William Lyon Mackenzie's radical agrarian ideology and espousal of egalitarian principles, rhetoric that became more potent amidst the devastating depression. If radical Democrats could not form the type of republic they desired in the United States, then why not create it in Canada? U.S. actions against the patriots only solidified their willingness to create a republic elsewhere. The patriots' appropriation of Democratic ideology proved a problem for Democratic papers that condemned the Patriot War, for they had difficulty countering the patriots' conception of the American Union – unlike Whig papers, which consistently maintained the supremacy of federal law. Not wanting to admit they feared war with Britain, and unable to debate the patriots ideologically, Democratic papers effectively ceded to American patriots their valid constitutional arguments and changed tactics. Instead of attacking American patriots for their illegal actions vis-à-vis U.S. laws, they attacked them for their alliance with the Canadian rebels, contending that the weakness of Canadian rebels mandated staying out of the conflict. If the Canadians were really meant to have freedom, so the argument went, then they would have taken it for themselves.[80] Instead the Canadian rebels had shown themselves "subservient" and "leaderless" – and therefore did not deserve American help.[81] Judging by the continued popularity of the patriots into the fall and winter of 1838, these arguments were not persuasive.

However, despite the prevalence of this radical Democrat language and ideology, American patriots deliberately portrayed their movement as nonpartisan. As the patriot newspaper *The Canadian* proclaimed at the heading of its first (and seemingly only) issue: "*The Canadian* is edited by a refugee – published by a Democrat – printed by a Whig, and read by the whole world."[82] One Detroit official even wrote Secretary of War Poinsett that the patriots comprised a political party of their own.[83] Proclaiming their explicit nonpartisanship was partially propaganda, but it also rested on a key truth: although outnumbered by Democrats, there were many Whig Hunters.[84] While these men may not have identified as much with patriot politics, as already noted there were other factors to entice them. For a prominent Whig like Rensselaer Van Rensselaer, for example, this was military glory and potential political power. For many other Whigs, it was the Great Lakes borderland: American political stances became irrelevant when Canadian friends and business partners' very liberty was at stake.

Patriots on both sides of the political spectrum valued this cross-party nature of the struggle, as evidenced with the outrage expressed towards Mackenzie when he began openly engaging in U.S. party politics. Mackenzie had stepped down from his leadership position after Navy Island, believing his own talents would best be used starting a pro-patriot press to rally more supporters. By the summer of 1838 Mackenzie could not help his political nature, and began lambasting Whig policies in his paper, arguing that Whigs were no different from British Tories. The blowback was immediate, as outraged Whig patriots cancelled their subscriptions, while frustrated Democratic patriots admonished him for getting involved in American politics.[85] Even Mackenzie's son James, living in the New York town of Lockport, pointed out to his father that, while the Whigs in the federal government in Washington were unsympathetic, the Whigs in New York were "our best friends."[86] One patriot from Watertown put it more succinctly: "The die is cast, and you are cursed by all good patriots, both Jackson and Whig."[87] The writer was correct; subscriptions to *Mackenzie's Gazette* dropped dramatically, as the nonpartisan patriot movement left the Democrat Mackenzie by the wayside.[88]

Beyond the simple fact that many Whigs did join the Hunters, the patriots' emphasis on their nonpartisanship suggests something more was at work than not trying to alienate these members: the patriots hoped U.S. partisanship would not follow them into a Canadian republic. They were not just *non*partisan, but *anti*partisan, displaying what Mark Voss-Hubbard has described as "antipartyism."[89] In 1838 the American patriot disenchantment with party politics was not surprising. Between the dreadful depression and the combined efforts of both national Democrats and Whigs to destroy the patriots, partisanship offered little. James Mackenzie, an astute observer of the political climate, described this feeling: "Neither of the political parties of the day will assist or countenance equal rights and privileges" for monopoly had become "so deeply rooted."[90] Moreover, it was a Democratic president who was primarily responsible for anti-patriot actions. Therefore, while Democratic Hunters could argue for their actions on traditionally Democratic grounds, they did not want to link themselves to the Democratic Party. The geography of the Patriot War gives further hints of this disillusionment. Throughout the Jacksonian era, counties along the northern border, especially those in New York and Ohio, were especially prone to populist third party candidates that offered answers to problems neither major party could. It was in these counties that the Anti-Masonic Party in the late 1820s and especially the Free Soil Party in the 1840s drew support.[91] In 1838, the third party was represented by the patriot movement, which in Upper Canada would create the ideal – nonpartisan – republic.

The popularity of the Free Soil Party in 1848 in northern New York and Ohio, a party founded by former Democrats frustrated with the Democracy's compromise with slavery, points to another important aspect of the vision of a Canadian Republic ten years earlier: its explicit antislavery posture. William Lyon Mackenzie had always been a vehement opponent of slavery, and he included a clause in his proposed constitution for Upper Canada acknowledging that the colony had been a haven for escaped slaves in the past ("People of Colour, who have come into this State, with the design of becoming permanent inhabitants thereof").[92] This attitude clearly resonated with individuals like Preston King, who would be elected on the Free Soil ticket in 1848.[93] Other patriots also expressed antislavery sentiments, although, due to the dearth of patriot sources, it cannot be known how many American patriots eventually became Free Soilers in 1848, or antislavery adherents more generally.[94] Nevertheless, since both movements drew their support from the same segment of society in the same region, crossover clearly existed.

Yet the patriots' antislavery stance was hardly radical: various flavours of antislavery existed throughout the northern U.S. at the time. The patriots were not abolitionists as the term was defined in the Jacksonian United States, for, unlike radical abolitionists like William Lloyd Garrison or more moderate abolitionists like the Tappan brothers, they did not seek to abolish slavery where it already existed. Rather, like the Free Soilers of 1848, they were not concerned with slavery's effects on enslaved black people, but its supposedly pernicious effects on free whites – taking up land that ought to be owned and worked by white yeomen, undermining the dignity of labour, and creating a dangerous mixed-race society. The patriot movement did not harbour sentiments of abolitionism or racial equality. Upper Canada would be a free soil, *white*, republic.

At first this assertion seems to contradict several of Mackenzie's statements expressing remarkable racial egalitarianism, in which he blamed perceived uncivilized qualities in the black population in North America on the effects of slavery.[95] Yet the loyalism of the Canadian black population grated on him. Less than a year before the rebellion, he stated: "[Black people] are so extravagantly loyal to the Executive, that to the utmost of their power they uphold all the abuses of government, and support those who profit by them."[96] In the days before the rebellion, Mackenzie played on white Canadian fears of loyalist black people, claiming British authorities would unleash them, as well as Indigenous peoples, on a defenceless populace if Canadians did not swiftly revolt. His paranoia was even expressed in his proposed constitution. To remain in Canada, black people would be required to take an oath to the new republic, something no white person was required to do. While Mackenzie primarily disliked black people for their loyalism, his racial rhetoric could also play well with racist American patriots who disliked them simply because they were black. The patriot movement was, in essence, united by whiteness – antislavery whiteness, but whiteness nonetheless.[97]

The patriots never explicitly expressed this racial unity; considering the population of the Great Lakes region on both sides of the border was overwhelmingly white, the lack of overt racial rhetoric was unsurprising. Nevertheless, when racial "others" entered the discourse, it was evident that race played a role in the conflict. Patriots often directed racism towards black Canadians, which, in a certain respect, was logical, for they joined the loyal militia in percentages far exceeding white Canadians. As Mackenzie understood even before the rebellion, black Canadians were ready and willing to fight for an empire that protected their freedom from the slaveholding republic to their south, and British officials often praised them for their loyalty.[98] Yet the patriots did not just condemn black Canadians; African Americans were also suspicious. They represented a potential British fifth column on American soil, who would stop at nothing to destroy the patriot cause. In the first weeks at Navy Island, rumours spread among the patriots that black cooks planned to poison them, leading Thomas Jefferson Sutherland to warn Van Rensselaer, "For God's sake look out for the negroes."[99] In Detroit, reports circulated that the "negroes are destroying things" across the river in Canada, and would soon lose their destruction on Detroit itself.[100]

American patriots also demonized Indigenous populations. Rumours of a British-incited Indigenous invasion arose on a regular basis. Like the animosity towards black people, these rumours also had some rationale: Canadian natives, like Canadian black people, proved overwhelmingly loyal to the British during the rebellion.[101] One letter-writer even feared the British would unleash both black and Indigenous populations in a multi-pronged attack on the patriots, arming slaves in the south and inviting them north, and simultaneously rousing Indigenous peoples in the west to attack east.[102] Of course, these reports were outlandish. While both Canadian black people and Indigenous peoples were indeed overwhelmingly loyal to the British, at no point did their small numbers merit the panic of patriot imagination. Nevertheless, behind the inflated rumours was an important truth: from the very outset of the conflict the patriots were united by their whiteness. By preserving Upper Canada as a white republic, they would completely avoid – and therefore solve – the racial issues increasingly engulfing the United States.

The racial dynamic of the conflict was prominent enough that it quickly filtered out from the northern borderland to other parts of the United States. To patriots and their sympathizers, Upper Canadians were "white slaves," and deserved the aid of their fellow white brethren. Even more galling, black people who had found freedom within Canadian borders were now – as Mackenzie quoted a sympathetic New Yorker – "assisting in destroying the political liberty of the colonists as the price of personal liberty for themselves."[103] Radical abolitionists in the United States were having none of this rhetoric and responded with outrage, arguing that it was black slaves in the United States, not white subjects in Canada, who were being truly oppressed. As *The Liberator* approvingly quoted an antislavery editorial from Massachusetts, "When the non-colored people any where choose to fret a little under a government whose heaviest impositions are light as air, weighted against the oppressions of the American slaveholder, then comes up the shrill, loud cry of 'oppression! intolerable taxation! go for liberty – *we* are for liberty *every where*!'"[104] In turn, patriots responded to the abolitionists critique by simply ratcheting up their "white slaves" rhetoric. As one letter-writer noted to Mackenzie, abolitionists constantly discussed "poor *black* slaves, but you will not hear a word uttered in behalf of the *poor white* slaves in Canada."[105] Rhetoric like this served to both universalize and racialize the conflict. By calling the Canadians "slaves," Patriot rhetoric paid homage to the rhetoric of the American Revolution, in which revolutionaries claimed that Great Britain sought to enslave them.[106] At the same time, in the more racialized Jacksonian era, Canadian "white slaves," because they were white, were presumably entitled to the aid of their white American brethren well before black slaves.

The patriots' arguments about Canadians' enslavement, coupled with their constant references to the American Revolution, pointed to the Patriot War as representing a sort of nostalgic revolutionary struggle for those who joined patriot ranks, one that was not complicated with issues of slavery, the black race, or issues of American disunion. Indeed, as David Shields has argued, the Canadian Rebellions and the Patriot War that followed represented a dividing line between an era where Americans concentrated on their own and other Atlantic revolutions (with Haiti the all-important exception), and an era where they focused on conflicts over slavery in both their own country and throughout the western hemisphere.[107] To American patriots, freeing Upper Canada would once again bring white Americans into conflict with the three *bêtes noires* of the early republic: black people, Indigenous people, and the British. This struggle was one that had come before, and was, to patriots as well as many observers, one that could be easily understood, for it fit into the tropes of U.S. history. Radical abolitionists, in contrast, envisaged a new type of struggle, one in which the British were allies, while slaveholders – and those that abetted them – were the enemy. This new struggle over slavery that men like William Garrison predicted disturbed many Americans, who loathed both radical abolitionists and equally radical southern fire-eaters. In other words, for American patriots the struggle to free Canada acted as a refreshing throwback, one in which white Americans aided white Anglo-Canadians (many of whom were descended from white Americans) to create a free soil – read: white – Canadian Republic.[108]

If Upper Canada could become the idealized white republic, so too could it become the idealized masculine republic, where traditional understandings of manhood would triumph. From the outset, issues of masculinity permeated the patriot movement, starting with the role of the Hunters' Lodges. Needless to say, these were strictly male organizations. Modelling themselves on Masonic Lodges – one region of lodges was initially known as the "Patriot Masons" – the Hunters reportedly established elaborate initiation rituals, secret signs and passwords, and a complicated hierarchy of rank ranging from "Snowshoe" (the lowest) to "Patriot Hunter" (the highest).[109] It is uncertain how many Hunters were also Freemasons, but during a time when Freemasonry was under attack, the Hunters provided an alternative, more legitimate form of organization.[110] They also offered large feasts and copious alcohol to their members, providing what historian Mary Ann Clawson defined as a "culture of fraternalism."[111] Moreover, the Patriot War provided something deeper, too: validation of their manhood. The patriots believed that their belligerence demonstrated masculinity, mirroring the masculinity of their fathers and grandfathers who fought in the Revolution. Even dead patriots were deemed "manly corpses."[112] In contrast, the federal government's pro-British measures represented a fundamental shift away from a masculine United States; in this too, the republic had lost its way. As one American patriot wrote, "We think more of the establishment of Banks, the price of stocks ... prosperity of our foreign trade, the preservation of our ledges, bales and silks, than the preservation of that ennobling and glorious spirit of manly independence, that guided and directed the conduct of our fathers in the 'Age of Revolution.'"[113] Van Buren received particular opprobrium. To one observer, in contrast to his predecessor Andrew Jackson, Van Buren had "not acted with manly forwardness."[114] That Van Buren was deferring to Queen Victoria of all people was especially galling to some; she was, in one writer's eyes, a "two legid strumpet" to whom no "states men or soldier" should "bow."[115]

Not only did the patriots believe they were demonstrating their masculinity, but on a deeper level both the fight for Canadian freedom and life in the future Canadian republic promised a return to a conception of manhood currently disappearing in American society. As the increasingly market-oriented North eroded many men's personal independence, the patriots gave this ideal renewed life.[116] Patriot volunteers could prove their martial prowess at a time when both state militias and the U.S. Army offered diminishing prospects for glory and personal advancement.[117] Additionally, they could acquire a significant amount of free land in a Canadian republic that still possessed ample undeveloped regions, which would allow them to maintain the custom of bestowing all of their sons with significant landholdings.[118] To preserve this traditional economic custom, thousands of American families would move west in the early 1840s, but in 1838 this option seemed available in much closer Canada. The economic plans of Mackenzie and his radical Democratic allies pointed to just such a system, in which men would be less beholden to the market and more in charge of their own – and their family's – future. One British official even believed that many Americans who failed to secure land in the west now "looked to the Canadas" for similar remedies.[119] Thus, the patriot cause provided a means to reassert the ideal of manhood in a world of increasingly unsettled gender categories.

More generally, between the acquisition of cheap land, the free soil impetus, and the quest for glory and adventure, the entire Patriot War echoed aspects of the American westward movement, in both its possibilities and its disappointments. By the time of the Canadian Rebellions, Americans had overrun much of the trans-Appalachian west, but this process did not yield the benefits that many agrarian yeomen had envisioned. Instead of solving the economic and social ills of the masses, westward settlement usually benefited speculators and wealthy landowners. To thousands of hopeful migrants, the western movement was a story of, in historian Stephen Aron's words, "possibilities lost."[120] Perhaps, then, these possibilities – land ownership, white egalitarianism, uncorrupted republican governance, assertions of masculinity – could be realized in Canada. If only for a brief time, Canada took its place alongside such places as Florida and Texas, Oregon and California, as a place for Americans to fulfill their settlement dreams.

Indeed, after the failures of the rebellions and the Patriot War that followed, anecdotal evidence suggests that many of the Canadian patriots who fled to the United States did eventually move farther west, many to Illinois, but some as far as California.[121] Whether any American patriot moved west is uncertain. Those who had joined the movement out of their own destitution most likely lacked the means to move west; it had been much easier to invade well-known Canada only a few miles away than move hundreds of miles to an unknown region. It seems most American patriots, both poor and rich, returned to their former lives on the American side of the Great Lakes borderland, some chagrined at joining a cause that had become such an utter failure.[122] However, throughout this region memories of the Patriot War remained vivid for decades after the struggle, for it had captivated much of the population.[123] Meanwhile, the rest of America moved on, as events on the southern border accelerated the United States into a war with Mexico. After the 1842 Webster-Ashburton Treaty seemed to solve all border issues between the U.S. and Great Britain, Canada became an afterthought.[124]

## CONCLUSION

It was to this much different United States that the American patriots exiled to Van Diemen's Land returned in the mid-1840s. Considering their remarkable journeys, it is no surprise that their homecomings were announced in many American newspapers. Realizing their newfound celebrity status, many of the exiles decided to turn their tales into financial gain by publishing memoirs of their travels. All of these memoirs focused on the dramatic story of exile, not on the Patriot War itself; after all, survival and return from the other side of the world was a triumphant story, while the Patriot War was tragic and embarrassing. Yet their willingness to fight for the patriots needed to at least be explained. How could this be done to a United States that no longer cared about the Patriot War?[125]

Several patriots turned to Texas, noting the similarities between each struggle. This strategy not only helped to rehabilitate their actions, but also allowed them to blame U.S. hypocrisy for the patriots' failure. Exile Daniel Heustis lamented that, in the case of Upper Canada, "[U.S.] Troops were sent to the frontier, not to punish our insatiable foe, but to assist her in crushing the republican spirit which threatened to uproot British power in Canada." Yet during the Texas Rebellion troops came and went "without molestation" by the American government.[126] Asked fellow exile William Gates, "What spirit could have actuated our government [to suppress the patriots] but … the knowledge that human servitude could find no extension at the north?"[127] To Gates, the government's laissez-faire attitude with Texas, in contrast to Canada, pointed to slave interests controlling the government. Neither Heustis nor Gates wanted to admit the truth: British power forced U.S. neutrality, and the combined power of Britain and the United States was too strong for the patriots to overcome.

While these men wrote from decidedly self-serving and biased perspectives, historians ought to heed their comparisons of the Patriot War to Texas. There may have been a great contrast between the Texas Revolution and the Patriot War on an international level, but the internal American dynamics of each conflict were indeed remarkably similar; in each, thousands of American men left the United States for political and economic opportunities offered in a land settled by people just like them. Yet by the time the exiles wrote in 1850, Texas fit into the pattern of American expansion and the ideology of

Manifest Destiny, part of a long list of regions – Louisiana, Florida, California, Oregon, and New Mexico – whose incorporation into the Union seemed foreordained. Part of the supposedly unsettled and under-populated American West and Southwest, these regions were seemingly always ripe for American settlement and U.S. conquest. British Upper Canada, in contrast, never presented an opportunity for expansion, and therefore the Americans who volunteered for the patriots must have been deluded. Thus the Patriot War was not failed expansion but a marginal movement that could be ignored and forgotten. Yet, for those Americans who joined or supported the patriots, Upper Canada *was* an opportunity for settlement and expansion, and as such it seized the imagination of thousands of Americans along the border. The Patriot War demonstrated that American migration and invasion until 1838 was not yet directed southward and westward, and instead directed outward, simply depending on where political and economic opportunities lay.

## NOTES

1 For numbers of American patriots, see Donald E. Graves, *Guns across the River: The Battle of the Windmill, 1838* (Prescott, ON: Friends of Windmill Point, 2001), 70, 227.

2 More recent studies that involve the patriots in some manner include Andrew Bonthius, "The Patriot War of 1837–1838: Locofocoism with a Gun?" *Labour/Le Travail* 52 (Fall 2003): 9–43; Marc L. Harris, "The Meaning of Patriot: The Canadian Rebellion and American Republicanism, 1837–1839," *Michigan Historical Review* 23 (April 1997): 33–69; Kenneth R. Stevens, *Border Diplomacy: The Caroline and McLeod Affairs in Anglo-American-Canadian Relations, 1837–1842* (Tuscaloosa, AL: University of Alabama Press, 1989); Sam Watson, "U.S. Army Officers Fight the 'Patriot War,'" *Journal of the Early Republic* 18 (Autumn 1998): 485–519; Reginald Stuart, *United States Expansionism and British North America, 1775–1871* (Chapel Hill, NC: University of North Carolina Press, 1988), 126–47; Stuart D. Scott, "The Patriot Game: New Yorkers and the Canadian Rebellions of 1837–1838," *New York History* 68 (July 1987); Francis M. Carroll, *A Good and Wise Measure: The Search for the Canadian-American Boundary, 1783–1842* (Toronto: University of Toronto Press, 2001), 202–20; Cassandra Pybus and Hamish Maxwell-Stewart, *American Citizens, British Slaves: Yankee*

*Political Prisoners in an Australian Penal Colony, 1839–1850* (Lansing, MI: Michigan State University Press, 2002), 7–45; John Duffy and H. Nicholas Muller, III, *An Anxious Democracy: Aspects of the 1830* (Westport, CT: Greenwood Press, 1982), 43–86; Jean-Paul Bernard, "Vermonters and the Lower Canadian Rebellions of 1837–1838," *Vermont History* 58 (Fall 1990): 250–63. Older but still valuable works include Edwin Clarence Guillet, *The Lives and Times of the Patriots; an Account of the Rebellion in Upper Canada, 1837–1838, and of the Patriot Agitation in the United States, 1837–1842* (Toronto: University of Toronto Press, 1968); Oscar Arvle Kinchen, *The Rise and Fall of the Patriot Hunters* (New York: Bookman Associates, 1956); Albert B. Corey, *The Crisis of 1830–1842 in Canadian-American Relations* (Toronto: Ryerson Press, 1941), 27–101; Orrin Edward Tiffany, *The Relations of the United States to the Canadian Rebellion of 1837–1838* (Toronto: Coles Publishing Co., 1972 [repr. 1905]). For a discussion of the failure of both American and Canadian historians to look across each other's respective borders, see Stephen Kenny, "The Canadian Rebellion and the Limits of Historical Perspective," *Vermont History* 58 (Summer 1990): 179–98. Other than the articles by Bonthius and Harris, all of these works give little to no attention to what drove Americans to volunteer for the patriots. For a list of works on the Canadian Rebellions and related historiography, see n4 below. Recent syntheses of the Early Republic have given the Patriot War short shrift or ignored it entirely: Daniel Walker Howe, *What Hath God Wrought: The Transformation of America* (New York: Oxford University Press, 2007), 518–19; Sean Wilentz, *The Rise of American Democracy: Jefferson to Lincoln* (New York: Norton, 2005). Additionally, recent works on American expansion, filibustering, and empire also ignore the Patriot War, or at best give it cursory attention: Richard Kluger, *Seizing Destiny: How America Grew from Sea to Shining Sea* (New York: Knopf, 2008); Walter Nugent, *Habits of Empire* (New York: Knopf, 2008); Robert E. May, *Manifest Destiny's Underworld: Filibustering in Antebellum America* (Chapel Hill, NC: University of North Carolina Press, 2002), 10–13; Amy S. Greenberg, *Manifest Manhood and the Antebellum American Empire* (New York: Cambridge University Press, 2005), 30, 33.

3 The only partial exception to this statement is Sam Watson, but he details the motivations of U.S. military officers tasked with defeating the patriots, not the patriots themselves. See Watson, "U.S. Army Officers Fight the 'Patriot War.'"

4 Works that reveal the complicated motivations and actions of American migrants/filibusters in the south and west include Eric Schlereth, "Privileges of Locomotion: Expatriation and the Politics of Southwestern Border Crossing," *Journal of American History* 4 (March 2014): 995–1020; Andrés Reséndez, *Changing National Identities at the Frontier: Texas and New Mexico, 1800–1850* (New York: Cambridge University Press, 2005); Andrew Cayton, "Continental Politics: Liberalism, Nationalism, and the Appeal of Texas in the 1820s," in *Beyond the Founders*, ed. Pasley, Robertson, and Waldstreicher (Chapel Hill, NC, 2005); Sarah Rodriguez, "'Children of the Great Mexican Family': American Immigration to Northern Mexico, 1810–1861" (PhD diss., University of Pennsylvania, 2015); Andrew McMichael, *Atlantic Loyalties: Americans in Spanish West Florida, 1785–1810* (Athens, GA: University of Georgia Press, 2008); David Weber, *The Mexican Frontier, 1821–1846: The U.S. Southwest under Mexico* (Albuquerque: University of New Mexico University Press, 1982).

5 Richard White, *The Middle Ground: Indians, Empires, and Republics in the Great Lakes Region, 1650–1815* (New York: Cambridge University Press, 1993); Alan Taylor, *The Civil War of 1812: American Citizens, British Subjects, Irish Rebels, & Indian Allies* (New York: Vintage, 2010); Gregory Evans Dowd, *A Spirited Resistance: The North American Indian Struggle for Unity, 1745–1815* (Baltimore: John Hopkins University Press, 1993); Jeremy Adelman and Stephen Aron, "From Borderlands to Borders: Empires, Nation-States, and the Peoples in between in North American History," *American Historical Review* 3 (June 1999): 814–41.

6 Marcus Lee Hansen, *The Mingling of the Canadian and American Peoples* (New Haven, CT: Yale University Press, 1940), 105–12; Stuart, *United States Expansionism and British North America*, 109–10; Colin Read, *The Rising in Western Upper Canada, 1837–1838: The Duncombe Revolt and After* (Toronto: University of Toronto Press, 1982), 23; Adam Fergusson, *Practical Notes Made during a Tour in Canada and a Portion of the United States in MDCCCXXXI* (Edinburgh, 1833), 148–9; Jane Errington, *The Lion, the Eagle, and Upper Canada: A Developing Colonial Ideology* (Kingston, ON: McGill-Queen's University Press, 1987), 121–5; Bonthius, "Locofocoism with a Gun?," 19; Stuart, *United States Expansionism and British North America*, 106–24; Donald Creighton, *The Empire of the St Lawrence* (Toronto, 1956), 249–54; Jane Dorothy Baglier, "The Niagara Frontier: Society and Economy in Western New York and Upper Canada, 1794–1854" (PhD diss., State University of New York-Buffalo, 1993), 178–252.

7 On the Eastern Townships, see J.I. Little, *Loyalties in Conflict: A Canadian Borderland in War and Rebellion, 1812–1840* (Toronto: University of Toronto Press, 2008), 57–77.

8 *Compendium of the Sixth Census of the Enumeration of the Inhabitants and Statistics of the United States* (Washington, DC), 18.

9 Duffy and Muller, *An Anxious Democracy*, 21; Bernard, "Vermonters and the Lower Canadian Rebellions," 251–2.

10 For a summary of the historiographical debates and trends of the Canadian Rebellions, see Allan Greer's influential article, "1837–1838: Rebellion Reconsidered," *Canadian Historical Review* 1 (March 1995): 1–18. For the rebellions considered together, see Michel Ducharme, *The Idea of Liberty in Canada during the Age of Atlantic Revolutions, 1776–1838*, trans. Peter Feldstein (Montreal: McGill-Queen's University Press, 2014); Michael Mann, *A Particular Duty: The Canadian Rebellions, 1837–1839* (Wiltshire, UK: Michael Russell, 1986). For the Lower Canadian Rebellion, see Allan Greer, *The Patriots and the People: The Rebellion of 1837 in Rural Lower Canada* (Toronto: University of Toronto Press, 1993); Elinor Kyte Senior, *Redcoats and Patriotes* (Stittsville, ON: Canada's Wings, 1985); Jack Verney, *O'Callaghan: The Making and Unmaking of a Rebel* (Montreal and Kingston: McGill-Queen's University Press, 1994); Little, *Loyalties in Conflict*, 57–99. For the Upper Canadian Rebellion, see Read, *The Rising in Western Upper Canada*; Colin Read and Ronald J. Stagg, "Introduction," in *The Rebellion of 1837 in Upper Canada: A Collection of Documents*, ed. Read and Stagg (Toronto: University of Toronto Press, 1985), xix–lxxxiii; Betsy Dewar Boyce, *The Rebels of Hastings* (Toronto: University of Toronto Press, 1992); Gerald Craig, *Upper Canada: The Formative Years, 1784–1841* (New York: Oxford University Press, 1963), 226–51. Much of the work on the Lower Canadian Rebellion is in French. For a brief summary of this French language historiography, see Ducharme, *The Idea of Liberty*, 160.

11 Nathaniel Wilson Brooks to Caroline Brooks, 29 December 1837, Nathaniel Wilson Brooks Papers, Burton Historical Collection, Detroit Public Library (hereafter BHC).

12 For a summary of the attitude of the Vermont press, see Duffy and Muller, *An Anxious Democracy*, 59–72, esp. 59–60.

13 Duffy and Muller, *An Anxious Democracy*, 64–5; Senior, *Redcoats and Patriotes*, 152; Greer, *The Patriots and the People*, 345; Bernard, "Vermonters and the Lower Canadian Rebellions," 261. For a contrast between New York and Vermont, see Tiffany, *The Relations of the United States to the Canadian Rebellion of 1837–1838*, 85–6.

14 Several historians, by including both Upper and Lower Canada into their studies, implicitly define the Patriot War as *all* of the border battles and skirmishes that occurred after both Canadian Rebellions. These studies define the Patriot War by place (the entire U.S.-Canada border) and not people (Guillet, *Lives and Times*; Kinchen, *The Rise and Fall of the Patriot Hunters*; Tiffany, *The Relations of the United States to the Canadian Rebellions*). I have followed several historians of Lower Canada by separating the second Lower Canadian Rebellion from the Patriot War: Senior, *Redcoats and Patriotes*, 149–63; Greer, *The Patriots and the People*, 332–56. An imperfect but helpful comparison can be found on the United States' southern border. The Texas Revolution began due to changing leadership in Mexico City, and Texas was one of several Mexican states and territories to rebel. Yet, while its origins could be found in Mexico, the Texas Revolution quickly became an American phenomenon as Anglo-Texans gained control of the rebellion and Americans crossed the border to help their perceived brethren. Meanwhile, in places like New Mexico and California, Americans played a role, but never directed the rebellions. Upper Canada was akin to a northern Texas (as, we shall see, the patriots argued), while Lower Canada echoed the rebellions in other Mexican regions, at least in its relationship to American participants.

15 Memorandum on the Formation of the Buffalo Committee of 13 December 1837, MS 516, Mackenzie-Lindsey Fonds, Ontario Archives (hereafter MLF); Tiffany, *The Relations of the United States to the Canadian Rebellion of 1837–1838*, 27.

16 *Buffalo Commercial Advertiser*, 12 December 1837; *Buffalo Daily Star*, 12 December 1837; Mary D. Taber to Mrs Richard Williams, 17 December 1837, Hawes-Taber family letters, William L. Clements Library, University of Michigan (hereafter CL). For reports of this Buffalo meeting, see also Tiffany, *The Relations of the United States to the Canadian Rebellion of 1837–38*, 27–8; Guillet, *Lives and Times of the Patriots*, 71–2.

17 C.H. McCollom to William Lyon Mackenzie, 22 December 1837, MLF; John Henderston to William Lyon Mackenzie, 28 December 1837, MLF.

18 Nathaniel Wilson Brooks to Caroline Brooks, 29 December 1837, Nathaniel Wilson Brooks Papers, Burton Historical Collection, Detroit Public Library (hereafter BHC).

19 For the Navy Island campaign, see Ernest A. Cruikshank, "The Invasion of Navy Island," in *Papers and Records: Ontario Historical Society* (1937): 7–84. It is impossible to pin down the exact size of the Patriot Army on Navy Island. Because firsthand reports from the time vary, secondary works also vary their estimates. In all likelihood numbers were fluid,

increasing during the end of December, reaching their high point in early January, and diminishing in mid-January after U.S. intervention. For example, the *Buffalo Daily Star* reported 6–700 men on 16 December, while one observer reported 1,000–1,200 men on 10 January: *Buffalo Daily Star*, 16 December 1837; Augustus Porter to Peter Porter, 10 January 1838, Reel 10, Peter Porter Papers, Buffalo and Erie County Historical Society (hereafter BECHS).

20 *Detroit Free Press*, quoting the *Buffalo Daily Commercial Advertiser*, 27 December 1837; Winfield Scott to Joel Poinsett, 2 Febuary 1838, Folder 10, Number 23, Joel Poinsett Papers, Historical Society of Pennsylvania (hereafter HSP).

21 John Anderson to Alexander Anderson, 15 January 1838, John Anderson Papers, Bentley Historical Library, University of Michigan.

22 Donald McLeod to William Lyon Mackenzie, 1 November 1838, MLF; Graves, *Guns across the River*, 227.

23 Lillian F. Gates, "*Mackenzie's Gazette*: An Aspect of W.L. Mackenzie's American Years," *Canadian Historical Review* 46 (December 1965): 331–6.

24 *Mackenzie's Gazette*, 14 July 1838. One Canadian patriot who fled to the U.S. felt the need to write letters pretending to be in Canada, in order to inspire more Canadians to rebel: E.B. O'Callaghan to Mackenzie, 9 September 1838, MLF.

25 A comparison can be drawn to American participation in the Revolutionary War. As Charles Royster has demonstrated, 1775 witnessed a "*rage militaire*" among the colonial populace, as Americans volunteered in remarkable numbers to fight the British. This enthusiasm would never again be replicated during the Revolution. Yet simply because the rage militaire was an immediate emotional response does not mean it was not sincere or worthy of study. Charles Royster, *A Revolutionary People at War: The Continental Army & American Character, 1775–1783* (Chapel Hill: University of North Carolina Press, 1979), 3–53.

26 J. Woolsey Burchard to Rensselaer Van Rensselaer, 22 December 1837, MLF.

27 Lemuel Cook Jr to William Lyon Mackenzie, 28 December 1837, MLF.

28 Statements supporting Canadian freedom occur too frequently in both letters and the American press to all be named here. A good sampling appear in the letters to Navy Island in December 1837–January 1838 in the Mackenzie-Lindsey Fonds: George Clinton Westcott and Beakes Rossell to William Lyon Mackenzie and Rensselaer Van Rensselaer, 28 December 1837; John Gates to Rensselaer Van Rensselaer, 29 December 1837; George Washington Morgan to Rensselaer Van Rensselaer, 30 December 1837; E. St John to Rensselaer Van Rensselaer, 1 January 1838; Robert

McMullen to Rensselaer Van Rensselaer, 2 January 1838; George Russell to William Lyon Mackenzie, 3 January 1838.

29 Thomas Jefferson Sutherland to editor of the *New York Daily Express*, 26 April 1838, MLF.

30 Thomas Jefferson Sutherland, "The Sword and the Pen: A Journal of Literature, Politics, and Military Science" (New York, 1840), 1–2.

31 Oliver Brodier to William Lyon Mackenzie, 26 November 1838, MLF; Edwin Stacy to Nathaniel Stacy and Susan Clark Stacy, Nathaniel Stacy papers, CL-UM; L.S. Martin to William Lyon Mackenzie, MLF; Lemuel Cook Jr to William Lyon Mackenzie, 29 December 1837, MLF; John Henderston to William Lyon Mackenzie, 28 December 1837, MLF; John Gates to Rensselaer Van Rensselaer, 29 December 1837, MLF. As Michael Kammen noted, the 1830s and 1840s were decades during which Americans sought to fulfill and preserve the Revolutionary generation's achievements: Michael Kammen, *A Season of Youth: The American Revolution and the Historical Imagination* (New York: Knopf, 1978), 51.

32 Newspapers reported the popularity of the struggle, and many of them jumped on the pro-patriot bandwagon. The *National Intelligencer* reported that 99 out of 100 people from New York City supported the rebels: *National Intelligencer*, 7 December 1837. The *Democratic National Review* heartily wished the rebels success: *United States Democratic Review* 1 (Jan. 1838), 215–20. For the American attitude towards the British during this era, see Sam W. Haynes, *Unfinished Revolution: The Early American Republic in a British World* (Charlottesville, VA: University of Virginia Press, 2010), esp. 118–26 and 209–10.

33 Sentiments of revenge for the Caroline appear in B.A. Hill to William Lyon Mackenzie, 3 June 1838, MLF; *Detroit Morning Post*, quoting the *Rochester Democrat*, 29 December 1838; Winfield Scott to Joel Poinsett, 12 January 1839, 11–150, Poinsett Papers, HSP; Edwin Stacy to Nathaniel Stacy and Susan Clark Stacy, Nathaniel Stacy papers, CL-UM; William Upjohn diary, 8 January 1838, BHC; Lucy Williams Hawes to Lawrence Grinnell, 30 December 1837, Hawes-Taber Family Letters, CL-UM; C. Hudson, "Poem: For the Volunteer," Sept. 1838, MLF; Buffalo *Daily Commercial and Advertiser*, 2 January 1838; Baltimore *Sun*, quoting the Albany *Argus*, 6 June 1838.

34 The one mention of the Caroline Affair occurs in Account of a patriot Meeting, 4 January 1838, MLF.

35 For accounts that maintain the Caroline Affair spurred patriot recruitment, see Tiffany, *The Relations of the United States to the Canadian*

*Rebellions of 1837–1838*, 42; Guillet, *Lives and Times of the Patriots*, 82. Both authors cite Rensselaer Van Rensselaer for this information, but give no page numbers in his published letters. While Van Rensselaer did mention that Navy Island was "rapidly reinforced" to 7–800 after the Caroline Affair, this number is only slightly larger than his pre-Caroline force. Van Rensselaer's letters and memoirs: Catharina V.R. Bonney, *A Legacy of Historical Gleanings*, 2nd ed. (Albany, 1875), 2, 83. For a thorough account of the diplomacy surrounding the Caroline Affair, see Stevens, *Border Diplomacy*.

36 For an example of the idea of peaceful convergence in the case of Canada, see *Democratic National Review* 1 (Jan. 1838): 217–18; see also Stuart, *United States Expansionism and British North America*, 97–9, passim.

37 *Mackenzie's Gazette*, 1 September 1838.

38 John Smyles to Mackenzie, 4 September 1838, MLF. On Smyles, see Gates, *After the Rebellion*, 89.

39 For the ambiguous visions of U.S. empire, see Rachel St John, "Contingent Continent: Spatial and Geographic Arguments in the Shaping of the Nineteenth-Century United States," *Pacific Historical Review* 86, no. 1 (Feb. 2017): 18–49; Peter S. Onuf, *Jefferson's Empire: The Language of American Nationhood* (Charlottesville, VA: University of Virginia Press, 2001), esp. 53–80. The phrase "sister republic" was quite common. Originally used towards France during the French Revolution, it came to be used for essentially any republic. See, for example, for Texas: *Pennsylvania Inquirer*, 30 September 1837; for Mexico: "Message of the President of the United States," *Baltimore Sun*, 5 December 1838; and, more broadly, Caitlin Fitz, *Our Sister Republics: The United States in an Age of American Revolutions* (New York: W.W. Norton & Co., 2016).

40 A. Chappell to Rensselaer Van Rensselaer, Dec. 1837 or Jan. 1838; Robert McMullen to Rensselaer Van Rensselaer, 2 January 1838, MLF.

41 George Russell to William Lyon Mackenzie, 3 January 1838, MLF.

42 The motivations for volunteering for the patriots anticipate those given for volunteering for militia service during the U.S.-Mexican War. See Paul Foos, *A Short, Offhand, Killing Affair: Soldiers and Social Conflict during the Mexican-American War* (Chapel Hill: University of North Carolina Press, 2002), 31–43.

43 Alexander Powell to Daniel Webster, 25 November 1841, in *The Papers of Daniel Webster*, Vol. 5: Correspondence, 1840–1843, ed. Harold Moser (Hanover, NH: University Press of New England, 1982), 172.

44 For statements asking for a certain rank in the Patriot Army, see Robert McMullen to Rensselaer Van Rensselaer, 2 January 1838, MLF; Stephen

Nateson to William Lyon Mackenzie, 26 December 1837; George Clinton Westcott and Beakes Rossell to William Lyon Mackenzie and Rensselaer Van Rensselaer, 28 December 1837; John Gates to Rensselaer Van Rensselaer, 29 December 1837; George Washington Morgan to Rensselaer Van Rensselaer, 30 December 1837; Eleaser Lewis to Rensselaer or Mackenzie, 5 January 1838, MLF.

45 For the Jacksonian ethos, see John William Ward, *Andrew Jackson: Symbol of an Age* (New York: Oxford University Press, 1962); Marvin Meyers, *The Jacksonian Persuasion: Politics and Belief* (Stanford, CA: Stanford University Press, 1957). Although he does not include the Patriot War in his study, Robert May identifies filibustering as a more attractive military endeavour than joining the antebellum U.S. Army, because it promised more glory, excitement, and possibility for advance. See Robert May, "Young American Males and Filibustering in the Age of Manifest Destiny: The United States Army as Cultural Mirror," *Journal of American History* 78, no. 3 (Dec. 1991): 874–5. Additionally, many of the motivations American cited for joining the patriots anticipated those given by Americans volunteering to serve in the militia during the U.S.-Mexican War. See Foos, *A Short, Offhand, Killing Affair*, 45–59.

46 Bonney, *A Legacy of Historical Gleanings*, 79.

47 On Van Rensselaer, see Bonney, *A Legacy of Historical Gleanings*, 63–80; Lillian F. Gates, *After the Rebellion: The Later Years of William Lyon Mackenzie* (Toronto: Dundurn Press, 1988), 18–19. For his drinking, see C.H. Graham to "Daniel Brooks" (aka Mackenzie), 10 February 1838; Graham to Mackenzie, 8 March 1838; Van Rensselaer to Mackenzie, 18 December 1838, all in MLF. For evidence of Van Rensselaer's insecurities, see Rensselaer Van Rensselaer to Solomon Van Rensselaer, 8 January 1838, in Bonney, *Legacy of Historical Cleanings*, 74–5; "Rensselaer's Van Rensselaer's Own Notes on His Military Life," in Bonney, 77.

48 As the cause became more desperate, the land reward increased to 400 acres: Gates, *After the Rebellion*, 22; "Regulations and Pay of the Northwestern Army, On Patriot Service in Upper Canada," 24 September 1839, Broadsides, CL-UM. For undeveloped land in Canada, see Douglas McCalla, *Planting the Province: The Economic History of Upper Canada, 1784–1870* (Toronto: University of Toronto Press, 1993), 189.

49 Gates, *After the Rebellion*, 22.

50 S.C. Frey to Mackenzie, 9 October 1838, MLF; "Regulations and Pay of the Northwestern Army, On Patriot Service in Upper Canada," 24 September 1839, Broadsides, CL-UM; Patrick Shirreff, *A Tour through North America* (Edinburgh, 1838), 16.

51 H.L. Allen to Mackenzie, 26 December 1837, MLF.

52 James Brewer to R.V.R., 27 December, MLF.

53 For the fear of unemployed men on the northern frontier, see for example, the Philadelphia *Public Ledger*, 16 June 1838.

54 E.B. Ward to Eben Ward, January 18, 1838, Ward Family Papers, BHC.

55 On the Panic of 1837, see Jessica M. Lepler, *The Many Panics of 1837: People, Politics, and the Creation of a Transatlantic Financial Crisis* (New York: Cambridge University Press, 2013); Alasdair Roberts, *The First Great Depression: Economic Crisis and Political Disorder in the United States, 1837–1848* (Ithaca, NY: Cornell University Press, 2012). On the Panic's effects on Buffalo, see H. Perry Smith, *History of Buffalo & Erie Co., New York*, vol. I (Syracuse, NY: D. Mason and Co., 1884), 213; on Michigan, see Don Faber, *The Boy Governor: Stevens T. Mason and the Birth of Michigan Politics* (Ann Arbor, MI: University of Michigan Press, 2012), 99–101, 111–37.

56 Dodge's whereabouts and actions: Matilda Anderson to John Anderson, 24 January 1838; John Anderson to Alexander Anderson, Feb. 4, 1838; Eliza Wing to Alexander Anderson, 25 February 1838; John Anderson to Alexander Anderson, June 9, 1838; all in John Anderson Papers, BHC. J.S. Neysmith to Mackenzie, 12 November 1838, MLF. W.W. Dodge to J.R. Field, 20 July 1839, Hugh Brady Papers, BHC. Dodge's escape was widely printed in U.S. papers. See for example *Detroit Morning Post*, 26 November 1838.

57 Albert Corey calculated that out of 157 patriots captured at the Battle of the Windmill, 140 were day labourers: Corey, *The Crisis of 1830–1842 in Canadian-American Relations*, 78, also 27–43 for a general characterization of the patriots as from the labouring ranks, with some "gentlemen" leaders. Many historians use financial distress as the sole explanation for patriot volunteering: Taylor, *The Civil War of 1812*, 455–7; Corey, *The Crisis of 1830–1842 in Canadian-American Relations*, 27–43; Walker, *What Hath God Wrought*, 518. Others have noted that there was quite a bit of economic diversity in patriot ranks: Duffy and Miller, *An Anxious Democracy*, 51; Kinchen, *The Rise and Fall of the Patriot Hunters*, 19–20; Bonthius, "Locofocoism with a Gun?," 15–16. Greer, "Rebellion Reconsidered," 14. On American emigration to Canada in the late 1790s and early 1800s, see Taylor, *Civil War of 1812*, 45–73. On the "Gone to Texas" phenomenon, see Mark E. Nackman, "Anglo-American Migrants to the West: Men of Broken Fortunes? The Case of Texas, 1821–1846," *Western Historical Quarterly* 5 (Oct. 1974): 441–55; Edward E. Baptist,

*The Half Has Never Been Told: Slavery and the Making of American Capitalism* (New York: Basic Books, 2014), 287–8.

58 For denigration of the patriots as lower class, see Sir George Arthur to Lord Fitzroy, 20 December 1838, *The Arthur Papers*, ed. Charles R. Sanderson (Toronto: University of Toronto Press, 1957), 1: 475; Arthur to Lieut.-Col. Dundas, 22 June 1838, *Arthur Papers*, 1: 204; Guillet, *Lives and Times of the Patriots*, 106; Winfield Scott to Joel Poinsett, 12 January 1839, Folder 11, Letter 150, Poinsett Papers, HSP; Kelley to Peter Porter, 16 January 1838, Roll 10, Volume 6, Peter Porter Papers, BECHS.

59 Charles Royster, *A Revolutionary People at War: The Continental Army and American Character, 1775–1783* (Chapel Hill: University of North Carolina Press, 1979), chapters 2 and 3; Edward C. Skeen, *Citizens Soldiers of the War of 1812* (Lexington, KY: University of Kentucky Press, 1998); Peter Guardino, *The Dead March: A History of the Mexican-American War* (Cambridge, MA: Harvard University Press, 2017), chapters 1 and 2.

60 For much more detailed accounts of the U.S. response to the patriots, see Reginald Stuart, *United States Expansionism and British North America*, 126–47; Stevens, *Border Diplomacy*, 18–47; Carroll, *A Good and Wise Measure*, 202–8; Watson, "United States Officers Fight the 'Patriot War.'"

61 Thomas Storrow Brown to Mackenzie, 23 May 1838, MLF.

62 Hugh Brady to General Jones, 6 December 1838, "Reports of General Brady on the Patriot War," ed. Francis Paul Prucha, *Canadian Historical Review* 31 (March 1950): 67.

63 Lucy Williams Hawes to Richard Williams Sr and Jr, 29 December 1837, Hawes-Taber Family Letters, CL-UM; *Buffalo Daily Commercial Advertiser*, 22 January 1838.

64 Scott, *Memoirs*, 308.

65 Worth to Poinsett, 30 January 1838, 9–159, Poinsett Papers, HSP; Worth to Poinsett, 17 February 1838, Gilpin Papers, HSP.

66 For other statements on patriot sympathizers who impeded federal officials, see B. Bagley to Mackenzie, 14 June 1838, MLF; William Worth to Joel Poinsett, 25 December 1838, 11–114, Joel Poinsett Papers, HSP; Arthur to Lord Fitzroy Somerset, 30 October 1838, *Arthur Papers*, 1: 335; Stevens, *Border Diplomacy*, 42–3; Bradley Miller, "The Law of Nations in the Borderlands," in *Essays in the History of Canadian Law, Vol. 11: Quebec and the Canadas*, ed. G. Blaine Baker and Donald Fyson (Toronto: University of Toronto Press, 2013), 237–44. For a more comprehensive

overview of the interactions between U.S. Army officers and the patriots, see Watson, "United States Officers Fight the 'Patriot War,'" 507–15.

67 Miller, "The Law of Nations in the Borderlands."

68 Works that argue the border enthusiasm for the patriots was fleeting and superficial, and more related to the Caroline Affair than the patriot cause, include Howe, *What Hath God Wrought?*, 518–19; Stevens, *Border Diplomacy*, 20–1; Haynes, *Unfinished Revolution*, 209–10.

69 There is no published biography of King, although his influence over three decades of politics suggests the need for one. The most recent full-length study is Ernest Muller, "Preston King: A Political Life" (PhD diss., Columbia University, 1957.) See 200–38 for King's involvement in the Patriot War. For King's continued subscription to *Mackenzie's Gazette*, see Preston King to Mackenzie, 2 October 1838; King to Mackenzie, 5 October 1838, MLF. King's family tree is discussed in Richard P. Eckels, "Preston King: A Preliminary Memoir," in Folder 60A, Preston King/ Simeon Smith Papers, St Lawrence University.

70 Muller, "Preston King," 200–38, Eckels, "Preston King"; Graves, *Guns across the River*, 112. King's aunt was Sarah Galloway, and her son John Dulmage was killed during the battle. Muller never made this family connection to the Battle of the Windmill, suggesting King himself either never knew of the connections or never discussed it. The former is certainly possible, but King was an intensely private man in certain respects, and his lack of discussion of the topic is not reason to think he was unaware of his cousin's death. Indeed, knowing his cousin was killed in the battle – even if they had little contact – adds further to King's tragedy and the weight of his devastation.

71 *Washington Daily National Intelligencer*, 11 June 1838.

72 Webster's report was written in 1842, when the MacLeod Affair threatened to reignite passions on the border. The Hunters' Lodges re-emerged during the hysteria, and President Tyler sent Webster, then secretary of state, to report on their activity. Despite its later date, Webster's statement holds true for the Lodges in 1838, when they were even more popular and powerful than they were in 1842: Webster to Tyler, *Letters of Daniel Webster*, ed. C.H. Van Tyne (New York: McClure, Philips, and Co., 1902), 132–3.

73 Schlereth, "Privileges of Locomotion."

74 Robert W. Coakley, *The Role of Federal Military Forces in Domestic Disorders, 1798–1878* (Washington, DC: Centre of Military History, 1988), 50–3, 98, 110–19. Indeed, both the Nullification Crisis and the Whiskey Rebellion are apt comparisons to the Patriot War; like them, the

Patriot War represented a complete breakdown of federal authority, to which the federal government was forced to respond militarily.

75 *Detroit Morning Post*, 6 December 1838.

76 E.A. Theller to Mackenzie, 5 January 1839, MLF.

77 George Herron to Mackenzie, 5 December 1838, Mackenzie Papers, BHC.

78 E.A. Theller, *Canada in 1837–1838: Showing, by Historical Facts, the Causes of the Late Attempted Revolution, and of Its Failure*, vol. 2 (New York, 1841), 304, 308–10. These statements capture the rich "states' rights" rhetoric in the North, which many scholars have missed due to an over-reliance on John C. Calhoun and his southern version of states' rights. Other examples of northern states' rights language and action during this era include the "Aroostook War" in Maine, the MacCleod Case in New York, and the "Toledo War" between Ohio and Michigan.

79 Ronald Formisano, *The Birth of Mass Political Parties: Michigan, 1827–1861* (Princeton, NJ: Princeton University Press, 1971), 189–90; Bonthius, "Locofocoism with a Gun?"

80 Of the many Democratic papers, I have surveyed, only one argued for suppressing the patriots due to a potential war with Britain: *Albany Argus*, quoted in *Detroit Daily Commercial Advertiser*, 25 December 1837. Whig papers that made the argument that the Canadians did not deserve help include: *New York Spectator*, 7 December 1837; *Washington Daily National Intelligencer*, 21 December 1837; *Detroit Daily Advertiser*, 31 January 1838. See *Detroit Free Press*, 10 December 1838, for a collection of Democratic papers making this same argument, including the *New York Sun*, *Albany Argus*, and *Onondaga Standard*. This attitude parallels the findings of Francois Furstenberg on the Jacksonian justification of slavery: only slaves who fought for freedom deserved freedom. See Furstenburg, *In the Name of the Father: Washington's Legacy, Slavery, and the Making of a Nation* (New York: Penguin, 2007), 218. For the politics of "Anglophobia" – where the Democrats usually proved more belligerent – see Haynes, *Unfinished Revolution*, 106–32. For the differing ideologies of the Second Party System, see Lawrence Kohl, *The Politics of Individualism: Parties and the American Character in the Jacksonian Era* (New York: Oxford University Press, 1989).

81 *Detroit Daily Commercial Advertiser*, 6 January 1838.

82 *Canadian*, 1 January 1838. Although printed "1838," the date was actually 1839: the Patriot War events of 1838 were mentioned explicitly in the text.

83 J. Doty to Poinsett, 30 April 1839, 12–97, Poinsett Papers, HSP.

84 Newspaper reports on the Hunters' Lodges also reported their nonpartisan stance. See, for example, *Detroit Free Press*, 19 December 1838. For a

differing attitude towards the patriots that emphasizes their partisanship, see Bonthius, "Locofocoism with a Gun?"

85 *Mackenzie's Gazette* (New York) 4, 12, 18, 25 August 1838 and 1 September 1838. Gates, *After the Rebellion*, 44–5; Duncan Koerber, "Political Operatives and Administrative Workers," *Journalism History* 36 (Fall 2010): 164–5.

86 James Mackenzie to William Lyon Mackenzie, 2 October 1838, MLF.

87 D. Hungerford to Mackenzie, 9 August 1838, MLF.

88 It is important to note that though the patriots themselves were nonpartisan, their cause was used for partisan purposes throughout the Great Lakes region. Both Democrats and Whigs tried to tie their opponents to the U.S.-British side. Democrats proclaimed Whigs were the same as British Whigs – and tories. Whigs pointed out that it was Van Buren, a Democratic president, and Marcy, a Democratic governor, who were responsible for cracking down on the patriots. It seems the Whigs had the better argument; both Van Buren and Marcy were defeated in New York in 1840, and some evidence suggests it was due to their hostility to the patriots. See especially Julien Maudit's essay in this volume, as well as Tiffany, *The Relations of the United States to the Canadian Rebellion of 1837–1838*, 102–12; Carroll, *A Good and Wise Measure*, 207–8; Muller, "Preston King: A Political Biography," 241.

89 On antipartyism, see Mark Voss-Hubbard, "The 'Third Party Tradition' Reconsidered: Third Parties and American Public Life, 1830–1900," *Journal of American History* 86, no. 1 (June 1999), 121–50; Glenn Altschuler and Stuart Blumin, *Rude Republic: Americans and Their Politics in the Nineteenth Century* (Princeton, NJ: Princeton University Press, 2000), 14–46. Most of Altschuler and Blumin's evidence that argues for lack of political interest came from western New York where patriot activity was rampant, but they do not mention the Patriot War – but the Patriot War suggests a reason for these attitudes.

90 James Mackenzie to William Lyon Mackenzie, 6 August 1838, MLF. James Mackenzie would have a successful career in Ohio politics as a Free Soil Democrat in the Ohio congress in the 1850s.

91 On the Anti-Mason Party, see Ronald P. Formisano, *For the People: American Populist Movements from the Revolution to the 1850s* (Chapel Hill, NC: University of North Carolina Press, 2008), 91–158, esp. 91–115 for New York. On Free Soil, see Jonathan H. Earle, *Jacksonian Antislavery: The Politics of Free Soil, 1824–1854* (Chapel Hill, NC: University of North Carolina Press, 2004), 49–77 on New York, 144–62 on Ohio; Eric Foner, *Free Soil, Free Labor, Free Men: The Ideology of the*

*Republican Party before the Civil War* (New York: Oxford University Press, 1970), 149–85.

92 "Mackenzie's Constitution," in Read and Stagg, ed., *The Rebellion in Upper Canada*, 97.

93 On Preston King's feelings on antislavery and racism, see Muller, "Preston King: A Political Biography," 265–6, 335–6, 378–9.

94 For other patriot antislavery statements, see William Gates, *Recollections of Life in Van Diemen's Land* (1850), 14–15; Sutherland, "The Sword and the Pen," *Detroit Morning Post*, 3 December 1838.

95 Mackenzie, *Selected Writings*, 156, 173.

96 Fourth Annual Report of the American Anti-Slavery Society," ed. Elizur Wright, *Quarterly Anti-Slavery Magazine* 2 (1837): 350.

97 Read and Stagg, "Introduction," in Read and Stagg, ed., *The Rebellion of 1837*, xl, lvi; Gerald Horne, *Negro Comrades of the Crown: African Americans and the British Empire Fight the U.S. before Emancipation* (New York: New York University Press, 2012), 116. For other anti-black statements, see *Detroit Daily Advertiser*, 1 January 1838; *Mackenzie's Gazette*, 3 November 1838; *Mackenzie's Gazette*, 9 June 1838. See also Read, *The Rising in Western Upper Canada*, 62, 71, 73. On the racism of white labourers in the northern U.S., see David Roediger, *Wages of Whiteness: Race and the Making of the American Working Class* (New York: Verso, 1991), Alexander Saxton, *The Rise and Fall of the White Republic: Class, Politics, and Mass Culture in Nineteenth-Century America* (New York: Verso, 1990). On the federal level, it was slavery that kept most southerners vehemently opposed to the Patriot War, for it brought with it a potential war with Great Britain. Whatever the outcome it would be poor for southerners. In the worst-case scenario, Britain would incite slave rebellions; if the war were won, Canada would be annexed, adding more free territory to the Union. See John Calhoun to James Edward Colhoun, 8 January 1838 and Calhoun to Micah Sterling, 26 February 1838, both in *The Papers of John C. Calhoun*, vol. 14, ed. Clyde Wilson (Columbia, SC: University of South Carolina Press, 1981), 70, 160; *Memoirs of John Quincy Adams*, vol. 9, ed. Charles Francis Adams (Philadelphia, 1876), 467.

98 For the black defence of Canada during the Canadian Rebellions, see Horne, *Negro Comrades of the Crown*, 114–19; Van Gosse, "'As a Nation, the English Are Our Friends': The Emergence of African American Politics in the British Atlantic World, 1772–1861," *American Historical Review* 113 (Oct. 2008): 1012–13; Fred Landon, "Canadian Negroes and the Rebellion of 1837," *Journal of Negro History* 7 (Oct. 1922): 377–9. Praise of black

loyalty: Arthur to Colborne, 28(?) May 1838, *Arthur Papers*, 1: 126. Lucy Hawes to Richard Williams, 29 December 1837, Hawes-Taber Family Letters, CL-UM; S.C. Frey to Mackenzie, 4 January 1838, MLF; *Detroit Morning Post*, 15 November 1838.

99 Sutherland to Van Rensselaer, December 1837 or January 1838.

100 Eliza A. Wing to Alexander Anderson, 5 January 1838, John Anderson Papers, BHC. For other anti-black sentiments, see Wilson Brooks to Caroline Brooks, 29 December 1837, Brooks Papers, BHC, MLF; A. Barber to RVR, 28 December 1837, MLF; Lucy Hawes to Richard Williams, 1 January 1838, Hawes-Taber Family Letters, CL-UM.

101 Chippewa Chiefs to S.P. Jarvis, 21 December 1837, in *The Rebellion of 1837 in Upper Canada*, 328; Adam Hope to his father, 11 December 1846, in *Letters of Adam Hope 1834–1845*, ed. Adam Crerar (Toronto: Champlain Society, 2007) 241; Graves, *Guns across the River*, 46.

102 Samuel C. Frey to Mackenzie, 4 January 1838, MLF.

103 *Mackenzie's Gazette*, 3 November 1838.

104 *Liberator* [Boston], 7 December 1838.

105 Anonymous to Mackenzie, 8 September 1838, Mackenzie Papers, BHC. See also J.S. Vail to Mackenzie, 7 December 1838, MLF.

106 Peter Dorsey, *Common Bondage: Slavery as Metaphor in Revolutionary America* (Knoxville: University of Tennessee Press, 2009).

107 David Shields, "The Power to be Reborn," in *The American Revolution Reborn*, ed. Patrick Spero and Michael Zuckerman (Philadelphia: University of Pennsylvania Press, 2016), 293–8. See also Fitz, *Our Sister Republics*, for a similar period division in the attitude towards Latin America.

108 This racial dynamic also helps explain the lack of American participation in the Patriote invasions of Lower Canada in late 1838. While white Americans did not denigrate French Canadians as akin to black people or Indians, they certainly were a race – or, at least, an ethnicity – apart. As one letter-writer put it, "The 'habitants,' generally, are an illiterate and peaceably disposed body of men, rather inclined to be penurious, and caring more for their 'peculiar habits of life' than for the kind of government under which they live": *Pennsylvania Inquirer*, 15 December 1837. Robert Nelson's Declaration of Independence for Lower Canada, in which he called for equal rights for all Canadian Indians, would only have further disenchanted Americans from volunteering.

109 For patriot rituals, see Kinchen, *Rise and Fall of the Patriot Hunters*, Appendix II, 127–31; Thomas Fitnam to Mackenzie, 13 February 1839,

MLF, T.R. Preston, *Three Years Residence in Upper Canada, from 1837 to 1839*, vol. 1 (London, 1840), 159–66.

110 The end of the Hunters' Lodges coincided with the revival of Freemasonry in the 1840s, although this could be more correlation than causation. See Steven Bullock, *Revolutionary Brotherhood: Freemasonry and the Transformation of the American Social Order, 1730–1840* (Chapel Hill, NC: University of North Carolina Press, 1996), 316.

111 Mary Ann Clawson, *Constructing Brotherhood: Class, Gender, and Fraternalism* (Princeton, NJ: Princeton University Press, 1996), 109.

112 "Mrs Lount's Letter," *Canadian*, 1 January 1838.

113 Hobart Berrian to Mackenzie, 21 November 1838, MLF.

114 John Tracey to Mackenzie, 29 August 1838, MLF.

115 John Griffon to Mackenzie, 28 January 1839, MLF. Portraying Van Buren as feminine was prevalent for his opponents: Haynes, *Unfinished Revolution*, 122–3. On the relationship between filibustering and manhood, see Amy Greenberg, *Manifest Manhood*, 12–13.

116 On manhood and the threat of the market revolution, see Joshua R. Greenberg, *Advocating the Man: Masculinity, Organized Labor, and the Household in New York, 1800–1840* (New York: Columbia University Press, 2008), 49–118; Greenberg, *Manifest Manhood*, 5–13; David Pugh, *Sons of Liberty: The Masculine Mind in Nineteenth-Century America* (Westport, CT: Praeger, 1984), 3–44; E. Anthony Rotundo, *American Manhood: Transformations in Masculinity from the Revolution to the Modern Era* (New York: Basic Books, 1993), 167–221.

117 Robert May, "Young American Males and Filibustering in the Age of Manifest Destiny," 874–5.

118 On the desire to pass down land to all sons and its relationship to western migration, see Kathleen Neils Conzen, "A Saga of Families," in *The Oxford History of the American West*, ed. Milner, O'Connor, and Sandweiss (New York: Oxford University Press, 1994), 315–58.

119 Sir George Arthur to John Colbourne, 20 March 1839, Charles Burow Papers, BHC.

120 Stephen Aron, *How the West was Lost: The Transformation of Kentucky from Daniel Boone to Henry Clay* (Baltimore: Johns Hopkins University Press, 1996), 192.

121 Canadians had left for the American West before the rebellions, but numbers substantially increased after them. See especially Fred Landon, *Western Ontario and the American Frontier* (Toronto: Ryerson Press, 1941), 198–204; also *Mackenzie's Gazette*, 26 May 1838; Martin Switzer

to Mackenzie, 7 December 1838, MLF; Read, *The Rising in Upper Canada*, 163.

122 Lucius Bierce, a patriot leader in Michigan, later expressed embarrassment: J. Fletcher Brennan, *A Biographical Cyclopedia and Portrait Gallery of Distinguished Men* (Cincinnati, 1879), 177.

123 For the Patriot War in memory, see Robert Ross, "The Patriot War," *Michigan Historical Collections XXI* (Lansing, MI: 1894), 601–9.

124 The Patriot War did not completely end until 1842, but after the various military disasters of 1838 most patriots abandoned the struggle. The few remaining hoped raids into Canada would kindle a U.S.-British war. During the height of the McCleod Case, the patriots briefly reemerged as a force, but effective management by the Van Buren Administration once again quelled them.

125 On the exiles, see Pybus and Steward, *American Citizens, British Slaves.*

126 Daniel D. Heustis, *A narrative of the adventures and sufferings of Captain Daniel D. Heustis and his companions in Canada and Van Dieman's land during a long captivity [microform]: with travels in California and voyages at sea* (1848), 55–6.

127 William Gates, *Recollections of Life in Van Diemen's Land* (1850), 14–15.

# 4

# Bald Eagle over Canada

## *Dr Samuel Underhill and the Patriot Rebellion of 1837–1838*

ANDREW BONTHIUS

We shall advocate the rights of the laboring classes, and expose the spirit of monopoly. We shall advocate equal and universal opportunity for education for rich and poor, furnished by the State.[1]

Prospectus statement of the *Cleveland Liberalist*

In the fall of 1837, a nationwide bank panic, growing economic poverty in the United States, and a raging political war against corrupt banking combined for a trifecta of aggravating deep-layered developments that led to widespread support for the Rebellion in Upper Canada (UC). Political program, too, reverberated across and along the U.S.-Canadian border as William Lyon Mackenzie was widely known in the U.S. for his radical Jacksonian and agrarian-centred critique of the new and unforgiving commercial banking system, then attempting to sink its teeth on both sides of the border.[2] Mackenzie's proposed constitution for the new Upper Canadian Republic reflected this outlook, and he couched his rebellion in the rhetoric of the American Revolution to great advantage. Very quickly the "Spirit of 1776" was revived as American patriots along the borderland only awaited a commander to plant the flag of "Liberty and Equality" on Navy Island and finally sweep British oppression from the continent thereby truly finishing the American Revolution.[3]

Most unappreciated as the central cause of this cross-border insurrection was the raw ideological tension that sorely tested the bonds of the American Union and drew a direct line between the success of the Rebellion and the protection of liberty and equality in the U.S. This was to be accomplished by a wide distribution of land in pursuit of the Jeffersonian-Republican ideal of a nation of yeoman-farmer producers as a necessary bulwark against a grasping and "ruthless monied aristocracy."[4] It was a regional movement that engulfed the entire Great Lakes and which, as historians Maxime Dagenais and Julien Mauduit have shown, even drew support from states farther south such as Pennsylvania, Maryland, Virginia, and Louisiana.[5] Key to understanding Ohio as the epicentre of patriot activity on the American side is one Dr Samuel Underhill who, largely through the power of his pen and oratory, rallied supporters in Ohio and other states to these conjoined movements.[6] In my first article, I speculated that the Rebellion in Upper Canada was "Locofocoism with a gun." However, I cautioned that such a hypothesis deserved further investigation beyond "the profile of a single leader," as I specifically focused on Mackenzie. Dr Underhill's vanguard role provides additional key insights into the motivations behind the Rebellion and, to a great extent, a window into the future of what the self-declared Canadian Republic might have looked like in operation. His writings and activities are additional ballast for the growing historiography that conclusively situates the Rebellion, on both sides of the border, within the discourse of Locofocoite, radical Painite civic-republicanism.[7]

## DR UNDERHILL'S POLITICAL MEDICINE

Underhill's early years provide some insight into the intellectual evolution that eventually led him to become a radical leader. Born on 14 November 1795 in Dutchess County, New York, to strict Quaker parents, his physical horizons were mostly limited to a life on the family farm, Quaker meetings, and his rural school. Underhill was a precocious child though, and he recalls that, at age fifteen, he "began to think seriously about the great variety of religious sects and opinions" and thought "they cannot all be right … Am I not as liable to be wrong as any one? These considerations induced me to resolve, that, I would examine for myself and choose for myself."[8] At age nineteen, his self-described "passion" for science led him to the Albany School of Medicine where he concluded his studies with what he writes provided him an "honorable standing in that class."[9] By age twenty-one, he began to drift from Biblical scripture feeling the gravitational pull of "every work, theological, literary, scientific, or metaphysical that fell within my reach including Watt's Logic, Rohaut's system of natural philosophy, Milton's Paradise Lost, and much more." He relates that even while blacksmithing on his father's farm, he found himself reading Dr Oliver Goldsmith's histories on Greece and Rome in the heat and light of his shop's furnace.[10] Although his sharp wit had not yet been honed to demonstrate his impressive intellect, before he ever left upstate New York, Underhill was well on his way to becoming a "Renaissance Man" of the first order.[11] Few of Cleveland's carriage set would be able to match this commoner's expansive mind in depth and breadth of knowledge.

The 1820s held immense intellectual and life changes for Underhill. While still in Dutchess County, he was dismissed from his Quaker community (and pastorate) in 1821 "in consequence of doubts of original immortality and the existence of the Devil" and denial of other key Christian doctrines such as "original sin, atonement, Trinity the divine, [and] authority of Scriptures."[12] His philosophical evolution tracked (perhaps independently of) the spreading Hicksite apostasy emanating from Long Island, New York. He would admit in a missive to Robert Owen, "I was what the disciples of Elias Hicks are and am now what those doctrines lead to, a sceptic [*sic*]."[13] Not long after his Quaker expulsion, he moved beyond purely philosophical musings to the political task of actually creating a community of equality based on common property. In this quest for agrarian equality, and three years before he had read any of Owen's writings, Underhill related that he had been impressed by Cornelius Blatchly's *Essay on Commonwealth*, which in turn leaned heavily on the writings of Owen.[14] Sans the religiosity of Blatchly's philosophy, Underhill found sustenance in Blatchly's call for "pure communities [based on] a system of social, *equal and inclusive rights*, interests, liberties, and privileges to all real and personal property."[15] Distinctions in wealth, social status, and land, Underhill had come to believe, were the bane of happiness and true equality. "Privileged men," he wrote to Owen, "are bad timber in a community. No community can prosper unless each member is profitably engaged. For a member to have private funds by which he is enabled to dress and live better than others though at his own expense is a curse."[16] By this point in his life, Underhill had become what Dr William Osler has described as a "Gallionian physician": militantly skeptic, believers in medicine as science, and the Enlightenment tenets of rationalism.[17]

Thus, on 16 December 1825, the erudite blacksmith/farmer and commoner led his and four other families to form the Forestville Commonwealth at Coxsackie, New York, the type of which, he would later write, "constitute the society spoken of in the *New-Harmony Gazette.*"[18] It was only the second Owenite "community of equality" in New York and one of seven Owenite communities in the U.S. along with New Harmony, Indiana.[19] As a leading member of the community, Underhill set an example of virtuous industry by becoming, in the philosophy of the communitarian, eagerly and "profitably engaged" in a number of trades necessary to make the community prosperous, among them "the shop, the farm, the sawmill, the stonehammer."[20] He did his best to make a go of the effort and even enlisted as an agent of Owen's *Gazette*. However, within two years, indebtedness forced the community to sell its property, and, in October 1827, he would lead a move westward to join greener pastures in Kendal, Ohio in a community formed by Owenite disciples Paul Brown and Josiah Warren.[21]

Upbeat about his newly chosen community, Underhill threw himself into making Kendal as successful an example of Owen's new "System" as possible. However, the arduous journey overland from Coxsackie to Buffalo and then to Cleveland "in an unseaworthy schooner that was tossed about like a cork in stormy Lake Erie" foreshadowed difficult times.[22] Having cut his political eyeteeth at Forestville, he quickly rose to a position of leadership at Kendal by helping to amend the community's Bond of Social Compact and taking a seat as one of the association's commissioners.[23] Within a month after arrival, Underhill began to employ his oratorical skills in a program of public (lyceum-type) lectures on the "New Social System" that were attended by association members as well by outsiders.[24] His considerable writing skills were employed in a letter to *The Gospel Advocate and Impartial Investigator*, a newspaper in Albany, New York, to recruit new members to the Kendal community. The letter first pitched the economic viability of the community as having – among other attractions – 2,200 acres of excellent land, a woollen factory, and a saw mill, and followed with an invitation to "Persons of good character, having small capitals, and hearts devoted to the system."[25] The community's demise, however, was only months away.

With membership lagging, he might have suspected the end was near as planting time arrived in May 1828, but Underhill persevered and eagerly wrote to Owen himself encouraging him to visit Kendal. He touted it as "the best established of any one on the new System" and enticed him with the compliment (and one for himself) that "there are many liberal men in this county who anxiously enquire when you will be along. My lectures have made a severe shock on the Superstitions of the country and we have believed that your visit would induce the liberals to form a [illegible] like the free press at Canton 7 miles east of Kendal."[26] Poetically, however, as fall commenced, his hopes of building a model egalitarian and secular community were dashed. Membership in the community continued to atrophy steadily for a multiplicity of reasons, not the least of which, according to Underhill, was a summer fever which took "some of our best men" and "debilitated many others," as well as an impossible debt load.[27] A lack of internal cohesion due to the tensions created by the comingling of so many different religious sects, whose belief systems Underhill and other skeptics continually challenged (to the great consternation of many) in their lectures, certainly contributed significantly to the muffled death of the utopian experiment.[28]

He would later write that he had no regrets over the failed experiment, and as he began his post-communitarian phase, he remained buoyant, seeking political ballast in the camaraderie of a "small company" of other former Kendalites who subscribed to the *Free Enquirer* and were seeking type set to begin a press of their own.[29] Having turned to a pre-Marxian materialist worldview, his political program logically evolved toward an explicit class analysis and association with the party politics of "workeyism."[30] On 31 July 1830, Underhill composed a broadside "to the Public Spring Hill" (an area of Massillon) in which he warned of a spreading "aristocracy of wealth," coming from the Eastern states and causing in Ohio similar a litany of depredations: "an oppressively unequal system of taxation ... large tracts of uncultivated lands held by wealthy monopolists ... a militia system [that] is a useless expensive demoralizing establishment," and an educational system that serves the children of the rich "while so little is done for the children of the poor?"[31] Exhibiting an abiding faith in the potential of every common man and woman, he opined that "many a man has worn out a life in toil and poverty who, had he been well educated, would have shone bright in the councils of his country ... And many a female now passing her days in the most squalid wretchedness of mind and body … who, had she been well trained, would have had her name added to the list of those whose private virtues and puplic [*sic*] labors have made them a bright constellation of lights in the world."[32] The redress of these daily insults, he urged, was not to be found in either the party of Jackson or Adams. Rather, he asserted, "it is high time that we unite under the name of the 'working men's party' and after enquiring into our rights see that we select men who know what we want who are able and willing to claim for us what is just, what is equal, what is for the good of all." The broadside ended with a call for "all persons friendly to *equal* rights, *equal* taxation, *equal* education and an abolition or remodification of our militia system to meet at the house of Jacob Miller's in Massillon" on 7 August 1830.[33] With his endorsement of the Workingmen's Party, the annals of history should record Underhill as being one of the earliest and foremost proponents of this ideology in Ohio.

In the spring of 1835, Underhill moved his family north to Willoughby, Ohio, for a lectureship in chemistry at the local university and less than a year later he was on to Cleveland.[34] By character and philosophy, he gravitated to leading roles in civic life of that city as a Justice of the Peace, printer, and propagandizer of free enquiry, secular egalitarianism, and workeyism. Driven more by a desire to change the world than to heal it and possessing a natural talent for the written word, book binding, and printing, he opened an office where he began publishing, with his son James, an eight-page newspaper called the *Cleveland Liberalist*.[35] In politics and breadth of content it was reminiscent of the *New-Harmony Gazette*. The first issue was coloured in Painite civic-republican hues: "To the Friends of Free Enquiry … There never was a time when the friends of Liberty of Thought and Equality of Rights and Privileges had stronger motives to go ahead."[36] Underhill kept a distance from the Locofoco/Equal Rights Party label and party affiliation (as did Robert Owen and Fanny Wright), but in its advocacy of equal rights, opposition to special privilege and monopolies, and support for hard money ("anti-bank") policy the *Liberalist* was, in many ways, indistinguishable from Locofocoism.[37] With regard to socio-economic divisions Underhill explained, perhaps with some fear of charges of Skidmorism: "I am not a leveler of *natural* distinctions in society … But those specimens of bloated, purse proud, privilege, money made nobles … are an unnatural excrescence on society … Mind alone should graduate and distinguish the various ranks in a democratic society."[38] Thus, from its very first issue the *Liberalist* struck a sharp, polemical tone, and signalled its intention to be a full-throated agitator for social, political, and economic change.

Until the burning of the *Caroline* in December 1837, the first nearly year and a half of print was dominated by polemics against worthless medicines, phrenology, and animal magnetism with the most frequent and longest always being withering attacks on religion.[39] Neither Canadian reform efforts (in either of the two provinces) nor political party differences seemed much in Underhill's line of sight. In this first year of publication, he stood out mostly for his vigorous advocacy of women's rights (as did Paine) by calling "essentially unjust" the three to four shillings women received per hour for the nine shillings to two dollars men were paid. His sincerity on this issue was underscored by the regular column he gave to political pundit "Sybil," and his printing of the prospectus for Anne Royall's newspaper *The Huntress*.[40] In May 1837, he issued forth with the first of a long-running, twelve-part series on the political economy and banking.[41] It was explicitly "anti-bank" and positioned him well for his eventual support of Mackenzie's draft constitution and the call therein for a Canadian Republic and a truly republican "free" bank.[42] The series hammered the corrupt U.S. banking system of money credit, interest, dividends, and stock-jobbers, which he saw as tied to the hip of the Bank of England, largely seen as the handmaiden, in both origin and purpose, of the Bank of the United States. The series left no doubt as to his agrarian impulse: "Banking, interest paper money, charters, monopolies ... [are] quackery."[43]

In the series, Underhill also articulated another radical agrarian tenet – the labour theory of value, a widely held belief among yeomen and mechanics in the Jackson years, according to historian Bruce Laurie.[44] Underhill asked rhetorically how wealth accumulation was accomplished: "And by whom is all this done? Not by the retired capitalist surely for he is only consuming, he produces nothing!!! By the sweat of the producing classes most certainly."[45] By his leadership in the radical left wing of the joint-stock "free" banking movement and defence of the class interests of yeomen and urban mechanics, Underhill stirred in Cleveland a debate every bit as vigorous as those led by such better known east coast, urban-centred, workingmen's counterparts as Theophilus Fisk in Boston, John Vethake and Thomas Skidmore in New York City, and William Heighton in Philadelphia.[46] As a foremost agitator in Cleveland of radical "anti-bank" philosophy then sweeping the nation, Underhill left, perhaps, his greatest legacy.

The fears he had of Massillon becoming a "debauched" New Lanark, Scotland (prior to Owen's rescue), he now transferred to Cleveland.[47] In a poem he titled "The Bank of the Lake," penned just months before the Panic of 1837 hit, Underhill attacked banking by analogy to Cleveland's environs in a clever play on words, as a "sweet bank of the lake" and a "delightful terrace of land" threatened by "rude waves of desolation." It pleads "[o]r waken ye friends of our beautiful City / Our walk will be lost and thrown in disorder."[48] The "rude waves," of course, were those of the cyclical boom and bust of the new market economy, its "privileged" drive for profits and concomitant corrupt speculation. The "desolation" was the paradox of "[a] national treasury full to overflowing, a country abounding in every sort of production … and yet we find distress, starvation, and crowded poor-houses, like canker on the body politic producing excruciating pain to the sufferers and to philanthropists."[49] Underhill was keenly aware that city trustees were regularly approving the indenture of children and ordering individuals and entire families to depart the city for being potential charges to the township.[50] Such scenes of homeless vagabonds, left destitute by the emerging market economy, would soon enough become the grist for editorial cartoons such as the now famous "The Times" by Edward Williams Clay.

As these market-induced social dislocations proceeded apace and Cleveland's workers began to resist the degradation of their wages and working conditions, Underhill was poised to take up the banner of workingmen in a very public way, much to the objections of the city's entrepreneurial Whigs who bemoaned "the machinations of those who attempt to array one class of community against another."[51] As would become the case with the patriot cause, his stature often provided him the podium at public meetings. At a meeting of Cleveland's mechanics and workingmen on 3 August 1837, called to "take into consideration the present condition of the country and the course pursued by the Banks," he addressed the assembled who later formulated a preamble that attacked the state legislature for having "granted to Banking institutions … certain exclusive privileges, which in their nature are peculiarly liable to abuse … [and] which operate unjustly upon a very large portion of fee citizens; which in short are destructive of equal rights, and good government." The second paragraph of the preamble charged the banking "monopoly" with controlling "almost every department of enterprize [*sic*], greatly to the prejudice and detriment of honest industry ... thus overthrowing and revolutionizing the character of our government and creating distinctions incompatible with the genius of our institutions, ennobling the rich and depressing the poor."[52] Given the combination of his leadership role in this meeting and his views on banking, Underhill's hand is undoubtedly seen in this preamble and the resultant resolutions.[53]

The banking question in these times had such political valence that the workingmen passed ten resolutions, fully eight of which focused on the pernicious role of banks and concluded in distinct Locofocoite tenor that "labor is the only true source of wealth – that all losses either from casualty or fraud must be made up by labor, and ... the loss to the country originating from the high-handed abuses, and utter faithlessness of the banks, are direct taxes upon labor ... and too subversive of equal rights to be tolerated by freemen." The growing social and economic inequality had reaped a whirlwind of resistance and drove Cleveland's workingmen, in their seventh resolution, to call for "efficient action by the workingmen" to resist "all attempts on the part of bank directors, attornies [*sic*], and cashiers, to instruct us concerning our interests."[54] Underhill was joined at the meeting by mechanic and patriot confreres: masons C.B. Denio and Wm.V. Craw, and gunsmith L.W. Babbitt.[55]

Underhill's vanguard role in this movement caused him to be publicly called out by name in a local newspaper for having "uttered a base calumny" against Capt. Daniel Worley, "an estimable citizen," because Underhill had charged him with "dishonesty and fraud ... and deliberate perjury" in his position as Commissioner to inspect state banks. The attack on Underhill ended with a caution: "Let the Whigs among the mechanics keep their eyes open" and not let "those demagogues ... who, not workingmen themselves, but drones in the community, under [take] to hoodwink and lead them astray."[56] These were the days when, it is well to remember, those with unpopular ideas and the temerity to speak them were not infrequently the targets of mob violence, something Underhill had good reason to fear and the reason he authored a condemnation of the mob violence against Fanny Wright in the first issue of his paper.[57]

As Cleveland's enterprising master builders began to view their journeymen and apprentices less as equals and more as drones for the surplus value (profits) they produced, the craftsmen of Cleveland and Ohio City (just across the Cuyahoga River) responded in kind. They secured a space of their own, "Mechanics' Hall in Mr. Clark's brick block in the Flat," where mechanics of all trades met. Carpenters and joiners in both cities were feeling the "squeeze" of the new market forces, and they resolved to put master builders on notice that they had formed themselves into a society and were limiting their work day to a more humane ten hours so that "those who have families to provide for can thus have time to attend to their domestic affairs." "Mechanics generally in Cleveland and Ohio City" were invited to attend.[58] The next year they formed a Mechanic's ticket to run a slate of candidates for three city wards, mayor, treasurer, and marshal and were successful in electing John Barr, described in a local newspaper as "one of the regular candidates of the Locofocos."[59] In 1837, Cleveland's carpenters and joiners were meeting to demand a raise in their wages from $1.50 to $1.75/day and to consider "a strike or a stand out, in order to obtain a reasonable compensation for their labor." The craftsmen objected to the "Master Builders, who in their preamble say – 'that the only proper regulator of prices is the demand for labor.'"[60] As testament to the political traction class interests had in this period, even the Cuyahoga County Whigs found it opportune to describe their convention delegates as "the real Democracy – the farmers, mechanics, and workingmen the county."[61] This flew in the face of the Ohio Whig party's uncompromising support for "Czar" Biddle's Bank of the U.S.

The conflict between labour and capital being played out in the rapidly advancing cities of Ohio (and the nation more generally) was countered by the overwhelming bias for land, which even Ohio's first Whig governor, Joseph Vance, praised in his 1837 Thanksgiving message, the opening line of which read: "The fruits of the earth are matured, and abundant. The husbandman is now reaping the bounties of kind Providence as the reward of his toil."[62] So, it is not surprising that Underhill, undoubtedly influenced by Paine's treatise on *Agrarian Justice*, believed land, as the natural and common inheritance of all men, was also the antidote to the socio-economic ills of the corrupt banking system. Just as Mackenzie's draft constitution had advocated land in the public interest and denied it to speculators, Underhill wrote of unequal land distribution as being the nexus of the problem: "The monopoly of land is perhaps at the bottom of this system of corruption. No monopoly is more odious, because none are more unjust, and its injustice is so very palpable."[63] From this perspective, America's economy should forever rest on the shoulders of the useful mechanic and yeoman whom he extolled as "*natures* [*sic*] nobleman."[64] A wide and *equal* distribution of land then was the "fire wall" that would keep the political economy out of the hands of the growing "monied aristocracy" and "rag speculators" and safely under the control of the masses of yeomen and mechanics who would mutually interact to make it bear fruit. Underhill endorsed a position so far to the left that it stopped just short of the expropriatory prescription of Thomas Skidmore by embracing plans of land distribution à la Robert Owen and George Henry Evans, who thought Skidmore unrealistic.[65]

To eliminate the vulgarities of inequality created by the banking monopolists and capital credit system, Underhill urged that "No man should have been allowed to own more than one-hundred and sixty acres in the United States. It is enough for one man and his sons to work, and if he has been prudent he will be able to aid his sons as they grow up.[66] "A country life," he opined, "appears to be as favorable to the moral healthiness of a man, as to his physical well-being."[67] Underhill sought, as did Mackenzie, the Jeffersonian ideal of the industrious and honest life on the land. Ohio provided that opportunity, particularly since several liberal state Land Acts (1800, 1804, and 1820) had favoured families of lesser means seeking smaller farms.[68] In support of pre-emption laws, Underhill also dismissed the concern that they might advance speculation by noting that: "you only need to contrast the surveyed districts monopolized by the rich purchaser with the unsurveyed portions settled as claims, and you will be satisfied that a very democratic spirit has apportioned the claims."[69] In the northern borderlands, then so attractive and inundated with land seekers as Ohio was in the mid- to late 1830s, it is, perhaps, more understandable that not a few Americans might have found the Rebellion a serendipitous occasion to take some Canadian land while ridding the continent of imperial British rule.

If antipathy to banks and support of yeomen/working class interests were the first two cardinal tenets of the Locofoco and American patriots, then the third was that of state autonomy. State control was seen as an additional layer of protection for the industrious yeoman-farmers and village mechanics against a growing class of swashbuckling capitalist marketeers who, Underhill charged, "bow at the crowded shrine of gammon," and produce nothing.[70] As historian

Jason Opal has observed in Kentucky and Tennessee, the economic dislocations of 1819–22 produced "political movements that sought more economic security for more citizens" and "a deeper critique of the *laissez faire* rule of law" to "secure the independence of state residents."[71] The root of this same impulse in Ohio went back, at least, to the state's 1819 seizure of state-imposed taxes from two branches of The Bank of the United States (at Chillicothe and Cincinnati) and a prior Ohio House resolution on 19 January 1818 that defended Ohio's right to tax the Bank of the United States: "The states that compose the American union are independent *sovereign states*," and "the law incorporating this bank [Bank of the United States] … attempts not to confer upon the stock of the company any exemption from taxation, either by the *state or by the United States*."[72] Three years later, on 29 January 1821, the Ohio House threw down the gauntlet by reaffirming the doctrines of the 1798 Kentucky and Virginia Resolutions, which upheld the right of state interposition. In a companion act of defiance, the state legislature enacted a law to "withdraw from The Bank of the United States the protection and aid of the laws of this state, in certain cases."[73] Underhill was equally unambiguous in his state bias: "Let all the gains of banking go to the state, and let this go from the state for rational education … Let the several states confirm their professions of democracy by exerting themselves to establish the principles of *equality*."[74] Notwithstanding the U.S. Supreme Court's ruling against Ohio's tax seizure, so many Ohioans viewed the Bank of the United States as a "foreign corporation over which they had no control" that by 1830 the number of chartered banks in the state had dwindled to eleven.[75]

In the aforementioned "Prospectus" statement of the *Liberalist*, with its capitalization of the word "State," is embedded a preference for local control as well: the logical and ultimate distillation of the desire for a corrective on a federal centre in the clutches of a burgeoning "rag"-happy capitalist class.[76] While praising the American House in Cleveland as a fine hotel, Underhill noted that it would have been most desirable had the proprietors "hired Cleveland mechanics to make its furniture" and later reasoned that as the "honest and industrious [mechanics] render prosperity more certain, uniform and unvarying" towns and villages should "afford [them] ample support."[77] Even then-governor Ethan A. Brown averred that "there appears no evidence why those branches [Bank of the United States branches at Cincinnati and Chillicothe] should be exempt.

Their exemption would be a partiality unjust to the local banks."[78] The Locofocoite sentiment to keep all things state-centred was perceived by their Whig opponents as the unadulterated doctrine of Southern Nullification, or the states' right to reject federal laws. A Whiggish Cleveland daily caustically observed, "thus extremes meet. – Nullification and Loco Focoism have a strong affinity, both seek a destruction of the union. – Hence, they readily coalesce."[79]

In an insightful prosopographic study of the Patriot Rebellion, anthropologist Albert Schrauwers has conclusively demonstrated the intersection of the localist impulse with the politics of the Patriot Rebellion in the U.S.: "The Locofocos' political program sought to protect this alternative 'associational economy' predicated on the multiply intertwined networks of mutual debt and credit that fostered trust and built a 'harmony of interests' organized in joint-stock corporate communities."[80] In other words, the type of "honest Republican economy" Palmyra Democrats in Portage County, Ohio, also sought when they demanded that their county Commissioner "procure an equal distribution of this county's share of Surplus Revenue equally among the several Townships." Their address proclaimed: "Republics are founded on virtue," and the "remedy to the existing [banking] evils ... can alone be found in the correcting arm of a Free and Virtuous People."[81] Underhill could not have agreed more. "Support Your Mechanics," he rejoined, "there is scarcely any thing [*sic*] which tends more to the improvement of a town, than a fair support afforded to mechanics of every description ... prosperity of our villages should induce us to afford a reasonable support to our mechanices [*sic*] ... A little experience will have convinced many that it is in most cases, their interest to do so, independent of many considerations."[82]

Those such as Underhill were hardly outliers in their disdain for what a witticism of the times dubbed the "rag hampers of federalism."[83] From the highest office in the land, the ethos of state and local autonomy was given imprimatur. President Van Buren is mostly remembered for his Independent Treasury plan, which is regularly mourned by many historians and economists as a disastrous measure in the "Bank War." Divorced from ground-level developments, however, it becomes a caricature and purposeful misrepresentation of the firm desire by "anti-bank." Locofocoite forces (of which Van Buren was widely recognized the titular head) to re-locate economic and political control away from an aggrandizing federal centre, thus rescuing local and state economies from the depredations and "embarrassments" of the Bank of the United States so bitingly portrayed in Clay's cartoon "The Times." Van Buren's first two annual messages to Congress are instructive in understanding the breadth and depth of this objective and the bias for state (and local) control. In 1837, the president praised the nation which had "gradually risen from a feeble few and dependent colonies to a prosperous and powerful confederacy" and seamlessly blended his position on banks with his understanding of the relationship between the "General Government" and its *confederate* states. Their creation, privileges, responsibilities, and restrictions "belong to the *States* to decide. Upon their rights or the exercise of them the General Government can have no motive to encroach."[84]

In his 1838 message, the president again referred to the nation as a "Confederation" that had achieved "unrivaled prosperity" through internal improvements "fostered by the protection of the States." The Bank of the United States, Van Buren instructed, had been a "concentrated money power … tempted to become an active agent in political affairs" that had unnaturally gained control of state revenues, "threw the country into convulsions of panic," and prevented government from pursuing "a diffusion and equalization of its benefits" to the community at large. The Constitution, the president observed, was a framework devised by the Founding Fathers for "promoting individual happiness and private interests" and "banks have but to continue in the same course and be content in their appropriate sphere to avoid all interference from the General Government and to derive from it all the protection and benefits which it bestows on other State establishments, on the people of the States, and on the States themselves."[85]

## DR UNDERHILL: THE PATRIOT LEADER

These political views of Underhill were shared by a broad swath of Americans and Canadians and are the political prism through which the Rebellion is best understood. In the wake of the *Caroline* Affair and outbreak of Mackenzie's rebellion, tension between the ideologies of federalism and local/state autonomy became a question of immediacy, particularly in the states hugging the Great Lakes. Underhill was ready to pounce on the imperial insult to American pride and the republican values it had assaulted. He skilfully used the incident as political kindling to move from propaganda to the agitation. In one of his first expressions of support for retaliation and establishment of a Canadian Republic, he lashed out with an unmistakable thrust of local autonomy: "The mad movements of the Canadian Government will throw a tremendous army in upon them from the states despite of [*sic*] every effort of our Government to prevent it ... We should not wonder if ten thousand men from the States ran over to see what is going on, and perhaps to lend a hand to the Patriots ... Do they not know the that the ties of consanguinity unite many on this side with Patriots on that side? ... Blood is up, hot blood too, and woe betide those who would repress the spirit of freedom. S.U."[86]

Underhill continued a relentless public agitation in support of the patriot cause in an excited description of the Lyceum Association debate he had helped organize as "protracted through three weekly sessions, attended by crowds of spectators, all taking a deep and stirring interest in the question." Even accounting for hyperbole by half, it presents a picture of popular American enthusiasm for the uprising. The Lyceum question of the hour on which both he and Dr A.D. Smith spoke in the affirmative was: "Are the Citizens of the U.S. justified in furnishing arms, ammunition, money, and provisions to, and expressing their sympathies in public meetings for, the Patriots of Canada?" It was resolved, Underhill informed his readers, overwhelmingly in the affirmative with only eight in the negative.[87]

As an active member of the Cleveland Lyceum Association, he assisted in the formation of a Committee of 21 and the passage of a long resolution that expressed the support of "American freemen ... in every extremity, [to] make their cause our own."[88] A narrow majority of conservative Whigs in the committee attempted to tamp down the efforts by making much of the risk of prosecution for violating the new neutrality agreement between the U.S. and Britain. This presented a serious strategic difference between those seeking to limit the raising of armed militias to purely defensive operations and that of a militant vanguard, including Underhill, that manoeuvred to assist the Canadian Rebellions in every possible way. Conservatives held sway at one point and, according to Underhill, "advertised for one hundred able bodied men to go after the Emigrants, to see that they be not enticed to Canada. We think the hundred would go over too."[89] In an effort to grow the body of "emigrants," he informed those Cleveland mechanics and yeomen who wished to exchange their hammers and ploughs for a flintlock, dirk, or pike that "a large company are to leave tomorrow in a schooner for Navy Island."[90]

A year later, as a part of the same Committee of 21, Underhill helped draft seven resolutions for a memorial to Congress arguing that the Neutrality Law (proclaimed by Van Buren and passed by Congress in March 1838 to squelch American patriot activities) "strikes at the very root of American Liberty, by an indirect declaration of martial Law, in time of peace – subjecting our citizens to seizures and arrests, contrary to the constitution" because it violated the 4th and 5th amendments. The fifth resolution "resolved, that the right of citizens to expatriate themselves, and become citizens of another country, is inherent and unalienable, has always been contended for, by our Government – was one of the principle causes of the late war with Great Britain, and was at length conceded by that Government, at the treaty of Ghent."[91] Historian Eric Schlereth has cogently explained this "emigrant" mindset: "U.S. citizens who joined the Texas and Canadian rebellions ... embraced a notion of 'insurgents' rights' based on their understanding of expatriation as a recognized principle of national and international law."[92] Ever the "insurgent" printer, Underhill offered his own resolve to the memorial praising patriot militias for "attempting to introduce principles of equal rights and self-government" into Canada.[93] In this light, the Americans in the patriot army may be seen as so many Davy Crocketts who, instead of Texas, saw Canada as their rightful place to squat on land unlawfully held by the British monarchy and its aggrandizing royal appointees. In so doing, they contemptuously thumbed their noses at U.S. diplomatic desire to maintain peaceful relations with Britain.[94]

Interestingly, for most of 1838, his *Liberalist* seems to have been on hiatus with regard to Canadian affairs. His coverage included, however, some agitational, "play-by-play" news reports, mostly reprinted from regional newspapers, on both Upper and Lower Canadian conflicts, with upbeat commentary. From Rochester, Buffalo, and Detroit papers came eyewitness accounts of Mackenzie and General Van Rensselaer on Navy Island, Duncombe's capabilities near Malden and Hog Island, the battles at St Eustache and St Benoit, British troop movements, and the assurance that "The knell of tyranny in Upper Canada has been sounded, and the pæan of Liberty will soon ring over the land and through their valleys."[95] An inconspicuous four-line ad for Mackenzie's newspaper, which

Underhill described as "full of interesting details about the Canadas and the late attempted revolution," did run in May.[96] Any doubt though as to the depth of Underhill's passion, and for that matter much of Cleveland's populace, in arming American patriots is put to rest by the brazen ad he ran in two January issues by gunsmith compatriot (and radical Whig) L.W. Babbitt.

Below this ad were several others by Babbitt offering for sale a variety of weaponry, supplies, and accoutrements: percussion powder, shot belts, pocket pistols, rifle powder, brass, and snare drums.[97] The last line of the above advertisement is instructive, again, for the implication of "insurgents' rights," by its reference to "emigrants." It, too, underscores that Cleveland's conservatives were "on their heels" having lost out to those American patriots, who believed both a constitutional and natural right to assist Mackenzie in the overthrow of British Crown tyranny and the establishment an Upper Canadian egalitarian republic.

By late October of 1838, financial losses had finally put Underhill's efforts underwater, and, despite their significant personal sacrifices, they were forced to stop the *Liberalist*. How he was able, late the next month, to come blasting back onto the Cleveland scene with the publication of the *Bald Eagle* is not explained, but he likely had a benefactor. The masthead of the *Bald Eagle* displayed the spread-winged national symbol with the declaration of "liberty and equality" immediately beneath it that patriots had also flown on Navy Island.[98] In the upper left-hand corner of the paper, Underhill fleshed out the paper's mission statement: "The *Bald Eagle* is intended to support the PATRIOT CAUSE – GIVE THE EARLIEST Canada News – go against the Neutrality Bill, – and TO EXPOSE TORYISM wherever found. In short it is to be a Republican Paper. Published every Tuesday and Friday morning. Office – Hancock Block, Sign of the *Patriot Flag*, – corner of Superior and Seneca Sts."[99] This statement, along with the masthead motto, neatly distilled a Locofoco outlook that Albert Schrauwers has noted as being "associated with the emergence of Painite-civic republicanism and labour politics of the early republic and hav[ing] parallels in similar movements behind the Upper Canadian Rebellion."[100] The statement of purpose offered explicit support for the arming of patriot militias, the right of insurgent citizens to determine their own national borders in purposeful violation of the recently strengthened Neutrality Law, and, by his flying of the patriot flag, support for Mackenzie's Locofocoite-inspired limitations on chartered banking in his draft constitution for the new Upper Canadian Republic.[101]

The paper expressed unequivocal and undistinguished support for the leadership of both the Upper and Lower Canadian Rebellions and contained pieces introduced as "from *Mackenzie's Gazette*," along with related news and views of the struggle that urged American involvement. It carried no other news items of the day as the *Liberalist* had, providing space only on the last page of every issue for a dozen or so advertisements by Cleveland businesses. Maintaining his "workeyist" tendency, he also assured his patrons that the paper would "exert its energies especially to sustain and vindicate" the rights of "Mechanics and Workingmen."[102]

Underhill became a leading member of the Hunters' Lodge and was present at its convention in Cleveland in late September 1838 to organize American patriot militias and elect a provisional government for the intended new republic.[103] His *Bald Eagle* effectively functioned as an organizing tool and continued preparation for the one-year anniversary of the burning of the *Caroline* by labelling the British attack "BUTCHERY of American Citizens" and assisted in assembling a public meeting: "Let us have a County Meeting. Pass resolutions expressive of the sentiments of the People of Cuyahoga county, in relation to this outrageous transaction … Meetings will be held throughout the state of New York. Shall the People of Cuyahoga be backward? Let every Town in the County be well represented."[104] Showing just how willing the editors were to sacrifice financial solvency for politics, one issue replaced all ads with a full-page article on the "Battle at Windsor" written for the *Bald Eagle,* and another reduced the ads to four to make room for two poems, one against the divine right of kings and the other urging readers to fight for liberty in Canada.[105] To assist the movements of Patriot Army militias by the recently established military command, Underhill printed what *appears* to be Hunter code in, at least, three issues of the *Bald Eagle*: Wo,uv;tuŒ?hHn?fi;u,t;Ot;s!;uv;fv?Æ,ev,uU?!æœ,i;pvu[-].[106] To bolster militia numbers, readers were incited to arms in bold oversized type: "MARTYRS TO LIBERTY!! in Canada! Samuel Lount, Captain Matthews, Colonel Moreau, Colonel Von Shoultz, Dorephus Abbey, Daniel George, Colonel Woodruff, Sylvanus Sweet and Joel Peeler. 'Revenge or Death,' for the murder of these Brave Heroes, is the Motto of every PATRIOT."[107] Lengthy model resolutions in support of the patriot cause were reprinted from Garrettsville in Portage

County, Ohio, and one by the Buffalo Ladies' Benevolent Society after which he urged: "to the Ladies of Cleveland, we would say … 'Go thou and do likewise.'"[108] White-hot sentiment such as this was so rife in the northern borderlands that it caused Secretary of War Joel R. Poinsett to lament that he did not have "sufficient number of regular troops" to effectively guard the frontier.[109]

Undergirding these public appeals were political principles that went much deeper than the macro-critique of British Crown oppression of Canada and the desire to replace it with a democratic republic.[110] The *Bald Eagle* persisted in its vocal opposition to Van Buren's strengthened neutrality law with what historian Thomas Richards Jr argues were widely held legal arguments that employed the U.S. Constitution in defence of their military activity in Upper Canada.[111] This constitutional defence, already presented by the *Liberalist*, was carried forward in the *Bald Eagle* with the reprint of an excerpt from a "spirited speech" by E.J. Roberts, adjutant general in the Western Division of the Patriot Army, who with clenched teeth rhetorically queried: "Is treason to the United States suspected, that the Constitution should be suspended? Are we not allowed to bear arms? Is trade and commerce interdicted? … This is wrong, and the question may as well be tried now as any at [*sic*] other time, whether the sovreignty [*sic*] of the U.S. is of such a Constitutional character, as to clothe its agents with power to resist the legitimate and reserved jurisdiction of a sovereign [*sic*] state."[112]

More than half a century later, Enlightenment notions of equality and the natural rights of citizens were again being carried at the business end of a gun aimed at the British imperial lion. Remarks by Mr White – who, before setting out for Canada, asserted that patriots were "neutrals" who had every right to "sell arms and munitions of war to a belligerent" – are instructive in this regard. For that, Underhill offered him Cleveland's "unfeigned thanks." White also did not let slip the chance to pointedly make the analogy to Texas (without any hint of "Manifest Destiny") by noting Van Buren's duplicity "when our citizens were endeavoring to wrench from Mexico, the best and fairest portion of her territory."[113] White's rationale was nothing less than the reified descendant of Samuel Adams's assertion to the Committees of Correspondence in a Boston town meeting that "All men have a right to remain in a state of nature as long as they please; and … to leave the society they belong to, and enter into another. The natural liberty of man is to be free from any superior power on earth, and not to be under the will or legislative authority of man, but only to have the law of nature for his rule."[114] This philosophical and legal rationale cut to the core of the "separation of powers" principle.

The patriot view appropriated to the states (as if still in Confederacy), localities, and even to individuals, the otherwise generally understood right of the judicial branch to interpret the Constitution. Resolutions passed at a large and very public patriot meeting in Detroit and carried in the *Bald Eagle* stated the principle in stark terms: "resolved, that our army officers cannot and will not be recognized as clothed with state or municipal authority. They are not sheriffs or constables, but soldiers. Resolved, that the act of ordering soldiers to fire at American citizens, by a United States Officer of the Army is a dangerous outrage upon the liberties of the people; and that, if loss of life had ensued, such officer would be guilty of murder."[115] Deconstructed, the above remarks by E.J. Roberts further revealed the popularly held, threefold imperatives that placed the rights of citizens as superior to those of the General Government to: interpret the Constitution for themselves in defiance of any of the three branches of government; take hostile, even deadly, action against federal soldiers in defence of locally asserted rights; and clothe all such actions with a veil of "sovereign state" legality. Patriot Army general Donald McLeod insinuated this same view in a communiqué to manage militia movements and raise arms when he wrote of his expectation that the (U.S.) National Government would "as in the cause of Texas, leave us alone to manage our own affairs without its interpositions."[116] The national government was a "monstrous" obstruction to the virtuous republican pursuit of equality and happiness.

In the assertion of the right of American citizens to violently resist federal forces, patriot Colonel George Washington Case and soldier John H. Harmon engaged in court-like proceedings by swearing out affidavits stating they had been fired upon by "American Regulars" from the steamboat *Erie* near Hog Island, laying a basis for the *Bald Eagle* to fume: "Why was not the fire returned? Why did American citizens stand and be fired at by U.S. soldiers? Had they no powder and ball? Let General Brady come to Buffalo, and he shall have Shot for Shot, and More! These officers of the General Government, if they do not know their duty, must be taught it."[117] Mackenzie goaded the American patriots: "all the Wools and Bradys and Worths on this continent will prove a feeble barrier to the desire for vengeance which is deeply implanted in the American bosom."[118] This view, however, would have been beyond the pale for most Americans. Even those that supported the expatriation principle, which represented a significant section of the American press, upheld Van Buren's Neutrality Law.[119] Nevertheless, the vast majority of Americans were willing to give patriot militias a wink and a nod, as suggested by the almost non-existent reports of clashes between the patriot militia and U.S. soldiers.

To justify "the right of citizens to expatriate themselves, and become citizens of another country" and, if in so doing, fight U.S. government soldiers, Underhill and patriot leaders often drew analogies to the great dethroning of monarchs throughout history. Underhill snarled at what he called Van Buren's "lick spit Proclamation" and provided Mackenzie a full front page to condemn President Van Buren's mobilization of the U.S. Army against patriot militias as a "shame and a disgrace" worthy of King George III.[120] By thinly veiled inference then, Van Buren's actions to halt American patriot rebels were imperial overreach and citizens in turn had a natural right to violate it. Accordingly, Mackenzie opened his treatise with a comparison of American patriot assistance to that of the Dutch enlisted by English reformers during the Glorious Revolution of 1688, French aid to the American revolutionists of '76, the pleadings of Polish independence fighters "surrounded by the despotisms of Austria, Russia, and Prussia," and, of course, the Irish plight. He asserted: "If it was right in Holland to aid England, and for France to aid the Union, it cannot be morally wrong for a people owing a long debt of gratitude to the gallant sons of France to pay it with interest to the tortured countrymen of their generous and spirited benefactors."[121] "Away with the twaddle about banks and currency, and trade and traffic!" Mackenzie exhorted. Canadians, he offered, were appealing to American freemen just as the martyred Irish nationalist Robert Emmett had appealed to George Washington.[122] The theme was extended by Underhill in a front-page poem: "Of Equal Rights and Equal Laws! / Wake up!! ye who have drawn the sword / The scabbard fling, and pledge your word / ... From Lands where Freedom is distressed / From Erin, Scotin, England, France / And with the Sons of Seventy-six / In shouting jubilee shall mix."[123] This would be one of the last few times Underhill would speak to the public via the *Bald Eagle*.

The Whig press had often impugned radical Democrats as a "mobocracy." In the very first issue of the *Cleveland Liberalist*, Underhill expressed his concern about politically directed violence by turning the tables on the Whigs: "All the mobocracy are not modern infidels. We ask who mobbed Frances Wright Darusmont, in Philadelphia? – not her own party surely."[124] He was savvy enough to know that his *Bald Eagle* might be the target of such political violence as he was not one to give quarter when it came to his political fire, even to the point of naming names. Hence, he was quite lucky not to have been physically attacked on that Saturday, 28 January 1839 when, under cover of night, one of his aggrieved political targets, A.H. Curtis, and a small number of friends, broke into his print shop and destroyed his press with a hammer.[125] Underhill would not be able to replace his destroyed press, thus bringing to a violent close his premiere effort at agitational, print propaganda in the cause of a radical Jacksonian Upper Canadian Republic.

## CONCLUSION

It might be tempting to dismiss Underhill's efforts (and those of his patriot confreres) to sustain and advance the Canadian Patriot Rebellion as simply being a geographically other-directed attempt by a radical Jacksonian to advance a white-yeoman's republic northward. But such a view would be unfair. It would also evidence a blind spot no smaller than Underhill's (better described as "mixed-consciousness") about the centuries of depredations suffered by Indigenous and black people (except for his muted though principled abolitionism). In his support of the Patriot Rebellion, through the pages of the *Bald Eagle* and the *Cleveland Liberalist*, Underhill should long ago have earned a place within the pantheon of his better-known comrades and exponents of the era who sought to defend and extend republican values of equality, liberty, and happiness in the face of what they saw as an American republic being hijacked by a self-serving juggernaut of the privileged few seeking to "rig the democracy" against the many. Much more than that, he distinguished himself by having the foresight and principle, as few others did in that time, to connect the fight for workers' and women's rights to the larger all-encompassing struggle against the Bank of the United States. This he coupled with an unflinching optimism necessary to envision its fulfillment by the establishment of an Upper Canadian Republic.

My first article on the Patriot Rebellion presented the hypothesis that rebellion, on both sides of the border, was essentially Locofoco in its objectives and concluded by proposing that the broad brush-strokes laid out therein required more investigation to put that reinterpretation on more solid ground. It cautioned that an analysis of a mass movement such as this rebellion "requires a finer calculus than the political profile of a single leader (e.g. Mackenzie) allows."[126] Proposed were numerous questions that needed to be pursued, among them the extent to which other known American patriot leaders were also motivated by "the broader radicalism that dominated the age" – that panoply of radical Democratic expressions of times: Free Enquiry, Painite-civic republicanism, Locofocoism, and Workeyism.[127] This investigation of Dr Samuel Underhill, yet one more person in the patriot vanguard, has yielded fresh and abundant fruit that conclusively answers the question in the affirmative.

It may fairly be stated that the patriot Locofoco "anti-bank" movement did not fully appreciate the magnetic attractions of the new money-mediated commodity market system: the variety of goods it offered, the labour-saving machinery, the creative energies it tapped into, and the seemingly boundless opportunities for profit and social advancement. Having granted this, it must also be recognized that Dr Underhill and others of his camp (including many women such as Fanny Wright) correctly understood the inherent social and economic inequalities of that new more impersonal commodity-based market economy. They were the "fire-bell" in the night sounding the alarm, the moral compass of the nation, standing against a nascent capitalism that demanded amplification of social and economic inequality and market-created scarcity. They understood this to be a threat to the original intent of the founding documents of the nation and the inherent natural right of every man and woman to preserve an approximate equality of social status and economic condition. This required the appropriation of the value of their own labour, which capitalist money-mediated and banking practices denied, for only then would happiness be achieved. If happiness was not achieved, then by definition liberty was not. And for their part, the true believers of capital creation and commodity manufacture, who sought to replace the quest for happiness and equality with the quest for wealth accumulation and socio-economic inequality, may take ownership of all the attendant social and economic pathologies of that same system.

Finally, historian Eugene Link, in his fascinating look at the social ideas of American physicians, posits that Underhill's "lasting contribution" to history is his defence of Thomas Paine.[128] This chapter, however, suggests that Underhill's signal contribution for the ages was the leadership he took in advancing a penetrating Locofoco, radical republican critique of the encroaching capitalist banking system, which the Patriot Rebellion placed front and centre in its cause. Seen through Underhill's eyes, the American patriot movement and the Canadian Republic for which it stood were a seamless deep-layered event and take on a vastly richer and more complex profile than previous historiography has admitted.[129] The historiography of the last twenty years conclusively cements Patriot Rebellion motivations within the larger context of the cross-border radical agrarian, anti-bank Locofoco convulsions of the times.

## NOTES

1 "Prospectus of the *Cleveland Liberalist*," 24 September 1836, published by Dr Samuel Underhill.

2 For a fuller consideration of Mackenzie's political persuasions see Anthony W. Rasporich, *William Lyon Mackenzie* (Toronto: Holt, Rinehart and Winston of Canada, 1972), 4, 10, 60, 66–8 and Andrew Bonthius, "The Patriot War of 1837–1838: Locofocoism with a Gun?" *Labour/Le Travail* 52 (Fall 2003): 9–43.

3 For comparisons between the American Revolution and the Patriot Rebellion see: Edwin Guillet, *The Lives and Times of the Patriots: An Account of the Rebellion in Upper Canada, 1837–1838* (Toronto 1968), 71–2; *The Huron Commercial Advertiser*, 26 December 1837; *Cleveland Herald and Gazette*, 1 July 1837; *Ashtabula Sentinel*, 30 December 1837. The *New York Express* warning was also carried in *The Huron Commercial Advertiser*, 19 December 1837; Oscar Kinchen, *The Rise and Fall of the Patriot Hunters* (New York 1956), 13–14, 17, 20–1.

4 *Jeffersonian*, 19 September 1839; Thomas Richards Jr, "The Lure of a Canadian Republic," this volume.

5 Maxime Dagenais, '"[T]Hose Who Had Money Were Opposed to Us, and Those Who Were Our Friends Were Not The Moneyed Class.' Philadelphia and the 1837–1838 Canadian Rebellions," *American Review of Canadian Studies* 48, no. 1 (Spring 2017): 1–18; Julien Mauduit, "'Vrais républicains' d'Amérique: les patriotes canadiens en

exile aux États-Unis (1837–1842)" (PhD diss., Université de Québec à Montréal, 2016).

6 The disappearance of Dr Underhill's role from the history books tracks with the disappearance of his Hunter compatriots, such as Dr A.D. Smith, whose role historian Ruth Dunley chronicles in her revealing study: "A.D. Smith: The First – and Only President of Canada," 2017. Historians such as Gertrude Van Renssaeler Wickham, in her *The Pioneer Families of Cleveland*, 1796–1840, vol. II. (Cleveland: Evangelical Publishing House, 1914), 534, have contributed to this disappearance of Underhill's (and the Locofoco and Patriot Rebellion more generally) critical role by dismissing him in a mere sentence or two as having "queer doctrines" that "We may be sure [were] looked upon with horror, and tabooed in many a household."

7 Albert Schrauwers, "Tilting at Windmills: The Utopian Socialist Roots of the Patriot War, 1838–1839," *Labour/Le Travail* 79 (Spring 2017): 4, 10–12, wherein Underhill is associated with Painite civic-republicanism, broadly defined as a "secular republican culture" advocating the liberal principles of free thinking, Locofoco anti-bankism, and working-class interests that encouraged vigorous debate and civic engagement. See n37 for a fuller definition of Locofocoism.

8 "Reminiscences of Youth," *Cleveland Liberalist*, 19 November 1836.

9 Josephine C. Frost, ed., *Underhill Genealogy, Descendants of Capt. John Underhill*, vol. II (Brooklyn, New York: privately published by Myron C. Taylor in the interests of The Underhill Society of America, 1932), 324. Photocopy of original letter from Dr Samuel Underhill to Robert Owen, 4 May 1828, Rotch Wales Papers, Massillon Public Library, folder H-22. Robert Owen was a Scottish businessman and philanthropist who tried to build a better industrial society. He notably experimented with his theories in communities at New Lanark, Scotland, and New Harmony, Indiana. For more information on Owen, see Gregory Claeys, *Citizens and Saints: Politics and Anti-Politics in Early British Socialism* (Cambridge: Cambridge University Press, 1989).

10 "Reminiscences of Youth," and "Free Discussion," *Cleveland Liberalist*, 1 October 1836, wherein Underhill relates this anecdote of his days as a blacksmith.

11 The best source of Underhill's prodigious free-thinking, intellectual abilities on an impressive variety of subjects are the issues of the *Cleveland Liberalist* from 10 September 1837 to 27 October 1838 and seven issues of his *Bald Eagle* from 21 December 1838 to 15 January 1839, all of which are held by the Western Reserve Historical Society (WRHS) in Cleveland, Ohio.

12 Underhill to Owen.

13 Ibid.

14 Underhill to Owen; Albert Fried, ed. *Socialism in America: From the Shakers to the Third International, A Documentary History* (New York: Columbia University Press, 1992), 65–6.

15 Fried, *Socialism in America*, 65, emphasis added.

16 Underhill to Owen. "Profitably" here carries no capitalist sense of money profit-making, rather, it is used in the sense of activities of benefit to the larger community or commonwealth.

17 Eugene P. Link, *The Social Ideas of American Physicians, 1776–1976: Studies of the Humanitarian Tradition in Medicine* (Selinsgrove: Susquehanna University Press 1992), 85, 90. The other two categories of physician, each named for classical traditions of antiquity, were Laodiceans and Teresians.

18 "Forestville Community," *New-Harmony Gazette*, 7 November 1827. Case Western Reserve University (CWRU), *Free Enquirer*, series 1, vol. 2, 1826–27 (New York: Greenwood Reprint Corp., 1969). The foregoing was a letter to the N-HG signed by Samuel Underhill; *New-Harmony Gazette*, 13 February 1828 describes the Coxsackie community as being "under the superintendence of Mr Underhill."

19 Underhill to Owen letter wherein he indicates he was present at the "commencement of our society at Coxsackie." From Carol A. Kolmerten, *Women in Utopia: The Ideology of Gender in the American Owenite Communities* (New York: Syracuse University Press, 1998), 64; Arthur Eugene Bestor Jr, "Backwoods Utopias: The Sectarian and Owenite Phases of Communitarian Socialism in America, 1663–1829," *American Historical Association* (Philadelphia: University of Pennsylvania Press, 1950), 204, wherein he notes that the Forestville Community "were doubtless in communication with the Owenites in New York City."

20 Underhill to Owen; Richard J. Cherok, "No Harmony in Kendal: The Rise and Fall of an Owenite Community, 1825–1829," *Ohio History Journal*, 108, 199, 33. Carol A. Kolmerten, *Women in Utopia: The Ideology of Gender in the American Owenite Communities* (New York: Syracuse University Press, 1998), 65.

21 "Agents for Gazette," *New-Harmony Gazette*, 30 May 1827, wherein Underhill is listed for the first time as a New York agent at Coxsackie, Greene County; Cherok, "No Harmony," 32; "Forestville Community," *New-Harmony Gazette*, 7 November 1827 wherein Underhill is described as "one of the principal directors of the community."

22 "Death Recalls Local History," *Massillon Evening Independent*, 18 April 1910; "Kendal Community, Ohio," *New-Harmony Gazette*, 13 February 1828, wherein it states "The community here number about 200 members, including children – composed of 30 families." See n26, which shows Underhill's numbers at variance. The Kendal Community minutes do not record twenty new members between 12 January 1828 and 13 February 1828.

23 Cherok, "No Harmony," 33.

24 Underhill to Owen; Cherok, "No Harmony," 33–4; "Kendal Community, Ohio," *New-Harmony Gazette*, 13 February 1828.

25 "Social Communities," Kendal Community Clippings folder, Massillon Museum of Art (MMA). On 12 January 1828, Underhill writes that the community is composed of 180 members including children.

26 Underhill to Owen wherein he also indicated he had successfully procured one Mr Everitt, the editor of the *Gospel Advocate*, to join Kendal and edit its new paper.

27 *Ohio Repository*, 7 November 1828.

28 "Chronicles, Notes and Maxims of Dr Samuel Underhill," Kendal Community Clippings folder, (MMA), wherein Underhill sampled twenty-six Kendal members and identified: eight "sceptics" [*sic*], one "doubtful," two Baptists, three Methodists, three Universalists, one Quaker, five Presbyterians, two Unitarians, and one Campbellite.

29 "Chronicles, Notes and Maxims of Dr Samuel Underhill," Rotch Wales Papers, Massillon Public Library (MPL), folder H-22, #9. The letter to Warren is dated 7 May 1830. The *Free Enquirer* was a reference to the utopian socialist press begun by Robert Owen and Fanny Wright in 1828.

30 For an overview on Workingmen's and early labour movements, see Edward Pessen, *Most Uncommon Jacksonians: The Radical Leaders of the Early Labour Movement* (Albany, NY: SUNY Press, 1967).

31 "Chronicles, Notes and Maxims," MPL, folder H-22, #11. This folder includes his comments on the teachings of Hicksite (Quaker) minister Dr William Gibbons in which he wrote "Now you are still a spiritualist, but I have become a materialist," as well as his call to the Spring Hill public. Dr Gibbon's was one of the foremost outspoken critics of Robert Owen, Fanny Wright and Free Enquiry in general according to J. Smith Futhey and Gilbert Cope. *History of Chester County, Pennsylvania with Genealogical and Biographical Sketches* (Philadelphia: Louis H. Everts, 1881), 568.

32 "Chronicles, Notes and Maxims," MPL, folder H-22, #11.

33 Ibid., emphasis added.

34 Willoughby University No. 1," *Cleveland Liberalist*, 7 January 1837.

35 Cleveland became an incorporated city on 6 March 1836. In the entire ninety-three issues of the *Cleveland Liberalist* (10 September 1836 to 27 October 1838) held by the Western Reserve Historical Society, Underhill writes knowledgably of medicine regarding various concoctions being sold for their health benefits. He does write of being paid for his medical services while in the Kendal community and the Massillon area before moving to Cleveland in 1835.

36 "To the Friends of Free Enquiry," *Cleveland Liberalist*, 10 September 1836.

37 F. Byrdsall, *The History of the Loco-foco, or Equal Rights Party: Its Movements, Conventions and Proceedings* (New York: Clement & Packard, 1842), 27, wherein the Locofoco/Equal Rights Party platform resolves to be: for hard money currency, against monopolies, state banks, and the Bank of the United States, which are in opposition to a free state and the principles of commerce, and against "the odious distribution of wealth and power against merit and equal rights." See the *Cleveland Liberalist*, 21 January 1837 for the Kirtland bank charter, which was the type of (non-capitalist) banking endorsed by most radical "anti-bank" Democrats of Locofocoite tendencies such as Samuel Underhill. For the most part the radical "anti-bank" or bank reform forces did not embrace the term "Locofoco." In the ninety-three issues of *Cleveland Liberalist* I examined, I found only one use of this label in the 24 June 1837 issue and none in the seven issues of the *Bald Eagle*. Fanny Wright was a Scottish social reformist, free-thinker, and abolitionist who emigrated to the U.S. in the 1820s and travelled extensively in the U.S. speaking against banks and social privileges of the monied aristocracy.

38 "Hard Times – Money – Monopolies – No. 2," *Cleveland Liberalist*, 20 May 1837, emphasis added. Thomas Skidmore was the founder of New York City's Working Man's Party in 1829 and an advocate of land expropriation, which Underhill never endorsed.

39 The British military burned the American steamer *Caroline* on 29 December 1837 and let a burning hulk drift over the Niagara Falls because it had been supplying a largely American force of Patriots on Navy Island.

40 "Female Labor," *Cleveland Liberalist*, 26 November 1836; "Prospectus for the Huntress," *Cleveland Liberalist*, 4 February 1837. Consideration of women's issues and support of women taking an active role in the public

sphere such as Fanny Wright (D'Arusmont) is the reason Whig papers so often attempted to emasculate "anti-bank" and bank-reform Democrats as "petticoat slanderers" in "A Stumper," *Maumee City Express*, 6 October 1838, and often as "Fanny Wright men."

41 "Money, money, Hard times, hard times," *Cleveland Liberalist*, 13 May 1837. This series' title changed slightly more than once, for example, the 20 May 1837 no. 2 in the series was titled: "Hard Times – Money – Monopolies."

42 See Anthony W. Rasporich, *William Lyon Mackenzie* (Toronto: Holt, Rinehart and Winston of Canada, 1972), 10 and 66–8, for the draft constitution and sections 55 and 56, which placed the control of all banking in an elected legislature and outlawed private ownership of banks.

43 For Underhill's view on the Bank of the United States as offspring of the Bank of England see "Hard Times IV," *Cleveland Liberalist*, 9 September 1837.

44 Bruce Laurie, *Artisans into Workers: Labor in Nineteenth-Century America* (New York 1989), 66. Underhill often repeated his belief in the labor theory of value: "HARD TIMES – MONEY – USURY, no. VI," *Cleveland Liberalist*, 24 June 1837: "We repeat it, labor produce all wealth in the world; people should never forget this one moment in their reasonings upon political economy." And again in "The pressure – Hard times," *Cleveland Liberalist*, 6 May 1837: "Labor produces all wealth in the world except the soil, and this naturally, is equally the patrimony of all, whilst uncultivated." Mackenzie's draft constitution also stated: "Labor is the only means of creating wealth."

45 "Money, money, Hard times, hard times."

46 According to Kevin F. Kern and Gregory S. Wilson. *Ohio: A History of the Buckeye State* (West Sussex: John Wiley & Sons, Ltd, 2014), 165: since the bank Panic of 1819, "where people stood regarding The Bank of the United States became one of the most important defining issues of the Ohio politics in the 1820s and 1830s." Ohioans, they write, harbored an "immense resentment" toward the Bank of the United States, which was seen as having been the primary beneficiary of the financial distress and had become the largest landholder in the state through resulting land foreclosures. William A. Taylor and Aubrey O. Taylor, *Ohio Statesmen and Annals of Progress from the Year 1788 to the Year 1900*, vol. 1 (Columbus, OH: Press of the Westbqt [*sic*] Co., 1899), 150, 162, 169, 171, 174: the 32nd General Assembly (Dec. 1833–Mar. 1834) of the state passed two resolutions in support of President Jackson's Sub-Treasury system. The 34th Legislative Session (Dec. 1835–Mar.

1836), which was evenly divided between Whigs and Democrats, the former having a majority of two in the Senate and the latter having a majority of three in the House, passed "an act prohibiting the establishment within the state of any branch of The Bank of the United States." That same session also enacted requirements for all state banks to pay 20 per cent of their dividends into the State Treasury, unless they agreed not to circulate bills of denominations less than three dollars after the fourth of July 1836. These were two of the cardinal reforms of the "anti-bank" Locofoco movement. For the list of the twenty-eight very intrusive questions all state banks were to answer passed by the first session of the thirty-seventh Ohio General Assembly, see Samuel Medary, State Auditor, Journal of the Senate of Ohio, at the First Session of the Thirty-Seventh General Assembly (Columbus 1838). https://archive.org/details/journalofsenate01838ohio. This was the number and kind of questions capitalist bankers shrank from and to which neither the Bank of the United States nor any of its branches were subject.

47 Fried, *Socialism in America*, 66.

48 "THE BANK OF THE LAKE," *Cleveland Liberalist*, 1 October 1836.

49 "HARD TIMES – MONEY – USURY, no. VI."

50 Township Journal, 1838–1853, City of Cleveland, Cleveland City Archives, stamped 203, 8, 15–22. Jane C. Howland was only six weeks old when she was indentured out. In August 1838 forty-one entries were made, thirty-two of which were families, recording notices given to those "likely to become paupers" to leave the township.

51 "City Matters," *Daily Cleveland Herald*, 1 March 1837.

52 "A Great Public Meeting," *Cleveland Herald and Gazette*, 11 August 1837.

53 "Paine's Decline and Fall of the English System of Finance," *Cleveland Liberalist*, 26 August 1838; and "HARD TIMES – MONEY – USURY, no. XI," *Cleveland Liberalist*, 22 July 1837, wherein he ties the Bank of England to America "Scotch Banks," *Cleveland Liberalist*, 22 July 1837, wherein Underhill lauds the safety and community interests of the Scottish banking system.

54 "A Great Public Meeting." The public meeting was called specifically "to take into consideration the present condition of the country and the course pursued by the Banks. The article reports that the meeting adjourned "after several appropriate addresses were delivered by Messrs. Smith, St John, Underhill and Lloyd." Smith was undoubtedly Dr A.D. Smith, whose life and role in the Patriot movement is detailed by Ruth Dunley, "Dr A.D. Smith: The Vanishing Act of a Canadian President."

55 Their attendance at the Patriot meeting is recorded in the *Cleveland Daily Advertiser*, 3 January 1838. Exhibiting either a genuine "mixed-consciousness" or, perhaps rank opportunists, Denio and Babbitt vacillated between Workeyism and Whig politics. The *Cleveland Herald and Gazette*, 25 August 1837 lists both as being committee members at the Farmers', Mechanics', and Workingmen's convention. The same paper on 15 September 1837 records Denio as having helped author a resolution at a Whig meeting in Cleveland on 8 September 1837 and Babbitt as a delegate to a September 1837 Cuyahoga County Whig convention. Babbitt also held the Locofoco hard-money position as demonstrated by his speech for the negative side in a Cleveland Polemical Association debate in September 1837 on the question: as reported in the *Cleveland Liberalist*, 9 September 1837.

56 "For the Daily Herald and Gazette," *Cleveland Herald and Gazette*, 11 August 1837.

57 *Cleveland Liberalist*, 10 September 1836.

58 *Annals of Cleveland 1818–1935*, 18, part 1 (1835–1836 Works Progress Administration Ohio, District Four, Cleveland, Ohio), 23 March 1836 (abstract 481); *Herald*, 7 June 1836 (abstract 482).

59 "Charter Election," *Cleveland Daily Herald*, 2 March 1837; *Cleveland Liberalist*, 10 Feb. 1838; *Annals of Cleveland 1818–1935*, 21, part 1 (1838 Works Progress Administration Ohio, District Four, Cleveland, Ohio), *Herald and Gazette*, 29 September 1838 (abstract 1597.)

60 "Cleveland, April 8, 1837," *Cleveland Liberalist*, 15 April 1837.

61 "From Our Daily Edition of Saturday," *Cleveland Herald and Gazette*, 6 September 1838.

62 "Proclamation," *Maumee Express*, 9 December 1837. The U.S. tradition of celebrating Thanksgiving on the fourth Thursday in November was initiated by President Lincoln in 1863.

63 "HARD TIMES – MONEY – USURY, no. XI." His use of "perhaps" was, as the rest of the sentence makes very clear, no qualifier of any kind but rather a courteous pause in an otherwise categorical statement of principle. In "HARD TIMES – MONEY – USURY, no. VI." Underhill again cited mal-distribution of land as the major source of inequality and for the delay of "improvements" (implying infrastructure such as roads and bridges).

64 "HARD TIMES – MONEY – USURY, no. II," *Cleveland Liberalist*, 20 May 1837 (emphasis in original) and "But those specimens of bloated, purse proud, privileged, money made nobles … they are an unnatural excresence

[*sic*] on society." Underhill's affinity for the mechanic equally with the farmer is found in "Support Your Mechanics," *Cleveland Liberalist*, 19 Sept. 1838 in which he wrote: "There is scarely [*sic*] any thing [*sic*] which tends more to the improvement of a town, than a fair support afforded to mechanics of every description. Scarcely any place has arisen to much importance, even possessed with the most commercial advantages without a true regard to the encouragement of the mechanic arts ... Although trade and commerce in all their various branches, should be free and unshackled, a prosperity of our villages should induce us to afford a reasonable support our mechanices [*sic*]." This paeon of praise to the mechanic echoed the opening lines of Mackenzie's draft constitution which he addressed to "the farmers, mechanics, and laborers, and other inhabitants of Toronto," and declared that all state lands would be kept for the use of the people, safely in the possession of a Peoples' Republic for distribution to the "producing classes." Anthony W. Rasporich, *William Lyon Mackenzie* (Toronto: Holt, Rinehart and Winston of Canada, 1972), 4, 10, and 66–8.

65 George Henry Evans was an English émigré and a leading labour activist in New York City from the 1820s to the 1840s. He was notably inspired by Robert Owen's ideas. For more information, see Pessen, *Most Uncommon Jacksonians*.

66 "HARD TIMES – MONEY – USURY, no. XI"; "Dr Beecher Again," *Cleveland Liberalist*, 22 July 1837 – a short article by S.U. in defence of Fanny Wright and Robert Owen.

67 "The License System," *Cleveland Liberalist*, 26 November 1836.

68 Kern and Wilson, *Ohio: A History of the Buckeye State*, 128.

69 "The Political Party Newspaper," *Cleveland Liberalist*, 3 March 1838.

70 *Cleveland Liberalist*, 26 December 1836.

71 Jason Opal, "Patriots No More: The Political Economy of Anglo-American Rapprochement, 1818–1838," 2, 6–7. See also R. Douglas Hurt. *The Ohio Frontier: Crucible of the Old Northwest, 1720–1830* (Bloomington: Indiana University Press, 1996), 277, who confirms the popular Jeffersonian Republican ethic of state control even when Ohio was a territory.

72 *Ohio Archaeological and Historical Publications* (OAHP), vol. XXIV, no. 1, Columbus, Ohio, Published by Fred J. Heer, 1915, online version, 313–15, wherein Ohio's decision to tax the Bank of the United States had followed those of Maryland, Tennessee, North Carolina, and Georgia, emphasis added.

73 OAHP, 324–5.

74 "HARD TIMES – MONEY – USURY, no. VI," emphasis added.

75 OAHP, 326, 341, 348–9.

76 Andrew Bonthius, "The Patriot War of 1837–1838," 35–7, wherein is presented the "household economy as a protector of equality" and an appreciation of historian Michael Merrill's thesis that the locus of socio-economic conflict of the early nineteenth century reflected a tension between commodity production for profit and what he termed the "household mode of production."

77 "The American Hotel of Cleveland," *Cleveland Liberalist*, 9 September 1837. "Support Your Mechanics," *Cleveland Liberalist*, 16 September 1838. This latter article also argued that despite the market forces of innovation and competition that often siphoned off cash from local mechanics: "A Little experience will have convinced many that it is in most cases, their interest to do so, independent of many considerations."

78 OAHP, 316–17.

79 *Daily Herald and Gazette*, 2 November 1837. This daily was criticizing a Democratic newspaper, the *Advertiser*, for praising the speeches of Senator John C. Calhoun and likening him to the Roman Senator Cataline. Of course, this charge of Nullification had a double meaning as it was also meant to tar northern Democrats with support of slavery, which northern Whigs were increasingly opposing.

80 Albert Schrauwers, "Tilting at Windmills: The Utopian Socialist Roots of the Patriot War, 1838–1839," *Labour/Le Travail* 79 (Spring 2017): 27.

81 "Address to the Democratic Electors of Portage County," *Western Courier*, 21 September 1837.

82 "Support Your Mechanics," *Cleveland Liberalist*, 16 September 1838. This same preference for the localized economy was widely expressed as in: "Help One Another," *Jeffersonian*, 19 September 1839; *Cleveland Herald and Gazette*, 1 July 1837.

83 "Martin Van Buren," *Cleveland Liberalist*, 27 October 1838.

84 John Wolley and Gerhard Peters, "Martin Van Buren, First Annual Message, December 5, 1837," *The American Presidency Project*, emphasis added. http://www.presidency.ucsb.edu/ws/?pid=29479.

85 Wolley and Peters, "Martin Van Buren, Second Annual Message, 3 December 1838."

86 "Canada – Canada," *Cleveland Liberalist*, 6 January 1838. Unfortunately, the WRHS archive is missing issues of the *Cleveland Liberalist* between 16 September 1837 and 6 January 1838. Its collection ends with the 27 October 1838 issue.

87 "The Lyceum," *Cleveland Liberalist*, 3 February 1838. Joining Underhill and Smith in the affirmative were Mr Bishop, J.R. St John, and C.B.

Denio. St John seems to have been the quintessential political opportunist as he sought nomination on both the Democratic and Whig tickets in 1837, according to the *Herald and Gazette*, 3 October 1837. Denio was both a Mason and a Whig. Eighty volunteers from Cleveland arrived in Toledo on a steamboat with Col. Sutherland to await delivery of a stand of 500 arms from Perrysburg: "The Cry Is Still, They Come!" *Toledo Blade*, 10 January 1838.

88 "Great Meeting of the Friends of the Patriot Cause in Cleveland," *Cleveland Daily Advertiser*, 3 January 1838.

89 "The Canada War," *Cleveland Liberalist*, 6 January 1838.

90 Ibid.

91 "Public Meeting on the Anniversary of the Burning of the Caroline," *Bald Eagle*, 1 January 1839.

92 Eric R. Schlereth, "Insurgents' Rights: Choosing Allegiance in North America's Borderlands Rebellions" (unpublished manuscript, 2017), 1.

93 Public Meeting on the Anniversary of the Burning of the Caroline," *Bald Eagle*, 1 January 1839.

94 For the comparison of Texas and Canadian emigration and the analogy of Davey Crockett see also Thomas Richards Jr, "The Lure of a Canadian Republic: Americans, The Patriot War, and Upper Canada as Political and Economic Alternative, 1837–1840." Also see Jacqueline Jones, Peter H. Wood, Thomas Borstelmann, Elaine Tyler May, Vicki L. Ruiz. *Created Equal, vol. I to 1877* (New York: Pearson Education, Inc., 2009), 328–9, 335–7 for the bravado of the folksy woodsman and populist politician Davey Crockett who exemplified the widely held cultural and political bias of states' rights and antipathy toward "eastern-based institutions of wealth and privilege."

95 *Cleveland Liberalist*, 13 January 1838.

96 "Mackenzie's Gazette," *Cleveland Liberalist*, 26 May 1838.

97 L.W. Babbitt gun ad. *Cleveland Liberalist*, 13 January 1838 and 20 January 1838.

98 The earliest issues I was able to access begin with the 21 December 1838 issue and run through 15 January 1839.

99 *Bald Eagle*, 28 December 1838, all emphasis in original.

100 Schrauwers, "Tilting at Windmills," xx, 4; "Canada Meetings in New York," *Maumee City Express*, 2 February 1839 notes that "Alexander Ming, the Locofoco takes an active part in the meetings." Also see Bonthius, "The Patriot War of 1837–1838," 27, wherein is detailed a fuller explanation of Mackenzie's identification with Locofocoism.

101 For more information on Mackenzie's banking policies, see Albert Schrauwers, "'The Road Not Taken.' Duncombe on Republican Currency: Joint Stock Democracy, Civic Republicanism & Free Banking," 8 and Lillian F. Gates, "The Decided Policy of William Lyon Mackenzie," *Canadian Historical Review* 40, no. 5 (1959): 185–208.

102 "To Our Patrons," *Bald Eagle*, 8 January 1839.

103 Schrauwers, "Tilting at Windmills," 2, 5; Edward P. Alexander, Kharles Dunkombe, and W.L. Marcy, "The Hunters' Lodges of 1838," *New York History* 19, no.1 (January 1938): 66.

104 "Remember the Caroline!!," *Bald Eagle*, 21 December 1838.

105 These were respectively: 21 December 1838 and 28 December 1838.

106 These were issues 21 December 1838, 28 December 1838, and 1 January 1839. A cautionary note: I have no confirmation as to whether this is, in fact, code. It has been noted that this is not the same code as used by Lucius Versus Bierce in his 18 August 1837 communiqué found in the WRHS archives. The answer may never be known though I speculate it is reasonable to assume that it was not a printer's error or garble given its repetition in these three issues. The reader should know that there is one character missing in this code that could not be replicated.

107 "MARTYRS TO LIBERTY," *Bald Eagle*, issues dated 1, 4, 8, 11, and 15 January 1839. The 1 January issue does not include the names of Sweet and Peeler. These two men were Americans hung at Kingston on 22 December 1838. Their executions brought to six at the time the number of Americans who had been captured at Wind Mill Point and subsequently executed. See also Gertrude Van Rensselaer Wickham's *The Pioneer Families of Cleveland, 1796–1840*, vol. II (Evangelical Publishing House, 1914), 535, wherein she states that Underhill, as publisher of the *Liberalist,* was more interested in advancing ideas than making a profit. This is also borne out by his statement to readers in his last issue of the *Cleveland Liberalist*, 27 October 1838.

108 "From the Buffalonian, AT A MEETING," *Bald Eagle*, 8 January 1839; "Buffalo Meeting," *Bald Eagle*, 8 January 1839.

109 Among more recent authoritative studies that recognize the widespread Patriot support below the 49th parallel are: Mauduit, "Vrais Republican d'Amérique" and Richards, "The Lure of a Canadian Republic." The following Ohio newspapers also reveal the same: The arrival in Toledo of eighty volunteers from Cleveland on a steamboat with Col. Sutherland to await delivery of a stand of 500 arms from Perrysburg was reported in "The Cry Is Still, They Come!" *Toledo Blade*, 10 January 1838. "The Battle on Pelle

Island," *Western Courier*, 5 April 1838, wherein the 300 Patriot forces are described as "composed exclusively of Americans." See "Of What Does Canada Complain?," *Bald Eagle*, 28 December 1838 for Poinsett's assessment: "I regret to say that not only have the citizens of the U.S., living on that frontier, aided the feeble efforts of the Canadians ... but others bordering on Upper Canada ... are banded together in secret societies for the express purpose of invading the province of a friendly power ... and it is a subject of regret with this department, that it has not at its disposal a sufficient number of regular troops effectively to guard this extensive frontier from all attempts, on the part of our fellow citizens, tending either to disturb the peace of Upper Canada, or to support the insurgents in the Lower Province," quoted by Mackenzie from a widely circulated report by Poinsett to President Van Buren on 28 November 1838.

110 "Of What Does Canada Complain?," wherein were listed the numerous grievances including: "absence of security for life and property – of taxation without representation – of the destruction of the liberty of the press – of the suspension of the *habeas corpus* ... the division of public lands among swarms of foreign stock-jobbers and speculators ... to the injury and degradation of industrious agriculturalists and emigrants."

111 Thomas Richards Jr, "The Lure of a Canadian Republic."

112 "Great Public Meeting in Detroit," *Bald Eagle*, 21 December 1838. Roberts's rank is found in an original, signed document in the Lucius Versus Bierce Papers, WRHS container four.

113 "Mr White's Address," *Bald Eagle*, 15 January 1839.

114 Samuel Adams, *The Rights of Colonists*, 20 November 1772. https://history.hanover.edu/texts/adamss.html#franklin

115 "Resolutions," *Bald Eagle*, 21 December 1838.

116 Donald McLeod to Honorable James Thompson, 16 February 1838 in the Publications of the Buffalo Historical Society, vol. VIII ed. by Frank H. Severance, Buffalo Historical Society, 1905, 139. McLeod signed his communication as Adj. Gen'l and Brig. Gen'l, Acting P.A. U.C. (Patriot Army of Upper Canada).

117 "Great Public Meeting in Detroit," *Bald Eagle*, 21 December 1838. Among other meetings reported were those in Auburn and Albany, New York, in "Public Meeting" and "Presentation of a Cloak to Commodore Johnson," *Bald Eagle*, 11 January 1839 respectively. A Patriot meeting in Buffalo, NY, was reported on in the 4 and 8 January 1839 issues.

118 "From Mackenzie's Gazette," *Bald Eagle*, 28 December 1838. Wool, Brady, and Worth were U.S. army officers operating along the northern border.

119 Refer to Harvey's chapter in this edited volume: Louis-Georges Harvey, "John O'Sullivan's 'Canadian Moment': The *Democratic Review* and the Canadian Rebellion."

120 "New-Year's Address of the *Bald Eagle* to Its Patrons," *Bald Eagle*, 1 January 1839; "To the Reformers of Upper Canada," *Bald Eagle*, 28 December 1838.

121 "To the Reformers of Upper Canada."

122 Ibid.

123 "New-Year's Address of the *Bald Eagle* to Its Patrons," *Bald Eagle*, 1 January 1839.

124 *Cleveland Liberalist*, 10 September 1836.

125 "News Matters," *Maumee City Express*, 2 February 1839.

126 Bonthius, "The Patriot War of 1837–1838," n61.

127 Ibid., 28, 42–3.

128 Link, *The Social Ideas of American Physicians*, 91.

129 Deep-layered change is a reference to the French Annales School's concept of "longue durée," which emphasizes the slow speed and multi-influences of historical change over time in contrast to the discrete, convulsive historiographical narrative.

# 5

# "The Road Not Taken"

## *Duncombe on Republican Currency: Joint Stock Democracy, Civic Republicanism, and Free Banking*

ALBERT SCHRAUWERS

Dr Charles Duncombe remains permanently in the shadow of William Lyon Mackenzie, having lacked the brash newspaperman's self-aggrandizing abilities. As an elected representative of the Upper Canadian Assembly, he fell only fitfully in step with Mackenzie's legislative reform coalition and was at one time even placed on Mackenzie's "legislative blacklist" of those "uncompromising enemies of the peace, happiness, and welfare of the people."[1] The London rebellion led by Duncombe remains a footnote to Mackenzie's assault on Toronto; and he remains a shadowy figure in the equally secretive Hunters' Lodges that helped organize the Patriot War. No full biography of him has been written, although he receives praise for a commendable list of personal achievements, including co-founding Upper Canada's first independent Masonic Lodge and its first medical school; and for authoring a number of progressive – if unimplemented – legislative reports on prisons, a lunatic asylum, and educational system reforms.[2] Yet few refer to Duncombe's persistent interest in the "dismal science," economics, and in banking where, perhaps, his greatest achievement lies. His interest, I will argue, stemmed from his participation in an international social and political movement seeking to overthrow "aristocratic" banking and establish "republican banking" in its place. Each of Duncombe's interventions on banking sought to provide a sound basis for republican forms of governance by guaranteeing economic "equality of opportunity" if not "equality of condition." In this chapter, I place

Duncombe's economic ideas in context in order to highlight his theoretical contributions to monetary theory as they were adopted by this republican movement.

Duncombe's own background as a well-educated and urbane American immigrant to Upper Canada – a "later Loyalist" – gave him a depth of insight into an unusually broad range of issues on both sides of the border that marked him off as an exceptionally perceptive – and liberal minded – leader. He was equally adept politically in both countries, having been elected to serve in legislatures both in Upper Canada (1830–37) and in California (1858, 1863–65). As an Upper Canadian MLA he was repeatedly delegated to investigate best practices on matters as diverse as dredging equipment, schools, prisons, and banks in the U.S.; Duncombe had also been delegated to present the "Constitutional Reform Society's" petition against the alleged electoral frauds perpetuated by Lt. Gov. Sir Francis Bond Head to the British House of Commons.[3] He was a consistent if shadowy leader of the Hunters' Lodge in Cleveland, the driving force behind the Patriot War. He was said to have played an organizing role in the Patriot Convention that elected the officers of the Patriot Republic of Canada in 1838, and in establishing their Republican Bank of Canada. It was in Cleveland, in 1841, that he published "Duncombe's Free Banking."[4] Duncombe's was a trans-Atlantic perspective, yet one firmly rooted in the republican idealism of his youth.

Duncombe's initial foray into banking in Upper Canada in 1835 sought to undercut the aristocratic Bank of Upper Canada, an unaccountable extension of the colonial government, by publicizing the legality of the Scottish system of joint stock (i.e., non-corporate) banking in Upper Canada.[5] His introduction to the Scottish system was by means of the American "Equal Rights" or Locofoco Party who were fighting a similar battle for "free banking" against the "licensed monopolies" of the "aristocratic" chartered banks in the United States at the same time. Duncombe's prospectus for a "Republican Bank of Canada" in 1838 envisioned a joint stock bank as a national institution, as an integral basis for a republican form of government, in an attempt to draw that Locofoco audience into supporting the Patriot War.[6] His 1841 treatise on "Free Banking" elaborated on that project in the context of the ongoing Congressional debate on the rechartering of the Second Bank of the United States.[7] Duncombe here serves as a red thread tying together apparently disparate national movements that shared a republican ideology and an anti-chartered corporation bias; they favoured, instead, a banking system predicated upon "equality of opportunity" (free banking), unlimited liability, a "hard" paper currency accessible to all without transaction costs, regulation by local norms of "public economy," and democratic accountability to their shareholders and the public. In the British and Canadian context this movement has been referred to as "joint stock democracy," and in the U.S. as "free banking."[8] These cases of joint stock driven democratization thus raise the "vexed" old problem of the relationship of liberal democracy to capitalism.[9]

In recounting the development of these transnational banking movements, the historical and sociological literature has noted the relationship between the political form of corporate governance and their contribution to politics in the public sphere. Given the multiple national contexts for this movement and its uneven development it is important to underscore the shared republican roots of each of its offshoots. Even in the aristocratic United Kingdom, Timothy Alborn has identified a period after the repeal of the Bubble Act between 1826 and 1844 when new banks were part of a social movement that fostered "joint stock democracy" by combining "strictly economic goals with subsidiary political aims."[10] This florescence of joint stock democracy can be placed in the context of the Great Reform Act and the growth of voluntary associations and "deliberative democracy" in the public sphere.[11] Mark Freeman, Robin Pearson, and James Taylor show a broader change in Britain to 1850 from a "mini-parliament" model of corporate governance to a model based on the authority of the CEO with the virtual representation of shareholders as passive investors protected by limited liability.[12] They note that political debate on types of franchise in local government (municipal corporations) mirrored the debate on the form of governance in joint stock companies.[13]

A similar popular credit movement was a core driver of the reform coalition in Upper Canada before the Rebellion of 1837 and of the Locofoco Party in the United States;[14] all three cited banking as central to the creation of a democratic polity. Addressing the question of joint stock democracy as a popular social movement in this tempestuous period thus requires a recognition that joint stock companies and chartered corporations were in the public political, not private sphere and hence a voluntary association like any other. Voluntary associations fostered a civil society that was "the training ground, and eventually the power base of a stratum of bourgeois men, who were coming to see themselves as a 'universal class' and preparing to assert their fitness to govern" in the public sphere.[15] As we shall see, as a political theorist, Duncombe had an idiosyncratic civic republican solution to that conundrum, "the road not taken."

There is now a growing sociological literature that examines the correlation between corporate governance and the political form of national states in Britain, America, and Germany.[16] Duncombe's call for a "republican bank" fits well within these arguments, as we shall see. A second literature examines the inter-linkages *between* cross-corporate governance networks and the political institutions of the state in order to assess the convergence in leadership of chartered corporations and state governance into one interlocked network;[17] I explore these connections in the Upper Canadian context elsewhere.[18] An important subset of this last literature focuses upon "gentlemanly capitalism," and is applicable to both Upper Canadian and British cases: it emphasizes the historical networks of intermarried aristocracy and the financial elite that dominated chartered bank and civil polity governance and are said to have served as the motor for European imperialism.[19]

This chapter, however, is less about this political sociology (which I have recounted elsewhere) than it is about a history of banking theory and Duncombe's place within it. Here, I place "Duncombe's free banking" in this legal, cultural, and political economic context in order to illuminate his theoretical innovations in monetary theory as they were utilized by this social movement for joint stock democracy. Writing on banking and currency in the era before classical economic theoretical hegemony was successfully asserted, Duncombe presaged the oppositional "historical school" of economics; this school focused on the sociological consequences of money mediated exchange.[20] Duncombe's theoretical innovations drew attention to precisely those elements of monetary theory that liberalism and classical economic theory glide so easily over. Duncombe, like the "historical school," focused on money as a "means of paying debt" rather than as a mere "medium of exchange." This shift in focus allows analysis of the banknotes of the period ("negotiable paper") as a "payment technology" (like a credit card) and reveals the social, political, and economic costs of that technology to the interconnected web of debtors who used it and to society at large.[21] Duncombe's views on currency did not encourage his readers to view banknote mediated market transactions in liberal terms as anonymous exchanges of equal values by strangers. Rather, he emphasized the way in which the chartered banks of his day were "licensed monopolies" whose privileged access to this technology created a new, threatening "monied aristocracy" that was undermining the republic.

## CHARLES DUNCOMBE: BANKER AND MONETARY THEORIST

In all of his life's endeavours – banking included – Duncombe was an autodidact. The trace of his economic learning curve was succinctly recorded in the introduction to "Duncombe's Free Banking" (1841); there he recounts that as chair of the Committee of Finance in the Upper Canadian Assembly in 1835, he was deputed by the House to travel to the United States in order to "obtain information upon various subjects of public economy" including "exchanges, finance, currency and banking."[22] Duncombe noted that "while in the United States, he was very politely furnished with every facility necessary to the accomplishment of the object of his mission, by political economists, financiers, bankers and merchants; by the members of the administration, as well as by those out of office, and opposed to the administration of the day."[23] This well-rounded grounding in the complexities of banking served as the basis for legislative action and his later theoretical innovations. Although he emphasized its American sources, the committee report that he was to ultimately author drew almost entirely on documents pertaining to the United Kingdom. The example "deeds of settlement" used to establish "joint stock banks" provided in the report appendix were all drawn from the florescence in "free banking" in England after 1826, when the Scottish banking system was introduced in England. Duncombe's life trajectory, and the sources that he drew on, thus demonstrate the multiple international contexts within which "republican banking" – or what I will more generally dub "joint stock democracy" – emerged as a transnational social and political movement in this period.

These criss-crossing international movements have a number of themes in common, beginning with an anti-corporate, "anti-aristocratic" bias. These two themes are related in that the *legislatively chartered* banks of England at the time were controlled by a new class of financier peers, the "gentlemanly capitalists" who also controlled both Houses of Parliament.[24] As Duncombe recognized in

1838, "The national institutions of a country should be based upon the same political foundation. In a Monarchical Government there should be a landed aristocracy; a church and state union, a restricted system of education ... [and] one great Government Bank as the basis of the monied aristocracy."[25] The gentlemanly capitalists he described were no arch Tories; rather, they comprised an alliance of "improving landlords in association with improving financiers who served as their junior partners. This joint enterprise established a tradition of modernization and was itself a modernization of tradition that both conserved gentlemanly values and carried them forward into a changing world."[26] Control of Parliament gave the peerage control over the process of "licensing monopolies," i.e., the legislative chartering of bank corporations with "separate personality" and limited liability for their aristocratic shareholders.

The early nineteenth century chartered corporation was, in the catchphrase of the era, a "political engine" of great power disparaged for its anti-democratic animus (hence President Andrew Jackson's prolonged "war" on the Second Bank of the United States in the 1830s); such was certainly the case in Upper Canada where the major corporations in the pre-Rebellion years were proxies of the state created to escape legislative review.[27] These were the corporate tools of the British Court Party, a group that oversaw the expansion of state administration, public credit, and the financial and commercial revolutions that strengthened the power of the Crown over Parliament. If we are to create a chronology of the ascendency of this "Liberal Order" in Upper Canada, 1825 would be a critical date;[28] in that year, the political economy of the embattled colonial state was reformed on a liberal basis. Its land *granting* policies that had rooted citizenship in loyalism were replaced with the New South Wales system of land *sales*. The two-sevenths of the province's land that had been set aside as Crown and Clergy Reserves were sold to two new land corporations; they provided annuities to the colonial administration, partly freeing it from dependence on taxes raised by the legislature. And in 1825, the Bank of Upper Canada was created and authorized to introduce a paper currency, through which it gained control of much of the province's trade. These corporations were managed by a group of "gentlemanly capitalists" who served to link state and economy.[29] The ascendency of the Liberal Order, I am arguing, was abetted by a corporate revolution that served as a "shadow state," propping up the colonial administration yet isolated from legislative oversight. This corporate revolution played a key role in monetizing the province's economy, thereby encouraging a self-regulating market economy in place of its existing "licensed" public economy.[30]

It was through "aristocratic" institutions such as chartered banks that the province's elite sought to *create* a local peerage. We need look no farther than the scion of the Family Compact, the Rev. John Strachan, the first Anglican bishop of Toronto, who sought to establish the Church of England here, sat on the province's Executive and Legislative Councils, and played a controlling role in both the Clergy Corporation (holding title to the province's Clergy Reserves) and the Bank of Upper Canada. "Strachan's attachment to social hierarchy, episcopacy and a religious establishment must not be interpreted simply as Canadian expressions of aristocratic conservatism. In early Upper Canada, there was little to conserve. For Strachan the present order of society was one of his worst enemies. He was surrounded by the wilderness of man's fallen nature. He had to be creative and build a social order before he could defend it."[31] A critical element in his strategy of building that aristocratic order was the Bank of Upper Canada. Of the forty-four men who served as bank directors of the Bank of Upper Canada in the 1830s, eleven also sat on the Executive Council, fifteen on the Legislative Council, and thirteen were magistrates in the city of Toronto; there was a clear link between the bank and the province's social and governmental elite, who used its chartered "licensed monopoly" to "print money" as a means of consolidating their wealth and social position.[32]

Duncombe's 1835 legislative report on banking to the reform-dominated Assembly was a highly successful attack on this tory controlled process of legislatively chartering banks for their own benefit; Duncombe's report declared the 1826 English law authorizing Scottish-style unincorporated "joint stock" banks with *unlimited* liability for shareholders was valid in Upper Canada, and it provided a template for their creation through "deeds of settlement" that subverted the organizational need for legislative chartering. The English had been wary of the corporate form since the collapse of the "South Sea Bubble" in the stock of the South Sea Company of 1711; this collapse led to the passing of the "Bubble Act" of 1720, which forbade the incorporation of companies without royal charter. This act never applied to Scotland, thus allowing the creation of a system of independent, unincorporated banks operating as extensive partnerships under partnership law there; these banks were marked by the *unlimited* liability of their shareholders for the bank's debts, thus holding them accountable in a way that the *limited* liability of shareholders in chartered banks were not. The English repealed the Bubble Act only in 1825 in the aftermath of a financial crisis, and passed a new banking law authorizing the Scottish system in England in 1826. The growth in joint stock banks in England after 1826 was repeated in a little noted "banking mania" in Upper Canada following the release of Duncombe's report and the legalization of joint stock "free" banking between 1835 and 1837;[33] this movement was explicitly designed to crack the monopoly of the "aristocratic" Bank of Upper Canada. As William Lyon Mackenzie declared, "Archdeacon Strachan's bank (the old one) ... serve[s] the double purpose of keeping the merchants in chains of debt and bonds to the bank manager, and the Farmer's acres under the harrow of the storekeeper. You will be shewn how to break this degraded yoke of mortgages, ejectments, judgments and bonds. Money bound you – money shall loose you."[34] The end result of this intense struggle for political reform was the "Bank of the People," an institution used to fund Mackenzie's radical reform newspaper, *The Constitution*.[35]

The title of Duncombe's 1841 tome, *Free Banking*, undoubtedly points to the influence of the American Equal Rights Party, or Locofocos, on his thinking. This party, the left wing of the Jacksonian democrats, shared equally in Duncombe's anti-corporate, anti-aristocratic sentiments; the proposal for a New York state constitution they prepared in 1837 served as an inspiration for Mackenzie in drafting a republican Upper Canadian constitution at the beginning of the Rebellion of 1837, and was noted for its limitations on chartered banking. The Locofocos advocated a form of joint stock "free" banking like the Scottish system predicated upon a "hard" currency and unlimited liability for bank shareholders. Their political charter was aptly summarized in the 1838 prospectus for a "republican Bank of Canada" attributed to Duncombe. In it, Duncombe wrote: "In a Republic, where the government is made for the good and equal protection of the whole people and not the people for the use of governors all the institutions of the country should be made for the protection and equal benefit of the whole people; there should be no landed aristocracy, no exclusive privileges to any; no church and state union or dominant religious denomination; no bank monopoly nor union of a monied aristocracy with the Executive."[36] The Patriot War has been dubbed "Locofocoism with a Gun" since both their propaganda and their leadership (Duncombe included) clearly articulated a Painite republicanism that stridently opposed the evangelical/anti-masonic/Whig electoral alliance.[37] The Locofoco's Painite insistence on equality of opportunity, separation of church and state, as well as their position against anti-corporate privilege all stood in stark contrast to the Whigs' defence of the new market economy.

An 1838 prospectus for the Republican Bank of Canada issued by the Hunters' Lodge, of which Duncombe was the author, did, however, reflect the evolution of his ideas given the radically different political context within which he was working.[38] Whereas the 1835 Legislative Report sought to introduce what he would later refer to as "republican banking" to the aristocratic context of Upper Canadian chartered banking, the 1838 document calls for the creation of a national bank of the new Republic of Canada. The 1841 treatise on "Free Banking" applies the concept of a national bank of issue to the American context, and more clearly elaborates on the nature of "republican" banking and its contrast with the aristocratic potential of the existing chartered bank system.

Unlike his first two practical forays into banking (1835, 1838), "Duncombe's Free Banking" (1841) was an extensive exercise in "building castles in the air." His model of a "republican currency" issued by a "republican bank of issue" was never implemented in the form he envisioned, although it clearly articulates the political economic principles motivating a significant sector of the banking public. As such, the book was an important intervention in two major banking controversies in the period; the congressional debate on the liquidation of the Second Bank of the United States (BUS) in 1841, and a competing plan for a new Bank of the United States based on the failed Ohio Life Insurance and Trust Company.[39] The liquidation of the BUS was the final moment in Andrew Jackson's "war on the bank" beginning in 1833, which had propelled the Anglo-American world into financial crisis, and thus ended America's experiment with a national bank on the Bank of England model to manage its national currency. It was the Congressional debate on the BUS that Duncombe explicitly addressed in a "Memorial to Congress upon the subject of Republican Free Banking" prefacing the book. In it, he presented his plan "based upon the principles of the Declaration of Independence, and of the Constitution, [which] centralizes the government of the currency; thereby furnishing us with all the national advantages of a United States bank, while it avoids its apprehended, financial and political evils."[40] Thus, like most Jacksonian Democrats, Duncombe objected less to a national bank as is usually supposed; he was more concerned with its political implications.

Duncombe's book was a response to Martin Van Buren's loss of the presidency in 1840, and the subsequent rejection of the Independent Treasury plan (as exists today) by his Whig successors, Harrison and Tyler. Congressional debate immediately restarted on chartering a new national Bank of the United States; these plans were instigated by New York financier Arthur Bronson. Bronson and his father Isaac were conservative "hard money" bankers like Duncombe. Isaac Bronson had first proposed a national bank in 1833 to replace the BUS.[41] To demonstrate how such a conservative institution could safely operate, Bronson organized the Ohio Life Insurance and Trust Company (OLTC) in 1834. The OLTC was chartered, in part, to forestall Ohio Democrats from chartering a competing State Bank of Ohio, which would have "nationalized" the profits of commercial banking in the state.

The OLTC was an innovative banking institution; unlike most banks, the OLTC was a "trust" which managed the fortunes of widows and orphans by investing their funds in long-term mortgages. However, to this investment trust, the Bronsons added the right to issue banknotes and engage in commercial banking, combining mortgage lending with commercial banking. The significant funds held in deposit plus the landed assets backing their mortgages in combination with conservative note issue and commercial loans policies had the potential to make the OLTC a stabilizing influence in expanding and regulating the money supply in Ohio. Its assets soon topped $4,000,000 – almost half of the state's bank capital.

However, the New York based Bronsons lost control of the OLTC in 1837, and their local Ohio partners abandoned these conservative policies and rapidly expanded their issuance of notes just as the Panic of 1837 was beginning. The OLTC was soon forced to suspend its specie payments like other banks, after which the Bronsons sold their majority share. As its charter right to issue banknotes was coming under review in 1843, a lengthy debate began on its failure and the need for a state bank to replace it. As a result, the failure of the Bronson national bank model in Ohio equally impacted the congressional debate sparked by Arthur Bronson on a new charter for the Bank of the United States in 1841. Duncombe, with intimate knowledge of the Ohio experience, thus entered this debate with his plan for a national bank and a "republican currency."[42]

## THE LEGAL AND SOCIAL CONTEXT OF BANKING

Understanding the politics of bank chartering and Duncombe's place in it requires detailed knowledge of the changing legal, social, and cultural context of the corporate form in the antebellum era. In the early nineteenth century corporations were delegations of state authority to favoured subjects for public purposes, usually religious, educational, or municipal.[43] They were granted legal standing through incorporation by state (not national) legislatures on a case-by-case basis, with each corporation defined by their local public rather than private character. As delegations of state authority, they were frequently indistinguishable from the states themselves; early trading companies acted like a "company-state" or "a state in the disguise of a merchant."[44] Hence it should be no surprise that companies frequently assumed the same governance structures as the state that created them – whether democratic or otherwise.[45] Corporations were a political strategy that delegated governmental (not specifically "economic") tasks to subsidiary jurisdictions that in the twentieth century would fall under the purview of the nation-state; in the case of banking, this delegation was ostensibly of the state monopoly rights on the "coinage" of currency.[46] "In all cases, while private profit was served, what justified the delegation of state powers were the public benefits resulting from incorporation."[47] As long as associations were defined as extensions of government, as an exercise in public governance, such rights were usually uncontested.

Since most considered the corporation as an extension of the state, and its governance assumed the same structure as the state that created them, corporations were intimately related to early conceptions of citizenship; the joint stock company was equally voluntary civil association and business, i.e., an "experiment in democratic sociability."[48] The "right to association" therefore assumed a very different meaning from modern definitions of liberal citizenship that presume a uniform allocation of universal rights to a unified legal subject of a modern nation-state.[49] In early American common law, legal privileges and immunities were doled out according to a person's membership in a vast array of supplementary local associations including a broad array of joint stock companies (some incorporated, some not) that operated churches, schools, banks, bridges, canals, and toll roads amongst others. As a result, membership in "a range of differentiated self-governing associations determined one's bundle of privileges, obligations, and immunities much more than the abstract and underdeveloped constitutional category of national citizenship."[50]

In other words, corporations were quasi-state enterprises accountable to all in the public sphere rather than a private business as conceived today; even Adam Smith concluded that corporations were incapable of efficient management and should be created only to handle highly capitalized, low-profit projects like canals.[51] It was only later in the antebellum era that they "shifted from a quasi-public agency – in principle accountable to all, embedded within an institutional structure that served the public sector – into a private agency, protected from government accountability by individual rights and legally accountable to no one but its owners."[52] It is precisely that shift in emphasis in banking from serving the public interest to promoting private gain that Duncombe objected to most strongly in his arguments for a "republican currency."[53] Like most Jacksonians, Duncombe viewed corporations – and banks in particular – as inherently "political machines" coming under the power of "aristocratic" elites.[54] His critique of banking was written less as economic text than as moral treatise on the proper balance between state and corporate governance.

Duncombe's book was thus concerned with the political effects of the new banking corporations that he cast, in the language of the Court and Country parties invoked by Jackson,[55] as aristocratic bodies "forever tending to sever the bonds of republican union founded upon liberty and equality."[56] The discourse of political economy had always faced a "'tricky adjustment' between a liberal element concerned with commercial freedom and a pastoral element concerned with the welfare of the population."[57] This pastoral or regulatory element meant that almost all modes of selling and a variety of occupations were considered "privileges" to be specially licensed by local government.[58] This was especially true of corporations, "licensed monopolies" for the exclusive right to earn profits in the provision of a public service.[59] Given these attitudes, more recent historico-legal studies argue that local aspects of American economic activity were publicly regulated according to a common law vision of the "well-ordered market" and "public economy" (as opposed to private enterprise); in other words, the public/private divide was differently configured, with government being intimately involved in the marketplace.[60]

This new common law legal approach to "public economy" contrasts the broad range of local regulatory practices governing commodified exchange with the lack of a concept of a self-regulating national private economic sphere as envisioned in later economic theory.[61] Public economy was not entrenched in a national constitutional framework, but rather, in state and local government. These domains of authority have been only tangentially examined, despite banking being an almost entirely state regulated activity.[62] Although "the notion of 'public economy' is not so much an intellectual construction based on abstract theorizing as a historical shorthand for the social practices of economic and legal actors that established the conditions for hiring, working, manufacturing, buying and selling," these practices were described and defended in the discourse of political economy.[63] Municipal and state laws were used to regulate products, licensing (of inns, trades, etc.), and the marketplace itself. Everyday governmental regulations rendered property rights "social, relative, and historical, not individual, absolute, and natural."[64] These arguments disrupt the late nineteenth-century liberal hegemonic mythology of absolute property rights and a disembedded economy.

As a result of his broader concerns about the corporate impact on government and individual citizenship, Duncombe did not directly address the immediate political debates emerging out of the Jacksonian war on the Bank of the United States (which, as we shall see, was the immediate context for the book and his memorial to Congress), but chose instead to write in the more philosophic (ethical) genre of political economy. The discourse of political economy concerned itself with the economic policy of the state, and of the close relationship between the polity and the social and economic order.[65] Political economy as it developed in the late eighteenth century combined mercantilism, political arithmetic, bullionism, and physiocracy into a conception of government as householding, with the sovereign as steward tasked with fostering and increasing available resources; it thus described many of the governmental strategies of "public economy" just discussed. Before the middle of the nineteenth century, however, it was rare to separate political economy from ethics.[66] Both republicans and "liberal Tories" shared this moralizing emphasis, which set them apart from Benthamite Liberals.[67] For example, in Upper Canada's Kings College, the Rev. John Strachan, titular leader of the Family Compact, contemplated a single department of "Mental Philosophy; moral and intellectual philosophy; Christian ethics; and political economy."[68]

For republicans, this ethical stance was considered crucial to maintaining those regulatory policies necessary to curtail the "monied aristocracy" created by banking and to thus sustain the virtuous character of a republic; they argued that "the concentration of wealth in a small number of hands undermined political freedom and thereby threatened the very foundations of society." Republicanism's ethical stance towards the regulation of wealth made it liberalism's bête noire.[69] It is critical to understand the nuances of this stance, since the Jacksonians declared an equal repugnance for the "levelling" demands of the agrarians. The Democrats defended those relatively minor inequalities in wealth that originated in the differing innate qualities of individuals, finding only that the vast wealth originating in special access to institutional privilege was of moral danger to the republic.[70] Hence, Duncombe argued that the exponential wealth acquired through the "licensed monopoly" of chartered banking created a dangerous anti-republican aristocracy. Preventing the development of this aristocracy required strict governmental regulation according to the interventionist norms of "public economy" on the one hand, and equal access to the opportunity to bank on the other.[71] He did not demand "equality of condition" for all citizens, merely "equality of opportunity" – a demand for "free banking" accessible to all and organized democratically.

Public antagonism and fear of bank monopolies in the period appears to be well founded, as studies of early American corporations shows that monopoly was a characteristic of the corporate economy from its inception and is not the result of a decrease in competition with the growth of large national and international conglomerates at the turn of the twentieth century.[72] Republicanism, as enunciated by Duncombe and other free-banking Locofoco politicians, thus placed great emphasis on creating a state that could ensure this "equality of opportunity" for all citizens.[73] It is this general stance that underwrote the Atlantic revolutions of which the Patriot War can be considered the last. Duncombe's Republican banking was initially intended, after all, as the means of financing the Patriot cause and the founding of a Canadian Republic.

## DUNCOMBE'S FREE BANKING

Duncombe's solution to the aristocratic tendencies of antebellum banking was to open banking to all, but in so doing, to deny the new banks the right to issue their own banknotes. The "soft" currency of the aristocratic banks would be replaced with a "hard" paper currency (a "republican currency" that mimicked the characteristics of specie) issued by a national bank of issue. To understand what Duncombe meant by a "republican currency" requires the unlearning of neoclassical economic theory and its restricted understanding of money as a medium of exchange. Economists today devote little theoretical attention to the nature of money; for the "dismal science," money is a mere "medium of exchange," a *symbolic* commodity that serves as a "veil" or neutral lubricant for exchanges of "real objects" that would otherwise be conducted through barter.[74] As a medium of exchange, it need not have intrinsic value, but must be universally accepted in exchange. While this understanding of money suits current economic conditions well, it ignores the key functions of banknotes in the antebellum era as a technology for the payment of debt.

Economists' restricted concern with money is rooted in an apocryphal theory of barter exchange, of humanity's propensity to "truck, barter, and trade" stretching back to primordial times. In this barter theory, money evolved to overcome the inconvenience of the "double coincidence of wants" on which direct exchange depends; i.e., that the two participants in an exchange should happen to want what the other had to trade. Money, as a universal commodity desired by all, eased exchange by eliminating this roadblock. In Marx's elegant transcription, it transformed the problematic exchange of commodities (C-C') into one mediated by money (C-M-C').[75] By eliminating the "double coincidence of wants," money-mediated trade was depersonalized, becoming an anonymous exchange between strangers whose agreed-upon prices now formed the basis of an impersonal market. Hence "money does not consist of unique objects at all. At least in principle, it is absolutely generic, any one dollar bill precisely the same as another. As a result money presents a frictionless surface to history … This is why transactions involving money can be said to be 'anonymous': the social identities of those transacting need not become part of the stakes of any transaction – in fact they do not have to play any part of the transaction at all."[76] Neoclassical economics' sole focus upon money as a medium of exchange is thus correlated with the late nineteenth century conceptual development of a "free market economy" distinct from "society" and composed of atomized "market actors" responding to "market cues." This depersonalized model thus legitimated the separation and development of the fields of economics and sociology.[77] Historian William Reddy points out that "the problem with any such approach to understanding exchange systems is that the very things human beings need most to understand about them, the unintended consequences of their operation, are explained away … the subject and enslavement of persons whose labor is used to create commodities for international trade, the systematic curtailment of political liberty – all such things tend to be treated as merely functional elements of a beneficial equilibrating process."[78] He calls this process of concealment the "liberal illusion."

Duncombe, however, wrote in the earlier genre of "political economy" and focused upon other functions of money that were eventually summarized in the late nineteenth century by the German "historical school" of economics (including Marx's "historical materialism"), and elaborated on by Max Weber and Karl Polanyi, and thereafter by economic anthropology more generally.[79] The German "historical school" emphasized those functions of money that lay outside of market exchange and stressed the role of the state in the creation of monetary systems. This is Duncombe's point of entry for his proposed "republican currency." The "historical school" saw the origins of money as lying in the *debts* between a polity and its members before later acquiring its role as a medium of exchange. They thus emphasized the functions of money as a "measure of value" (or unit of account), as a "store of value," and as a "medium of payment" for a range of obligations including fines, tithes, and taxes.[80] Rather than a "neutral veil" enabling depersonalized "free market exchange," money was a "structure of social relations" expressing ties of credit and debt.[81] These social relations become most apparent when we look at money as a *technology* for settling debts; such transfers require a technological infrastructure – a "means of payment" such as "negotiable paper" or a "banknote" (or, today, a credit card), which in this period were predicated on long-term chains of entangled creditors and debtors rather than the anonymous market actors of neoclassical economics.

This last point is perhaps best clarified through Duncombe's own arguments, although he wrote long before the "historical school." Duncombe rejected the barter theory of money's origins in large part because the banknotes serving as money in his day were not a commodity with intrinsic value like specie but representations of debt (i.e., an IOU). Government coined specie, a real commodity with an "intrinsic worth" distinct from its state-sanctioned nominal value, was in very short supply throughout North America. In the absence of specie, merchants would carry book debts for years, recording the balance of crops bought and goods sold, without any exchange of money (i.e., the use of money as a "unit of account" in an otherwise barter economy). At any point, a merchant could demand that these years of exchanges be summarized and that the customer record his balance owed in a "promissory note" (an IOU) due on a particular date. It was then common that the merchant would transfer this debt owed (i.e., "sell" it) to others to settle his own debts by "endorsing it" like a cheque and thereby guaranteeing its ultimate payment; although the debt had been passed on, he remained as responsible for its ultimate repayment as the note's originator.[82] Payment of these credit transactions was governed by the "principle of negotiability," whereby private contractual agreements (such as these promissory notes and bills of exchange) could substitute for money as a circulating medium of exchange (i.e., to replace specie); *they functioned just as later banknotes did.*[83] The circulation of these notes created chains of debtor relations that persisted until the note was finally, successfully, redeemed by its ultimate recipient from its original issuer on its due date. This meant that almost all transactors were simultaneously both creditors and debtors, and that all these relationships were recorded as endorsements on the note as it circulated to settle a whole chain of other debts. Here, "negotiable paper" is a payment technology that embroiled its users in intimate, long-term social relations by the mere act of accepting and passing a note.[84]

As a medium of payment, these notes were a "structure of social relations" rather than a depersonalized medium of exchange. The chains of debt created by the passing of negotiable paper created long-term relations of mutual indebtedness – and trust – in a way that paying in specie (which immediately ends the relationship) could not. These webs of debt, and the trust they required and engendered, persisted over years thereby making community members mutually dependent upon each other; they exhibited a Durkheimian organic solidarity, or what Henry C. Carey, a prominent political economist of the era, referred to as a "harmony of interests."[85] *Respectability* was a critical expression of this trust, a public expression of "credit worthiness." In the absence of this trust, lawsuits for the recovery of debts would be launched, livelihoods would be lost, and the debtor jailed indefinitely until the debt was repaid.[86] These community-based networks of mutual indebtedness and the ongoing trust they elicited were a source of social capital; they were a network of social relationships that could be converted into economic capital in the form of negotiable paper – an IOU that circulated as a medium of exchange.[87] A large part of the commercial transactions of the era were carried out by these means.

Duncombe's ideas about bank-issued paper currency – then a relatively new phenomenon – were thus rooted in this system for the payment of debts, and were contrasted with specie as a medium of exchange and store of value. In the antebellum era, paper currency was negotiable paper of this kind: a circulating banknote recorded a debt, a "promise to pay" in specie whenever the note was presented to its issuer (the bank) for payment. Duncombe repeatedly reminded his readers that paper currency was circulating debt, and "not capital": "The moment it is required to assume the character of capital, its true and legitimate powers fail, and it vanishes like smoke, – nothing remains but stained, worn and soiled rags of paper."[88] The bank loaned its customers its negotiable paper (its IOU), not its store of specie; and since they loaned in excess of three times more notes (on which they drew interest) than they had specie, their circulating debt could easily bankrupt them should the public's faith in their respectability fail, and a "run" be made on the bank to redeem its notes in specie. Alternately, by expanding the note supply by loaning ever larger amounts, they multiplied their profits; since their shareholders were protected by corporate limited liability, the risks of expanding the note supply seemed "reasonable" to bankers. The average lifespan of a bank at this time was about five years for this reason.

These banknotes differed from other forms of negotiable paper in at least one important respect. Other forms of negotiable paper were predicated upon the recorded chains of endorsers who passed the note as means of payment; passing a note thus created a mutually obligated social network. Banknotes, as a means of payment, obscured this network of social relations so that the note could circulate, like specie, between anonymous parties, although this was not without its own risks; as Duncombe reminded his readers, to obtain a banknote, borrowers had to provide the bank with a personal note "with two good endorsers all three of them being liable for the whole amount of the endorsed note to the extent of their entire fortunes" and in exchange they received an unendorsed unbacked banknote – with the bankers' personal fortunes protected by limited liability, leaving the borrower on the hook should the bank suspend payments. "And this is the *equality* of incorporated banking companies!"[89] The right to issue such an unendorsed unbacked banknote was a corporate privilege, the right to "manufacture money" for private gain that Duncombe declared the "least defensible of all aristocracies ... they obtain their exclusive privileges, argue, reason, and administer to the *gullibility* of mankind, until their earnest and apparently sincere protestations in favor of bank paper, its convenience, its excellence, and its value to the community, captivates thousands of honest men, who are charmed into a belief that bank paper is money, and that such money is real capital."[90] The creation of an impersonal market economy was thus indelibly linked in Duncombe's mind to the development of "monied aristocracies" who transgressed the most basic element of commercial trust: accountability for the notes they issued.

Despite these problems, the issuers of paper currency claimed it offered advantages to the borrower as a technology for paying debts, and to the community as a medium of exchange. By focusing on the banknote as a technology (like a credit card) for the payment of debt, Duncombe was also able to point to the costs, as well as the benefits, paid by both borrowers and more generally by the public, for their use. The benefits of the banknote primarily accrued to the borrower whose credit worthiness might not be known in a distant market; in this case, the local bankers would substitute their better-known banknotes for the personal notes of the borrower. This advantage, Duncombe argued, had to be of greater worth to the borrower than the 6 per cent interest they paid for the privilege.[91] Personal notes from distant sources were frequently only accepted at a steep discount (up to 50 per cent), given the difficulty of seeking repayment across legal jurisdictions.

Duncombe also noted that there were other attendant costs than the interest paid for the use of this payment technology since paper currency was not a "store of wealth" like specie, but circulating debt. These costs were paid by both the borrower and, more importantly, by society at large. The expansion of banknote issues frequently led to their devaluation, for instance, resulting in general inflation that disadvantaged the poor the most. Banknotes frequently circulated far from home and decreased in value in proportion to that distance. Yet all who were forced to accept their wages in "uncurrent notes" at its par value ended up losing, especially when they needed to obtain small change in specie. Specie – a real store of value – thus passed "at a premium" but was irreplaceable in everyday transactions.[92] Duncombe calculated that this cost averaged about ten cents a day, or about $146 over a four year period. This "tax" ("his bankers and brokers bill") paid by each member of the general public for the circulation of paper currency was sufficient, he argued, to make or break the pioneering farmer who had to pay it; "How long will men, who claim to themselves the exclusive privileges of independence, and the boasted glory of equality, bow their necks to the paper money lender, and become tax-payers to Rag Barons, in their painted paper castles?"[93] Similar sentiments were expressed by William Lyon Mackenzie in opposition to the Bank of Upper Canada (and U.S. chartered banks),[94] and by Samuel Underhill, Locofoco publisher and Patriot organizer in Cleveland, who argued "dazzling pictures of [the] promise to pay [have] proved a chain equal, and more than equal, in enabling the strong to compel the weak to give of their substance than the superstition & slavery of ancient times ... Patented picture promises to pay, drawing usury, sucks the life blood of the laboring classes, chokes the fountains of benevolence, and exempts a large portion of able bodied men from the duty of living on the product of their own labor."[95]

The disadvantages of paper currency to the artisan and farmer were accentuated through dishonest trade practices. The rapid expansion of note issue followed by its contraction at the whim of a local bank monopoly could throw the commerce of a region into chaos, allowing those with cash (the bankers' cronies) to corner the produce market and depress prices, and allowing for huge profits when those goods were sold at a distance; allowing the currency to be controlled by "*private interest*" in this way was "*anti-republican*."[96] Duncombe thus argued that the history of banknotes was "one of dishonor, discredit, waste, extravagance, pride, vanity, ambition and disappointment;" and, in short, that if "the love of money is the root of all evil, the love of paper money is the evil itself, for it contains all the temptations to vice and immorality chargeable upon money, while it is only its shadow and not its substance; and it is none the less emblematical of the fountain of vice for its being but a semblance of what it professes to be."[97]

Duncombe's complaint was that the banker's monopoly right to "manufacture money" created economic and political inequalities that were hidden by the "liberal illusion." Reddy argues that liberal economic theorizing predicated upon the narrow conception of money as medium of exchange emphasizes the *equality* of the transactors as they meet impersonally in the marketplace; because all participants are assumed to be rational maximizers, these theorists assume that all transactions are fundamentally similar in social cause and effect and the participants walk away with equal "value." When money is viewed, however, from the perspective of its function as a payment technology as we have done here, the *unequal* effects of monetary exchange (the "monetary exchange asymmetries") are underscored. As Duncombe argued: "Whenever a privileged chartered banking company monopolizes any business, and by superior capital, superior credit, or superior local advantages, drives the regular dealers in the business out of the market, she regulates the price of buying and selling the articles in which she deals, and thus monopolizes them at her own will. Having all the money, she can have all the merchandize at her own price. The public are uniformly the losers."[98] Control of the money supply, the ability to expand and contract the number of bills in circulation, gave bankers great power. Because they clearly viewed the banks from this perspective, "the political writings of Jacksonian theorists such as William Gouge and Charles Duncombe and ... Jacksonian polemicists ... stated that their goal was to *control the money supply* (often to expand it for agricultural credit), not to release it to market forces."[99]

As an expression of the general Jacksonian desire for state control of monetary policy and the money supply, Duncombe's plan began by depriving commercial banks (banks of discount, or lending) of the right to issue banknotes. He called, in other words, for a reformed Bank of the United States similar to that initially envisioned by Jackson himself. In Duncombe's version, this national bank would retain the sole right to issue both specie and paper currency, which would be distributed through its state branches, who would offer commercial loans according to restrictive "hard money" policies. These state branches, having received their fair appropriation of the national share capital and blank notes from the national bank of issue, would be allowed to make loans "*not more* than three times the amount of specie actually in the bank" thus "confining the supply [of notes] to the actual demand for currency" as demonstrated by applications for loans. This would curtail rapid expansions and contractions of the availability of currency, and its inflationary effects. They would issue no small notes, so that only specie would be available for the local market transactions of workers, while making paper currency in large bills available to merchants for inter-state trade, giving "each class of the community ... that kind of currency least desirable to the other."[100] This paper currency would be exchanged at par throughout the union, thus easing the costs of doing business, while halting the "tax" paid by the general public for the use of banknotes; it would be a "hard" currency of uncontested value like specie, always convertible in specie at full value in any of the local state branch banks. Duncombe summarized his plan as a separation of the bank of issue from the banks of discount (commercial banks); this would centralize the government of the currency (the Jacksonian goal), but divide its administration among independent branches so that the business of making loans did not become a source of central political ("aristocratic") power.

As just outlined, Duncombe's plan followed the "hard money" policies of most conservative bankers of the period such as eastern financier Isaac Bronson, who had presented a similar plan to Jackson in 1833 as a replacement for the second Bank of the United States.[101] Where Duncombe differed was in the specifically *republican* emphasis he placed on bank governance, and hence its tendency to strengthen republican values and a sense of national citizenship. His bank plan sought to ensure equality of opportunity and prevent the creation of vast "aristocratic" differences by denying an institutional basis for inheritable wealth. This republican aim was to be achieved by republican methods, by making the management of both bank of issue and banks of discount directly electable – a process that he ironically claimed would eliminate politics from the currency and separate it from private interests. Since the national Bank of Issue simply determined the total national supply of money required, but distributed its blank bills to the state Banks of Discount for actual use, the governance of the currency supply was centralized (the control of the monetary supply so dear to the Jacksonians) but its loan was left to locally elected managers of state banks. These local bank directors would be precluded from making loans in which they had an interest; and since they were dependent on re-election, it was in their interest to give "loans of the bank equally to the fair traders of the place [on whose votes they counted], instead of being loaned in large sums exclusively to a few speculators."[102] Here profit was explicitly subsumed to the general public welfare and equality of opportunity in keeping with local common law conceptions of "public economy." While this paper currency would thus still entail a breakdown in the community of interest woven by chains of credit and debt in the move to a depersonalized market, this innovative form of governance would replace those ties with "a bond of union between the citizens and government of this country upon the all-powerful principle of self-interest."[103]

## JOINT STOCK DEMOCRACY IN BRITAIN, UPPER CANADA, AND USA

"Duncombe's Free Banking" was clearly a civic republican attempt to rein liberalism – and its growing extra-governmental "aristocratic" corporate power – within the bounds of "public economy," and provide an alternate model of "joint stock democracy." This alternate model was successively encoded in the unenacted republican constitutions of Upper Canada, of the Locofocos of New York, and of the Patriot Republic of Canada, "the path not taken." The early history of banking and the corporation in Britain, Upper Canada, and the United States was thus dominated by this social movement, and these debates were clearly reflected in the major political divisions of the period. "Duncombe's Free Banking," though never enacted in the form he had hoped, remains the clearest ideological expression of that movement's economic and political vision. While that vision ultimately succumbed to the ascendency of the "Liberal Order" it was a clear motivating factor in these, the "last of the Atlantic Revolutions."[104]

Here, however, I would also like to point to Duncombe's innovations as a political economist of banking corporations. Duncombe's *Free Banking* should not be viewed as a failed bank proposal, but as a cogent, astute analysis and critique of the monetary system of the time, and an expression of the economic culture of civic republicanism. Duncombe was particularly adept at highlighting the ideological blindness of the liberal theory of money that viewed it as a simple "medium of exchange" while ignoring its roots in a technology for the payment of debts. This insight allowed Duncombe to focus on the economic, social, and political costs of the banknotes of the antebellum period, and on the toll they took on the republican value of equality of opportunity. Duncombe noted that the substitution of an unbacked banknote for the previous circulation of endorsed "negotiable paper" eroded the "harmony of interests" that tied the community of mutually indebted and accountable businessmen together; bank paper used as mere "medium of exchange" left them as strangers in the marketplace. Duncombe foreshadowed Marx's analysis of the capitalist transformation, as money transitioned from a medium of exchange enabling the barter of commodities (C-M-C'), to the capitalist search for profits where the commodity was but the means (M-C-M'), to the banker's alchemical ability to manufacture money without engaging in commodity exchange (M-M'). The banker's alchemical ability was rooted in the fetishization of money as a mere "medium of exchange" – i.e., our attribution of agency to money by obscuring the social relationships (the banking technology) that create it. Treating money as a mere "medium of exchange" allowed the creation of a "moneyed aristocracy" with the charter rights to "manufacture money" that passed unnoticed.

Duncombe's Free Banking was thus an attempt to re-socialize money, to create a new kind of bond that tied equal *citizens* together in a national community through the money they circulated, and the republican bank they collectively operated. As such, he presaged the emergence of territorial national currencies out of the welter of local banknotes in the later nineteenth century whose nationalist symbolic value was matched by the united markets they created.[105] Duncombe also sought to root banking – as a licensed monopoly – in the regulatory values of "public economy," which demanded that the exercise of those rights must benefit all members of the community equally. This regulatory role – the intervention of the state in what was increasingly a distinct, liberal, economic sphere – was a strike at the "moneyed aristocracy" that he saw growing, through banking, in Britain, Canada, and the U.S. As I have noted, with the ascendency of the Liberal Order and its economic hegemony this became the path not taken.

NOTES

1 PAO, Mackenzie-Lindsey papers, clippings and notations, file no. 1841.
2 The most extensive biographical treatments of Duncombe's life can be found in: Michael S. Cross, "DUNCOMBE, CHARLES," in *Dictionary of Canadian Biography*, vol. 9, University of Toronto/Université Laval, 2003, last accessed 28 May 2018, http://www.biographi.ca/en/bio/duncombe_charles_9E.html; Colin F. Read, *The Rising in Western Upper Canada, 1837–1838: The Duncombe Revolt and After* (Toronto: University of Toronto Press, 1982); and George E. Thorman "Dr Charles Duncombe – His Life & Times," in *The Heritage Lodge no. 730, A.F. & A.M., G.R.C.: proceedings 1997*, ed. John Sutherland (Toronto). For a discussion of the social and cultural movements on which he drew (Freemasonry, Free banking, Free Thought), see Albert Schrauwers, "Tilting at Windmills: The Utopian Socialist Roots of the Patriot War, 1838–1839," *Labour/Le Travail* 79 (Spring 2017): 53–80.
3 Cross, "Duncombe."
4 Ibid.
5 Charles Duncombe, "Report of the Select Committee to which was referred the Subject of the Currency," No. 31 in *Appendix to the Journal of the House of Assembly of Upper Canada* Session 1835 Vol. 2 (Toronto: M. Reynolds, 1835).
6 Charles Duncombe, *An Address to the Different Lodges upon the Subject of a Joint Stock Banking Company Bank* (1838, manuscript copy found in "The Durham Papers," PAC MG 24, A 27, Vol. 21, Reel C-1854, 823–31).
7 Charles Duncombe, *Duncombe's Free Banking: An Essay on Banking, Currency, Finance, Exchange and Political Economy* (Cleveland, OH: Sanford & Co., 1841); Bray Hammond, *Banks and Politics in America: From the Revolution to the Civil War* (Princeton, NJ: Princeton University Press, 1957), 326–86.
8 For "joint stock democracy" see Albert Schrauwers, *"Union is Strength": W.L. Mackenzie, the Children of Peace and the Emergence of Joint Stock Democracy in Upper Canada* (Toronto, University of Toronto Press, 2009); Timothy L. Alborn, *Conceiving Companies: Joint-Stock Politics in Victorian England* (London: Routledge, 1998); for "free banking" Howard Bodenhorn, "Bank Chartering and Political Corruption in Antebellum New York: Free Banking as Reform," in *Corruption and Reform: Lessons from America's Economic History*, eds Edward Glaeser

and Claudia Goldin (Chicago: University of Chicago Press, 2006), 231–57.

9 Joyce Oldham Appleby, "The Vexed Story of Capitalism Told by American Historians," *Journal of the Early Republic* 21, no. 1 (2001): 1–18.

10 Alborn, *Conceiving Companies*, 4, 85–115.

11 Jeffrey L. McNairn, *The Capacity to Judge: Public Opinion and Deliberative Democracy in Upper Canada, 1791–1854* (Toronto: University of Toronto Press, 2000).

12 Mark Freeman, Robin Pearson, James Taylor, *Shareholder Democracies? Corporate Governance in Britain and Ireland before 1850* (Chicago: University of Chicago Press, 2012), 11.

13 Ibid., 35–6.

14 Schrauwers, *"Union Is Strength"*; Bodenhorn, "Bank Chartering," 231–57.

15 Nancy Fraser, "Rethinking the Public Sphere: A Contribution to the Critique of Actually Existing Democracy," *Social Text* 25/26 (1990): 60; William J. Novak, "The American Law of Association: The Legal-Political Construction of Civil Society," *Studies in American Political Development* 15, no. 2 (2001): 163–88.

16 Dobbin, "Why the Economy Reflects the Polity"; Colleen Dunlavy and Thomas Welskopp, "Myths and Peculiarities: Comparing U.S. and German Capitalism," GHI *Bulletin* 41, no. 4 (2007): 33–62; Roy, *Socializing Capital.*

17 Dunlavy and Welskopp, "Myths and Peculiarities"; William K. Carroll, *Corporate Power in a Globalizing World: A Study in Elite Social Organization* (Toronto: Oxford University Press Canada, 2004); Dobbin, "Why the Economy Reflects the Polity."

18 Albert Schrauwers, "The Gentlemanly Order & the Politics of Production in the Transition to Capitalism in Upper Canada," *Labour/Le Travail* 65 (Spring 2010): 9–45; "'Money bound you – money shall loose you': Micro-Credit, Social Capital and the Meaning of Money in Upper Canada," *Comparative Studies in Society and History* 53, no. 2 (2011): 1–30.

19 Mark Brayshay, Mark Cleary, and John Selwood, "Social Networks and the Transnational Reach of the Corporate Class in the Early Twentieth Century," *Journal of Historical Geography* 33 (2007): 144–67; Martin Bossenbroek, *Holland op zijn Breedst: Indië en Zuid-Afrika in de Nederlandse Cultuur omstreeks 1900* (Amsterdam: Uitgeverij Bert Bakker, 1996); Schrauwers, "The Gentlemanly Order" and "'Money bound you.'"

20 See for example, William M. Reddy, *Money and Liberty in Modern Europe: A Critique of Historical Understanding* (Cambridge: Cambridge University Press, 1987).

21 I am thus drawing on recent anthropological work such as Bill Maurer, "The Anthropology of Money," *Annual Review of Anthropology* 35 (2006): 15–36; Bill Maurer and Lana Swartz, eds, *Paid: Tales of Dongles, Checks, and Other Money Stuff* (Cambridge, MA: MIT Press, 2017).

22 During this extensive trip, Duncombe collected material for legislative reports on prisons and education as well. Duncombe's reports on the prison and education systems were largely unimplemented, but are frequently lauded for having introduced important modern innovations in institutional management to the political discourse of the province. His report on the currency (and banking) was equally innovative and had immediate and far-reaching economic and political (if short term) effects, but is rarely mentioned (Schrauwers, *"Union Is Strength,"* chapter 5).

23 Charles Duncombe, *Duncombe's Free Banking: An Essay on Banking, Currency, Finance, Exchange and Political Economy* (Cleveland, OH: Sanford & Co., 1841), 21.

24 P.J. Cain and A.G. Hopkins, *British Imperialism: Innovation and Expansion 1688–1914* (London: Longman, 1993), 58–9.

25 Charles Duncombe, "An Address to the Different Lodges upon the Subject of a Joint Stock Banking Company Bank" (manuscript copy found in "The Durham Papers," PAC MG 24, A 27, Vol. 21, Reel C-1854, 823–4).

26 Cain and Hopkins, *British Imperialism*, 101.

27 Schrauwers, *"Union Is Strength"*; for Britain, cf. James Taylor, *Creating Capitalism: Joint-Stock Enterprise in British Politics and Culture, 1800–1870* (Woodbridge, UK: Royal Historical Society/Boydell Press, 2006).

28 Ian McKay, "The Liberal Order Framework: A Prospectus for a Reconnaissance of Canadian History," *Canadian Historical Review* 81, no. 4 (2000): 616–45.

29 Schrauwers, "The Gentlemanly Order."

30 I am thus firmly placing this social movement in the broader context of the "transition to capitalism" debate in America. See Albert Schrauwers, "Revolutions without a Revolutionary Moment: Joint Stock Democracy & the Transition to Capitalism in Upper Canada," *Canadian Historical Review* 89, no. 2 (2008): 223–55.

31 William Westfall, "The Sacred and the Secular: Studies in the Cultural History of Protestant Ontario in the Victorian Period" (PhD diss., University of Toronto, 1976), 46.

32 Schrauwers, "The Gentlemanly Order."

33 Schrauwers, "*Union Is Strength*," 151–75.

34 *Correspondent & Advocate* (Toronto), 30 August 1835.

35 Schrauwers, "'Money bound you.'"

36 Duncombe, "Address to the Different Lodges," 824–5.

37 Andrew Bonthius, "The Patriot War of 1837–1838: Locofocoism with a Gun?," *Labour/Le Travail* 52 (Fall 2003): 9–43; Albert Schrauwers, "Tilting at Windmills."

38 Duncombe, "Address to the Different Lodges."

39 C.C. Huntington, "A History of Banking and Currency in Ohio before the Civil War," *Ohio Archaeological and Historical Quarterly* 24 (1915): 420–1.

40 Duncombe, *Duncombe's Free Banking*, 2.

41 Larry Schweikart, "Jacksonian Ideology, Currency Control and Central Banking: A Reappraisal," in *Historian* 51, no. 1 (1988): 86; John D. Haeger, *The Investment Frontier: New York Businessmen and the Economic Development of the Old Northwest* (Albany: State University of New York Press, 1981), 39–48.

42 John D. Haegler, "Eastern Financiers and Institutional Change: The Origins of the New York Life Insurance and Trust Company and The Ohio Life Insurance and Trust Company," *Journal of Economic History* 39, no. 1 (1979): 269.

43 Pauline Maier, "The Revolutionary Origins of the American Corporation," *William and Mary Quarterly* 50, no. 1 (1993): 55; R.C.B. Risk, "The Nineteenth Century Foundations of the Business Corporation in Ontario," *University of Toronto Law Journal* 23 (1973): 270–303.

44 Philip Stern, *The Company-State: Corporate Sovereignty and the Early Modern Foundations of the British Empire in India* (Oxford: Oxford University Press, 2011).

45 Frank Dobbin, "Why the Economy Reflects the Polity: Early Rail Policy in Britain, France and the United States," in *The Sociology of Economic Life*, eds Mark Granovetter and Richard Swedberg (Boulder, CO: Westview, 2001).

46 Each state declared a constitutional monopoly right to coin the country's specie and determine its metallic value. Banks of the period could circumvent this monopoly right because they circulated banknotes, which, as we will discuss, were specifically *not coins*, and had no value other than as IOUs for payment in specie.

47 James Taylor, *Creating Capitalism: Joint-Stock Enterprise in British Politics and Culture, 1800–1870* (Woodbridge, UK: Royal Historical Society/Boydell Press, 2006), 4.

48 McNairn, *The Capacity to Judge*, 63; Schrauwers, *"Union Is Strength,"* 254–7.

49 William J. Novak, "The Legal Transformation of Citizenship in Nineteenth-Century America," in *The Democratic Experiment: New Directions in American Political History*, ed. M. Jacobs et al. (Princeton, NJ: Princeton University Press, 2003), 86.

50 Novak, "Legal Transformation," 97–8.

51 Adam Smith, *The Wealth of Nations* (London: Penguin Books, 1999), 700.

52 William G. Roy, *Socializing Capital: The Rise of the Large Industrial Corporation in America* (Princeton, NJ: Princeton University Press, 1997), 41.

53 Duncombe, *Duncombe's Free Banking*, 163–4.

54 James R. Sharp, *The Jacksonians versus the Banks: Politics in the States after the Panic of 1837* (New York: Columbia University Press, 1970).

55 Major L. Wilson, "The 'Country' versus the 'Court': A Republican Consensus and Party Debate in the Bank War," *Journal of the Early Republic* 15, no. 4 (1995): 619–47.

56 Duncombe, *Duncombe's Free Banking*, 261.

57 Ann Firth, "From Economy to 'the Economy': Population and Self-Interest in Discourses on Government," *History of the Human Sciences* 11, no. 3 (1998): 20.

58 William J. Novak, "Public Economy and the Well-Ordered Market: Law and Economic Regulation in 19th-Century America," *Law & Social Inquiry* 18, no. 1 (1993): 32.

59 Robin Pearson, "Shareholder Democracies? English Stock Companies and the Politics of Corporate Governance during the Industrial Revolution," *English Historical Review* 117 (2002): 840–66; Naomi Lamoreaux, "Revisiting American Exceptionalism: Democracy and the Regulation of Corporate Governance. The Case of Nineteenth-Century Pennsylvania in Comparative Context," in *Enterprising America: Businesses, Banks, and Credit Markets in Historical Perspective*, eds William J. Collins and Robert A. Margo (Chicago: University of Chicago Press, 2015), 25–72.

60 The debate about whether a self-regulating market economy had emerged in this period is ongoing. However, contemporary models of a self-regulating market in the private sphere, distinct from the polity, were not made until Ricardo (in 1817); Gus Dix, "Ricardo's Discursive Demarcations: A Foucauldian Study of the Formation of the Economy as an Object of Knowledge," *Erasmus Journal for Philosophy and Economics* 7, no. 2 (2014): 1–29; Mary Poovey, *Genres of the Credit Economy: Mediating*

*Value in Eighteenth- and Nineteenth-Century Britain* (Chicago: University of Chicago Press), 224ff.

61 Timothy Mitchell has argued that the concept of a self-regulating economic sphere was introduced in economic thought only in the 1930s by John M. Keynes. *Rule of Experts: Egypt, Techno-politics, Modernity* (Berkeley: University of California Press, 2002), 83–4.

62 Appleby, "The Vexed Story"; Tony A. Freyer, *Producers versus Capitalists: Constitutional Conflict in Antebellum America* (Charlottesville: University Press of Virginia, 1994).

63 Novak, "Public Economy," 7.

64 William J. Novak, *The People's Welfare: Law & Regulation in Nineteenth-Century America* (Chapel Hill, NC: University of North Carolina Press, 1996), 83.

65 Drew R. McCoy, *The Elusive Republic: Political Economy in Jeffersonian America* (New York: Norton, 1980), 6; Graham Burchell, "Peculiar Interests: Civil Society and Governing 'The System of Natural Liberty,'" in *The Foucault Effect: Studies in Governmentality*, eds Graham Burchell, Colin Gordon, and Peter Miller (Chicago: University of Chicago Press, 1991), 119–50.

66 Keith Tribe, *Land, Labour and Economic Discourse* (London: Routledge & Kegan Paul, 1978); McCoy, *The Elusive Republic*, 6–8; Craig Calhoun, *The Roots of Radicalism: Tradition, the Public Sphere, and Early Nineteenth-Century Social Movements* (Chicago: University of Chicago Press, 2012).

67 Peter Mandler, "Tories and Paupers: Christian Political Economy and the Making of the New Poor Law," *Historical Journal* 33, no. 1 (1990): 81–103.

68 McNairn, *Capacity to Judge*, 144–5. Indeed, Boyd Hilton, *The Age of Atonemen: The Influence of Evangelicalism on Social and Economic Thought, 1795–1865* (Oxford: Clarendon Press, 1987) and Mandler ("Tories and Paupers") argue that Christian Political Economy was of greater popular impact in the British poor law reforms of the 1830s than the secular economic discourse of the Benthamites.

69 Michel Ducharme, *The Idea of Liberty in Canada during the Age of Atlantic Revolutions, 1776–1838* (Montreal and Kingston: McGill-Queen's University Press, 2014), 25; Wilson, "'Country' versus the 'Court.'"

70 Richard B. Latner, "Preserving 'the Natural Equality of Rank and Influence': Liberalism, Republicanism, and Equality of Condition in Jacksonian Politics," in *The Culture of the Market: Historical Essays*, eds

Thomas Haskell and Richard Teichgraeber III (Cambridge: Cambridge University Press, 1993), 198.

71 Schweikart, "Jacksonian Ideology," 86–7.

72 David Bunting, "Origins of the American Corporate Network," *Social Science History* 7, no. 2 (1983): 129–42.

73 Latner, "Equality of Rank," 208–16.

74 Geoffrey Ingham, "Money Is a Social Relationship," *Review of Social Economy* 54, no. 4 (1996): 511–16.

75 Ibid., 507–29.

76 David Graeber, *Toward an Anthropological Theory of Value: The False Coin of Our Own Dreams* (New York: Palgrave, 2001), 94.

77 Koray Caliskan and Michel Callon, "Economization Part 1: Shifting Attention from the Economy towards Processes of Economization," *Economy and Society* 38, no. 3 (2009): 381.

78 Reddy, *Money and Liberty in Modern Europe*, 80–1.

79 Joel S. Kahn, "Towards a History of the Critique of Economism: The Nineteenth-Century German Origins of the Ethnographer's Dilemma," *Man* 25, no. 2 (1990): 230–49; David Graeber, *Debt: The First 5,000 Years* (New York: Melville House, 2011), 47–8.

80 Duncombe, *Free Banking*, 37, 46ff, 324ff.

81 Ingham, "Money," 516ff.

82 William M. Gouge, *A Short History of Paper Money and Banking in the United States* (Philadelphia: T.W. Ustick, 1833), 18–20.

83 Freyer, *Producers versus Capitalists*, 59.

84 It is important to note the alternatives to debt based currency suggested in a multitude of experiments. The Owenites and Warren created labour notes on the premise "labour is the source of all value"; others sought creative alternatives to back their notes, with either land or commercial goods (Schrauwers, "*Union Is Strength*").

85 Henry C. Carey, *Principles of Political Economy* vol. 2 (Philadelphia: Carey, Lea & Blantchard, 1838), 230ff. Freyer, *Producers versus Capitalists*, 49ff.

86 Schrauwers, "*Union Is Strength*," 66.

87 Schrauwers, "'Money bound you.'"

88 Duncombe, *Duncombe's Free Banking*, 146.

89 Ibid., 156.

90 Ibid., 261.

91 Ibid., 50.

92 Ibid., 147, 209.

93 Ibid., 69–70.

94 William Lyon Mackenzie, *The Life and Times of Martin Van Buren* (Boston: Cooke & Co., 1846).

95 Mackenzie in *Correspondent & Advocate*, 30 July 1835. Samuel Underhill, "Hard Times – Usury – Money," part four of a twelve-article series on banknotes, *Cleveland Liberalist*, 10 June 1837.

96 Duncombe's emphasis, *Duncombe's Free Banking*, 60.

97 Ibid., 70.

98 Ibid., 192.

99 Schweikart, "Jacksonian Ideology," 80, my emphasis.

100 Duncombe, *Duncombe's Free Banking*, 17.

101 Schweikart, "Jacksonian Ideology," 86.

102 Duncombe, *Duncombe's Free Banking*, 19.

103 Ibid., 20.

104 Ducharme, *The Idea of Liberty*.

105 Eric Helleiner, "Historicizing Territorial Currencies: Monetary Space and the Nation-State in North America," *Political Geography* 18 (1999): 309–39.

SECTION THREE

# Continental Impact

# 6

# John L. O'Sullivan's "Canadian Moment"

## *The* Democratic Review *and the Canadian Rebellions*

LOUIS-GEORGES HARVEY

Founded in October 1837, *The United States Magazine and Democratic Review* has long been associated with the ideological and political effervescence of the Jacksonian Era, as well as the evolution of an expansionist American nationalism in the form of Manifest Destiny. However, historians tend to overlook the fact that the magazine's editors were confronted almost immediately with an international crisis on their northern border that spoke directly to both these aspects of its political and cultural message. Indeed, only a few weeks after the publication of the *Democratic Review*'s initial issue, republican revolutionaries in the British provinces of Lower Canada and Upper Canada challenged colonial rule in a series of ultimately unsuccessful violent uprisings and pitched battles that created instability and unrest on the United States' northern border. Moreover, Canadian revolutionaries garnered considerable support among Americans living in states neighbouring the rebellious colonies. The *Review* initially reported the news in its second issue, excitedly informing its readers of "Civil War in the British North American Provinces!" and adding that although the events in the Canadas were a surprise to most Americans, they were "neither strange nor unexpected" to those who had followed the progress of reform movements in the colonies of Upper and Lower Canada.[1] In the following years, the *Democratic Review* published numerous articles on the Canadian situation and generally they were sympathetic to the cause of the revolutionary movements active on the republic's northern frontier. John L. O'Sullivan's editorials heaped criticism on the British colonial regime and often drew parallels between the Canadian revolutionaries' struggle and that of American patriots who had challenged the same colonial rule in 1776. The *Review* also chastised other American papers and journals that seemed to side with either colonial tories or British administrators, accusing them of ignoring their own revolutionary heritage. Yet, despite O'Sullivan's sympathetic treatment of the Canadian revolutionaries, the magazine simultaneously promoted and defended the Van Buren administration's position of strict neutrality, condemned border raids into the Canadas, and admonished Canadian rebels in exile who worked to recruit American citizens to fight for their cause.

This apparently contradictory position would not seem amiss in an administration organ forced to defend a largely unpopular measure, particularly in states along the republic's northern border, were it not for the future trajectory of both the *Democratic Review* and its editor. For O'Sullivan is chiefly remembered for his role in defining the American brand of expansionist nationalism and settler colonialism associated with his term "Manifest Destiny," which came into usage in the mid-1840s as a justification for the annexation of Texas, and later for the annexation of a vast territory of Mexican land acquired in the aftermath of the Mexican-American War. Moreover, while the term Manifest Destiny entered political debate in the mid-1840s, its meaning had been developed in several articles published in the late 1830s and early 1840s – most notably in the famous 1839 article "The Nation of Futurity," which explicitly linked the *Review*'s democratic creed to providential notions of American exceptionalism and to the idea that the American federation would one day grow to engulf all of the western hemisphere.[2] The *Democratic Review*'s response to the Canadian rebellions, and to the general issue of the annexation of eventual Canadian republics, was formulated at the same time as these broad notions of American expansionism were crystallizing in a way that seemed to reinforce the common traits of the Canadian and American experiences. It is worth asking, then, how the impact of the Canadian rebellions contributed to the genesis of the idea of Manifest Destiny as it evolved in O'Sullivan's discourse and took form in the texts published in the *Democratic Review*. The *Review*'s representation of the rebellions, its view of the rebels and the colonial system, as well as its response to Lord Durham's *Report on the Affairs of British North America* (1839), were formulated in discursive patterns that not only emphasized the historical inevitability of American expansion, but also legitimized the agency of other settler populations in establishing sovereign, democratic governments. Articles dealing with the role of the French Canadian majority in Lower Canada also demonstrated a certain elasticity on racial notions connecting democracy exclusively to Anglo-Saxon settler populations. Indeed, O'Sullivan openly rejected such an association and defended Lower Canadian rebels against critics who saw French Canadians as a degenerate European people corrupted by racial mixing with Indigenous populations. What emerges from such an analysis also speaks directly to the differences between the notions of Manifest Destiny as they were first developed in the 1830s and the more categorical and aggressive expansionist rhetoric of the 1840s.

## THE *UNITED STATES MAGAZINE AND DEMOCRATIC REVIEW* AND MANIFEST DESTINY

John L. O'Sullivan's (1813–1895) early life and the circumstances surrounding the founding of the *Democratic Review* are well known. O'Sullivan's family had been involved in international intrigue and it was a claim related to his father's death abroad that led to the Van Buren administration financing the launch of the *Review* in 1837. As co-founder, O'Sullivan brought with him a freshly completed education at Columbia University, as well as a stint in French schools during his adolescence. His background would thus have made him more sympathetic to Latin American political movements, and perhaps even to that of the French Canadian Patriotes. By all accounts O'Sullivan was also an avid reader of Jefferson and Madison, and his biographer attributes an important intellectual influence to William Leggett, whose editorials appeared in the *New York Evening Post* and were highly influential among radical Democrats. Despite his strong connections to the Van Buren administration, O'Sullivan and his colleagues saw themselves as outsiders, particularly in the world of highbrow culture where existing magazines and literary reviews, a relatively recent genre, were dominated by British publications and what he saw as their American Whig imitators. The administration clearly saw the *Review* as one of its partisan organs, but it did not follow through with promised publication contracts, and its finances were consequently often in a precarious state.[3]

O'Sullivan modeled his new publication on the *Westminster Review* as a literary and political journal whose mission became the cultivation and representation of the uniquely democratic culture of the United States. This impetus gave the *Review* a certain stature among American literary figures and in intellectual circles. As a result of this, O'Sullivan was able to convince Ralph Waldo Emerson, Henry David Thoreau, Herman Melville, and Nathaniel Hawthorne to contribute to his journal. The *Democratic Review* constantly sought to counter what it saw as the cultural emulation of Great Britain so prevalent in rival publications and it liberally espoused Jacksonian positions and rhetoric. Published in the *Review*'s first edition, O'Sullivan's manifesto clearly stated that it would be unwaveringly devoted to the cause of democracy in terms of both politics and culture. Indeed, he linked the cause of democracy to providential design in this first editorial, adopting a tone of "secular religiosity," which Edward Widmer has associated with both the French Revolution and American millennialism. This messianic tone was often repeated in later articles O'Sullivan wrote for the *Review*, where he linked the cause of democracy and the future of the United States to the unfolding of God's divine plan.[4]

The *Review* and its editor are perhaps best known for their role in developing the ideology of Manifest Destiny, which historians have traditionally associated with an article simply titled "Annexation," which appeared in 1845, and which proclaimed that it was "the fulfillment of our manifest destiny to overspread the continent allotted by Providence for the free development of our yearly multiplying millions." The article was published as an endorsement of the annexation of Texas and called for aggressive expansionism in a very direct language. As far as British North America was concerned it noted: "indeed there is a great deal of Annexation yet to take place, within the life of the present generation, along the whole line of our northern border." Rejecting the notion that European powers might maintain the balance of power in the hemisphere, the article went on to add that "Whatever progress of population there may be in the British Canadas, is only for their own early severance of their present colonial relation to the little island three thousand miles across the Atlantic; soon to be followed by Annexation, and destined to swell the still accumulating momentum of our progress."[5] Historians have seen this aggressive rhetoric as a political tool deployed to overawe Whig critics of expansionism in the mid-1840, but also as the expression of a new vibrant nationalism associated with a younger generation of Americans.[6]

That being said, Manifest Destiny as a form of American nationalism incorporated aspects of American thought that had far deeper roots. Older treatments of the genesis of Manifest Destiny have insisted on its messianic nature and on the millennial tones that heralded the advent of the great American nation. The providential references in the 1845 article were limited in their development, but other texts that appeared in the *Review* dealing with republican culture and literature had fleshed out these themes in the years previous to the famous debate on Texas's admission to the Union. Given its emphasis on promoting a unique cultural and historical perspective that was a reflection of American political values, the *Democratic Review* is usually seen as an incubator of this particular brand of American nationalism, which emerged full-blown in the debate over expansionism in the 1840s and 1850s.[7] Historians have traced its origins further back, linking its millennial overtones to the First Great awakening and the concept that America would be the cradle of a global spiritual renewal.[8] This sense of American providentialism was further nourished by the American Revolution and the revolutionary generation's heralding of a new age being inaugurated in political and social organization.[9] With the adoption of the Constitution, American federalism seemed to also provide a mechanism for the endless expansion of the republican way of life. Indeed, as Madison explained in Federalist number 10, the multiplicity of interests regrouped under the aegis of a Federal government could actually help to preserve liberty.[10] The rapid territorial expansion of the United States and the experience of the War of 1812 fanned American nationalism in the 1820s and created a context within which grandiose ideas about American domination of the western hemisphere found fertile ground. According to most historical accounts, O'Sullivan in turn distilled these ideas into a coherent form in his *Democratic Review* precisely at the moment where the Canadian question was being debated in the period press, with seminal texts on Manifest Destiny appearing in the wake of the rebellions, from 1839 to 1845. In recent years there has been some disagreement over the authorship of key articles expounding the ideas associated with Manifest Destiny between 1839 and 1845, but there seems little doubt that O'Sullivan was responsible for the articles that dealt with the Canadian situation, since he remained in close control of the *Review* until the spring of 1839.[11]

## "DEMOCRATIC HISTORY" IN THE MAKING: THE CANADIAN REBELLIONS IN THE *DEMOCRATIC REVIEW*

Only a few weeks after the publication of the *Democratic Review*'s first issue, a rebellion broke out in Lower Canada that would put the journal in a delicate position. Much of the border population seemed to enthusiastically support the Canadian revolutionaries and O'Sullivan's sympathies ran naturally toward endorsing those he saw as latter-day patriots challenging British rule in America. However, on 5 January 1838 the Van Buren administration imposed strict neutrality that forbade American citizens from interfering in the affairs of the neighbouring British provinces under threat of arrest and imprisonment.[12] The president's policies were so unpopular in border states that they eroded support for incumbent Democratic regimes. In New York, Governor William Marcy's powerful electoral machine was unable to prevent his defeat against a Whig opponent in the 1838 election, and attempts to help enforce Van Buren's neutrality proclamation may well have been partially responsible for his defeat.[13] On a broader scale, as Julien Mauduit demonstrates in the following chapter, the federal government's response to the Canadian situation would have a discernable impact on the outcome of the 1840 presidential election.

Similarly, O'Sullivan and his *Democratic Review* had to defend the neutrality proclamation despite a marked sympathy for the cause of the Canadian rebels. In "The Canadian Question," published in the journal's January 1838 issue, O'Sullivan outlined the causes and main events associated with the rebellions in the Canadas. The *Democratic Review*'s editor took great pains to distinguish between the revolutionary movements that had arisen in the Canadian provinces, but he also sought to associate both of them with a broader movement of colonial liberation from European rule. Although he would go on to discuss the issue of the Upper Canadian rebellion in detail, and underline the important support it had garnered on the American side of the border, the first articles published in the journal went into much greater depth on the Lower Canadian situation and on the individuals involved, owing perhaps to a personal connection between O'Sullivan and individuals associated with the Lower Canadian movement.[14] The article thus reproduced large sections of the 92 Resolutions adopted by the Lower Canadian Assembly in 1834 and the Imperial Parliament's response, in the form of the

Russell Resolutions (1837), which O'Sullivan saw as the direct cause of the rebellion. He considered the Patriotes' demands reasonable, as they amounted to little more than a call for an end to corruption and misrule. In justifying the position of the Lower Canadian reformers, O'Sullivan frequently compared them to the American patriots who had contested British rule some sixty years earlier. The *Democratic Review*'s editor considered that the Canadian rebellions marked the death knell of British imperial rule, since maintaining control over the colonies through force was both untenable on the ground and highly unpopular with the British electorate. As for the Canadians, he considered that "a majority of the people of the Canadas desire to be free, to govern themselves on the pure representative principles of which they have so glorious a model perpetually before their eyes." Still, the editor was careful to warn against interference in the affairs of the republic's neighbours: Canadians had to gain their own independence. O'Sullivan explained that his sympathy for the Canadian rebels grew out of the belief that the "triumph of the people will be the triumph of liberty – of democratic principle – of the right of self-government." However, he added that it was the duty of the United States and its citizens to do nothing that would compromise its neutrality by taking sides with either protagonist in the conflict raging along its northern borders.[15]

Still, O'Sullivan saw sympathy for the Canadian revolutionaries as a "moral duty" of Americans and he used the issue of the Canadian rebellions to expose the antidemocratic leanings of his political enemies. He regretted the disposition of "not a few respectable presses, of the United States, to frown upon the infant revolution, to disparage the efforts of the Canadians, and the character and principles of the able and respectable men, who, like the Otises, the Adams, the Henrys, and the Franklins of our own Revolution, happen to be placed, by their patriotism, and the confidence of their countrymen, in the front of affairs." O'Sullivan noted that this was hardly surprising given the existence in the United States of "a party, respectable in numbers as well as in wealth and education, entertaining an inveterate distrust of, and dislike to, the people and popular principles." Always the advocate of democracy, he considered the reaction of Americans to the struggles of freedom loving rebels as a litmus test of their republican principles. The fact of the matter was that many American newspapers had received information about the rebellions from articles drawn from the tory press of Montreal and had consequently adopted a position less favourable to the Canadian rebels. To O'Sullivan, this position was untenable for any American patriot. He concluded, "as Americans, as the citizens of a country elevated to greatness by virtue of the very claims to self-government which the Canadians assert, it is impossible to repress the emotion of candid good will towards them, and of ardent aspirations for the honorable success of this new family of worshipers at the holy Shrine of Liberty."[16]

While the first article on the Canadian rebellions was not as detailed as those that came later, it did contain a rather striking passage that indicates the extent to which they stimulated thinking about expansion, republicanism, and America's place in history. For while O'Sullivan insisted on American neutrality in Canadian affairs, he also pointedly took the opportunity to answer those who argued that the United States could not expand to any great size without threatening its ability to maintain liberty. The impact of the federation's growth on its internal political stability had been raised by Texas' request for admission to the Union, which had been formulated in 1836 and rejected by the Jackson administration. During the debates on this question critics called on classical political theory, which held that republics could not maintain their liberty if they grew too large.[17] While O'Sullivan continued to claim he was not arguing for the annexation of the Canadian colonies, he did maintain that the American federation could eventually absorb republics that had been formed by peoples who were emerging from under the yoke of European imperialism. Indeed, it was part of the genius of the American political system that it lent itself to territorial expansion by guaranteeing the particular interests and the autonomy of the States. The role of the federal government was limited to ensuring the uniformity of laws in the republic and acting for the States in international matters and security, and this role was precisely delineated by the Constitution and the separation of powers it instituted. The article also distinguishes between two eras of human history separated by the American Revolution when referring to classical ideas about the limits to republican growth as belonging to "a past which was terminated when the American experiment first dawned upon the world as the commencement of a new era." "The peculiar characteristic of our system," O'Sullivan argued, "the distinctive evidence of its divine origin (that is to say, its foundation on those original principles of natural right and truth, implanted by the Creator, as the first moral elements of human nature) is, that it may, if its theory is maintained pure in practice, be extended, with equal safety and efficiency, over any indefinite number of millions of population and territory."[18] Here, the Constitution appears almost as a divine revelation, charting the future course of American expansion in a trope that would be further developed in the 1839 essay "The Great Nation of Futurity." Thus, while he remained uncertain as to the wisdom of eventually integrating the liberated Canadian colonies into the American federation, O'Sullivan asserted he could "see no reason why, at some future day, our experiment should not be in successful operation over the whole North American continent, from the isthmus to the pole."[19] At the very least, it seems the Canadian rebellions prompted O'Sullivan to formulate an early version of his providential vision of America's future.

A long two part article appeared in a double issue of the *Review* in the early summer of 1838 that chronicles the events that shook Lower Canada in the last months of 1837, and the unsuccessful attempt to re-invade the province early in 1838. It also recounts the uprising in Upper Canada in December of 1837 and describes in great detail the agitation that took hold of neighbouring American states, the attempts by American authorities to make sure that war would not break out as a result of tensions along the border, the *Caroline* incident, the events at Navy Island, and the unsuccessful attempts to invade Upper Canada. The perspective adopted is once again sympathetic, emphasizing the Canadians' cause as that of a North American people struggling against European colonialism. O'Sullivan depicts Lower-Canadian tories as cruel, corrupt, and desperate to preserve their privileged position within the colonial system. British administrators and officers are described as heartless bureaucrats bent on imposing unjust rule on an unwilling people, whose resistance they would brutally crush after the outbreak of the rebellions. Generally, patriot leaders and their followers in both colonies are seen as part of a movement of colonial liberation that O'Sullivan associates freely with the patriots of 1776 and with the struggle of all colonial peoples of the New World against European empires. His most critical comments regarding the revolutionary movements deal with the military strategies adopted by the patriot leadership, which he saw as disorganized and ill prepared, both in the fall of 1837 and in ill-advised frontier raids carried out in early 1838.[20]

These highly detailed articles served as a template for diffusing an interpretation of the rebellions on the international stage that told the story from a perspective more sympathetic to the revolutionaries.[21] The repression of the patriot press in both provinces created a void that would only later be filled by papers established by exiles in the United States. In the interim, the *Democratic Review*'s interpretations served to counter information that was coming mostly from the Montreal tory press and being relayed by American and British papers on the international level. Indeed, O'Sullivan himself was keenly aware that the tories had succeeded in circulating a largely negative view of the revolutionary movements and he considered it his duty to set the record straight by stating the case for the popular movement in both provinces. For the most part, the journal adopted almost in its entirety the explanations advanced by the rebels themselves, and in the case of the Lower Canadian rebellions the *Review* seems to have relied on sources very close to the movement. Not surprisingly then, the account of the uprising in Lower Canada described the rebellions as a "Civil War" largely instigated by the tories and their rabid press, which had been attacking the reform movement for years and distorting its aims and ambitions. Indeed, the tories had attempted to portray the Patriote movement as exclusively French Canadian in order to undermine its reformist and anti-colonial nature.[22] The *Democratic Review,* on the other hand, made the argument that the movement was not exclusively French Canadian, that its demands called for reform of a corrupt and partial system, and that it was not focused solely on gaining advantages for the French Canadian majority. O'Sullivan also contested the tory claim that the English population had risen as one to smite the rebels, and made much of the participation of English leaders in the uprising, providing a brief description of Wolfred Nelson's role both politically and as a Patriote military leader. He also noted the great enthusiasm created all along the Canadian border for the revolutionary movement among the American population, describing meetings organized in the main towns of New York and Vermont in aid of the Patriotes' cause.[23]

In describing the Patriotes' military defeats, O'Sullivan insisted on the depredations of British troops and loyal volunteers upon the people of the regions and villages sympathetic to the rebels and reported in great detail tory attempts to humiliate the Patriotes and their supporters. The battle at St-Eustache in December of 1837 is portrayed as a massacre, and the subsequent sacking and burning of the village of Saint-Benoît appears as a senseless act of cruelty. In the end though, these tactics of the Crown's officers and supporters are seen as further proof of the harshness of colonial rule and as a harbinger of the end of British rule in the colonies. O'Sullivan writes that these events would not only mark the future of Canada, but would ultimately damage the reputation of the British crown: "The insurrection was indeed suppressed, but Canada has not been strengthened to the British Crown. Such events as these will hardly find a place in the proud pages of English history; but deep, deep will they burn into the heart of her distant province, and the blood of these patriot martyrs, so profusely shed at the altar of royalty, on an American soil, will hallow their cause with millions of the free, and forever dishonor the escutcheon of England's Virgin Queen, with an ineffaceable stain of blood, which, in this hemisphere, at least, will link a name auspicious to all the rest of her empire, with the doings of the TYRANT KING who left his parricidal print of blood upon the American soil, to form the seal of its freedom to all future time."[24]

The anti-colonial tone of the description of Canadian events is carried over into the narrative of those that had played out on Upper Canadian soil. O'Sullivan was careful to point out the difference in the population of the two provinces, referencing very intentionally the penchant of Upper Canadians for political discussion and speculation, qualities he associated with the American origins of many settlers. As to the movement and its leadership, William Lyon Mackenzie is first presented in a highly favourable light, with O'Sullivan drawing on Irish history to identify him to Wolfe Tone's republican movement of the late eighteenth century. The comparison no doubt pointed to the nature of the organization in Upper Canada, but it was quickly qualified by the assertion that the movement that arose in Upper Canada was entirely under the influence of ideologies and practices associated with the United States.[25] The rapid failure of the Upper Canadian uprising is again attributed to faulty military strategy, and the bulk of the commentary on the situation relating to the upper province quickly shifted to the effects of the movement on the border states and the significant political agitation that occurred in these areas.

O'Sullivan provides accounts of meetings organized by sympathizers in Buffalo and Ogdensburg that took place even before the Upper Canadian patriots had sought refuge on American soil. Throughout the description of these and later events, he attempts to strike a balance between his admiration for the republican fervour of the American sympathizers and his need to support the strict neutrality enacted by the administration's proclamation. This was less obvious in his description of events that took place before the burning of the *Caroline*, that is, before the neutrality proclamation, and the author thus repeatedly praises the patriotism of American citizens who flocked to support the cause. On arriving upon American soil, O'Sullivan writes, Mackenzie found himself in a "nation of friends." He reports a large meeting at Buffalo in a hall over which floated a tricolour flag with two stars apparently representing the Canadian republics, and describes the organization of American volunteers under Van Rensselaer who later marched to Navy Island. O'Sullivan goes on to describe this unsuccessful campaign and the burning of the *Caroline*, questioning only the military tactics employed.[26] However, the tone of the article changes once the account broaches the administration's adoption of a policy of neutrality, which is portrayed as a salutary gesture designed to restore calm on the frontier, maintain the peace, and prevent the United States from being dragged into a war. Along with the loss of Navy Island, as well as Mackenzie's return and subsequent arrest by American authorities, the article provides details of the four further campaigns aiming at invasion of Upper Canadian soil, all staged from various locations and often with arms that were obtained by raids on American arsenals, notably at Watertown, Batavia, and Elizabethtown. O'Sullivan emphasizes the illegal acts and unrest caused by the sympathizers without severely blaming them for their enthusiasm. The author also pointedly comments on the use of Aboriginal and free black troops by the British in their actions against the rebels near Detroit.[27]

Clearly, the Upper Canadian rebellion and the unrest it caused in the border states along the St Lawrence and Great Lakes proved a more difficult subject for the *Review*. On the one hand, O'Sullivan sought to applaud the republican spirit of those who flew to the aid of the Canadian rebels, while on the other, he was mindful of the need to support the administration's position and explain its necessity. The apparent contradiction between his anti-colonial stance and his support for the government measure limiting American participation in a war against British colonialism was reconciled by the idea that it fell to the Canadians to secure their own freedom. Still, O'Sullivan explained that the meaning of the events in Canada was far more significant in the longer view of "democratic history" than the immediate defeat of the patriots might suggest:

> We have described those confused, and unwarrantable operations, because they were inseparably connected with the subject, and possess an important interest, in developing, both to England, Canada, and the United States, the one irrefutable fact, that the PEOPLE in these contiguous regions cannot be separated in their feelings and interests; and that, however Britain may legislate, the hardy, simple, republican, people of the North, hold, at all times, the balance of power between her and her province in their hands, and that it rests, at any moment, with the Canadians themselves, to maintain the equipoise with European interests and European rulers, a cumbrous inutility of an irresponsible monarchy and its ten thousand alien bayonets or to make the scale preponderate, in a moment, with the priceless benefits of popular liberty, self-government, and national independence, chiefly and lastingly secured. This is but anticipating the language of history, and is a question with which government and their interests can have little bearing.

In this sense, even in failure the Canadian rebellions commended themselves to the attention of the American public: "let not, at least, democratic history be false to itself by refusing to record its sympathy not less strong in defeat than it would have been in victory in behalf of a cause which cannot be otherwise than sacred in the eyes of every sincere American friend of popular freedom."[28]

Moreover, Americans who expressed admiration for the British government might also take note that the British parliament had voted to suspend the constitution of Lower Canada, thus depriving the colonists of their fundamental political rights. Still, O'Sullivan did not entirely despair for the fate of liberty in Britain, since there was at least one "voice of manhood in that hall to tell the people of England, that success was more a matter of regret than gratulation, when a free nation was found tyrannizing over a people equally free."[29] O'Sullivan again here emphasizes in gendered language the historical significance of the Canadian rebellions. For while British colonists in North America espoused republican freedoms, representatives of their brethren in the metropolis found themselves dishonouring the historic mother of parliaments and the memory of previous champions of parliamentary freedom by imposing tyranny on an "equally free" people. Qualified as manly, Sir William Moleworth's objection to the measure is seen as an isolated demonstration of the virility necessary to defend and maintain freedom. The passage cited here anchors American freedom in the Anglo-Saxon past while emphasizing the divide created by the American Revolution, a fracture made evident by the historical anachronism of continued British rule over an American people.

## THE QUESTION OF ANNEXATION

Although the *Democratic Review* remained interested in the course of the Canadian revolutionary movement, and particularly its impact on the border states, articles dealing with the Canadian situation moved away from narrating the events of the rebellions to a more thematic and analytical coverage. In the months following the long surveys that appeared in 1838, the *Review* published poems and short articles that reinforced its historical portrayal of Canadian events as a chapter in the longer struggle of American peoples against the forces of European colonialism. A poem dealing with the Lower Canadian leader Louis-Joseph Papineau published in the fall of 1838, for example, presented him as tending "the sacred fire thy hand had lit" and eventually guiding the people of his newly released "young Republic" to "free and equal rights."[30] The news of British reprisals against patriot positions and villages sympathetic to the movement in both Upper and Lower Canada prompted the *Review* to publish another poem titled "Canadian Avatar," which this time highlighted the cruelty of soldiers and volunteers who gave no quarter to either rebels or innocent villagers brandishing white flags. The poem was preceded by an excerpt from the *Montreal Herald* advocating harsh treatment for rebels, arguing that "nothing but sweeping them from the earth and laying their habitations level with the dust, will prevent renewed rebellions south of the St Lawrence." It then opened by questioning the glory to be obtained by burning "the poor cottager's home, where innocence slept with her beautiful ones" and added that Britain would not escape divine retribution for these crimes. However, the author quickly shifted to the subject of American indifference to the cause of the Canadian cause, portraying an America that "Calmly folded her hands on her bosom of cold, as though the oppressed could no precedent find." The poem went on to urge readers to

> Take down your bright volumes from history's shelves,
> and open the seals from your forefathers' graves,
> Read out the proud story from letters of gold,
> And hurl back the libel that darkens their way,
> The stars and the stripes when in glory unrolled,
> Were the symbols of rebels as guilty as they.[31]

Once again, the Canadian rebellions were situated within the context of America's revolutionary and anti-colonial history and Americans were enjoined to at the very least sympathize with the cause of the rebels. In addition to these short poems, the *Review* would also publish accounts of executions carried out by the British.[32]

Returning to the "Canada Question" in a much longer piece published in January of 1839, O'Sullivan sought once again to address the question of American neutrality. Noting the policy's unpopularity in radical quarters and in the population sympathetic to the Canadian cause along the frontier, the article went to some length to counter critics who argued that it was born out of fear of British power or that it demonstrated a lack of sympathy for the cause of popular rights in Canada. In developing his argument, the *Review*'s editor turned immediately to the question of Texas. The successful uprising that led to the independence of Texas was organized and led by Americans who had migrated to Mexico, attracted by easily available lands. The Texas Revolution (1835–36) also attracted armed American sympathizers who joined the struggle against the Mexican government, and this interference of American citizens in the internal affairs of another state heightened tensions between the United States and its southern neighbour. The controversy surrounding American involvement in Texas proved for O'Sullivan that laws in place at the time were insufficient; it also demonstrated that the Federal government's actions in the Canadian case were amply justified. The Texas situation was a perfect example of "the success with which an actual war might be levied by individual enterprise, excited by the tempting allurement of a distribution of spoil and land, against a country to which we were bound by solemn treaty guarantees of peace and friendship," concluding that "the impartial pen of history must always record (it) as nothing more nor less than what it has been well termed, *the robbery of a realm*." In this analysis, the Texas Revolution seemed not to fit into the march of democratic history since it had been carried out by external agents. The further problem, from O'Sullivan's perspective, was that the laws in place left the American government powerless to prevent "the private war which was levied against (Mexico) by our citizens."[33] If the case of Texas proved that greater executive action was necessary to prevent America's neutrality from being compromised, this seemed even more evident in the case of the Canadian rebellions, since the Canadian uprisings had been organized by the British colonials themselves.

O'Sullivan also dismissed the charge that the administration's position had been adopted out of fear of war with Britain. Van Buren's neutrality proclamation was inspired by neither fear of Britain nor disdain for the cause of the rebels; rather it was an example of the "American system of foreign policy." Interference in the affairs of other nations and neighbouring countries was associated with the "Old European powers," while the American system of foreign policy proceeded from a concern for peace and an assumption of good faith towards other countries. From these positions flowed the duty of non-interference and neutrality regarding their internal affairs, despite whatever sympathy Americans and their government might have for the cause of one side or another in the conflict. Moreover, O'Sullivan argued that given the popular basis of government in the United States, that duty also extended to American citizens. Still, the *Review*'s editor recognized that patriot lodges were active in the northern states from Michigan to Vermont and he estimated that up to 90,000 Americans could be involved in secret societies supporting the patriots. This he saw as a direct threat to the stability of the republic, mostly born of the danger of secret societies established by unscrupulous Canadian exiles who would lead young Americans to their death in hopeless attacks against Canadian soil.[34]

What made this worse in O'Sullivan's eyes was that it was a needless carnage. Returning to the "democratic view of history," he predicted that left to their own devices the Canadian colonies must inevitably become independent, arguing that British ascendancy over the colonies was rapidly coming to an end. The cause of popular reform could not go backwards, and O'Sullivan ridiculed British attempts to re-establish colonial rule, most notably through the mission of Lord Durham, who he portrayed as an "aristocratic dictator."

It was abundantly clear to the *Democratic Review* that the British could only maintain the current regime through the use of force, and its editor considered it obvious that the British people would neither finance nor countenance such a regime. As for the Canadians, having embarked on the road toward liberty and independence, it was now impossible for that course to be reversed: "The human breast is too congenial a soil for such seed, to admit of their ever being eradicated. On the contrary, they must grow, and every year must only strike deeper their roots, and mature the fruits which it is their nature to bring forth. How, then, in the present instance, when the popular demand is for the privilege of self-government by elective legislation when the truth has gone abroad through the earth, of the sovereignty of the people and when the vicinity of such institutions as those of our Union must serve as a perpetual model and incentive, how can the British Government cherish the absurd delusion, of being ever able to appease the agitation once thus awakened, by anything short of the unreserved concession of such a demand?"[35]

In the end it was impossible for the British to govern the Canadas without eventually conceding the main demands of the Canadians for political reform that would give them control over their own government. Once that control was achieved, O'Sullivan firmly believed that the Canadians would use it to break away from the Empire and declare their independence. Given the inevitability of colonial liberation, the enthusiasm of the sympathizers was misplaced. History would unfold in the manner that it should, and consequently the era of European domination over the New World would soon come to an end. As O'Sullivan concluded, the question "is now one, not of a reform, but of independence. The Canadians can now never be satisfied with less."[36]

Of course, the logic of O'Sullivan's argument that the independence of the Canadian colonies was inevitable raised the question of their eventual relationship to the United States. He noted that certain commentators, among them Canadians in exile, urged that annexation of the Canadian colonies would be in the United States' best interest. Advocates of annexation argued that the addition of the independent Canadian colonies as two or more new states would increase in the union's population, provide access to the St Lawrence and to the vast resources of the Canadas, as well as put an end to Canada serving as a safe haven for fugitive slaves. Advanced by William Lyon Mackenzie, among others, the latter argument aligned the activities of abolitionists operating the underground railroad to British intrigues seeking to destabilize and weaken the republic by encouraging slaves escaping to the North.[37] In turn, these runaway slaves were incorporated into regiments that fought against the patriots and their American allies. In response to these arguments, it seemed clear to O'Sullivan that commercial relations with the colonies and later with free Canadian republics could be obtained without annexation and by pursuing the policy of good faith and non-interference. As to the issue of fugitive slaves, he refused to reduce this to a matter of British intrigue; there were "other motives" for this movement, a subject he pointedly did not pursue. Further, even once Canadian independence was achieved and recognized by all including the mother country, he believed that "neither their prosperity and happiness, nor our own, would be promoted by a union; which would require on our part an amendment to the Constitution according at least to the views of the State-Rights school now happily prevalent in this country." All other questions could easily be "arranged without an union, the manifest common interest of both, the spirit of the age, and the ascendancy, in both, of that popular will which can never in an industrious and commercial republic be in favor of war, will afford an ample guarantee against any danger of hostile collision between the two."[38]

## THE DURHAM REPORT, REFORM, AND RACE

Only a few months later, the *Democratic Review* returned to the Canadian question, this time in a long commentary on Lord Durham's *Report on the Affairs of the British North America.* Considering O'Sullivan's portrayal of Durham as an incompetent, aristocratic dictator, the *Review*'s generally positive reception of the *Report* marked a significant reversal. Indeed, the editor remarked that the document was generally far better than he had expected, and despite speculating that it might actually have been written by a member of the commission rather than by the British envoy himself, he ended the article by stating that Durham had henceforth to be regarded as a leading statesman. This reversal was primarily the result of the *Report*'s condemnation of the abuses of colonial rule, particularly as it related to corruption and favouritism. O'Sullivan insisted that the *Report* entirely vindicated the *Democratic Review*'s earlier analysis of the political situation in the Canadian colonies and he repeatedly chastised rival editors who had questioned the rebels' motives in challenging a colonial rule they considered benign.[39]

While the article noted the long list of colonial abuses in the provinces of Upper and Lower Canada, including those related to clergy reserves and land distribution, the antidemocratic role of the appointed council, and the role of colonial oligarchies, O'Sullivan devoted the major part of his text to refuting a central aspect of the *Report* as it related to the situation in Lower Canada. Indeed, one of the most telling aspects of Durham's analysis was his insistence that the conflict in Lower Canada proceeded from a collision of "nations," that is, that it grew from the animosity that had arisen between the British and French Canadian inhabitants of the province. Durham, as O'Sullivan noted, while recognizing the legitimacy of some of the issues raised by the Patriotes tended to undermine the significance of their struggle by insisting that the movement's goals were essentially conservative, involving the preservation of the French Canadian nation and its distinct institutions, including the seigneurial system of land holding and an antiquated system of French civil law. These in turn acted as a brake on the ambitions of the more progressive Anglo-Saxon population. While O'Sullivan found much to commend in the *Report*, he energetically refuted its emphasis on the national basis of the conflict in Lower Canada. He admitted that the rebellion itself had sharpened ethnic animosities, no doubt as a result of British reprisals on the population, but O'Sullivan saw this as a result of the uprisings rather than as their principal cause. In his opinion, Durham's view was imputable to the influence that Montreal tories had exercised on him during his stay in the province. It was also the expression of "good old English prejudice and pride, which no superadded cosmopolitan liberality, of a political school but little congenial to a proud English aristocrat, can ever overcome."[40] In order to prove the contrary, O'Sullivan went to great pains to insist on the significant participation of American and Irish segments of the population during the political phase of the Patriote movement, and he also once again included a long note on the character and political conduct of Papineau, refuting Durham's charge that his charismatic leadership had mobilized an ignorant *Canadien* population against the British in order to advance a conservative social agenda. Indeed, Papineau was a Democrat in the American mould, well versed in American history and politics, and his opinions "fully sustain and sympathize with the general policy of the late and present Democratic Administrations, with which he is very familiar, and especially in the great struggle for a financial reform, vitally important to the best interests, moral and material, of the country, in which both have been so deeply engaged."[41]

Having transformed Papineau into a full-blown Jacksonian Democrat, O'Sullivan attacked the concept of ethnic conflict by turning it on its head and recognizing it essentially as an instrument of colonial domination. Citing the case of Ireland, where a Protestant ascendancy held sway, he noted that the British ascendancy that Lower Canadian tories wished to instill and that Durham sought to reinforce was nothing more than a screen for control of one nation by another. The separation of French Canadians and their British neighbours that Durham described in the report was the product of colonial institutions that enforced inequality as a means of political domination, and in this they were reproducing the separation of Catholics and Protestants in Ireland. These differences could be overcome through common struggle for political reforms, as was the case with the cause of the Lower Canadian rebels, and they could be entirely removed by the establishment of free institutions. Citing Durham's use of Louisiana as an example for the assimilation of French Canadians, O'Sullivan noted that integration occurred in American society because free institutions removed barriers for holding office, the law making no distinctions between citizens.[42] This position may seem curious coming from an Irish American in an era during which the Irish faced significant discrimination, but O'Sullivan's argument rested on an idealized view of American society and politics that emphasized equal rights and opportunities for all white males, and he saw the Patriote revolution as sharing the same ideals. Moreover, many Irish Americans embraced political notions of American exceptionalism that emphasized the creation of a new man in the Americas, forging a new identity, often defined in racial terms, simply identified as "American."[43]

The same perspective informed his analysis of Durham's proposals for reforming colonial government and for dealing with the "French Canadian problem." Generally, O'Sullivan approved of the solutions Durham presented and particularly that of giving colonial legislatures control over the executive, which he also saw as the main source of the political problems in the colonies. He believed that this reform would merely accelerate the demands for the concessions of more democratic institutions, for the abolition of appointed councils and for the separation of the colonies from the mother country. The proposed union of the provinces he saw essentially as tending toward the same end. Concerning the union of the Canadas as a means of assimilating the French Canadians and dealing with the problem of conflict between ethnic groups, O'Sullivan generally agreed that this was far preferable to the creation of an unfair electoral system, which would have stacked representation in favour of the British population in Lower Canada. At least the Anglo-Saxon majority in the newly created province would be honestly achieved, and he had little doubt that with the democratic reforms proposed the French Canadian minority would be well treated by a reform minded majority. Moreover, he also quite accurately predicted that the French members would vote together to protect their interests, mirroring the conduct of Southern representatives in the United States Congress. Ultimately though, all these reform measures and the prospect of federating the provinces were but "the first step towards that total disconnection of the colonies from the mother country, which is now evidently close at hand." Inasmuch as the relative isolation and weakness of the provinces had bound them to the metropolis, the strength that would grow from union would pull them toward independence. Similarly, the checks on popular power that Durham proposed would also serve "to expedite the separation." In O'Sullivan's view the British North American colonies would fall away from the empire in short order and "that separation will then take place peacefully and tranquilly, for it is plain that Great Britain could not dream, in that case, of attempting to oppose it by force." British commercial interest would also dictate a course favouring colonial independence and ensuring the peaceful separation of the colonies as "a federation of republics whether in union with our own, or independently."[44]

Once again, then, the *Democratic Review*'s position on the Canadian situation was couched in a historical determinism that emphasized the inevitable separation of European colonies from their metropolis and their adoption of American political ideals and republican institutions. Such a position, expressed repeatedly in articles concerning the rebellions and activities along the Canadian frontier, was consistent with the Democratic culture that the *Review* sought to instill, and it fostered the notions of American exceptionalism that would be highlighted in the key texts that consecrated the ideology of Manifest Destiny. What appears rather unique in these analyses, however, is O'Sullivan's particular sensibility to the situation of Lower Canada. Indeed, throughout his writing on the Canadian troubles, the *Review*'s editor displayed greater knowledge of and concern for the Lower Canadian political movement, which he clearly considered more important and significant than that in Upper Canada. While the repercussions of the Upper Canadian rebellion were more serious in the border states, the uprising in Upper Canada itself seemed to him less organized and more spontaneous than that in Lower Canada. O'Sullivan may have had entries into the Lower Canadian movement in exile, and the detail with which he described events and individuals suggests that this was probably the case. At least two of the movement's leaders, Papineau and Edmund Bailey O'Callaghan, were well connected to the Albany Regency and this no doubt assisted in ensuring a more sympathetic portrayal of their movement in the *Review*.[45]

Nevertheless, O'Sullivan's treatment of the French Canadian component of the revolutionary movement was inconsistent with elements of Anglo-Saxon nationalism that have been linked to Manifest Destiny. It is clear that by the mid-1840s the racial and ethnic component of Manifest Destiny stood at the centre of discourse concerning the annexation of Texas and suggesting an aggressive American stance on the eventual absorption of California, and this was articulated in the famous 1845 article "Annexation." Moreover, the same attitude was quite evident in response of the Whig *North American Review* to Durham's report. In its own long treatment of the situation in British North America the rival journal registered its complete agreement with Durham's assessment of the French Canadians and his identification of the conflict of "races" as being at the base of the troubles in Lower Canada. The *North American Review* also endorsed his view of the French Canadians as clannish and overly nationalistic, being primarily motivated by their hatred of the English and being led by a group of unscrupulous demagogues.[46] By the 1840s dominant stereotypes of French Canadians in American discourse presented them as a degenerated European population, associating them with Aboriginal peoples, representing them as "mongrels and hybrids," and situating them in the same manner as Mexicans, below Anglo-Saxons in terms of their ability to govern themselves.[47] O'Sullivan may have seen French Canadians as more suited for government as a result of their having lived so long under British rule and because of his acquaintance with leaders such as Papineau. He may also have been aware of the struggle over Irish identity in Lower Canada, in which tory editors tried to convince Irish voters to side with the Anglo-Saxon minority, while Patriote papers emphasized the common struggle of Lower Canada and Ireland against British colonialism.[48] Whatever the cause, the expression of an Anglo-Saxon identity and its identification with the advance of democratic government remained muted in articles dealing with the Canadas, as it did in the 1839 essay "The Great Nation of Futurity."[49]

## CONCLUSION: THE *DEMOCRATIC REVIEW* AND THE "CANADIAN MOMENT"

Only a few months after the journal's last major article on the Canadian rebellions, the *Democratic Review* published an essay that is most often considered as the first coherent exposition of the doctrine of Manifest Destiny. In the "Great Nation of Futurity," doubts about the viability of American expansion seemed to have completely evaporated. Using the same historical framework that had inspired O'Sullivan's interpretation of the Canadian rebellions, it restated the belief that the American Revolution marked a turning point for humanity and that it consecrated America's mission: "our national birth was the beginning of a new history, the formation and progress of an untried political system, which separates us from the past and connects us with the future only; and so far as regards the entire development of the natural rights of man, in moral, political, and national life, we may confidently assume that our country is destined to be the great nation of futurity." The United States was thus endowed with a providential mission to perfect human government and effect the liberation of the subjected peoples of the hemisphere. Americans would erect a "temple" to liberty on a continental level: "Its floor shall be a hemisphere, its roof the firmament of the star-studded heavens, and its congregation an Union of many Republics, comprising hundreds of happy millions, calling, owning no man master, but governed by Gods natural and moral law of equality, the law of brotherhood of peace and good will amongst men."[50] The providential nature of this text and its focus on broad democratic principles linked Manifest Destiny to a millennial vision, but unlike the commentaries on the Canadian situation and the more aggressive "Annexation" of 1845, it remained a statement of principles rather than a direct blueprint for expansion. Other essays with a similar philosophical and religious bent appeared in the following years. "Democracy" published in March of 1840 reinforced the historical determinism evident throughout the writing in the *Review* by establishing the inevitable progress of democratic regimes and the subsequent decline of aristocratic and monarchical government. This particular analysis also attacked wealth as creating moneyed aristocracies that could threaten the republic and argued that the vigilance of citizens was essential to prevent government from falling into the hands of corrupt minorities. Still, the triumph of democracy – true democracy, both social and political – appeared inevitable since it corresponded to God's design.[51]

The progress of democracy and of democratic regimes, a view of history centred around the American Revolution and the decline of aristocratic, and thus European, regimes in the New World were all themes that had been developed in analyses of the Canadian rebellions published in 1838 and 1839. These discussions lacked much of the messianic language found in the later texts, and they openly rejected the aggressive annexationist stance that would be espoused in the mid-1840s. Several explanations have been advanced to account for these differences. A few authors have argued that articles such as the "Great Nation of Futurity," "Democracy," and even "Annexation" were not penned by O'Sullivan at all, but by a female associate, Jane McManus. McManus's role might explain the shift from the more cautious positions advanced in the earlier articles, but the basis of America's bright democratic future articulated in these seminal texts remained rooted in similar ideas. Despite the stance taken by the *Review* in 1845, McManus and O'Sullivan apparently shared a less overtly aggressive view of American expansion – this despite the former's involvement in Texas politics and land speculation.[52] Other historians have argued that these texts represented an idealistic initial representation of Manifest Destiny in which the agency of other settler populations tempered the emphasis on the territorial expansion of the United States. In this model, settler societies had to achieve independence on their own and only then could their eventual and voluntary adherence to a loose American federation be entertained.[53] Significantly, this pattern of discourse assumed that annexation would take place over the much longer term and with the consent of the newly created republics' citizens who would freely chose to join the American federation. This vision corresponded to the position often outlined in the Patriote discourse of the 1830s, and to contemporary American beliefs about the possibility of sister republics and even of other republican federations existing alongside that of the United States, for a time at least.[54] This tendency in both the *Review*'s writing on Canada and more general texts on the future expansion of republican government gave Manifest Destiny its more "progressive" face, and since it included a nod to the self-determination and agency of other peoples, historians long denied its imperial character. On that score, the work of Reginald Horsman convincingly demonstrated the strong racial component within this ideology that sought to submit Mexicans and Aboriginal Nations to the inexorable advance of Anglo-Saxon peoples. Manifest Destiny, a form of settler colonialism, was imperial from its very inception.[55]

The "Canada Question" differed precisely because it involved colonies populated by settlers of white European origin. As such, their annexation was not ensured by simple racial superiority since their inhabitants were deemed capable of establishing and sustaining democratic governments. On this issue, O'Sullivan departed from other commentators, including Durham and much of the Whig press, in insisting on the legitimacy of Patriote discourse and endorsing the idea that French Canadians could govern themselves. His affinity for the Lower Canadian movement can be explained by many factors, but more importantly it speaks to the fluidity of racial formulations in the late 1830s and early 1840s.

Still, the *Review*'s strong stance against American involvement in Canada stood in stark contrast to its later position on Texas and its open advocacy of the annexation of British North America in the mid-1840s. Of course, this position can be explained as political expediency. As an organ of the administration the *Review* was obliged to take a stance that reflected official policy: in 1838 that policy opposed the annexation of any new territory, while in 1845 it advocated the annexation of Texas, and perhaps even that of British North America. While this view has considerable validity, it should not obscure the context within which the Canadian rebellions occurred and were received in the United States. In a very recent article, Andrew C. Isenberg and Thomas Richards Jr have argued that the emphasis on Manifest Destiny in American historiography has created a teleological perspective that obscures the hesitancy about expansion that characterized the late 1830s. Citing the opposition to the annexation of Texas mounted by John Quincy Adams in 1835, they demonstrate rather convincingly that although the idea of

American hegemony over the continent was being floated in the late 1830s, the path towards territorial expansion remained unclear and various scenarios were envisaged, few of them culminating in the American federation occupying the entire continent, at least in the short term. Indeed, they refer to the period between 1836 and 1845 as the "Texas Moment," one where Texas continuing as an independent republic seemed feasible, and where both settler populations and Aboriginal nations in other parts of North America envisioned the creation of political entities that were not necessarily "destined" to fall under the sway of the United States.[56] As the other contributions to this volume make clear, American sympathizers to the cause of Canadian rebels often referenced Texas, and Canadian patriots came to see their potential republic as an independent entity. An examination of the *Democratic Review*'s treatment of the Canadian rebellions demonstrates that its editor had his own "Canadian Moment" and that his analysis of the rebellions within the context of American neutrality led him to develop an interpretation that leaned heavily on the agency of neighbouring colonial peoples as an argument against American participation. This approach was couched in anti-colonial language and drew on the historical determinism that would also shape the formulation of Manifest Destiny that in later texts appeared almost as an ideology of colonial liberation. As such, it may well be that the "Canadian moment" helped shape the ideology of Manifest Destiny in ways that would continue to define it long after the debate over Texas had been resolved by the republic's absorption into the Union.

## NOTES

1 John L. O'Sullivan, "The Canada Question," *United States Democratic Review* (USDR) I, no. 2 (January 1838): 205.

2 "The Great Nation of Futurity," USDR VI, no. 23 (November 1839): 426–30.

3 On O'Sullivan's early life and the foundation of the *Review* see Robert Sampson, *John L. O'Sullivan and His Times* (Kent, OH: Kent State University Press, 2003), 4–22.

4 Edward L. Widmer, *Young America: The Flowering of Democracy in New York City* (Oxford: Oxford University Press, 2000), 40; John L. O' Sullivan, "Introduction: The Democratic Principle, the Importance of

Its Assertion, and Application to Our Political System and Literature," *USDR* I, no. 1 (October 1837): 1–15.

5 "Annexation," *USDR* XVII, nos 85–6 (1845): 5, 7, 9–10.

6 Andrew C. Isenberg and Thomas Richards Jr, "Alternative Wests: Rethinking Manifest Destiny," *Pacific Historical Review* 86, no. 1 (February 2017): 4–17.

7 Thomas R. Hietala, *Manifest Design: American Exceptionalism and Empire* (Ithaca: Cornell University Press, 2003 [1985]), 177, 184; Robert W. Johannsen, "The Meaning of Manifest Destiny," in *Manifest Destiny and Empire: American Antebellum Expansionism*, ed. W. Johannsen (Arlington, TX: Texas A&M University Press, 1997), 9–12; Robert J. Scholnick, "Extermination and Democracy: O'Sullivan, the *Democratic Review*, and Empire, 1837–1840," *American Periodicals* 15, no. 2 (2005): 128; Amy S. Greenberg, *Manifest Manhood and the Antebellum American Empire* (Cambridge: Cambridge University Press, 2005), 11–17; Yonatan Eyal, *The Young America Movement and the Transformation of the Democratic Party, 1828–1861* (Cambridge: Cambridge University Press, 2007), 144; Brian Loveman, *No Higher Law: American Foreign Policy and the Western Hemisphere since 1776* (Chapel Hill: University of North Carolina Press, 2010), 59.

8 Anders Stephanson, *Manifest Destiny: American Expansionism and the Empire of Right* (New York: Hill and Wang, 1995), 13; Nathan O. Hatch, "The Origins of Civil Millennialism in America: New England Clergymen, War with France and the Revolution," *William and Mary Quarterly*, third series, XXXI, no. 3 (July 1974): 407–30.

9 Loveman, *No Higher Law*, 56.

10 Hietala, *Manifest Design*, 175.

11 The authorship of key articles such as "The Great Nation of Futurity" (1839) and "Annexation" (1845) has been attributed to Jane McManus by her biographer. However, the entirety of the articles devoted to the Canadian situation predate her arrival as a collaborator to the *Review* in 1839. As for O'Sullivan, he assumed editorial duties until he left the journal in the spring of 1839. See Linda S. Hudson, *Mistress of Manifest Destiny: A Biography of Jane McManus Storm Cazneau, 1807–1878* (Austin: Texas State Historical Association, 2001), 41, 44–50; Widmer, *Young America*, 45.

12 Martin Van Buren, "Proclamation 45A – Neutrality with Respect to Canadian Affairs," 5 January 1838. Online by Gerhard Peters and John T. Woolley, *The American Presidency Project*. http://www.presidency.ucsb.edu/ws/?pid=67317.

13 I.D. Spencer, *The Victor And the Spoils: A Life of William L. Marcy* (Providence: Brown University Press, 1959), 99–100.

14 Patriote refugees were active in attempting to get their story into the American press. Edmund Bailey O'Callaghan, editor of the Montreal *Vindicator* and Louis-Joseph Papineau's political lieutenant, had extensive connections to the Democratic press in New York and contributed at least one article on Papineau to the *Saratoga Sentinel* which was eventually reprinted as a short pamphlet. Another English-speaking Patriote, Thomas Storrow Brown, penned several articles for the *New York Daily Express* in the months preceding the rebellions. See *A Biographical Sketch of the Hon. Louis Joseph Papineau: Speaker of the House of Assembly of Lower Canada* (Saratoga, NY: Sentinel Press, 1838); Amédée Papineau, *Journal d'un fils de la liberté*, ed. Georges Aubin (Quebec: Septentrion, 1998), 158; Louis-Georges Harvey, "The Forgotten Patriots: Ireland and the Irish in Lower Canadian Political Discourse and Anglophone Historical Consciousness," in *Ireland and Quebec Multidisciplinary Perspectives on History, Culture and Society*, eds Margaret Kelleher and Michael Kenneally (Dublin: Four Courts Press, 2016), 49–63; Jacques Monet, "O'CALLAGHAN, EDMUND BAILEY," in *Dictionary of Canadian Biography*, vol. 10, University of Toronto/Université Laval, 2003–, accessed 4 July 2017, http://www.biographi.ca/en/bio/o_callaghan_edmund_bailey_10E.html; Fernand Ouellet, "BROWN, THOMAS STORROW," in *Dictionary of Canadian Biography*, vol. 11, University of Toronto/Université Laval, 2003–, accessed 4 July 2017, http://www.biographi.ca/en/bio/brown_thomas_storrow_11E.html.

15 "The Canada Question," USDR I, no. 2 (January 1838): 216–18.

16 Ibid., 219–20.

17 On these arguments as they evolved into the 1840s see Michael A. Morrison, "Westward the Curse of Empire: Texas Annexation and the American Whig Party," *Journal of the Early Republic* 10, no. 2 (1990): 221–49.

18 O'Sullivan, "The Canada Question," 217–18.

19 Ibid., 218.

20 J.L. O'Sullivan, "History of the Recent Insurrection in the Canadas – Part First," USDR IV, no. 3 (March–June 1838): 73–87; and O'Sullivan, "History of the Recent Insurrection in the Canadas – Part Second," USDR IV, no. 3 (March–June 1838): 87–104.

21 On the diffusion of news in Paris, for example, see Aurélio Ayala and Françoise Le Jeune, *Les rébellions canadiennes de 1837 et 1838 vues de Paris* (Quebec: Presses de l'Université Laval, 2011).

22 On the tory press, see Harvey, "The Forgotten Patriots" and François Deschamps, *La rébellion de 1837 à travers le prisme du Montreal Herald: la refondation par les armes des institutions politiques canadiennes* (Quebec: Presses de l'Université Laval, 2015).
23 O'Sullivan, "History of the Recent Insurrection in the Canadas – Part First," 80–4.
24 O'Sullivan, "History of the Recent Insurrection in the Canadas – Part Second," 94.
25 Ibid., 87–8.
26 Ibid., 94–6.
27 Ibid., 99–100.
28 Ibid., 103–4.
29 Ibid., 104.
30 A.D. Woodbridge, "Papineau," *USDR* III, no. 10 (October 1838): 112–13.
31 "Canadian Avatar," *USDR* III, no. 12 (December 1838): 380–1.
32 See for example "The Execution in Canada," *USDR* V, no. 15 (March 1839): 343–4.
33 John L. O'Sullivan, "The Canada Question," *USDR* V, no. 13 (January 1839): 8–29, cited at 9.
34 Ibid., 11–14.
35 Ibid., 16.
36 Ibid., 18.
37 Such arguments cost Mackenzie support and attracted criticism from American and Canadian abolitionists. See Lillian F. Gates, *After the Rebellion: The Later Years of William Lyon Mackenzie* (Toronto: Dundurn, 1996), 82–3.
38 O'Sullivan, "The Canada Question," *USDR* V, no. 13: 9.
39 J.L. O'Sullivan, "Lord Durham's Report," *USDR* V, no. 18 (June 1839): 542–79.
40 Ibid., 554.
41 Ibid., 547–8.
42 Ibid., 554–5.
43 In so doing, Irish Americans became "white," associated with descriptions of the American character that included attributes often ascribed to Anglo-Saxons. See Reginald Horsman, *Race and Manifest Destiny: The Origins of American Racial Anglo-Saxonism* (Cambridge, MA: Harvard University Press, 2009), 164; Greenberg, *Manifest Manhood*, 45; James Belich, *Replenishing the Earth: The Settler Revolution and the Rise of the Angloworld* (Oxford: Oxford University Press, 2009), 62.
44 O'Sullivan, "Lord Durham's Report," 578–9.

45 On this question see Louis-Georges Harvey and Yvan Lamonde, "Origines et formes diverses du 'destin manifeste' dans les Amériques: les Papineau et la *United States Magazine and Democratic Review* de Washington et New York," *Cahiers des dix* 67 (2013): 25–73; Yvan Lamonde, *Fais ce que dois, advienne que pourra: Papineau et l'idée de nationalité* (Montreal: Lux, 2015), 83–95.

46 "British North American Politics," *North American Review* 49, no. 105 (October 1839): 373–432.

47 Horsman, *Race and Manifest Destiny*, 222; Jean M. O'Brien, *Firsting and Lasting: Writing Indians out of Existence in New England* (Minneapolis: University of Minnesota Press, 2010), 120.

48 Harvey, "The Forgotten Patriots."

49 Indeed, this essay tended to emphasize a break with the diverse national pasts of those who had migrated to become Americans: "The American people having derived their origin from many other nations, and the Declaration of National Independence being entirely based on the great principle of human equality, these facts demonstrate at once our disconnected position as regards any other nation; that we have, in reality, but little connection with the past history of any of them, and still less with all antiquity, its glories, or its crimes." "The Great Nation of Futurity," 426.

50 Ibid., 427, 429–30.

51 "Democracy," *USDR* VII, no. 27 (March 1840): 215–29.

52 Greenberg, *Manifest Manhood*, 20, 227–9; Hudson, *Mistress of Manifest Destiny*, 38.

53 Scholnick, "Extermination and Democracy," 127; Eyal, *The Young America Movement*, 130–1.

54 Papineau's view on the question evolved: see Harvey and Lamonde, 57–60.

55 Scholnick, "Extermination and Democracy," 137–9.

56 Isenberg and Richards, "Alternative Wests," 7, 15.

# 7

# Canadian Interference in American Politics

## *The 1840 Presidential Election*

JULIEN MAUDUIT

In 1837, the Canadian patriots saw themselves as fulfilling history's "natural" progress towards more democracy. They assumed a favourable outcome: "the democratic swell irresistibly flowed [and] will overwhelm, without violent effort, the powerless obstacles that some will attempt to oppose." In this they were hardly alone. Indeed, most of the citizens in the northern states conveyed a similar vision of history, in which the American republic was destined to be reformed "in the direction of the general democratic movement of the age," squaring more and more with "democratic principles." The Constitution of 1787 was regularly presented as an "experiment," subjected to citizens' trial, error, and improvement. The more radical, early supporters of the Canadian Revolution also called for a regeneration of the Republic on a "genuine" democratic basis. Traditionally, "the Democracy" had conveyed that longing, but during the 1840 presidential campaign, William Henry Harrison and the Whig Party effectively challenged the Jacksonians on this front. The Whig candidate repeatedly reminded his compatriots that "the name does not constitute the Democrat." In this sense, Whig and Democrat electors, as well as Canadian patriots, were the actors of a larger era of political transformations and innovations, the so-called "Age of Revolutions."[1]

A *connected* history of the British colonies and the United States allows us to "move laterally" from national historiographical frameworks. Crossing borders and integrating transnational spaces within the same analysis disrupts familiar narratives.[2] The connection of the attempted revolution of 1837 in the Canadas to the American presidential election of 1840 is a striking example. Historians of the election rarely consider Canada, and for superficially good reasons: both Whig leaders and their Democrat counterparts denounced the illegitimacy of the patriots' activities. When the influential *United States Democratic Review*, stunned by Harrison's victory, tried to explain the act of "suicidal stupidity" committed by the American people in 1840, the editors did not mention the Canadian question, nor the diplomatic crisis with Britain.[3] Therefore, it is not surprising to read only scattered historiographical remarks on Van Buren's unpopular foreign policy in 1840, and nearly nothing about Canada.[4]

Yet a Canadian perspective on the election shows how the patriots' activities undermined Van Buren's electoral basis in the northern states, shattering the alliance Jackson had secured in the mid-1820s between the south and the more popular elements of the free states. Many of the citizens supporting the Canadian Revolution ended by voting Harrison despite their "*locofocoist*" principles, usually associated with the Democratic Party. They did not endorse many of the Whigs' attributed tenets, such as the re-establishment of a national bank, the superiority of the law, or skepticism towards popular sovereignty. Those electors even regularly criticized the national leaders and their press. The "Party Period" concept, which often assumes that voters followed the party line, cannot explain this support for Harrison.[5] Those Whigs-on-the-ground remained self-consciously radical: they were opposed to monarchies and to the British presence in America, they challenged the authority of the president and Congress, and they condemned the legitimacy of the American army's interventions on behalf of the British Crown. Why would these citizens turn their backs on the Democratic Party and fill the ranks of the Whig Party, known to praise the British commercial power and the power of the law?

A reconsideration of the 1840 election through a Canadian lens reveals some tendencies in American politics. The radicals' support for the Whigs connects, for example, with the antiparty tradition and the rebellious spirit in the Republic. "Parties were always required to operate within an ideological environment that was in some way hostile to their existence," remarks one of the most ardent advocates of the "Party Period" concept.[6] Canadian and American patriots regularly criticized the two main parties' national leaders, notably for their opposition to the Canadian republican cause. They also called for the formation of a new party, a "radical party" whose principles would, among other things, support their revolution. The spreading "culture of antipartisanship," as Mark Voss-Hubbard terms it, threatened a republican order that claimed the rightful power of representation. The impact of the Canadian crisis illustrates how, in the late 1830s, party loyalism was loose, complex, and fluid. It also reveals citizens' political and intellectual autonomy: they could support a candidate with reluctance and even vote for them without being convinced by their platform, and had rational reasons to do so. In 1840, they also had *Canadian* reasons.[7]

The patriots' political activities also speak to a wider dynamic, directly connected to the transatlantic "Age of Revolutions" and indeed to our conceptions and assumptions about democratic politics.[8] Stimulated by the attempted revolution in the Canadas, hundreds of armed citizens publicly questioned the nature of the Republic and its established rulers. Simultaneously, the 1840 presidential election generated high enthusiasm, while major public figures remarked that the United States was "in the midst of a revolution." To be elected, and to stabilize the Union, the Whigs had to address this anger and use careful words when mentioning Canadian events.[9]

## POLITICAL WARFARE AND WAR FOR INDEPENDENCE

The 1830s was a decade of political unrest. The recently established "Second Party System," a bipartisan opposition at a national level between Jackson's "Democracy" and the Whig Party,[10] only channelled a fraction of the population's cultural and social demands and grievances. These national structures were as much artificial electoral constructions as they were ideological platforms.[11] In the mid-1830s, the alliance supporting the Democratic Party began to wither, notably because its more radical components were tired of empty phrases. In New York City, the founding of the Equal Rights Party during the winter 1835–36 by the "Locofocos" epitomized this frustration. The national opposition party's name, "Whig," a symbolic revolutionary term, further illustrates the stormy political context.

If Andrew Jackson in 1832, and Martin Van Buren in 1836, managed to retain the radicals' vote, members of their party shared the impression that a political "war" was occurring: "we distinctly trace the war upon our State institutions to the doctrines promulgated in this city in 1829 … [a] contest between the antagonist principles of Democratic Republicanism and Loco Focoism." The pro-Democrat *New York Times* denounced the Equal Rights Party as "Revolters," "Renegade anti-Masons," "Pests of Party," "Fanny Wright Men," "Carbonari," and so on. The *New York Herald* even asked: "Are we not on the eve of another revolution?" Nicholas Biddle, the president of the Bank of the United States and a strong Whig supporter, echoed this aggressiveness when he said that he hoped to see those who opposed his bank, some "banditti," "scourged back to their caverns." French observer Michel Chevalier concurred that "a crisis is at hand" because, he thought, the Republic had too many active citizens.[12]

Many radical citizens agreed. To them, constant political struggle was necessary for a healthy republic needing democratic reforms. If they could secure political alliance in particular elections, the Equal Rights Party's "Locofocos" nevertheless considered that "the leaders of the two great political parties under which the people have arrayed themselves are selfish and unprincipled … they are the enemies of the equal rights of the citizens." Congressman Ely Moore, a former labour activist, declared that the "aristocracy" was sustaining a "clandestine but vigorous war" against democracy, which explains the radical answers and the "public violence and disorders" of the time.[13]

The "party warfare," as it was then termed, fed the turbulent atmosphere. Political parties used military symbols in their activities, such as "parades" mounted by citizens dressed in "uniforms." They called voters the "army" of their cause or enlightened "republican soldiers" ready to save the Republic. Leaders asked that voters sacrifice their individual interests, a form of military heroism. Frequently, political leaders were army veterans proudly exhibiting their record of patriotic violence. Public discourses were vehement, notably during the "bank war" or the "holy war" over the currency issue. Some historians even consider that physical violence became a common political tool during the 1830s, from the streets of western cities to the halls of Congress.[14]

The Panic of 1837 deepened the schism. "Where will it all end? – In Ruin, Revolution, perhaps Civil War," lamented New York City's former mayor, Philip Hone. In September 1837, the Utica constitutional convention, organized by the Equal Rights Party, openly embodied this rebellious spirit: "No leading politicians, no lawyers or professional gentlemen of any kind, have been consulted or employed in constructing [this proposition of constitution]. It is the work of working men – of unambitious, humble men – who have long been compelled to feel most bitterly the cruel oppressions of the system founded and upheld by the aristocracy of wealth and its mental prostitutes."[15] These demands from "unambitious" men were threatening not only the republican practices, but also the very nature of the Republic. Contrary to 1787, their proposed constitution demanded a new social compact based on the "democratic principles."

This was the heated context in which the Canadian revolutionaries spread their ideas and shared their experiences. The Canadian crisis immediately became another source of violent political tensions. The exiles also brought a new agenda for democratic reforms; the British colonies appeared to be a natural territory to establish new republican experiments. Yet as soon as the first shots were fired, president Martin Van Buren, the American government, and a majority of Congress all renounced the Canadian republicans and their American supporters. The country's weak response following the destruction of the *Caroline*, the new Neutrality Act of March 1838, and the military cooperation between the American and British armies illustrate the United States and Van Buren's counter-revolutionary path taken during the Canadian crisis. In the winter of 1838–39, the president declared that the patriots were "a nefarious set of outlaws" who perpetrated "criminal assaults" against the rightful government of the British colonies. He recalled to the nation that the government had the "obligation to repress all attempts on the part of its citizens to disturb the peace of a country where order prevails or has been re-established." Van Buren's commitment to defeating the patriots led them to see the imprisonment of William Lyon Mackenzie as a presidential decision taken to please and appease the British.[16]

Active supporters of the Canadian Revolution pointed out the contradictions between Van Buren's democratic discourse and the reality of his foreign policy. The long pleas published by the *United States Democratic Review* reveal the passion and political conundrum generated by the Canadian attempted revolution. The editors considered the revolt legitimate and "nearly analogous to that of our own Revolution." They also maintained that suppressing the revolution would be "repugnant to the first principles and natural sentiments of a true democracy." Nevertheless, they remained loyal to their party, never criticized Van Buren, and used their newspaper to defend him. In this way, it was the president's duty to avoid any direct (official) or indirect (private) involvement. Peace with the British was an economic necessity, and supporting the government's discretion was crucial even if "this duty is disregarded by any considerable number of citizens." In January 1839, the *Review* acknowledged that "the Government has found itself compelled to undertake the unpleasing and unpopular discharge of this duty," that "the Administration has been severely assailed" because of the "Canadian question," and that "along the frontier" this policy had "a very serious effect against the Administration."[17]

Van Buren's opposition to the revolutionaries, combined with his pro-British stance, clearly undermined his reputation – and his authority. Evidence suggests that many citizens, including members of the Democratic Party, were deeply upset. This feeling was, of course, very strong along the border. Some Democrats in the borderland tried to limit the disastrous consequences of Van Buren's stance. In Vermont, for instance, in an attempt to preserve the patriots' favourable view of Jackson's party, one Democrat had to critique Van Buren himself by acknowledging that all the inhabitants of this state were "mortified" by his declarations. From various places in New York State Democrats were convinced that Mackenzie's confinement was doing "much prejudice" to Van Buren. They described his liberation as a potentially "very popular act." Furthermore, they feared that the president would "lose the state" at his re-election because of his pro-British policies.[18]

Before 1837, the majority of Canadian patriots supported Jackson, sharing his position against the "money aristocracy." They were in favour of the Jacksonian discourse glorifying the "democratic principles of natural and equal rights." And yet, many of the most active supporters of the patriots were members of the Whig Party. When Mackenzie attacked the Whigs in his *Gazette*, he was flooded by warnings. In upper and western New York, everyone recalled that the officers who joined the patriot army in Navy Island were mostly Whigs, not Democrats. From Watertown, where the population was mobilized for the Canadian cause, messages were sent to Mackenzie asking him to stop attacking the Whigs if he wanted to keep his subscribers and support for the patriot cause. At Lockport, it was said that the Whigs were friends of the cause, while the Democrats were their secret enemies. The situation was similar near Rochester and Buffalo.[19] Evidence from the other bordering states corroborates this. When Mackenzie distanced himself from party warfare, during the summer of 1838, and stopped criticizing the Whigs in his newspaper, he gained subscribers in Vermont. In western New York, as with the "freemen of Green Mountains," opposition to slavery was explicitly mixed with the Canadian question, nurturing support for the Whig Party. In Ohio and Michigan, reports stressed that there were significant consequences against federal attempts to prevent patriot invasions. Van Buren, it was regularly argued, "has not the confidence of the men." The pro-Whig wave was strong among the highest revolutionary figures, including Edward A. Theller, William "Bill" Johnston, and the Nelson brothers. In 1840, Mackenzie was the only patriot leader actively supporting the Democratic Party.[20]

While the leaders of the two national parties did not support the Canadian Revolution, the electoral struggle also undermined their revolutionary enterprise. It divided patriot ranks and blurred their political message. Some bemoaned the new and active Whig tendency in their ranks: "Nelsons are gone Whig, God help us!!!" Their heated discussion regarding the electoral warfare was public, vehement, and finally devastating. "This is lamentable," admitted an exile, "lamentable that Canadians should be their own destroyers."[21] The exiles participated in electoral public debates throughout 1840 by publishing letters in several newspapers, in both French and English.[22] Even though the election and party opposition eroded their unity, and consequently their strength, their attempted revolution helped fracture Van Buren's electoral support. The Canadian exiles' electoral shift, or meandering, was very similar to that of many American voters.

The backlash against Van Buren's Canadian policy reached far beyond the borderland region. Disappointed members of the Democratic Party were especially active in the biggest cities. *L'Estafette*, a French New York City newspaper, wrote during the first weeks of the Canadian Revolution that despite their adherence to the party, they were "mortified" by the president's "pusillanimity." An important fraction of the city's radicals – many of them actively engaged in the Canadian cause – were no longer Van Buren's supporters by 1840. Influential members of the Equal Rights Party organized pro-Canadian meetings, raised money, set up battalions, and sent petitions to Washington demanding Mackenzie's liberation. In their newspapers, they advocated military support for the Canadian Republican cause, even if their articles "excited a great deal of bitter feelings" in Washington. One of their leading editors, Theron Rudd, expressed "the unequivocal expression of public indignation" when he explained that he was now a "stranger" to the Democratic Party as a result of Van Buren's obvious dishonesty, with regards to both the Canadian question and the currency issue.[23]

The situation was similar with Philadelphia's Democrats. The *Public Ledger*, a Democratic pennypaper, was hardly alone in criticizing the president's unwise authoritarianism. It wrote: "the chief magistrate of the United States has no right, in an official document, to denounce the Canadians as traitors or pirates, we must say that never have our republican predilections been so shocked." Jackson's former secretary of the treasury, William Duane, circulated a petition asking for Mackenzie's release, eventually signed by more than three hundred "of the best citizens." When he wrote to Mackenzie, he added that "nine tenths of the citizens of this place are your friends." A member of the party also reported that "the feeling manifested in this remote section of the country from the frontier ... will militate much against Mr Van Buren's re-election." According to him, "influential men," who were also "friends" to the president, "*swear* that [Van Buren] will receive no support from them whilst Wm L. Mackenzie is permitted to occupy a prison." Corroborating Duane's statement, he noted that thousands of people had signed petitions and that "every class of persons in the community" were Mackenzie sympathizers. In Washington, Georgian Democratic senator Wilson Lumpkin admitted to a Canadian exile that Van Buren "was rapidly falling in the estimation of his own party upon the Canadian question!"[24]

The Canadian crisis directly influenced and interfered with the United States' political and electoral dynamics. It generally worked against the president and his party, and consequently in favour of the Whigs. It also raised fundamental questions about the nature of the Union's republicanism.

## THE 1840 PRESIDENTIAL ELECTION

Between 1836 and 1840, Martin Van Buren lost most of the northern states that were essential to the Jacksonian coalition: New York, Pennsylvania, Michigan, and Maine. Among the border states, New Hampshire was the only one to stay in the democratic fold. This realignment was also accompanied by a notable rise in voter participation, from 57.8 per cent to 80.2 per cent.[25]

The many peculiarities of the 1840 campaign have been highlighted, such as the entertainment generated by the two parties, the involvement of women, the influence of religion and family ties, and the new tactical efforts of the Whigs. Most historians, however, privilege an economic explanation, focusing first on the consequences of the hard times that had begun just as Van Buren took office in early 1837. To them, the people rejected Van Buren's "hard money" policy and adopted the Whig leaders' view about a national bank. This interpretation echoes the Whig campaign that put the responsibility for the depression on Jackson and Van Buren. Such an explanation means that the voting citizens agreed with and accepted the leaders' discourse. However, many historians challenge this interpretation.[26] The attempted Canadian revolution's impact substantiates those critics. If Van Buren and the Democratic Party were criticized for their management of the Canadian troubles, most of the Whig leaders shared the president's view. Henry Clay qualified the *Caroline* affair as an "outrage" and declared that it would be a "just war" if the U.S. were involved, but he also sought to reduce the risk of a military conflict from the very beginning. Daniel Webster was less ambiguous since he travelled to England in 1839, and began the negotiations for an Anglo-American peace treaty then and there.[27]

In Congress, however, some members of the Whig Party defended the revolutionaries and mocked their rivals' hypocrisy. After all, the Democrats did support slave-holding settlers in Texas, while opposing anti-slavery patriots in the North. Some Whig representatives – notably Caleb Cushing from Massachusetts – boldly questioned Van Buren's anti-patriot policy. A few Democratic representatives also expressed pro-patriot sympathies with vice-president Richard M. Johnson being the most important example. Canadian exiles and members of both parties in Washington reported that there are "a few enthusiastic friends here," as well as "some warm 76-patriots" in the executive cabinet. A Canadian who spent several weeks in Washington even believed that the patriots enjoyed "the opinion of the majority of the Democratic *Senators* assembled."[28] Though the dominant feeling among national leaders was against them, the patriots received support from members of *both* parties, both at the national and at the local levels. This indirectly confirms the intra-party factionalism in the 1830s.[29] As early as December 1837, New York governor William Marcy, Van Buren's close ally, admitted that "the Canada Business threatens to become more embarrassing than was anticipated."[30]

Marcy's defeat in 1838 was a first electoral sign of things to come. This result does not fit in Michael Holt's explanation stressing economic factors, since the brief recovery of 1838 should have logically favoured the Democrats. The *Democratic Review* tried to explain this defeat with different elements, the Canadian question being an important one for the "northern tier of the counties." To the patriots, this election foretold a political shift against Van Buren: "other states may follow the example of New York." To them, the fall 1838 electoral results revealed that their political power was growing as it translated in favourable opinion at the polls. They were convinced that they "have more friends in Congress than last session," and that Van Buren "never will be elected as President." At Detroit, one of their adversaries shared a similar opinion, and believed that the Hunters "will make the next president unless Van Buren gives them a war."[31]

The impact of the Canadian crisis on the electoral and political agenda is fully illustrated through the case of Democratic congressman Augustus Hand. According to *The Native American*, a newspaper published in Washington and opposed to the patriots, Hand was under the influence of the "modern Goths and Vandals who are swarming our shores and over-running our fair land." The editor was scandalized by the fact that the "myriads of [Canadian] vagabonds" could force the representative of Essex county, New York, to introduce a bill that allowed naturalization two years after one's arrival in the "fair land." To the *Native American*'s irritated editor, Hand needed this legislative move – otherwise, he said, "next November's flood will leave him high and dry at home." This particular episode shows how the Canadian revolutionaries – without actually voting – influenced American electoral and legislative activities. Furthermore, while the presidential election approached, the editor admitted that he had been "roughly handled by the administration press, in this city and elsewhere" after his rush of blood against the Canadian "vagabonds."[32]

Economic issues sometimes mingled with the Canadian crisis. In July 1840, the *Madisonian*, a pro-Whig newspaper published in Washington, printed a long letter from Alburgh, Vermont. Penned by a "low and humble" citizen, and written in the name of "the farmers and workingmen" of this borderland county, the letter virulently attacked their Democratic representative in Congress, John Smith, who became famous thanks to his recent speech on the

Independent Treasury. The angry elector began his letter by reminding the public that they all voted for Smith. He also specified that he had his own "plain way of thinking." His reflection opposes any form of party loyalism. Echoing the Whigs' national message, the Vermonter argued that Smith's views on banking and currency were a "mistake." "But Sir," added the citizen, "when you pretend it was the question [of the Independent Treasury] that gave to you your election, I am bold to say you mistake facts … When Mr Everett called on you to know if the Canada question had no influence on your election, you, sir, as an honorable man, should have acknowledged it … You were elected to support the Canada cause, and not as a sub-Treasury man, if you were nominated as such, and there is deception." The attempted Canadian Revolution was, in this particular and rare case, explicitly used by an influential Whig publication in the midst of a tense political campaign. "It is true you have not, as the President has, insulted us," continued the Vermonter, "but you have totally neglected and deceived us." He concluded his letter with a warning: "we will have a reckoning with you. Let me tell you, sir, that the eyes of 'we, the people,' are on you, and on all our public men, and we will have a settlement of these long accounts."[33] In the next elections, Smith and Van Buren were defeated in Vermont.

In many parts of the northern states, public opinion was strongly in favour of the revolutionaries. The patriots, both American citizens and Canadian exiles, also personified Mark Voss-Hobbard's idea of "antipartisanship culture." Candidates had to address this trend in favour of the Canadian revolutionary cause. During the campaigns, patriots disdainfully remarked that all the candidates "all at once turned about and became amazingly patriotic." They often denounced this opportunism, deepening the divide between them and the two parties. Among those who expressed defiance against the parties and declared that they would vote Whig because of Van Buren's opposition to the Canadian Revolution were a group of inhabitants from Ogdensburg. This border town in upstate New York had been a hotbed of patriot agitation. In the summer of 1838, a dozen citizens of the town renounced their individual subscriptions to the pro-Democrat *Mackenzie's Gazette*. They hoped to see the creation of a continental republic based on the principle of "equal rights." They also concurred with Mackenzie's criticism of the "greedy, selfish, and unfeeling" Whig leaders and their papers on the coast that were favourable to "British capital, British feelings, and British interests." While they agreed with Mackenzie on these points, they nevertheless considered Van Buren a "traitor" who had revealed his Anglophilism when he was the American ambassador in London. They sided with the Whigs to "oppose [Van Buren's] reelection, for that, he has used all means within his reach *to put down the insurrection in Canada*, and to prosecute & harass the unfortunate exiles from thence." They wanted "to rid that wretched country of the *miscreants* who are misgoverning it." To these voters, they represented a sample of the party's majority, the "bone and sinew Whigs." In other words, though they were Whigs, they still opposed their national leaders, their press, and their stance on major issues, including their response to the Canadian crisis.[34]

Mackenzie's imprisonment had a particular impact on American public opinion, convincing many sympathizers of the Democratic Party to vote for Harrison. Symbolically, a lover of democracy had been sent to jail for having attempted to recreate the spirit of '76. The trial itself drew close attention. Partisans of the patriots were outraged. They considered Mackenzie's liberation an electoral necessity for Van Buren. "Van Buren is not the people. No. No." complained a patriot, he "is not going to put down the feelings of the whole countrymen – who are already ashamed." His complaint ended with a perfect example of the American rebellious spirit: "[Canadian] Independence will be achieved without the assistance and in defiance of the tyrannical veto of Van Buren." William Duane, a notably disillusioned Democrat, offers a privileged observation. The former member of Jackson's cabinet remarked that Mackenzie's imprisonment was working "against the President's reelection in the frontier states." Van Buren "has given to the Whigs a whip," his collaboration with Britain, "that will be used to much advantage against himself." As a Canadian exile wrote from Washington, his hostility to the patriots "has afforded his glorious opponents a glorious opportunity to canvass against him!"[35]

Opposition to Van Buren's Canadian policy was widespread. In Cleveland, the Hunters' capital, members of both parties signed petitions demanding Mackenzie's release. One of them included two hundred and fifteen "of the first citizens of this place." "The election next fall," repeated Clevelanders, "will convince [Van Buren] that the majority of the people, and not an occasional flying Dutchman, or Bashaw of Kinderhook, governs this vast republic." Because of Van Buren's unpopular foreign policy, "the most influential of his former supporters, in this city, are going with the Harrison ticket." Harrison's Ohioan background was never mentioned, but it probably helped. Harrison was the son of a signatory of the Declaration of Independence, and "they hope in him to find still a little (at least) of the leaders of '76." Their main goal was to get rid of Van Buren because he proved to be an impassable obstacle to an Anglo-American war; a general military conflict was then seen as their primary option to force Canadian independence.[36]

In 1840, Van Buren was denounced by both the patriots and the Whigs as an illegitimate "majesty" who dismissed public opinion. The Democratic Party became the "Federalist Party," at least insofar as it opposed a third Anglo-American war. The Federal power was becoming "anti-republican," "tyrannical," and entirely submissive to the British. This view was particularly shared by radicals who combined it with economic issues: both proved that the Union had not yet established a real independence. The Whigs in the borderland used the Canadian question to label their adversaries "Federalists," "federal British tories," and so on. This semantic strategy sustained their willingness to call themselves "Democratic Whigs." It also helped Harrison to diffuse the image of a patriotic General who fought the "tories" in 1812, now a saviour of a Republic threatened by would-be "Federalists" who were, indeed, aiding the British empire repressing their neighbours' call for democracy. Furthermore, the Whig candidate personally knew the patriots' commander-in-chief on Navy Island, Rensselear Van Rensselear.[37]

At the Whig convention, William H. Harrison was chosen as candidate against two open adversaries of the Canadian Revolution: General Winfield Scott, who tirelessly travelled along the border to maintain the peace, and Daniel Webster, an unapologetic anglophile, legal advisor of English bankers in the United States, and adversary of "Locofocoism." The fourth candidate, Henry Clay, was a more discreet opponent, as was Harrison. According to the Whig newspapers, the "unexpected" chosen candidate was "the People's favourite," "emphatically the choice of the yeomanry, the farmer, the laboring man, and the mechanic." Historians have also stressed the Antimasons' influence. If Harrison's family was among the aristocratic "Virginia First Families," he still lived on a farm. The party constructed a popular image of the man, in direct reaction to Clay's alleged elitism. This angle was also used against Van Buren, an "aristocratic" consumer of luxury goods, perfumed with the "Double

Extract of Queen Victoria," a rhetoric immortalized in the famous "Golden Spoon Oration."[38]

If the president no longer counted as a friend of the Canadian democratic cause, he nevertheless tried to appease its supporters. Mackenzie – whose imprisonment had hurt the Democratic Party at the 1839 elections – was liberated in May 1840. Van Buren presented himself as an "enemy" of British capital. The Canadian question was important enough to force some members of the party to play down the electoral consequences of Van Buren's foreign policy. Some pro-Democrat editors were actively maintaining Mackenzie's positive opinion of their party, including Samuel Langtree of the *Democratic Review*. But after an interview with the president, Langtree could only promise that "everything in [Van Buren's] power will be done to make your confinement as comfortable as possible." These efforts were primarily made on a local or individual scale. They tried to convince the exiles that their party was the natural ally of the Canadian patriots, an alliance of "democratic principles." A citizen from Philadelphia promised, for example, that if Mackenzie was willing to advocate for Van Buren's candidacy in his newspaper, the Democrats would support the Canadian Revolution.[39]

Harrison also tried to seduce the patriots, but he hesitated to exploit anti–Van Buren feelings regarding his foreign policy. He never condemned the supporters of the Canadian Revolution, unlike Van Buren, Webster, or Scott. On 10 September 1840, at Dayton, Ohio, he reminded the public of his military actions during the War of 1812. The candidate avoided the words "British" or "England," for the more vague "foreign foe" or "the enemy." He claimed to be a sincere "Anti-Federalist," and expanded on patriotism to highlight the Federalists' opposition to the war now personified by Van Buren. Without mentioning the Canadian Revolution, this kind of rhetoric spread vague allusions that he was not entirely opposed to a new war against the British Empire, and it helps to explain why some patriots hoped to find in him an heir of the spirit of '76. It also illustrates how the Canadian events helped the Whigs to argue that Harrison was a "Democrat," against the "Federalist" and pro-British Van Buren.[40]

Harrison was sometimes more explicit. At a June 1840 public meeting in Cleveland, he addressed four to five thousand people. "It was literally pure democracy" according to a Canadian revolutionary. Audience members included many active patriots. According to an exile whose heart was with the Democratic Party, Harrison openly presented himself as a friend to the Canadian Revolution. While the patriot was not convinced the candidate was sincere, he remained nevertheless "at a loss" on how to advise his friends with regards to the election. At the gigantic rally in Fort Meigs, Ohio, during this same Great Lake tour, the air was "filled with shouts, music and guns." Harrison celebrated his old victory against the British, twenty-seven years earlier. Amidst songs like "La Marseillaise" and "The Hunters of Kentucky," which were regularly heard during the patriot meetings, one of the speakers stressed that the presidential candidate was, during the War of 1812, one of the first to "land on the Canada shore in pursuit of the British," and a rare American officer who "had captured a whole army in their own Territory." After his election, in his inaugural speech, Harrison finally announced his desire to maintain friendly relations with all nations, and to oppose "any claim and pretension" from "their subjects" or "our citizens." However, he noted that "my fellow-citizens will not see in my earnest desire to preserve peace with foreign powers any indication that their rights will ever be sacrificed or the honor of the nation tarnished." After all, this tactical elusiveness on the Canadian question echoed his "artfully ambiguous" position on the currency issue.[41]

No one personified the political shift caused by the Canadian question better than John Griffin, an Irish shoemaker who became an innkeeper in Philadelphia. Griffin had always been an active Democrat. He voted three times for Jackson and once for Van Buren. In his own words, he was "one of the greatest Van Buren's man in this country before his Royal Damned Proclamation [of November 1838] came out." The Irish-American had been busy working for Mackenzie's liberation from a "Van Buren and Victoria Bastile." He even participated in the organization of a military company for the prospect of a war. Because of such irreverence, he was expelled from the party. He confessed that he was "disgusted" with the "crouching mock demagogues" who controlled the Democratic Party, and claimed that he "could see [Van Buren] lynched with pleasure": "He is a dangerous man to this Republic." For citizens like Griffin, "extermination ought to be the American password with everything English if they value Liberty." In the spring of 1840, he became a tireless Whig activist and announced that, in Philadelphia, "the Jackson Irish and natives are all going for Harrison."[42]

Pro-patriots who voted for Harrison often questioned his declarations. The so-called "Whigs' tenets" were never mentioned to justify their realignment, such as the national bank issue. A real distance remained between patriots and national leaders. Edmund Bailey O'Callaghan, the former editor of a Lower Canadian patriot newspaper, remarked disdainfully that as the election approached, many politicians declared themselves to be "warm friends of Canadian independence": "Indeed so are all the leaders here of *both* parties – Whig and Locofoco ... But when we recollect how much is done in this country with a view to affect political objects – to carry an election – either state or Federal and remember the great Presidential contest which approaches, we are at a loss to conclude whether all we hear and read is pure 'jaw,' for mere political effect, or whether it be a bona fide precursor of a game of fight-cuffs." Patriots complained about party warfare and the damage it was doing to republican principles. They regularly called for a new party to represent their radical and patriotic stance. "To look at any *present* party for true, pure, Democratic principles is wrong," wrote a Canadian exile from Lockport, "both have an Augean stable or aristocratic tendencies which will require a *new* party to change." The moral crisis generated by the Canadian events fed the "third party" and anti-elite spirit, and ultimately benefited the Whig Party. This violent antipartyism also suggests that, in the late 1830s, the legitimacy of the political institutions – regulated by "party warfare" – faced a serious crisis.[43]

## CONNECTED POLITICS

The disgust inspired by the political struggle of two hierarchical factions, sometimes labelled "antipartyism" by historians, shaped outcomes on both sides of the U.S.-Canadian border. The Whig patriots distrusted their leaders. They focused on other important political questions of the time. They regularly called for a regeneration of the Republic, echoing various American citizens, regardless of their party preferences, who during the 1830s urged the establishment of a "true" republic: "time has arrived when the people of the United States must decide whether they will be a Republic in fact, or only a Republic in name."[44] Their quest for a "true" republic meant a new republican compact based on the equality of social conditions, beyond a relative equality before the law or the right to vote.

This political trend can be traced, at least, to the American Revolution. During the 1790s, the "Painites," as Seth Cotlar has named them, denounced the existence of a two-class society, the "labor" and the "few," calling for "another revolution [which] must and will be brought about in favor of the PEOPLE." The Workingmen's parties of the late 1820s took over this tradition of protest against the "1 per cent" who monopolized private property and held the "many" in a state of dependency, if not of (white) "slavery." During the second half of the 1830s, the Equal Rights Party, or the genuine "Locofocos," became the heirs of this history of protest. Their influence was national, and even continental, when we read that Canadian republicans claimed to be inspired by them – William Leggett in particular.[45]

The Locofocos were clearly challenging the political and economic order, as Albert Schrauwers's chapter demonstrates regarding the currency issue. On 13 February 1837, they organized a gigantic public meeting in New York City where they denounced their living conditions. The financial mechanisms were blamed: "The voice of the people emphatically declares, and in fact demonstrates, that our monstrous banking system is the prime original cause of the present state of things." Following this meeting, some audience members marched to the docks where they destroyed dozens of flour barrels.[46] After Van Buren took his seat and after the Panic blew up, the Equal Rights Party became more subversive. They wanted to "seize the present occasion as favorable to overcome [the] enemy," the American "aristocracy" of Wall Street and their political associates. The hard times were to them a signal to regenerate the American republic. They questioned multiple republican pillars: the nature of law, the power of their representatives, the financial mechanisms, the citizens' rights, and so on; "It is not the less true that America is not yet a republic; Man is the slave of Money. 'Law rules the poor, and Money rules the Law.'" Their proposed constitution describes the political revolution they called for, and is so important that it deserves to be quoted at length:

> There never was a time when human law was so perfect that there was no room for improvement, or so just and upright that there was no public wrong to reform. The time has now arrived when reform is not merely desirable, but indispensable to our very existence ... The original organizers of our state government ... merely constructed a temporary shelter out of the least odious parts of the system they had warred against, leaving it to their descendants, when enlightened by study and

> refreshed by peace, to establish a social edifice based entirely on the immediate principles of equality and justice ... It is time – the disastrous results of aristocratic legislation prove that it is high time – that our state constitution should define the powers and duties of legislators; and above all other instruments, it should afford the clearest pledge, the safest guarantee of the rights of the people against legislative usurpation – against the creation of those vested wrongs, monopolies – and against the fostering of a system of artificial credit, calculated to sap all public and private morals, not only placing the advantages of credit within reach of the dishonest, but enabling hordes of promise-printers and speculators to engross all the provisions and goods produced by the industry of the people, and then deal them out at prices limited only by fear of popular vengeance.[47]

In his *History of the Working Men*, the British émigré, radical leader, and Mackenzie's friend George Evans echoed the Locofocos when he stated that the American Revolution only "secured the means of obtaining Equal Rights," the members of the Working Men Party of 1829 being the "first" to try to "[turn] those means to account." The workingmen's goal was a "radical revolution," with New York as the epicentre of a worldwide process. And Evans was *naturally* optimistic: "man's regeneration is at hand ... a revolution is in embryo."[48]

This radicalism was also expressed by members of the Whig Party. For instance, New York editor Horace Greeley openly recognized the positive influence of socialists such as Robert Owen and Charles Fourier. William Seward, elected governor of New York in 1838, also embraced radical ideas. His speeches were quoted by radicals as he explained that despite the "equality of civil rights," "we have only approximated towards, what is even more important, equality of social condition ... aristocràcy has home even in this land of freedom." Having previously shown affinities with some of the Workingmen Party's ideas, former Antimasons fed the radicalism within the Whig ranks, which in turn seduced the patriots. In New York state house, they supported radical reforms on imprisonment for debt, the educational system, the judiciary system, or taxation. The Whig Party managed to lose its elitist image thanks to this Antimasonic heritage, particularly in Michigan, Ohio, New York, and Vermont, states that were deeply shaken by the Canadian Revolution. Therefore, it is not surprising to see Antimason leaders – such as Solomon Southwick

– actively supporting the Canadian patriots, denouncing Van Buren's judicial manoeuvres against Mackenzie and, more generally, his collaboration with the British. This does not mean that the supporters of the Canadian patriots were the Antimasons, but it does help us understand the anti-elite and anti-party background that pushed the patriots towards the Whigs.[49]

The Whig tendency among the patriots illustrates how fluid and volatile party lines could be. Each party attracted radicals who shared similar principles. The Free Banking law voted by the New York Whig majority in 1839 is an example of how party loyalism could disappear, since the (radical) Whigs adopted the Equal Rights Party–inspired reform against the conservative members of both parties. Whig radicalism was nationwide. A good example is the *True American*, a New Orleans–based Whig paper opposed to the "credit aristocracy" and the commercial elite. This trans-party radicalism corroborates the "decline of deference" that historians have stressed with regards to the 1840 election. It also questions the idea of "hegemony of partisanship" or "party loyalism" during the Jacksonian era.[50]

Historians have mentioned the fear expressed during the 1840 election and the "extraordinary intensity" of the campaign. For some witnesses, it was straight "sink or swim" for the Republic's future. In North Carolina, a citizen felt that in the event that Harrison should fail, "'The People' will never elect another President, till we have had another Revolution." This fear of – or hope for – an eventual political revolution was not only shared by anonymous citizens who could be accused of having a restricted, or local, perspective. Even former president John Quincy Adams believed that Harrison's popularity was "artificial," and worried about his capacities to handle the country's issues: "The whole country is in a state of agitation upon the approaching Presidential election such as was never before witnessed ... Not a week has passed within the last few months without a convocation of thousands of people to hear inflammatory harangues against Martin Van Buren and his Administration! ... Here is a *revolution* in the habits and manners of the people. *Where will it end?* These are party movements, and must in the natural progress of things become antagonistical ... *Their manifest tendency is to civil war* ... Harrison came in upon a hurricane; God grant he may not go out upon a wreck."[51]

Revolutionary songs such as "La Marseillaise," "The Star-Spangled Banner," and "The Yankee Doodle" were always heard in Harrison's rallies – melodies of the Age of Revolutions *en marche* across the Western world. Threatening cries resonated from pro-Harrison songs: "The People lead forward the gathering storm." "Tipp's Invitation to Loco, Patriotic Glee" expressed the radical desire to challenge the rulers hand in hand, much as the Equal Rights Party tried to unify the citizens against the two national parties:

> Locofoco drink hard cider with me,
> This the watchword of all men resolv'd to be free.
> Our Country is fill'd with oppression and woe,
> Brought on by our Rulers, Van Buren and Co.;
> Now therefore Loco Foco remember next fall,
> Is the end of the oppressors, with their cabbage and all.

During Harrison's campaign, an atmosphere of rebellion against the established rulers seemed to hover above the country. Though the campaign was indeed remarkably entertaining, it could not hide the "serious issues" that were raised by public opinion.[52] One of these issues was the tension between London and Washington regarding the British American colonies. From the beginning of the Canadian crisis, there were concerns that an uncontrollable series of events threatened to destroy peaceful relations with Britain. Thomas Richards Jr's chapter perfectly illustrates how the republican order in the northern states was shaken by the attempted revolution. Prior to signing the 1842 peace treaty, British and American officials feared, in Lord Ashburton's words, that "the border population may go to war and eventually involve the two countries." Both armies had to be sent to the northern border despite both countries' desire to remain in peace.[53]

Federal authorities were horrified by the independence of mind shown by American patriots who, according to Daniel Webster, "do not propose to join the forces of the United States" if a war breaks out, but instead to "unite themselves with the disaffected in Canada, declare the province free, and set up another government." "A respectable inhabitant" of Detroit warned that the Hunters' Lodges "will be the engine that is to shake the United States to the very center." The government's mission was then to maintain "the peace of the country against the mischievous consequences of the [patriots'] acts." From Toronto, Governor Arthur considered that the Hunters could "revolutionize the United States and certainly decide who shall be the next president" should Van Buren fail to annihilate the organization. Even if they acknowledged the right to overthrow a "tyrannical power," the *Democratic Review* recognized that Van Buren's "unpleasant" and "unpopular" duty was to crush the patriots who were "hostile to the spirit of American institutions." They represented a threat against American institutions, "there can be no doubt either of the magnitude or of the imminence of the danger."[54]

Hence, the patriots' attempted revolution was also directed against the corruption of republican "privileges." They attacked the patrician realities of the United States: its tendency to build an elected aristocracy, to silence the public debate through party warfare, to legislate for the benefit of the upper classes, and to refuse a general policy based on the idea of "public good."[55] The political and social power of lawyers was regularly censured.[56] Many citizens criticized the degeneration of some original revolutionary ideas, including the creation of a community-minded economy and independent citizens. To them, this particular ideal was incompatible with wage-earning labour. Money and banking activities were subject to violent attacks. From New York City to small towns along the border, they denounced the "American nobility," bankers, great proprietors, "capitalists," and so on. They opposed the two national parties because they contributed to this situation. The radicals were also pleased to repeatedly mention that there was a "faint and distant murmur" among the population: "It is no longer a question of 'bank reform'; it is a question of destruction ... How much longer will you be governed by these licensed rogues, these legalised swindlers?"[57]

The patriots, regardless of their electoral preferences, questioned the nature of the United States' republican spirit, "if it is republican." In Buffalo, one of them suggested that Van Buren's disdain for public opinion was not only an act "putting a chain & extinguishing on the further growth of democracy in America," but also "an act ... tacitly threatening the existence of this country." Another patriot declared: "Should Harrison attempt to pursue the same course [as Van Buren] in regard to Great Britain & Canadas, all the BANKS, CORPORATIONS, CAPITALISTS JOBBERS & SPECULATORS, will not save him from the Censure and disapprobation of the great mass of the people! In truth this Nation must soon either become a kingly power or kingly power must be drove from the Continent."[58]

Thousands of Americans saw Mackenzie's imprisonment as an obvious abuse of the institutions, boosting the loss of legitimacy of the established political order. In Michigan and Vermont, juries always refused to condemn patriots despite the president's and Congress's opposition to them. In December 1838, after two days of deadly battles near Windsor, the patriots met at Detroit's Town Hall and denounced Congress, the government, and the federal army. Van Buren's policy was deemed "unconstitutional." They viewed the federal army as an armed force obeying Queen Victoria, and the American republic as a "territory of Great Britain." In Vermont, a patriot declared that "[Van Buren's] life would be in jeopardy if he should dare pass through Vermont ... Some say he must be insane." According to many, the crisis generated by the Canadian Revolution could "light up the torch in this country that all the influences and power of both governments will be unable to smother or quench." It would become a revolutionary fire against the Anglo-American "tory" power or, as the *Democratic Review* termed it, "an excitement which no efforts of our Government *can* repress." To Canadian republican leader Wolfred Nelson, Van Buren's re-election would push the American republic towards a "civil war," led by an authoritative administration against a people anxious for democratic reforms, such as in Europe.[59]

The practical definition of "democratic principles" was at stake. The patriots were fighting to "finish" the Revolution in two particular ways. First, they meant to continue efforts from 1775 and 1812 to bring all the North American British colonies in the republican realm. Second, and somewhat more vaguely, they sought to build a new world, entirely separate from the European aristocratic heritage. Supporters of this political revolution hoped that it would establish a more egalitarian and more "true" republic. The envisioned outcome was the destruction of a two-class society condemned by those who had been deceived by the American Revolution. Through the Canadian crisis, the patriots and their radical supporters hoped to overwhelm the patrician republican order. They viewed the violent struggle on the northern border as the best way to annihilate "American nobility," which they thought to be nurtured by British capital.

New England intellectual Orestes Brownson said, of a war for a Canadian republic, that: "[it is] the only thing which to me seems capable of saving the republic, and the sooner it comes the better." A provocative and disillusioned Mackenzie even warned: "People of America, your cause and that of Canada is one. If the Canadians are enslaved through your apathy, hope not to escape the punishment your selfishness will have merited." Pro-patriots disseminated the idea that the rights of the people north and south of the border "have been encroached upon by the officers both civil and military, and by the Representatives of the people in Congress assembled." They regularly warned the citizens against their "domestic tyrants" who were serving British interests by crushing the Canadian Revolution. "The friends of American institutions and American Liberty must be vigilant," a pro-patriot newspaper also declared, because "the spirit of despotism is abroad in the land." And it was directing the republic toward an "unnatural" path.[60]

In a similar fashion, the New York City Locofocos believed that this continental war would occur "sooner or later," and hoped that it would destroy the roots of corruption in the republic: British commercial power and influence. U.S. economic dependency was perceived as "unfavorable to our prosperity as an independent nation," but also "insidiously subversive of our republican institutions." Theron Rudd explained: "the independence of Canada is with me a secondary consideration ... I wish a war with Great Britain on our account, if nothing else but to get rid of our infernal funding and banking system." During the public debate on the advantages and disadvantages of a third Anglo-American war, they declared that, in terms of "national independence," of "republicanism" and of "sound internal prosperity," the Union has "everything" to win with this war: "We should sacrifice money and human life, and so did our forefathers when our country was but little more under the control of England than it is at this moment; but we should renew and perpetuate our national existence as a republic – an existence impaired and endangered by the immense monied power of our ancient superior. If our present commercial relations with Great Britain were to remain uninterrupted twenty or thirty years longer, every vestige of democratic republicanism would be hopelessly crushed ... The Canadians themselves tell us this, and we believe them."[61] This thirst for democracy was addressed by the candidates in 1840 – especially by the Whigs, who recognized the merits of the radicals' critiques. One of their major campaign pamphlets declared that "the people have had enough of the democratic principle ... what they want now, is, a little democratic practice." By acknowledging it, they legitimized this anger, and of course pushed radicals towards Harrison, an "honest patriot." The Whig candidate was presented as a viable actor to transform the republic into a real democracy, "the commencement of a new era."[62]

Harrison's inaugural speech also addressed, at length, the radicals and the "antipartisanship culture." He qualified the radical "hard money" theory as a "well intended" perspective, even though he did not endorse it. Above all, the new president recognized that some "errors" were made by the framers of the Constitution, which had resulted in "defects." Contrary to some interpretations, his inaugural speech was a complex reflection on necessary constitutional reforms, resulting from his own analysis of the Constitution and from fifty years of republican experimentation.[63]

## PIVOTAL MOMENT

The attempted Canadian revolution is not the only reason why Van Buren lost his seat in 1840. However, it clearly helps explain the electoral shift witnessed in the northern states. Connecting the 1840 election to the Canadian Rebellion epitomizes the heuristic interest of not only looking at different national histories together in order to compare or contextualize, but also studying transnational historical phenomena that could radically nuance national narratives. For instance, and even if it is impossible to affirm on a large scale who voted for whom and why, Van Buren suffered a political backlash due to his anglophilism and strict opposition to the patriots. Harrison was significantly more cautious and ambivalent about the Canadian crisis. In addition to internal issues – first of all the banking question and the devastating Hard Times – one would connect the pro-patriot (and therefore anti–Van Buren) feelings in the northern states with the small margins that allowed Harrison to conquer Pennsylvania, New York, Michigan, and Maine. The Canadian Rebellion did not alone *make* the new president, but it decisively sealed the Little Magician's fate.

The electoral warfare is but one of the transnational political impacts. As third parties had done throughout American history, the angry patriots "assailed corrupt politics as often as they attacked corporate greed or exploitation." Parties or factions were still widely viewed as evil, and party loyalism was not considered honourable behaviour by the patriots. The "party warfare" between the two main factions was a *demoralizing* reality, to re-actualize Noah Webster's first definition of the word, "corrupting or destroying morals or moral principles." The 1840 campaign was a tense political moment, notably because channelling the citizens' confidence was not an easy task. The "fever of party passion … inflamed men's mind," during "one of the most excited and interesting period of our political existence." Whigs, Locofocos, and patriots were calling for a "new era," but they had divergent ambitions. The political, economic, and continental order was threatened by the revolutionary activities, which were not limited within the borderland areas. Patriots viewed their cause "a more necessary revolution than that of the Fathers of the Republic," because the United States became the "tools for monarchy." Their revolution would have brought new practical definitions of republicanism into North America. They were opposed to the common "*country*" discourse or the "liberal capitalist consensus" – as historians call it – shared by the two national parties. President Harrison endorsed part of their discourse, but he mainly tried to appease the nation with some promises on constitutional reforms, and sent thoughtful messages towards the rebellious Americans. This election was then far from being a campaign regularly qualified by historians as "mainly fun and games," an interpretation that dramatically reduces both the meaning of the political issues and the intellectual agency of the American people.[64]

## NOTES

1 "Democratic Swell": translation from Louis-Joseph Papineau's speech at Saint-Laurent, 15 May 1837, reprinted in Yvan Lamonde and Claude Larin, eds, *Louis-Joseph Papineau: un demi-siècle de combats* (Montreal: Fides, 1998), 417–49, "Le flot démocratique a coulé irresistiblement [et] renversera sans violents efforts les impuissants obstacles que l'on peut tenter de lui opposer." "Movement," "experiment," "trial": *United States Democratic Review* (hereafter USDR), June 1840, 475–6. "Name": Harrison's speech at Dayton, 10 September 1840, printed in the *Burlington Free Press*, 2 October 1840. On the Whigs' use of "democracy": Robert Gray Gunderson, *The Log-Cabin Campaign* (Lexington: University of Kentucky Press, 1957); John William Ward, "The Whigs Take to the Woods," in *Andrew Jackson: Symbol for an Age* (New York: Oxford University Press, 1955), 79–97. The full insertion of the Canadian attempted revolution in the transatlantic revolutionary context remains recent: Louis-Georges Harvey, *Le printemps de l'Amérique française:*

*américanité, anticolonialisme et républicanisme dans le discours politique québécois, 1805–1837* (Montreal: Boréal, 2005); Michel Ducharme, *The Idea of Liberty in Canada during the Age of Atlantic Revolutions, 1776–1838* (Montreal and Kingston: McGill-Queen's University Press, 2014 [2010]).

2 Alan Taylor's work illustrates the interest of an integrated North American history, notably: *American Revolutions: A Continental History, 1750–1804* (New York: W.W. Norton & Co., 2016); *The Civil War of 1812: American Citizens, British Subjects, Irish Rebels, & Indian Allies* (New York: Alfred Knopf 2010); "Continental Crossings," *Journal of the Early Republic* 24, no. 2 (2004): 182–8. Connected history is one method of transnational history among others. For an overview on transnational history, Akira Iriye and Pierre-Yves Saunier, eds, *Palgrave Dictionary of Transnational History* (Houndmills: Palgrave Macmillan, 2009). For the connected history, see Sanjay Subrahmanyam's works: *Explorations in Connected History: From the Tagus to the Ganges* (Oxford: Oxford University Press, 2005); "Connected Histories: Notes towards a Reconfiguration of Early Modern Eurasia," *Modern Asian Studies* 31, no. 3 (1997): 735–62. "Moving laterally" is Subrahmanyam's expression.

3 "The Late Election," *USDR* (November–December 1840): 387–8.

4 Donald B. Cole notes the impact of his foreign policy, *Martin Van Buren and the American Political System* (Princeton: Princeton University Press, 2014 [1984]), 327. However, Morton Keller believes that the uncontentious foreign relations played a marginal role during the 1830s, *America's Three Regimes: A New Political History* (New York: Oxford University Press, 2007), 86. The Canadian events' impact on the American elections is briefly mentioned by a handful of historians: Orrin Tiffany, *The Relations of the United States to the Canadian Rebellion of 1837–1838* (1905), 105–7; Albert B. Corey, *The Crisis of 1830–1842 in Canadian-American Relations* (New Haven: Yale University Press, 1941), 93–101; Oscar A. Kinchen, *The Rise and Fall of the Patriot Hunters* (New York: Bookman Associates, 1956), 43–4, 104; Lillian F. Gates, *After the Rebellion: The Later Years of William Lyon Mackenzie* (Toronto: Dundurn Press, 1988), 52–3, 70–1; Kenneth R. Stevens, *Border Diplomacy: The* Caroline *and McLeod Affairs in Anglo-American-Canadian Relations, 1837–1842* (Tuscaloosa: University of Alabama Press, 1989), 44–7, 56–8.

5 Richard P. McCormick's work is seminal for the "Party Period" concept: *The Party Period and Public Policy: American Politics from the Age of Jackson to the Progressive Era* (New York: Oxford University Press,

1986). In *The American Political Nation, 1838–1893* (Stanford: Stanford University Press, 1991) Joel H. Silbey defends the idea of the "hegemony of partisanship." On the historiography of electoral behaviour: Ronald P. Formisano, "The New Political History and the Election of 1840," *Journal of Interdisciplinary History* 23, no. 4 (1993): 661–82. For a critic of the rigidity of the "Party Period" concept: Formisano, "The 'Party Period' Revisited," *Journal of American History* 86, no. 1 (1999): 93–120; Formisano, "Deferential-Participant Politics: The Early Republic's Political Culture, 1789–1840," *American Political Science Review* 68, no. 2 (1974): 473–87. For a more critical perspective: Mark Voss-Hubbard, "The 'Third Party Tradition' Reconsidered: Third Parties and American Public Life, 1830–1900," *Journal of American History* 86, no. 1 (1999): 122–8.

6 McCormick, *Party Period*, 5. Whigs' use of Antipartyism: Major L. Wilson, "The 'Country' versus the 'Court': A Republican Consensus and Party Debate in the Bank War," *Journal of the Early Republic* 15, no. 4 (1995): 639–41.

7 Voss-Hubbard, "Third Party," 121–4, 148–50. The study of the citizens' political skepticism is remarkably undertaken by Glen C. Altschuler and Stuart M. Blumin, "Limits of Political Engagement in Antebellum America: A New Look at the Golden Age of Participatory Democracy," *Journal of American History* 84, no. 3 (1997): 855–85. On antipartyism: Formisano, "Political Character, Antipartyism, and the Second Party System," *American Quarterly* 21, no. 4 (1969): 683–709; Gerald Leonard, "The Ironies of Partyism and Antipartyism: Origins of Partisan Political Culture in Jacksonian Illinois," *Illinois Historical Journal* 87, no. 1 (1994): 21–40; Marc W. Kruman, "The Second Party System and the Transformation of Revolutionary Republicanism," *Journal of the Early Republic* 12, no. 4 (1992): 509–37; Edward L. Mayo, "Republicanism, Antipartyism, and Jacksonian Party Politics: A View from the Nation's Capitol," *American Quarterly* 31, no. 1 (1979): 3–20.

8 An example is Daniel Walker Howe's study of the Whig "culture" rather than "party," *The Political Culture of the American Whigs* (Chicago: University of Chicago Press, 1979). Among others: Jeffrey L. Pasley, "Minnows, Spies and Aristocrats: The Social Crisis in Congress in the Age of Martin Van Buren," *Journal of the Early Republic* 27, no. 4 (2007): 602–3, 613–16; Formisano, "Party Period Revisited," 112–20; Paula Baker, "The Domestication of Politics: Women and American Political Society, 1780–1920," *American Historical Review* 89, no. 3 (1984): 622; Voss-Hubbard, "Third Party," 135–7; Norma Basch, "A Challenge to the Story of Popular

Politics," *Journal of American History* 84, no. 3 (1997): 903; Jean Harvey Baker, "Politics, Paradigms, and Public Culture," *Journal of American History* 84, no. 3 (1997): 898; Altschuler and Blumin, "Political Engagement," 879, 885; Mary Hershberger, "Mobilizing Women, Anticipating Abolition: The Struggle against Indian Removal in the 1830s," *Journal of American History* 86, no. 1 (1999): 15–40.

9 "Revolution": Henry Clay quoted in Pasley, "Minnows," 607. Historians tend to consider that the revolutionary threat during the Jacksonian era was an overstatement. Some disagree, such as Pasley, "Minnows," 606–8. On the question of legitimacy, Julien Mauduit, "'Vrais républicains' d'Amérique: les patriotes canadiens en exil aux États-Unis" (PhD diss., UQAM, 2016); and in this volume, Thomas Richards Jr, "The Lure of a Canadian Republic: Americans, the Patriot War, and Upper Canada as Political and Economic Alternative, 1837–1840," and Andrew Bonthius, "Bald Eagle over Canada: Dr Samuel Underhill and the Patriot Rebellion of 1837–1838."

10 Richard P. McCormick, *The Second American Party System: Party Formation in the Jacksonian Era* (Chapel Hill: University of North Carolina Press, 1966); Formisano, "'Party Period' Revisited."

11 For an argument on the absence of ideology within the national bi-partisanship: Edward Pessen, *Jacksonian America: Society, Personality, and Politics* (Chicago: University of Illinois Press, 1977), 149–260.

12 Biddle and Chevalier are quoted in Pasley, "Minnows," 604–5, 629. See also 616 on the meaning of the political struggle for the radicals. The *Herald* is quoted in Edwin G. Burrows and Mike Wallace, *Gotham: A History of New York City to 1898* (New York: Oxford University Press, 1998), 606. *New York Times* is quoted in Fitzwilliam Byrdsall, *History of the Loco-Foco Party, Or Equal Rights Party* (New York: 1842), 28–9. "War upon Our State": *Proceedings of the Great Democratic Republican meeting in the City of New York, New York, 1838*, 4–7.

13 Moore is quoted in Pasley, "Minnows," 629. "Enemies": Pessen, *Jacksonian America*, 278.

14 Marc W. Kruman, *Parties and Politics in North Carolina, 1836–1865* (Baton Rouge: Louisiana State University Press, 1983); Kruman, "Second Party System," 522–4; Jean H. Baker, *Affairs of Party: The Political Culture of Northern Democrats in the Mid-Nineteenth Century* (Ithaca: Cornell University Press, 1983): 287–97; Jean H. Baker, "From Belief into Culture: Republicanism in the Antebellum North," *American Quarterly* 37, no. 4 (1985): 545–7; Robert H. Wiebe, *The Opening of American Society: From the Adoption of the Constitution to the Eve of Disunion* (New York: Alfred

A. Knopf, 1984), 98–104; Glen C. Altschuler and Stuart M. Blumin, "'Where Is the Real America?': Politics and Popular Consciousness in the Antebellum Era," *American Quarterly* 49, no. 2 (1997): 231; "The War of the Five Campaigns," USDR (June 1840): 477–8, 485.

15 Address of the Utica Convention, September 1837, Byrdsall, *Loco-Foco*, 169. Philip Hone is quoted in Jessica Lepler, *The Many Panics of 1837: People, Politics and the Creation of a Transnational Financial Crisis* (Cambridge: Cambridge University Press, 2013), 189.

16 President Annual Message to the Congress, 3 December 1838, available at http://www.presidency.ucsb.edu/ws/?pid=29480. On Van Buren's willingness to repress the revolutionaries: Stevens, *Border Diplomacy*, 33–47; Corey, *Crisis*, 97–8. On Mackenzie's incarceration: see below.

17 "The Canadian Question," USDR (January 1839): 8–13, and "The New York Election," USDR (January 1839): 5. Emphasis added. The same explanation is exposed by a member of the Democratic Party in Vermont: *Mackenzie-Lindsey Papers*, PAO (hereafter MLP), Moore to Mackenzie, 12 December 1838.

18 MLP: Moore to Mackenzie, 12 December 1838 ("mortified"); Birge to Mackenzie, 15 July 1839 ("prejudice" and "popular act"); Lower to Mackenzie, 30 March 1839 ("lose").

19 MLP: James Mackenzie to Mackenzie, 6 August 1838; Bagley to Mackenzie, 2 August 1838; "Jefferson" to Mackenzie, 18 September 1838; Hungesford to Mackenzie, 9 August 1838; Johnston to Mackenzie, undated (#2009); McConnell, *Orleans Republican*'s editor, to Mackenzie, 31 August 1838; James Mackenzie to Mackenzie, undated (#2161); Durand to Mackenzie, 22 October 1838; Cowen to Mackenzie, 6 December 1838; Hunt to Mackenzie, 7 February 1839; Hunter to Mackenzie, 18 October 1839. Whigs' expansionism has mostly been studied through the Texas case: Michael A. Morrison, "Westward the Curse of Empire: Texas Annexation and the American Whig Party," *Journal of the Early Republic* 10, no. 2 (1990): 221–49. For the pro-Democrat stance before 1837: Harvey, *Printemps*; Robert Richard, "Bank War in Lower Canada," in this volume.

20 MLP: Johnston to Mackenzie, undated (#2009); Citizens of Ogdensburg to Mackenzie, 8 August 1838; Vail to Mackenzie, 7 December 1838; Fry to Mackenzie, 14 December 1838; O'Birne and Heron to Mackenzie, 28 and 30 September 1839; Doyle to Mackenzie, 22 December 1839; McLeod to Mackenzie, 13 June 1840; McLeod to Mackenzie, 15 October 1840.

21 "Own destroyers": *Plattsburgh Republican*, 3 October 1840. See also Tiffany, *Relations*, 103–7.

22 For a debate in French: *Plattsburgh Republican*, 31 October 1840. For a debate among leading Canadian patriot figures: *New York Must Be Redeemed!* (Rochester), 19 September 1840; MLP, W. Nelson to Mackenzie, 10 October 1840; *Mackenzie's Gazette*, 31 October 1840.

23 *L'Estafette*, 20 March 1838. MLP: Rudd to Mackenzie, 4 November 1839; Rudd to Mackenzie, 12 May 1840. Locofocos: *New York Evening Post*, 27 and 28 December 1837; *Mackenzie's Gazette*, 29 September 1838. On the tensions between Van Buren and the Locofocos: Sean Wilentz, *The Rise of American Democracy: Jefferson to Lincoln* (New York: W.W. Norton & Co., 2006): 533–4.

24 MLP: Duane and Sutherland to Mackenzie, 1 July 1839; Fitman to Mackenzie, 13 July 1839; Fitman to Mackenzie, 21 July 1839; Petition from citizens of Philadelphia to Van Buren, undated (#3219). "Falling in the estimation": MLP, A.K. Mackenzie to Mackenzie, 24 January 1839. The *Public Ledger* is reprinted in *Mackenzie's Gazette*, 1 December 1838. On the positive reception of the Canadian patriotic cause among Philadelphia editors, Maxime Dagenais, "'[T]Hose Who Had Money Were Opposed to Us, and Those Who Were Our Friends Were Not the Moneyed Class.' Philadelphia and the 1837–1838 Canadian Rebellions," *American Review of Canadian Studies* 48, no. 1 (Spring 2017).

25 Michael F. Holt, *The Rise and Fall of the American Whig Party: Jacksonian Politics and the Onset of the Civil War* (New York: Oxford University Press, 1999), 75–6, 112. The total number of voters was 60 per cent higher than in 1836, representing a raise of 900,000 electors.

26 Among historians who have focused on the economic issues: James R. Sharp, *The Jacksonian versus the Banks: Politics in the States after the Panic of 1837* (New York: Columbia University Press, 1970); Holt, *Whig Party*, in particular 61–115; Silbey, *Political Nation*, 26–7; William N. Chambers, "Election of 1840," Arthur M. Schlesinger Jr and Fred L. Israel, eds, *History of American Presidential Elections, 1789–1968* (New York: Chelsea House, 1971), 682–3. Historians also stress the division among the Democratic Party provoked by Van Buren's hard money policy: Major L. Wilson, *The Presidency of Martin Van Buren* (Lawrence: University of Kentucky Press, 1984); Watson, *Liberty and Power*; Donald B. Cole, *Martin Van Buren and the American Political System* (Princeton: Princeton University Press, 2014 [1984]); Charles Sellers, *The Market Revolution: Jacksonian America, 1815–1846* (New York: Oxford University Press, 1991), 332–427; Wilentz, *American Democracy*, 478–81. On the 1840 election: Elizabeth R. Varon, "Tippecanoe and the Ladies, Too: White Women and Party Politics in Antebellum Virginia,"

*Journal of American History* 82, no. 2 (1995): 494–521; Ronald J. Zboray and Mary Saracino Zboray, "Whig Women, Politics, and Culture in the Campaign of 1840: Three Perspectives from Massachusetts," *Journal of the Early Republic* 17, no. 2 (1997): 277–315; Richard Carwardine, "Evangelicals, Whigs, and the Election of William Henry Harrison," *Journal of American Studies* 17, no. 1 (1983): 47–75; Leslie L. Hunter, "The Role of Music in the 1840 Campaign of William Henry Harrison," *Bulletin of Historical Research in Music Education* 10, no. 2 (July 1989): 107–10. For a critique of the alleged intellectual submissiveness of the voters: Formisano, "Party Period Revisited," 103–7; Altschuler and Blumin, "Political Engagement."

27 Whig leaders: MLP, A.K. Mackenzie to Mackenzie, 18 January 1839. Clay: *Burlington Free Press*, 18 January 1838; Jason M. Opal and Julien Mauduit, "La Panique financière de 1819 et les Patriotes de 1837: nouveau regard sur le rapprochement anglo-américain et la 'démocratie jacksonienne,'" *Bulletin d'histoire politique* 25, no. 2 (2017): 194. Webster: J.R. Baldwin, "The Ashburton-Webster Boundary Settlement," *Report of the Annual Meeting of the Canadian Historical Association/Rapports annuels de la Société historique du Canada* 17, no. 1 (1938): 121–33.

28 On the support from Democratic representatives: MLP, A.K. Mackenzie to Mackenzie, 18 January 1839; MLP, A.K. Mackenzie to Mackenzie, 24 January 1839; MLP, Doyle to Mackenzie, 22 December 1839; MLP, Cushing to Mackenzie, 20 March 1841. On Cushing: John Belohlavek, *Broken Glass: Caleb Cushing and the Shattering of the Union* (Kent, OH: Kent State University Press, 2005), 92–120. On R.M. Johnson: MLP, Duane to Mackenzie, 30 March 1840; MLP, McLeod to Mackenzie, 20 September 1840; Kinchen, *Hunters*, 41–2; Gates, *After Rebellion*, 69. On the critiques regarding Texas and Canada: *Vermont Republican*, 17 August 1842; *Le Courrier des États-Unis* (New York), 28 December 1837; Tiffany, *Relations*, 70–3; Corey, *Crisis*, 53; William L. Mackenzie, *Life and Times of Martin Van Buren* (Boston, 1846), 294–5; Donald McLeod, *A Brief Review of the Settlement of Upper Canada* (Cleveland, 1841), 225–6, 231–2; MLP, Magrine to Mackenzie, 18 December 1838.

29 An example is the bank question in Pennsylvania between 1835–40: Charles McCool Snyder, *The Jacksonian Heritage: Pennsylvania Politics, 1833–1848* (Harrisburg: The Pennsylvania Historical and Museum Commission, 1958), 71–80; Formisano, "Election of 1840," 667–70. On the difficulty of interpreting electoral results, Donald Ratcliff, "Popular Preferences in the Presidential Election of 1824," *Journal of the Early Republic* 34, no. 1 (2014): 44–77.

30 Marcy, 31 December 1837, quoted in Gates, *After Rebellion*, 26–7. According to Mackenzie, Marcy was first a supporter of the Canadian Revolution, *Martin Van Buren*, 293.

31 "Next president": "Extract from a letter addressed by a respectable inhabitant of Detroit to a gentleman in Toronto," 26 December 1838, quoted in Kinchen, *Hunters*, 44. Holt, *Whig*, 71–4. According to I.D. Spencer, Marcy's defeat was largely due to his anti-patriots stance: *The Victor and the Spoils: A Life of William L. Marcy* (Providence: Brown University Press, 1959), 99–100. USDR, January 1839, "The New York Election," 5. "May follow": MLP, Durand to Mackenzie, 24 November 1838. "More friends" and "never will be elected": MLP, Neysmith to Mackenzie, 11 December 1838.

32 *The Native American*, 21 March, 4 April, and 20 June 1840. Hand's cause was defended in Washington by the *Metropolis*.

33 *Madisonian*, 18 July 1840.

34 MLP, Citizens of Ogdensburg to Mackenzie, 8 August 1838. "Amazingly Patriotic," and for a similar critique of the party's leaders by upstate New York Whigs: MLP, "Jefferson," Sherman and Winston, to Mackenzie, 18 September 1838.

35 On public opinion: MLP, Durand to Mackenzie, 24 November 1838; MLP, Mackenzie to O'Reilly, 15 August 1839; Cole, *Van Buren*, 327. "No. No.": MLP, "Martin Van Buren & the Canadas" by Charles Durand, 1 December 1838. MLP, "HJ Sawner" (W.J. Duane) to Mackenzie, 11 February 1840. "Whip": MLP, "For Mackenzie's Gazette," anonymous from Washington DC, 28 December 1838.

36 "76": MLP, Fry to Mackenzie, [1840?] (#3418). On Clevelanders: MLP, McLeod to Mackenzie, 3 April 1840; MLP: McLeod to Mackenzie, 14 May 1840. Van Buren as an obstacle to a war: *Fonds Duvernay*, ANQ, W. Nelson to Duvernay, 31 December 1839; W. Nelson to A. Papineau, 11 January 1841, Georges Aubin, ed., *Wolfred Nelson: écrits d'un patriote* (Quebec: Comeau et Nadeau, 1998), 133–6; MLP, Theller to Mackenzie, 29 May 1840; MLP, W. Nelson to Mackenzie, 10 October 1840; Gates, *After Rebellion*, 67–9.

37 "Democratic Majesty": MLP, James Mackenzie to Mackenzie, undated (#2161). For the discrepancies between principles and practices: *Mackenzie's Gazette*, 29 September and 1 December 1838; MLP, [O'Callaghan] to Mackenzie, 4 July 1840; *Burlington Free Press*, 6 November 1840. Harrison as a patriotic soldier: Paul Boller, *Presidential Campaigns: From George Washington to George Bush* (New York: Oxford University Press, 2004), 68. On his acquaintance with Van

Rensselear: Marc L. Harris, "The Meaning of Patriot: The Canadian Rebellion and American Republicanism, 1837–1839," *Michigan Historical Review* 23, no. 1 (1997): 56n. For the link with the economic issues: *The Beacon* (New York), quoted in *The North American* (Swanton), 24 July 1839. In 1823, Van Buren already put party loyalism before public opinion: Ratcliff, "Popular Preferences," 71–2.

38 *Vermont Watchman*, 23 December 1839, collected the Whig press reactions after Harrison's victory. Boller, *Campaigns*, 66–9; Holt, *Whig*, 49–50; Ronald P. Formisano, *For The People: American Populist Movements from the Revolution to the 1850s* (Chapel Hill: University of North Carolina Press, 2008), 150–3; Pessen, *Jacksonian America*, 169. For the designation of the Whigs' candidate: Wilentz, *American Democracy*, 493–8.

39 "Comfortable": MLP, Langtree to Mackenzie, 7 November 1839. Another example is Hobart Berrian, editor of the *Metropolis*: MLP, Berrian to Mackenzie, 5 September 1838. Efforts: MLP, Moore (Vermont) to Mackenzie, 12 December 1838; Doyle (Philadelphia) to Mackenzie, 29 May 1840; *Mackenzie's Gazette*, 12 October 1839; *The New World*, 18 April 1840.

40 Speech available at: https://archive.org/details/genharrisonsspeeooharr.

41 Harrison's speech at Cleveland: MLP, McLeod to Mackenzie, 15 June 1840. On his tour: *Ohio State Journal*, 10 June 1840; *Log Cabin* (Dayton), 27 June 1840 ("guns"); Wilentz, *American Democracy*, 504–6. "Artfully ambiguous": Holt, *Whig*, 108–10. On the patriots' skepticism: A. Papineau to L.-J. Papineau, 29 May 1840, Georges Aubin et Renée Blanchet, eds, *Amédée Papineau: correspondance, 1831–1841*, vol. 1 (Montreal: Michel Brûlé, 2009), 282–3; MLP, Johnston to Mackenzie, 20 September 1840. Harrison's nickname was "General Mum" due to his habit of being unclear, but Van Buren was performing in a similar fashion: Pessen, *Jacksonian America*, 150–1, 168–9.

42 Information on John Griffin is available in the MLP: Griffin to Mackenzie, 28 January 1839; A.K. Mackenzie to Mackenzie, 24 March 1839; Griffin to Mackenzie, 26 June 1839; Griffin to Mackenzie, 20 July 1839; Fitman to Mackenzie, 21 July 1839; Doyle to Mackenzie, 17 August 1839; Griffin to Mackenzie, 25 October 1839; Doyle to Mackenzie, 28 November 1839; Griffin to Mackenzie, 3 January 1840; Griffin to Mackenzie, 10 February 1840; Fitman to Mackenzie, 12 March 1840; W.J. Duane to Mackenzie, 30 March 1840; Griffin to Mackenzie, 3 May 1840 ("*Van Buren & Victoria Bastile*"); Fitman to Mackenzie, 20 May 1840; Doyle to Mackenzie, 29 May 1840.

43 New party: *MLP*, James Mackenzie to Mackenzie, 6 August 1838 ("new party"); *MLP*, Duncombe to Mackenzie, 27 July 1841. "Jaw": *MLP*, O'Callaghan to Mackenzie, 1 April 1840. For their difficult position regarding the "party warfare": *MLP*, James Mackenzie to Mackenzie, 10 December 1838; *MLP*, James Mackenzie to Mackenzie, 23 August 1839. For the Whig Party as a receptacle of antipartyism: Kruman, "Second Party System," 522; Holt, *Whig*, 30–2; Formisano, "Political Antipartyism," 709.

44 "Republic in fact": George Evans, *The Man* (1834), quoted in Sean Wilentz, *Chants Democratic: New York City and the Rise of the American Working Class* (New York: Oxford University Press, 1984), 237.

45 Seth Cotlar, *Tom Paine's America: The Rise and Fall of Transatlantic Radicalism in the Early Republic* (Charlottesville: University of Virginia Press, 2011), 121–58; Joyce Appleby, *Capitalism and a New Social Order: The Republican Vision of the 1790s* (New York: New York University Press, 1984). On the influence of New York City Locofocos: Lillian F. Gates, "The Decided Policy of William Lyon Mackenzie," *Canadian Historical Review* 40, no. 3 (1959): 185–208; Andrew Bonthius, "The Patriot War of 1837–1838, Locofocoism with a Gun?," *Labour/Le Travail* 52 (2003): 9–43; Mauduit, "Vrais républicains"; Louis-Georges Harvey, "Banques, société et politique dans le discours d'Edmund Bailey O'Callaghan, 1833–1837," *Cahiers des dix* 69 (2015) : 251–79.

46 "Voice": Byrdsall, *Loco-Foco*, 101. Burrows and Wallace, *Gotham*, 610–11; Wilentz, *Chants*, 288–9; Wilentz, *American Democracy*, 445; Lepler, *Panics*, 67–9.

47 "Vengeance": Byrdsall, *Loco-Foco*, 167–9. "Enemy": Byrdsall, *Loco-Foco*, 99–100. "Money rules": Byrdsall, *Loco-Foco*, 147–51. On these meetings: Burrows and Wallace, *Gotham*, 611–14; Wilentz, *Chants*, 288–95.

48 George Evans, "History of the Origin and Progress of the Working Men's Party in New York," *The Radical* (New York), 1842.

49 Antimasons and Workingmen's parties: Formisano, *For the People*, 104–6; Pessen, *Jacksonian America*, 261–9. Antimasons and Whigs: Holt, *Whig*, 27–32; Formisano, *For the People*, 134–5, 145–57. Southwick: Mackenzie, *Van Buren*, 26. Seward is quoted in Robert Townsend, *An Inquiry into the Cause of Social Evil; With its Remedy* (New York: Reform Association, 1839), 5, 30. Horace Greeley, *Recollections of a Busy Life* (New York: J.B. Ford and Company, 1868), 144–58. On the rebellious spirit in this area, and the political meanings of the Antimasons movement, see Thomas Richards Jr's chapter in this volume.

50 *True American*: Lepler, *Panics*, 117–18. "Decline of Deference": Formisano, "Election of 1840," 678. Free Banking Law: Wilentz, *The American Democracy*, 493–4.

51 John Quincy Adams is quoted in Boller, *Campaigns*, 65, 71–2. Italics are mine. The North Carolina citizen is quoted in Kruman, "Second Party System," 523–4. "Intensity": Formisano, "Election of 1840," 680.

52 Boller, *Campaigns*, 67. "Gathering storm": *The People are Rousing* (available at: https://www.loc.gov/resource/sm1840.470970.0?st=gallery). *Tipp's Invitation to Loco, patriotic glee* is available at: https://www.loc.gov/item/sm1840.371460/. Entertaining campaign: Wilentz, *American Democracy*, 502–4. For a different interpretation: Altschuler and Blumin, "Political Engagement," 881–4; Howe, *American Whigs*, 7–8 ("serious issues").

53 Lord Ashburton is quoted in Jay Sexton, *Debtor Diplomacy: Finance and American Foreign Relations in the Civil War Era, 1837–1873* (Oxford: Oxford University Press 2005), 30. Van Buren's strategy: *MLP*, O'Callaghan to Mackenzie, 1 April 1840. Fear: *North American* (Swanton), 3 February 1841. Patrick Lacroix, "Choosing Peace and Order: National Security and Sovereignty in a North American Borderland, 1837–1842," *International History Review*, online (2015): 5–6.

54 "Shake": "Extract from a letter addressed by a respectable inhabitant of Detroit to a gentleman in Toronto," 26 December 1838, quoted in Kinchen, *Hunters*, 44. "Join": Secretary of State Daniel Webster, quoted in Kinchen, *Hunters*, 108–9. "Mischievous": President Tyler, quoted in Kinchen, *Hunters*, 141. Governor Arthur to Hamilton, 3 January 1839, quoted in Kinchen, *Hunters*, 44. USDR, January 1839, "The Canada Question," 13.

55 On the elected aristocracy: Pessen, *Jacksonian America*, 152–260; Altschuler and Blumin, "Political Engagement"; Pasley, "Minnows," 605–6, 623–5. On the reduced public debates: Pessen, *Jacksonian America*, 152–260; Altschuler and Blumin, "Political Engagement." Class-oriented legislation: Edward Pessen, "The Social Configuration of the Antebellum City: An Historical and Theoretical Inquiry," *Journal of Urban History* 2, no. 3 (1976): 294; Edward Pessen, *Riches, Class, and Power before the Civil War* (Lexington: D.C. Heath & Co., 1973): 251–301; Robert H. Wiebe, *The Opening of American Society: From the Adoption of the Constitution to the Eve of Desunion* (New York: Knopf, 1984), 349–52; Ronald P. Formisano, "Toward a Reorientation of Jacksonian Politics: A Review of the Literature, 1959–1975," *Journal of American History* 63, no. 1 (1976): 51. Against the "public good": Louis Hartz, *Economic*

*Policy and Democratic Thought: Pennsylvania, 1776–1860* (Cambridge: Harvard University Press, 1948); McCormick, *Party Period*, 21.

56 In the 1830s, lawyers represented approximately 65 per cent of the Congress: Pasley, "Minnows," 600. Altschuler and Blumin, "Political Engagement," 880; Formisano, "Deferential-Participant"; Walter Hugins, *Jacksonian Democracy and The Working Class: a Study of the New York Workingmen's Movement, 1829–1837* (Stanford: Stanford University Press, 1960), 142–3.

57 "Murmur" and "destruction": *The Spirit of the Age* (Woodstock, VT), 16 October 1840. On the original republicanism: Kruman, "Second Party System," 512–13; Drew R. McCoy, *The Elusive Republic: Political Economy in Jeffersonian America* (Chapel Hill: University of North Carolina Press, 1980), 131.

58 "If it is republican": *MLP*, [McLeod] to Mackenzie, 13 June 1840. Charge against the "capitalists": Charles Duncombe, *Duncombe's Free Banking* (Cleveland: N.A., 1841), 178. "Threatening": *MLP*, Durand to Mackenzie, 24 November 1838. "Speculators": *MLP*, A.K. Mackenzie to Mackenzie, 7 January 1840.

59 "Territory": *MLP*, Brossing to Mackenzie, 4 August 1839. On the Detroit meeting: Kinchen, *Hunters*, 137–9. "Light up": *MLP*, Moore to Mackenzie, 12 December 1838. *USDR*, January 1839, "The Canada Question," 27. "Insane": *MLP*, Neysmith to Mackenzie, 11 December 1838.

60 Brownson: Mackenzie, *Van Buren*, 143–4. "People of America": Mackenzie, *Caroline Almanack* (Rochester: N.A., 1840), 65. "Vigilant": *North American* (Swanton), 10 April 1839. John J. Duffy and H. Nicholas Muller, III, *Anxious Democracy, Aspects of the 1830s* (Westport: Greenwood Press, 1982), 71.

61 "Believe them," "insidiously," and "unfavourable": *New Era and American Courier*, 30 June 1838. Rudd is co-editor of the *New Era*. *MLP*, Rudd to Mackenzie, 4 November 1839. Influence of the British economic domination, among many others: "War or Peace? Why Does England Hold Fast in Canada?," *Mackenzie's Gazette*, 12 October 1839.

62 Richard Hildreth, *The Contrast: or William Henry Harrison versus Martin Van Buren* (Boston: 1840), 64.

63 Inaugural address available at: http://www.presidency.ucsb.edu/ws/?pid=25813. Ronald Formisano stresses the antiparty dimension of this speech: "Antipartyism," 686–7. On Harrison's view of the president's role: Howe, *Whigs*, 90. Harrison died one month after this inaugural speech – as a result, it is said, of a cold he caught during it.

64 "Corrupt politics": Voss-Hubbard, "Third Party," 129–30; "Inflamed": USDR, November 1840, 387; "Interesting Period": USDR, January 1842, 57. "More necessary": MLP, James Mackenzie to Mackenzie, 23 August 1839. "Tools": MLP, Sawner (W.J. Duane) to Mackenzie, 11 February 1840. "Country": Wilson, "Bank War." "Liberal capitalist consensus": Keller, *Three Regimes*, 82–5; "Fun": Boller, *Campaigns*, 65.

AFTERWORD

# "The Practicability of Annexing Canada"

## *Or, the Manifest Destiny of Canada, According to the United States*

AMY S. GREENBERG

> The practicability of annexing Canada is very often spoken of with great sincerity by our citizens ... The annexation of one country to another is a troublesome undertaking, even under the most favorable circumstances. How much more so ... when circumstances are adverse, when at least one of the parties to the project is unwilling. Such an illustration applies to Canada. Its inhabitants are not in the condition the people of Texas were, when they came in collision with Mexico. A few years ago perhaps there was a visible analogy between them, when at least the half of the population of Canada felt a sincere hostility to their rulers ... While there was a strong tendency in the Canadian mind to look abroad for help and sympathy, the confidence reposed by them in the people of the United States was never strong ... by far the majority of the Canadians never forgot, even in their wrath, that a sacrifice of their dear nationality would follow a political union with this republic ... At the present moment Canada is ... more quiet than at any period within the last twenty years, and those who would calculate on the co-operation of this people to effect a union with this country, would find themselves mistaken ... We presume that none are so foolish as to advocate a forcible annexation.
>
> "Canada," New York *Herald*, 27 July 1845

Less than a year before the United States threatened war with Britain in order to gain half of the Oregon Country, and went to war with Mexico in order to forcibly annex California, the New York *Herald* mixed befuddlement over the continuing lust for Canada among the American citizenry with an almost envious evaluation of the political, social, and economic position of Canadians. While neither Canada's economy nor their political institutions were perfect, both were good. Since the failure of the Canadian Rebellion of 1837–1838, the moment when annexation was most likely – because, according to the *Herald*, "at least half of the population of Canada felt a sincere hostility to their rulers, and would have been glad to change its connection for any other without being very particular about the terms" – almost everything in Canada had improved for the better. In 1841 Lower and Upper Canada united into the Province of Canada, and Britain granted meaningful rights and privileges to its residents. "Without any reference to the admitted inferiority of monarchical institutions, no other subjects of a crowned head enjoy more liberty and protections than the Canadians," the *Herald* explained to its readers. "Religious freedom prevails, there are almost no taxes, direct or indirect; they enjoy a species of monopoly of commerce with the mother country," and "a great annual expenditure of money takes place in the payment of the army and the construction of military and public works." As for trade, "their wharves are covered with merchandise which is purchased by the consumer 40 per cent cheaper than here; the credit of its merchants and commercial classes is unbounded and stable."

All things considered, it was worth wondering if Canadians, "participators in all the advantages derivable from a connection with a rich and powerful country; and exempt from nearly all the evils that affect their fellow subjects on the other side of the Atlantic," might be better off than their neighbours to the south. Even in the worst of times, in 1837–1838, the majority of Canadians were unwilling to cast aside their "dear nationality"; clearly they had no interest in doing so under vastly improved circumstances. "To talk of an annexation of Canada with the consent of its people, at present," betrayed "an ignorance of these facts," the *Herald* stated. But surely none of these pro-annexation expansionists were "foolish" enough to suggest that the United States take Canada without the blessing of its residents. Who would dream of a "forcible annexation" of Canada?[1]

Three years later, this same newspaper argued in favour of just such a forcible annexation on the other end of the continent. "It is a gorgeous prospect, this annexation of all Mexico" the *Herald* wrote in October of 1848, after the United States captured Mexico's capital. "It were more desirable that she should come to us voluntarily, but as we shall have not peace until she be annexed, let it come, even though force be necessary, at first, to bring her. Like the Sabine virgins, she will soon learn to love her ravisher."[2]

It has long been accepted by scholars of expansionism that Canada faded as a target of expansionist fervour after the Rebellion of 1837–1838. After decades when "the border between the two countries was not clearly defined" and "Canadian efforts at fighting ecclesiastical favoritism, high taxation rates, and limited representation" drew American sympathy and rapacity in equal measure, visions of Manifest Destiny spreading north were dashed by President Martin Van Buren's determination to enforce neutrality laws, the resolution of key boundary disputes, and British concessions to Canadian self-government. Canada was safe and expansionists were forced to turn "south and west to fulfill their dreams of a continental empire." [3] As Reginald C. Stewart concluded in his study of nineteenth-century U.S.-Canada relations, although Americans "continued to assume that their republican-democratic values would expand" to the north after the failure of the provincial rebellions, they also accorded Canadians "their own principle of self-determination." U.S. residents never lost their faith that "historical forces" were driving the union of the provinces and the United States, including "the temptations of sharing in American prosperity, and the infection of American republicanism." But press coverage of the Canadian Rebellion led most "reflective Americans" to recognize an important truth: a widespread "provincial dislike of the United States" prevented Canadians from recognizing how much better off they would be as U.S. citizens.[4]

Why Canadians were allowed the principle of self-determination, while Mexicans were not, and why the same New York newspaper made clear that a forcible annexation of Canada was inconceivable, but the rape of Mexico necessary, is no great mystery. It is not the purpose of this essay to reflect on the relationship between racial and sexual domination, in international relations or otherwise – beyond noting that, to my knowledge, no public speaker ever recommended that a crowd of expansionist men at a public meeting "take a trip of exploration" to Canada, and "look out for the beautiful senoritas, or pretty girls, and if you should choose to annex them, no doubt the result of this annexation will be a most powerful and delightful evidence of civilization," as did former Texas Republic president Samuel Houston while speaking to New York workingmen about Mexico in 1847. White women, and white nations, were entitled to certain rights and privileges that less "civilized" (and white) women and nations were not.[5]

The purpose of this afterword is to consider, rather, the views of those citizens who continued to pursue Canadian annexation after 1838. Despite the evidence that Canadians did not wish to be annexed, and the widely acknowledged right of self-determination for America's Anglo-Saxon neighbours to the north, certain Americans continued to lobby – quite loudly – for the fulfillment of their Manifest Destiny to incorporate Canada into the American Republic after events in 1838 supposedly brought an end to such musings.

This is not to suggest that American participation in the Canadian Rebellion was driven by the desire to annex Canada. As the essays in this volume make clear, among the many motivations of U.S. participants in the Canadian Rebellion, few if any of them were fighting to bring more land into the United States. Press coverage at the time by and large made it clear that the Patriots were motivated by the desire to see Upper and Lower Canadian citizens free, free both of British tyranny, and to a lesser degree, the economic tyranny of unbridled capitalism.

But the decision of the Van Buren administration to enforce the Federal Neutrality Acts of 1818 and 1838, as well as British reforms instituted in the wake of the rebellions, should have killed annexation fantasies altogether, particularly given the push by slave owners to gain political power through the annexation of new slave territory. In the 1840s and 1850s, slave owners held outsized power in the federal government, with a virtual lock on foreign policy. There was no possibility of introducing slavery into Canada. Indeed, as the home of many escaped American slaves, and a centre for antislavery agitation on the continent, Canada was a distinctly undesirable acquisition in the eyes of southerners.[6]

Given the power of slaveholders over foreign policy, it is unsurprising that the U.S. pursued a "dovish" and distinctly harmonious relationship with Canada in the 1840s and 1850s. The Webster-Ashburton Treaty of 1842 resolved boundary disputes in Maine and Minnesota. In return for ceding claims to the Maine frontier,

Britain gained the security of unimpeded control to the St Lawrence River. In 1845, the U.S. army closed the Hancock Barracks in Maine, reflecting the pacified situation as the U.S. turned its attention to the Pacific. An 1854 reciprocity treaty between Canada and the United States drew the two nations together through mutually advantageous trade, bringing economic relief to residents on both sides of the border.[7]

Yet somehow annexationist sentiment refused to die. Contrary to both historical narrative and common sense, many Americans continued to look longingly north, while the British looked warily south of the U.S.-Canada border. Although the Americans who pushed for the integration of Canada into the U.S. after the Canadian Rebellion were a minority, their actions influenced U.S.-British relations long after the era of Manifest Destiny had supposedly come to a close.

It is easy to forget that in the middle of John L. O'Sullivan's famous 1845 essay "Annexation," which begins with an order that "opposition to the Annexation *of Texas* ... cease," the author turned his sights northward. "There is a great deal of annexation yet to take place, within the life of the present generation, along the whole line of our northern border ... destined to swell the still accumulating momentum of our progress."[8] Although as Louis-Georges Harvey argues in his essay in this collection, O'Sullivan opposed the annexation of Canadian territory in the 1830s, there is no trace of such restraint in his later writings. O'Sullivan gestured to no particular province in "Annexation," but rather to the entirety of a very long border. And at every point on that border there were supporters of the cause. Oregon Country, jointly controlled by the U.S. and Britain, was the object of passionate desire by northern expansionists. Thousands of American settlers had made the arduous trek by covered wagon to farm its fertile soils, and were anxious to see British claims to the region extinguished. In 1844 James K. Polk campaigned on the annexation of the entirety of Oregon County, rhapsodizing about a United States that spread all the way to the Pacific, encompassing British Columbia and Vancouver Island. He settled for much less in 1846, dividing ownership of Oregon with the British.[9]

Not that this necessarily settled the question. William Seward, an abolitionist Whig who vehemently opposed war, understood that "the popular passion for territorial aggrandizement is irresistible." He urged compromise on Oregon, not because he respected British claims to the region, but because of his faith that Manifest Destiny would ultimately bring the entirety of the northern portion of North America into U.S. hands. "Let the Oregon question be settled when it may," he told an audience in his home state of New York. "It will, nevertheless, come back again. Our population is destined to roll its restless waves to the icy barriers of the north."[10]

Residents of Lake County, Ohio, gazing across Lake Erie toward Canada West (modern-day Ontario), agreed. They called a public meeting in Painesville to "consider the project of 're-annexing' Canada to the United States." The wording was meant to taunt southerners who called for the "re-annexation" of Texas, but the Detroit *Advertiser* "warmly" agreed that the Canadian territory directly to the east belonged in the United States. The newspaper further advocated "an exchange of Oregon for Canada."[11]

Economic distress produced by the British repeal of the Corn Laws in 1847 raised the distinct possibility that Quebec might also be annexed. Rioters agitating in Montreal for economic relief burned down the parliament building, and merchants in the city called for annexation to the United States. Governor Lord Elgin pleaded with London, "If England will not make the sacrifices which are absolutely necessary to put the Colonists here in as good a position commercially as the citizens of the States … the end may be nearer than we wot of."[12] After Montreal residents issued an annexation manifesto in 1849, U.S. papers thrilled to the possibility of immediate annexation. The Vermont *Watchman* called the annexation of Canada to the United States "*the greatest free soil movement of the day*."[13] A Wilmington Delaware newspaper agreed. In response to unnamed "Canadian papers" that "are freely discussing the propriety of annexing themselves to the United States," the paper clearly stated, "We are in favor of the annexation of Canada … It is a free population of about three millions, and would make from five to ten States. It must come to us sooner or later, and the British would be gainers by permitting it at once."[14]

As Montreal burned, William Seward's predictions about the Northwest appeared to be coming true. In 1847, the British Colonial Secretary warned the House of Lords that unless the Northwest was "regularly settled and regularly organized" it would be "irregularly colonized by squatters" from the United States. This was nothing new. The U.S. had long promoted expansion via settler colonialism, and Canada, which failed to attract immigrants, was an appealing target. Minnesotans hungered for the Red River Valley, north of Lake Traverse, while U.S. settlers on the West Coast gazed longingly towards Vancouver Island. The Hudson Bay Company, tasked with holding the entirety of the Northwest, warned that unless something was done, U.S. settlers would soon force a renegotiation of the border.[15]

Given the agitation across the entirety of the U.S.-Canada border, it is perhaps unsurprising that in 1849 an author going by the pseudonym "Halifax" published *Future Annexations and Their Effects*, a pamphlet laying out the means by which America's "destiny" to "subdue and replenish" a "portion, and not a *small* portion of the face of this earth." Halifax was convinced that "the revolutionary element in Canada is sufficiently strong and progressive to produce, within a few years, a struggle with Great Britain of a kind that must involve our own government, and consequently lead to annexation."[16] There were forces at work, such as gravity, that argued against the independence of Canada. "There is, no doubt, a latent attraction, which may cause such movement ... like that which a great and growing orb exercises over a smaller one, heretofore under the influence of another that is now waning." England was the waning orb; the United States was great and growing.

Geography supported annexation as well. "Whenever two spaces of country, under separate governments, are of such topographical structure that the same interior channels of trade and communication have to be much used by both, the condition of both is benefited by union." Thus the St Lawrence River, and Great Lakes, rather than serving as natural boundaries between two nations, instead argued for the union of Canada and the United States, because "the mutual benefit arising from the joint jurisdiction and more perfect common use of those waters" illustrated, to the author, "the advantages we would derive from the annexation of Canada."

Shared advantages were appealing, particularly given that the author acknowledged the right of Canadian self-determination, but ultimately their vision was nationalistic. As for the "expense and vexation of guarding a long and assailable" border between the two nations, Halifax rhapsodized over the possibility of "having for our Northern boundary a desert, 'where winter fortifies the realms of frost,'" and thus there was no need for "fleets, forts, nor custom houses."[17]

Not all who promoted annexation insisted on remaining anonymous. Given the territorial annexation of half of Mexico in the 1840s, and repeated demands by southerners to annex Cuba in the early 1850s, New York Representative and zealous abolitionist Gerrit Smith's expressed desire (in 1854) to annex antislavery land in compensation was not entirely irrational. But the scope of his desires, as expressed on the floor of the House of Representatives in 1854, is worth quoting. "I claim the right of the British provinces, north of us, to annex themselves to our nation, if we are willing to receive them; and that, too whether England does, or does not consent to it," Smith pronounced. "I hope, that, in due time, the right will be exercised; and that England will feel, that she cannot justly resist the exercise of it. But I hope, for more than such annexation. I hope for the annexation to us of every other part of North America."[18]

As sectional divisions derailed the possibility of northerners and southerners agreeing on any further annexations, the discovery of gold in British Columbia in 1857 provoked a rush of U.S. immigrants similar to that in 1849 San Francisco. By 1858 Victoria and New Westminster – on the mouth of the Frasier River – were connected to San Francisco by steamship service frequent enough that they had become, in effect, "economic outposts of the city by the Golden Gate."[19] A dispute over a pig in the San Juan Islands allowed a zealous American general – who believed Vancouver Island was "as important to the Pacific States as Cuba is to those of the Atlantic" – to attempt a military takeover of the San Juan Islands. President James Buchanan, a Southern sympathizer, refused to support him.[20] On the eve of the Civil War, William Seward was still looking northward. He commended the "ingenious, enterprising and ambitious" people of Canada for "building excellent states to be hereafter admitted to the American union."[21]

Given that the United States did not annex Canada it has been easy for historians to overlook these events, and dismiss the views of those who wished to annex Canada after 1838 as insignificant. But this was not how Canadians or the British at the time saw things. British fears that the United States government had designs over their Canadian territories were real enough to influence foreign policy throughout the hemisphere.

After President Franklin Pierce recognized the government of filibuster William Walker in Nicaragua in 1856, British diplomats worried that the U.S. government was using filibuster surrogates to fight British power in Central America. Rather than fight back, the British backed down, surrendering its claims to the Bay Islands to

Honduras, as well as contested territory along the southern border of Belize to Guatemala. According to historian Robert E. May, the British reasoned that by releasing their Central American colonies, they could avoid a military conflict with the United States "that might jeopardize its hold on Canada."[22]

Just as historians agree that the Rebellion of 1837–38 drove the creation of the Province of Canada, they recognize that British support for Canadian Confederation in 1867 came in response to the perceived threats from the United States.[23] Richard W. Van Alstyne has argued that Canada's purchase of Rupert's Land from the Hudson Bay Company was "a step comparable in importance to the American acquisition of Louisiana in 1803" because it ended U.S. dreams of an American Canada. By defining Canada as a continental nation, the purchase "insured" Canada's "independence as a North American nation." Filibustering in Central America in the 1850s so undermined international relations that it rendered lawful annexations impossible for Latin American countries to contemplate. Agitation in the United States for the annexation of Canada had similarly dramatic effects.[24]

Minority voices are not always marginal in their impact. A majority of northerners never supported abolitionism, but southerners' reactions to their agitation helped create an antislavery coalition that ultimately defeated slavery. Patriot supporters of rebellion failed in their quest to establish an independent Canada, but as the essays in this volume reveal, their efforts influenced economic and political policies on both sides of the border. As for the Americans who refused to recognize that 1838 marked the close of dreams of a northern Manifest Destiny, they may not have been as marginal as they seem. Nor was their impact necessarily limited to the hemisphere. As supporters and opponents of colonialism debated the practicability of an American overseas empire in 1898, they did so with a shared fundamental assumption about territorial expansion born in North America. According to Walter LaFeber, a majority on both sides continued to talk, and to believe, in the "inevitable drift" of Canada into U.S. hands.[25]

## NOTES

1 "Canada," *Herald*, 27 July 1845.

2 "Our Relations with Mexico – The Destiny of the Two Republics," *New York Herald*, 8 October 1847.

3 Amy S. Greenberg, *Manifest Manhood and the Antebellum American Empire* (New York: Cambridge University Press, 2005), 30.

4 Reginald C. Stewart, *United States Expansionism and British North America, 1775–1871* (Chapel Hill: University of North Carolina Press, 1988), 146–7.

5 "The Great War Meeting," NYH, 30 January 1848. For a discussion of the place of both consensual and non-consensual sex in American territorial expansionism, see Greenberg, *Manifest Manhood*; Mark E. Neely Jr argues that a recognition of shared whiteness among white troops in the Civil War prevented atrocities that were widespread in the U.S.-Mexico War, and by white Confederate troops against black Union troops during the Civil War. "The most powerful cultural force restraining white American volunteers on both sides in the Civil war was the perception that the enemy was of the same race," *The Civil War and the Limits of Destruction* (Cambridge, MA: Harvard University Press, 2007), 37.

6 Matthew Karp, *This Vast Southern Empire: Slaveholders at the Helm of American Foreign Policy* (Cambridge, MA: Harvard University Press, 2016), 19–20, 51–2.

7 Karp, *This Vast Southern Empire*, 20; Jeremy Black, *Fighting for America: The Struggle for Mastery in North America, 1519–1871* (Bloomington, IN: University of Indiana Press, 2011), 220–1.

8 John L. O'Sullivan, "Annexation," *United States Magazine and Democratic Review* 17, no. 1 (July–August 1845): 5–10, quotes on pages 5 and 7–8.

9 Amy S. Greenberg, *A Wicked War: Polk, Clay, Lincoln, and the 1846 U.S. Invasion of Mexico* (New York: Vintage, 2013), 15, 34.

10 William Seward, "To the Chautauqua Convention," 31 March 1846. *The Works of William H. Seward*, vol. III, ed. George E. Baker (New York: Redfield, 1853), 409.

11 "Our Neighbors of Lake County," *Cleveland Herald*, 8 February 1845.

12 Elgin quoted in J.L. Granatstein and Norman Hillmer, *For Better or For Worse: Canada and the United States to the 1990s* (Toronto: Copp Clark Pitman Ltd, 1991), xv.

13 "Annexation of Canada," *Vermont Watchman and State Journal*, 29 November 1849.

14 "Canadian Annexation in Delaware," *Milwaukee Sentinel and Gazette*, 22 November 1849.

15 Richard W. Van Alstyn, *The Rising American Empire* (Oxford: Basil Blackwell, 1960), 117. Van Alstyn may have been the first author to recognize that "irregular colonization by squatters was in fact the established rule in American society," 117.

16 "Halifax," *Future Annexations and Their Effects* (n.p., 1849), 16, 7.

17 Ibid., 9–10.

18 *Congressional Globe*, 33rd Congress, 1st session: 27 June 1854: 1016–17.

19 Van Alstyn, *Rising American Empire*, 118.

20 General Harney to General Scott, 19 July 1859 *Papers relating to the foreign relations of the United States: transmitted to Congress with the Annual message of the President*, vol. 2 (USGO 1860): 109.

21 Seward, *The Works of William H. Seward*, vol. IV: 333.

22 Robert E. May, *Manifest Destiny's Underworld: Filibustering in Antebellum America* (Chapel Hill: University of North Carolina Press, 2002), 245.

23 Black, *Fighting for America*, 350; Van Alstyn, *The Rising American Empire*, 121–2; Stewart, *United States Expansionism and British North America*, 239.

24 Van Alstyn, *The Rising American Empire*, 123; May, *Manifest Destiny's Underworld*, 240–1.

25 Walter LaFeber, *The New Empire: An Interpretation of American Expansion 1860–1898* (Ithaca: Cornell University Press, 1998), 201.

# Contributors

ANDREW BONTHIUS received his MA in U.S. history from San Francisco State University in 1991. His undergraduate thesis, "The Origins of the Longshoremen's and Warehousemen's Union," was published in the *Southern California Quarterly*. His first article on this subject, "The Patriot War 1837–1838: Locofocoism with a Gun?" was published in *Labour/Le Travail* (2003).

MAXIME DAGENAIS is an adjunct assistant professor at McMaster University and the coordinator of the Wilson Institute for Canadian History. He holds a PhD from the University of Ottawa and postdoctoral fellowships from the Wilson Institute and the McNeil Center for Early American Studies. He is the author of *The Land in Between: The Upper Saint John Valley: Prehistory to World War I* and numerous academic articles, including in *Quebec Studies*, *Bulletin d'histoire politique*, *Canadian Military History*, and *American Review of Canadian Studies*.

RUTH DUNLEY is an independent scholar who has been researching the life of A.D. Smith for the better part of two decades. A veteran journalist with bylines in newspapers across Canada, she holds undergraduate and graduate degrees in journalism from Carleton University as well as a teaching degree and a PhD in American history from the University of Ottawa. She was a Fulbright Scholar at the College of William & Mary and is the author of *The Lost President: A.D. Smith and the Hidden History of Radical Democracy in Civil War America*.

AMY S. GREENBERG is the George Winfree Professor of American History and Women's Studies at Penn State University. She is the author of five books, including *Manifest Manhood and the Antebellum American Empire*, *A Wicked War: Polk, Clay, Lincoln and the 1846 U.S. Invasion of Mexico*, and most recently *Lady First: The World of First Lady Sarah Polk*. She is currently at work on a study of failed U.S. territorial annexations.

LOUIS-GEORGES HARVEY is a retired professor of history at Bishop's University. He is the author of *Le Printemps de l'Amérique française* (2005), a seminal work that reconceptualized Quebec's socio-cultural history. He has published widely in Canada, the United States, and Europe and was inducted into the Société des dix in 2011. His recent publications include "Confédération, capitalisme et carbone: la difficile conciliation des origines politiques avec les valeurs contemporaines" and "Confédération et corruption: la critique républicaine des Résolutions de Québec."

JULIEN MAUDUIT holds his PhD from UQAM (2016) and is the Lynton R. Wilson Assistant Professor at McMaster University. He received the Quebec National Assembly's 2017 Prix de la Fondation Jean-Charles-Bonenfant for his PhD dissertation, and he has notably published an award-winning article (CHA's Jean-Marie Fecteau Prize) on the patriots' political economy in the *Bulletin d'histoire politique*. He is interested in the history of democracy and the transition to capitalism in North America and is currently working on the political meanings of monetary theories.

JASON M. OPAL is an associate professor in the Department of History and Classical Studies at McGill University. He is the author of *Beyond the Farm: National Ambitions in Rural New England* (2008) and *Avenging the People: Andrew Jackson, the Rule of Law, and the American Nation* (2017) and is broadly interested in colonialism, slavery, and law in the early Americas. He is now working on a global history of Barbados. His writings have also appeared in the *Los Angeles Times*, *Washington Post*, *Newsweek*, *The Walrus*, and *Jacobin*.

ROBERT RICHARD is a PhD candidate in the History Department at the University of North Carolina–Chapel Hill, focusing on North

American political and financial history. His dissertation, "Panic and Power: The First Great Depression in North Carolina, 1819–1833," explores the profound political-economic legacy of the first modern financial collapse in U.S. history through the lens of one critical yet understudied Southern state. He has also published an article on Jacksonian fiscal populism in the *Tennessee Historical Quarterly*.

THOMAS RICHARDS JR received in his PhD in American history from Temple University (2016) and he was the 2017–18 David S. Weber Fellow at the Clements Center for Southwest Studies at Southern Methodist University. He is the author of several articles, including "Farewell to America: The Expatriation Politics of American Overland Migration, 1841–1846," which won the WHA's Michael P. Malone Prize for best article on state or territorial history, and the co-author (with Andrew Isenberg) of "Alternative Wests: Rethinking Manifest Destiny." His book project *Breakaway Americas* is currently under contract with Johns Hopkins University Press.

ALBERT SCHRAUWERS is an economic anthropologist in the Department of Anthropology at York University. He is the author of *"Union Is Strength": W.L. Mackenzie, the Children of Peace and the Emergence of Joint Stock Democracy in Upper Canada* (2009) and other monographs. His work focuses on early forms of corporation in the British and Dutch colonial empires and their political implications – in particular, the ways in which chartered corporations with unlimited liability fostered "gentlemanly capitalism" and imperialism.

# Index